SHAKESPEARE
FROM
BETTERTON
TO IRVING

HENRY IRVING AS SHYLOCK
From a copyrighted photograph by Lock and Whitfield of London

SHAKESPEARE - FROM BETTERTON TO IRVING

By

GEORGE C. D. ODELL

PROFESSOR OF ENGLISH AT COLUMBIA UNIVERSITY

VOLUME II

BENJAMIN BLOM   New York / London

First Published by Charles Scribner's Sons, 1920
Reprinted 1963, with permission of the publishers
by Benjamin Blom, Inc., Bronx, N.Y. 10452
and 56 Doughty Street, London, W.C. 1

Library of Congress Catalog Card Number 63-23277

Printed in U.S.A. by
NOBLE OFFSET PRINTERS, INC.
NEW YORK 3, N. Y.

CONTENTS

VOLUME II

BOOK VIII. THE AGE OF IRVING (1879–1902)

ILLUSTRATIONS

VOLUME II

BOOK IV

THE AGE OF KEMBLE

(1776–1817)

CHAPTER XVII

THE THEATRES

THE two royal theatres are all that need detain us here; the Haymarket, to be sure, in 1777 passed to the elder Colman, who retired from Covent Garden, and enlarged the Haymarket for the better accommodation of actors and spectators. But so far as notable productions of Shakespeare are concerned, the history still limits itself to Drury Lane and Covent Garden.

As to the first of these houses, Garrick, immediately on his retirement, sold out to the younger Sheridan, who had just won brilliant success with The Rivals and The Duenna. Percy Fitzgerald, in his Lives of the Sheridans, supplies details of the transfer. Sheridan at first brought in Ewart, a brandy merchant of sound financial standing, and his (Sheridan's) father-in-law, Dr. Linley. The whole Drury Lane property was valued at £70,000, of which Garrick was to dispose only of his half, Lacy still retaining his. Four purchasers were involved, Ewart furnishing £10,000, Linley £10,000, Sheridan £10,000 and a Dr. Ford £5,000. Eventually Ewart withdrew from the negotiations, and Dr. Ford "went in" for £15,000. It was also proposed that they take over a mortgage of £22,000 which Garrick held on Lacy's share. The contract was concluded on June 24, 1776. Historians of the theatre long wondered where Sheridan secured the money with which to carry on these weighty operations. Professor Brander Matthews, in the introduction to his edition of Sheridan's Comedies (1885), has shown that the brilliant young author of The Duenna covered most of his tracks with mortgages, and really raised in cash only £1,300 of the £10,000 for which he was responsible; furthermore, when, in 1778, he took over Lacy's share, he not only bought it, as it were, by merely

3

assuming mortgages and obligations for annuities, but, far from paying any cash, he actually received back the £1,300 he had originally expended in the purchase of Garrick's share!

From June, 1776, then, until the burning of the theatre in 1809, Sheridan was ostensibly the manager of Drury Lane, playing it off against the expenses of his social and political activities, and really almost running it on the reef of disaster. He left the disagreeable part of the direction to some actor-manager, to his father, at first, and then to King, and, for some years after 1788, to John Kemble. It was, no doubt, the shifty, ruthless, selfish policy of Sheridan that finally drove Kemble from the theatre in the spring of 1802, and forced him to negotiate for the share in Covent Garden that he soon obtained from Harris. From the autumn of 1803 till his retirement Kemble made Covent Garden what Drury Lane had previously been, the leading theatre of the English-speaking world. Perhaps, at its highest moment, it was the finest in the world.

In the age of Kemble important physical changes, as well, occurred in the two great houses. Twice by human consent—in 1782 and in 1792—both houses were entirely altered and renovated; once—in 1808 and 1809, respectively —by divine interposition, as many thought—they were consumed by fire and rebuilt from the ground.

The result of the first change—that of 1782—is neatly described by W. C. Oulton, in his Continuation of Victor's Theatres of London, published in 1796. Of Drury Lane, he says "the theatre was very much improved now; Boxes neatly papered with a light pea green, and ornamented with crimson curtains to all the doors: the seats covered with baize of the same colour. His Majesty's box and the opposite one were rather more advanced than before, and the side scene lights were much encreased."

Covent Garden the same season was also greatly improved. Harris had intended to tear it down and rebuild, but "other alterations less expensive were deemed equally good."

The roof was raised eight feet over the stage; and to a proportionate height to the back of the second gallery, which opened a full view of the stage, even to the spectators in the back seats. The first gallery projected equal to the front of the boxes; and four seats beyond the front of the second gallery. By these means the theatre had a light appearance, and the Gods a full view of the stage.

The boxes, which were constructed on a very advantageous plan, were considerably elevated and built upon the stage, as far as the space before occupied by the side stage doors. The boxes were separated by corinthian columns, white with gold flutings . . . in the front of each box was a crimson drapery, and the linings were of the same colour.

One receives the impression, from reading these old chronicles, that the theatres had to be repaired or altered frequently. In ten years the decorations thus agreeably described by Oulton were demolished, and both theatres were again in the hands of carpenters and masons. The old house that Sir Christopher Wren had built in Drury Lane was now found to be insecure and dangerous; it was necessary to tear it down and rebuild from the foundation. Harris, at Covent Garden, contemplated a similar procedure, but at last decided merely to alter and refurbish. For the result of his attempt we are again indebted to Oulton:

In 1792, Mr. Harris having expended £25,000 on this place, by an entire alteration of the interior parts, and an addition to the exterior, rendered it a new theatre. . . The Amphitheatre is entirely new, and contains three rows (or as they are now called) circles of boxes, and a gallery surrounding the whole . . . The front of the stage advances something more than the old one into the pit, and is in a straight line. . . .

The first circle of Boxes is, by a new contrivance, continued round the house. The Boxes are separated from each other by partitions which are low in front, rise behind, and are placed in a new and commodious direction. They are lined and ceiled with wainscot, and not papered for the advantage of sound. They are coloured red . . . Their fronts project in a manner very accommodating to those who sit in . . . the front rows.

The ceiling is painted as a sky . . . The Proscenium is composed of pilasters and columns of the corinthian order, fully enriched, having between them the stage doors over which are the balcony boxes. In the entablature to the order is introduced the old motto, " *Veluti in Speculum.*"

Many prints of this interior are extant; perhaps a sufficiently good idea of it may be obtained from that of 1804, showing the stage during a performance of Pizarro (see page 98); a charming one is the aquatint in Ackerman's Microcosm of London, with Handel's organ on the stage. At first, according to Boaden (Life of Kemble), all was not to the satisfaction of the audience. "Mr. Holland [the architect] had constructed . . . a theatre in the lyral form, rather solid than light in its appearance, and of which the fronts of the boxes bulged something in the curve of a ship's side. The effect was grand and imposing, as to the tiers and number of the boxes; but the gallery called the first, or two shilling gallery, had been hoisted up to the mansions of the gods; and those turbulent deities were indiscreetly banished the house altogether." In other words, the shilling gallery, heretofore under the roof, had been abolished, and the lower gallery, now the top, had been raised to its place—at two-shillings admission. This was done to make room for an extra or third tier of boxes. After much disturbance, a shilling gallery was added, and the regular prices became fixed at 6 shillings for a box seat, three and sixpence in the pit. Boaden implies that the alterations were flimsy. "Twenty-five thousand pounds were said to be expended upon this new erection; and yet when, fifteen years after, it was destroyed by fire, it was said that it could not have stood many years longer."

Sheridan's reasons for enlarging Drury Lane have been said by Percy Fitzgerald to be partly financial. He had run the property into such debt that he hoped by greatly increasing the size of the house to increase the profits correspondingly and relieve his financial embarrassment. While the new theatre was building, the Drury Lane Company was housed at the King's Theatre in the Haymarket; on April, 1794, the grand new building was opened with Macbeth. Boaden cries excitedly of this magnificent building by Holland: "Had I the construction of twenty theatres, this should be their model. It seemed to grow out of the pointed architecture, from its effect; though its parts did

INTERIOR OF DRURY LANE THEATRE

From an aquatint by Rowlandson and Pugin in Microcosm of London, 1808

not imitate that mysterious order, perhaps disorder of composition." Oulton is far more specific:

The accommodations for the stage are upon a much larger scale than those of any other theatre in Europe. The opening for the scenery is 43 feet wide, and 38 high; after which the painter and machine contriver will have a large space 85 feet in width, 92 in length, and 110 in height, for the exertion of their respective abilities.

In the roof of the theatre are contained, besides the barrel-loft, ample room for the scene-painters, and four very large reservoirs, from which water is distributed over every part of the house, for the purpose of instantly extinguishing fire. . . An iron curtain has been contrived, which, on any such occasion, would completely prevent all communications between the audience and stage. . . .

The audience part of the theatre is formed nearly on a semicircular plan. It contains a pit, eight boxes on each side the pit, two rows of boxes above them, and two galleries, which command a full view of every part of the stage. On each side of the galleries are two more rows of boxes, rising to a cove, which is so contrived as to form the ceiling into a complete circle.—The proscenium, or that part of the stage which is contained between the curtain and the orchestra, is fitted up with boxes, but without any stage door or the usual addition of large columns.—The boxes are furnished with chairs in the front rows, and behind with benches. The trimming and covering are all of blue velvet.

In this spacious and magnificent playhouse, John Kemble, as we shall see, inaugurated that system of special Shakespearian production that led the way for Macready, Phelps, Charles Kean and Irving.

The twin fortunes of the two royal theatres brought them to destruction by fire, Covent Garden on September 20, 1808, and Drury Lane on February 24, 1809. This coincidence impelled the righteous to hint at the wrath of God, and the unrighteous to think of incendiarism on the part of the unlucky directors of Drury Lane. The losses were enormous—partly covered by insurance. The company of Covent Garden acted at the King's Theatre in the Haymarket, and that of Drury Lane at the Lyceum. Plans for rebuilding were at once instituted, and in about a year's time the costly new Covent Garden was ready for occu-

pancy. Drury Lane had recently been so unsuccessful
that there was, for a time, question as to rebuilding it.
Matters progressed so slowly that it was not till the autumn
of 1812 that the new theatre was opened. By a singular
stroke of good fortune, Edmund Kean appeared mid-way
the second season. After that, all was well with Drury
Lane for some months or even years to come.

Boaden furnishes us ample material concerning the new
Covent Garden, which, by the way, he seems to have
admired not at all, though Kemble, the god of his idolatry,
was chief adviser there. "Mr. Robert Smirke, jun.," he
says, "was selected to be the architect of the new Theatre
Royal; and the anticipation of classical structure was carefully kept awake by reports of his travels and his taste,
and his peculiar study of theatres. The site of the new
play house . . . . was somewhat extended—some adjacent
houses were bought, so as to open the area: the architect
might have surrounded the house by a colonade, and facili-
tated the departure of spectators by stair-cases of considerable width, and doors to be open only at the close of the
amusement. He did not choose such a plan; but loaded
his design with a bleak, a barren, and portentous portico,
and strengthened his walls, as though they were bound to
resist every thing but the 'crack of doom.' So solid an
edifice required funds of no mean amount even in the outset, and 50,000*l.* in 500*l.* shares, were subscribed in a very
few days. They secured a *deposit* of 40 per cent, and the
remainder was conveniently enough arranged; the whole,
with 44,500*l.* from the fire-offices, was to be paid into the
banking-house of Stephenson, Batson, & Co., there to be
expressly and solely appropriated to the erection, and completion, and furnishing of the new theatre. The most
costly materials were always chosen; the proprietors seemed
never to recollect their *personal* responsibility for everything—they were building a *temple* and a *palace*, as if it had
been voted by the people of England, and their representatives had constituted them the committee of taste for its
erection."

In speaking of the completed theatre, Boaden is very
severe. "There is, externally, not a particle of taste—a
heavy portico of four doric columns, the largest in any
modern building, astonishes by its ponderous inutility; the
columns are 5 feet 6 inches in diameter. . . . We are told
that the Bow-street front is an imitation of the Temple of
Minerva in the Acropolis. Partially it may be; but it has
no interior columns, no point of sight from which it can be
viewed, or its proportions discerned. The lower part of
the building is of stone, the upper of cement very dingy and
liable to scale off or crack." Kemble's biographer cannot
be ironical enough about either the classic or the Shakespearian statues on the outside of the theatre, or the figure
of Shakespeare inside. Furthermore, the halls and stair-
cases of this theatre, its lobbies and saloons, are really
wretched, when compared with the contrivances of Wyatt
at Drury Lane.

But at last he finds something to praise. "In speaking
of it as a play-house, its highest excellence was the stage
itself, constructed by Mr. Saul; certainly the most perfect
with which I am acquainted."

Dibdin gives these measurements for the stage:

	ft.	in.
Width of the proscenium in front	42	6
Width at pilasters	38	8
Height to the centre of arch	36	9
Height at spring of arch	33	3
Depth of stage from front lights to the sliding pilasters	12	3
Depth of stage from front lights to the back wall	68	0
Width from wall to wall	82	6
Height of flats	21	0
Width of flats (14 feet each half)	28	0
Width of side scenes	4	0

It will be seen that these proportions are smaller than those
cited by Oulton for the Drury Lane built by Holland in
1792; but the stage, at that, is considerably larger in width
and depth than that of the New Amsterdam Theatre in
New York.

The boxes, [proceeds Boaden] were calculated to hold as many people as they did in the former [i. e. Covent Garden] theatre; only, from the encroachment of the private circle, now occupying the whole of the third tier, 140 persons were accommodated in the lower circles. Six feet six inches were now the average depth of the three rows, which had been only six feet three inches in the old theatre, and but six feet in Drury Lane.

The pit had still its former twenty seats [i. e., rows of seats or benches], but the declivity, instead of being, as formerly, only three feet, was now four feet nine inches.

In the two-shilling gallery of Drury Lane, a person seated in the back row was one hundred feet from the stage-door; in the old Covent Garden he was eighty-eight feet, and in the present only eighty-six. In the upper gallery these relative distances were one hundred and four feet, ninety-three feet, and eighty-five feet.

The house was lighted by glass chandeliers in front of each circle —270 wax-candles was the nightly supply; 300 patent lamps lighted the stage and its scenery. The prevailing colour of the house was white; the ornament, gold upon a light pink ground; the box doors were all of solid mahogany.

The first and second circles of the boxes were appropriated to the public. From the third circle they were entirely excluded—the boxes were let annually, and each of them had a small anti-room about six feet wide, opening outwards into a general saloon, appropriated to these renters, as that below was to the public. To these boxes the entrances were private. . . . .

The proprietors of the Theatre Royal, Covent Garden, demonstrated that they could only be reimbursed for their enormous outlay, by a rise in the prices, which would place the boxes at seven shillings, the pit at four, leaving the still far distant galleries at the old rates of two shillings and one.

The riots which took place at the opening of this theatre caused every previous disturbance to pale into insignificance. The two points that King Public, or Tyrant Public, objected to were those I have last quoted from Boaden —the establishment of private boxes, rented by the year, which excluded the people from a certain part of the house, and the advance in prices, an advance of one shilling for admission to the boxes, and sixpence to the pit. The row continued for exactly sixty-six nights; no play given was ever heard in the smallest part—all was acted as in pantomime. The chief targets of public boo-ing and execration were members of the Kemble family, particularly John and Charles; Mrs. Siddons refused to appear after the first night. The "gentlemen" who conducted this disgraceful uprising spared no one—neither the actresses nor ladies in the boxes. At last the theatre was closed. Kemble and Harris were at length forced to yield. A compromise dinner was finally held at the Crown and Anchor, and while the seven-shilling entrance was retained for the boxes, the three shillings-sixpence was restored for the pit. Kemble agreed to give up the private boxes, though with them he renounced a sure profit of some thousands of pounds per annum. At the opening of the house in the following season—the boxes had been graciously allowed by the rioters to be kept for the rest of the first season—it was discovered that some of the private boxes still remained; further rioting resulted, and they were finally removed. These month-long disturbances are known as the O. P. or Old Price Riots, and are among the most disgraceful in English theatrical annals. One can only wonder what the legal authorities were good for, or why Kemble had not sufficient "nerve" to invoke them. I suppose an actor cannot afford to antagonise any part of his public.

The affairs of Drury Lane dragged pitiably between the time of the fire and the opening of the new house. In the first place, there were debts of £436,000 to consider. Finally, a compromise was effected with creditors for one-fourth of their claims. The new house—the present Drury Lane—was to cost £150,000; as a matter of fact £212,000 was laid out in the venture. It succeeded principally because of Samuel Whitbread, brewer, who managed affairs honestly and efficiently. The prime object was to get rid of Sheridan. This was finally brought about, and at its opening the house was managed by a committee of nobles and gentry, Lord Byron being one. In 1819 this committee, in utter boredom, and with an accumulated loss of £90,000 to their discredit, turned the management over to Elliston, the actor. For these items, I am indebted to various works by Percy Fitzgerald.

The theatre thus built and opened in 1812 is still standing in London, one of the most beautiful structures of its
kind in existence. "It is, in truth," says Percy Fitzgerald
in his New History of the English Stage, "a noble, spacious,
and finely conceived edifice, reflecting the traditions of a
good classical school. It is impossible to enter and pass
through its halls, vestibules, and rotundas without a sense
of dignity and proportion. The architect [Wyatt] had
formed a true conception, which he was allowed to carry
out untrammelled. This sense of just proportion and dignity is sadly lacking in modern temples. The exterior is
indeed not imposing, but it has never been completed. It
should be added, however, that it is professedly modelled
after what is perhaps the finest theatre in Europe—the one
at Bordeaux. This can be seen by a comparison of the
plans, though the beautiful arrangement of short balconies,
supported between pillars, has not been followed in the
English house. On entering the theatre the visitor finds
himself in a great vestibule or crush-room, which opens
again on the rotunda, a noble and imposing circular hall
reaching to the roof, with a gallery running round, whence,
to the right and left, open all the approaches to the various
stairs. These are laid out in a bold airy way, and are
very striking." Any one who has visited this beautiful
theatre will agree with Mr. Fitzgerald's estimate and
applaud his adjective—"noble." I have never seen a
more attractive entrance-hall or anything so charming as
the rotunda. The auditorium is spacious, finely propor-
tioned and excellent for hearing. It can be judged by
the view given of Macready's performance of As You
Like It.

The architect of this exquisite theatre has left an admirable account of his problem and its solution in his Observations on the Design for the Theatre Royal, Drury Lane,
as Executed in the Year 1812.

Drury-lane Theatre [he writes] consisting of three-fourths of a
circle, with a Proscenium limiting the Stage-opening to 33 feet, contains, in four different heights, 80 Boxes, holding 1098 persons; with

four Boxes (of larger size than the rest) next to the Stage, on each side of the Theatre, capable of containing 188 Spectators in addition to the 1098 before mentioned; amounting in an aggregate to 1286 persons.   A Pit capable of containing 920 persons, a Two-Shilling Gallery for 550 persons, a One Shilling Gallery for 350 persons, exclusive of four Private Boxes in the Proscenium, and 14 in the Basement of the Theatre, immediately under the Dress Boxes.

.   .   .   .

I confined the distance from the front of the Stage to the *back* wall of the Boxes, facing the Stage, to 53 feet 9 inches . . . . 38 feet 6 inches laterally.

I have already stated, that the extreme distance from the front line of the Stage to the *back* wall of the Boxes, facing the Stage, according to my plan, is 53 feet 9 inches; in the late Theatre in Drury Lane it was 74 feet, or 20 feet 3 inches more than at present; in the Old Theatre in Covent Garden (I mean as it was built about the year 1730), the distance between the front of the Stage, and the back wall of the front Boxes, was 54 feet 6 inches, or 1 foot 3 inches more than in my design.   In the Old Opera House, built by Sir John Vanburgh, in the Haymarket, it was 66 feet, or 12 feet 3 inches more than in my design.

.   .   .   .

In the present Theatre at Covent Garden it is 69 feet 8 inches, or fifteen feet eleven inches more.

. . . . The height of the Ceiling from the centre of the Pit, is 48 feet. . . . The height of the Ceiling in the late Theatre in Drury-lane was 56 feet 6 inches.

From the Dramatic Censor of February, 1811, we derive some idea of the expenses and receipts of the two great theatres, just a little before the fires of 1808 and 1809.   The following is said to be a correct statement of what the two metropolitan theatres would hold, in money and people, in July, 1805:

COVENT GARDEN

Boxes, four tiers	1230
Pit	632
Two Shilling Gallery	822
One Shilling Gallery	360
Total Persons when full	3044
In Money, when full, about	£600

When Master *Betty* performed *Romeo* at this Theatre, the Receipts in Money were £634, exclusive of Renters' shares, and Persons on the Free List.

The Nightly Expences were	£160
Average Nightly Receipts during the Season	£300

DRURY LANE

	Persons		£.	s.	d.
Boxes	1828	at 6s.	548	8	0
Pit	800	3s. 6d.	140	0	0
First Gallery	670	2s.	67	0	0
Upper Gallery	308	1s.	15	8	0
	3611 [*sic*]		770	16	0

The Boxes were known, on some few particular occasions, to have holden 1,960 persons;—the pit 930;—the First Gallery 682;—and the Upper Gallery 426.

The Expences, including Performers, Lights, Ground-rent, Taxes, and every contingent, were upwards of £200 per night.

The Salaries were as under:

	£	s.	d.
One at	31	10	0
Four at	17	17	0
Four at	15	15	0
Twenty at	10	10	0
Ten at	8	8	0
Ten at	7	7	0
Six at	6	6	0
Six at	5	5	0
Ten at	3	3	0
Ten at	2	2	0
Fifty at	1	11	6
Ten at	1	10	0

Total £740 per week, or about £124 per night. The Season in both Theatres, consisted of 35 weeks, or 200 nights.

CHAPTER XVIII

INTRODUCTORY: BELL'S SHAKESPEARE, 1773

STANDARD TEXTS FOR ACTING VERSIONS

A CAREFUL study of material at hand will prove that the period under discussion availed itself of generally accepted stage versions of Shakespeare's plays. Acting editions now began to appear, not separately, but in series. The decade 1770–80 saw the inception of this interesting custom. The first important set of such a nature was Bell's Shakespeare, edited by the Authors of the Dramatic Censor, and printed from the prompt-books of the theatres royal, in 1773. This invaluable collection furnishes the first clue to Shakespeare as acted throughout the number of his plays that habitually graced the boards; and from it—I see no reason to doubt the authenticity of the texts—we can learn exactly what portions of those plays attendants at the theatre were privileged to behold. Similar series followed rapidly, that of John Harrison appearing in 1777–80; anonymous sets, also, are found. From the time of John Kemble's actual directing of the stage of Drury Lane, almost to the end of his career, he made his own versions of the plays and printed them for sale in the theatre. In general one can review the milestones in his career by the dates of his acting versions. From his first days of stage-directing in 1788 to his collected series of Shakespearian plays in 1815, there were four periods when circumstances allowed him to indulge his desire to revive Shakespeare with great pomp and splendour. At each of these times he published the pieces exactly as he produced them. Hence from his own publications we can judge him. Each of those periods I shall review in the progress of this narrative. Mrs. Inchbald's famous British Theatre, published in 1808, is to all intents and purposes, so far as the Shakespearian

15

plays are concerned, but a re-issue of Kemble's versions. This I have proved by collation. The matter was, no doubt, easily arranged, since the same firm published both series.

In addition to these standard editions of the stock plays, a few sporadic attempts were made to re-write Shakespeare, in the old way that the century and more from Davenant to Garrick had not entirely discredited. So late as 1816, Reynolds made an onslaught on A Midsummer Night's Dream, and, just before and after that lamentable affair, Kean appeared at Drury Lane in re-workings of Richard II and Timon of Athens, respectively. But the day for such things was nearly past, and we shall not need to consider many more. Those I have mentioned will be taken up in their proper place; for the major part of the discussion, however, I shall rely contentedly on the editions of Bell and Kemble. What I am trying to say is that, by the time of the period at which I have arrived, the consciences of both managers and playgoers were suffering a change into something rich and strange, and that the standardisation of texts was now something feasible and desired.

BELL'S SHAKESPEARE

I shall begin, then, with some account of Bell's acting edition of the plays of Shakespeare—"regulated from the prompt-books, by permission of the managers," and published in the years 1773–75. This is quite different from the edition published by Bell in 1788; the latter is merely a library edition in small volumes, from the text of Johnson and Steevens. The earlier collection is a guide to the theatre, and purports to be no more. As an edition of Shakespeare, it is, as Isaac Reed called it, the worst imaginable; as an indication of what was acted in the theatres, it will, now that scholarship is turning its attention to such things, become increasingly valuable with the passing of the years. It is, as I have found, rather difficult to come by; it is not worth money, but it is hard to find.

In view of the fact that this edition began to be issued three years before the retirement of Garrick, it might be asked why I had not considered it as a close to the preceding period. I debated doing so; but since that period was one long struggle toward such standardisation as Bell's represents, and since the beginning of the period we are now entering upon was—until the scholarly Kemble began, in 1789, to make new versions of Shakespeare's most frequently acted works—a mere time of reliance on the heritage of the former age, I decided here, at the beginning of the Kemble *régime*, to survey as broadly as possible the versions or perversions included in Bell, and undoubtedly regulated from the managers' copies at both theatres. Here, then, let us examine what London theatre-goers were permitted to witness in the name of Shakespeare from 1773 and before, until 1789 and after.

The two leading forces in the enterprise of publishing Bell's Shakespeare are worth a moment's attention. John Bell—"the mischievous spirit, the very Puck of booksellers," as Charles Knight calls him—had a knack of bringing out pretty books that pleased the eye and stimulated to reading. He was responsible for the edition of the British poets in one hundred and nine 18mo volumes, launched as a counter-irritant to Johnson's edition, brought out by the Association of Publishers in 1779. He also got together the British Theatre, a collection of plays long pillaged for the character portraits of players prefixed to the separate works. I am greatly indebted to him, also, for Bell's Weekly Messenger, published on Sundays from 1801 to the time just succeeding the accession of Queen Victoria, though Bell himself died in 1831. The Weekly Messenger teems with dramatic criticisms (as does the Examiner of John and Leigh Hunt), very helpful to the student who would revisualise old performances in the theatre.

Francis Gentleman, the editor of this series of acting versions of Shakespeare, was an Irishman who began as actor, appearing for a while in Foote's company at the Haymarket, and wrote some plays, The Modish Wife, The

Tobacconist (adapted from Jonson's Alchemist) and The
Coxcomb (adapted from The Silent Woman). He also
was the author of the Dramatic Censor (1770), from which
I quoted perhaps too liberally in the chapters on Garrick.
The foot-notes in Bell's Shakespeare are so fresh and charming, so naïvely humorous where Gentleman apparently
least intended them to be, that it is with a surprise of disappointment we come upon the last stage of all in the life
of the unhappy editor. Perhaps his pleasing name mis-
leads us, but the final days as a dependent on the bounty
of Garrick, who refers to him as Gentleman only in name,
and the last snuffing out of the candle in Dublin, somehow
disconcert a reader predisposed to think of Gentleman as
a fine flower of Eighteenth-Century civilisation. Alas,
Grub Street, how many failures hast thou housed and made!

The plays of Shakespeare printed in this edition from the
prompter's copies are exactly those that were performed in
the theatres, before and during and after the years of the
publication. These acting versions are twenty-four in
number, eighteen from the prompt-books of Drury Lane
(Mr. Hopkins, Prompter), and six from the books of Covent
Garden (Mr. Younger in the same capacity). The come-
dies so given are, as we might expect, All's Well that Ends
Well, As You Like It, Measure for Measure, The Merchant
of Venice, The Merry Wives of Windsor, Much Ado about
Nothing, The Tempest, Twelfth Night, and The Winter's
Tale; the tragedies, Coriolanus, Cymbeline, Hamlet, Julius
Cæsar, King Lear, Macbeth, Othello, Romeo and Juliet,
Timon of Athens; the histories, both parts of King Henry IV,
Henry V, Henry VIII, King John, Richard III. Of these,
Hamlet, Henry V, Henry VIII, Julius Cæsar, Measure for
Measure and The Winter's Tale are regulated from the
Covent Garden prompt-books.

The twenty-four above cited are, as we have seen, the
plays that had standardised themselves as the regular
Shakespearian repertoire at the two houses; others, on
revival, in "adapted" (i. e., mutilated) version, had had
but a temporary life. In general, the same statement may

be made of the first years of the period we are about to
discuss, and even of its later years. Kemble revived a few
of the less frequently acted plays—The Two Gentlemen of
Verona, The Comedy of Errors, Antony and Cleopatra—
but his lack of success with any or all was discouraging.
The other plays of Shakespeare—other, that is, than the
twenty-four specified—except Pericles, which is not included, are printed in Bell entire, as in a library edition of
the poet's works; Gentleman marks by inverted commas
lines that he thinks might be omitted in representation.
But he does not pretend that these are acting-versions.
He has not gone beyond the authority of prompt-books
actually in existence; hence he gives from such books plays
only that are acted, and hence, as a result, one derives a
comfortable assurance as to the authenticity of the texts
actually printed "as regulated by the theatres." The
edition therefore becomes exactly what the producers meant
it to be—a *vade-mecum* to the theatres of the time. To
scholars of a later date it is invaluable.

GENEST'S RECORD, 1776–1817

A careful tabulation of performances recorded by Genest
for the period of Kemble shows no such result as was discovered in a similar study of the Garrick times. Hardly
any play at either house was acted so regularly, year after
year, as were the great tragedies in the time from 1742 to
1776. In fact, Hamlet, King Lear, and the rest sometimes
disappear from the boards of either house for several seasons
in succession. For instance, John Kemble made his first
appearances with great success in Hamlet, yet he did not
enact the character during the following season, and, having satisfied all theatre-goers in the part for four years
thereafter, for some unaccountable reason he dropped it
from his list for six successive seasons. Even at that, it
failed to appear in the forty-one years we are considering
for only thirteen seasons at Drury Lane, and but eight at
the rival house. King Lear was kept from the boards for

several years (as Mrs. Inchbald implies) because of the
ticklish public feelings engendered by Napoleon and the
incapacity of George III. Macbeth fared better; it was
absent from Covent Garden bills only five of the forty-one
seasons now under review, but from seventeen at Drury
Lane. This discrepancy is accounted for by the fact that
when Mrs. Siddons, in 1803, carried her great performance
of Lady Macbeth to Covent Garden, the number of performances of the tragedy at the house she deserted diminished to a marked degree. After all, it was—and is—a
question of the actors. This is again notable in connection
with the Falstaff plays. In the early years of our period
Henderson kept them alive, first at one house, then at the
other; toward the latter years of the *régime*, Cooke revived
them at Covent Garden. Between the times of these two
great representatives of the Fat Knight, both parts of
Henry IV and The Merry Wives languished or sickened
unto death. With this view, the reader will not be surprised to learn that As You Like It was more frequently
acted from 1776 to 1817 than any other Shakespearian play
at Drury Lane; it missed but three seasons out of forty-
one. Why? Because a succession of great Rosalinds
graced the boards of that playhouse: Mrs. Barry, Miss
Younge, Mrs. Jordan—even Mrs. Siddons essayed the part.
At Covent Garden, where there was less comedy-talent on
the distaff-side, even in Kemble's time, the play failed of
performance—according to Genest—in very many of the
forty-one seasons. Conversely, the magnificence of Kemble as Coriolanus accounts for the frequency with which
that self-willed Roman emerged in the later days of Covent
Garden. Verily, great is Shakespeare, but the actors are
his prophets!

Desire for accuracy compels me to warn the reader that
the seasons of the companies of Drury Lane and Covent
Garden registered above include the periods when they
were acting at other theatres, by reason of the rebuilding
of their own playhouses.

THE COMEDIES IN BELL'S SHAKESPEARE

I shall begin the discussion of Bell's Shakespeare with the Comedies. All's Well that Ends Well has ever been a problem on the stage; the story is revolting, the heroine incapable of awakening sympathy, and the comic scenes either disgustingly low (to use an Eighteenth-Century expression) or mere reminders of earlier (?) successes in the Falstaff plays. Who would cut must needs wield an heroic axe. The Bell version of this play is one of the worst—if not the very worst—in the series. Almost all of the really fine poetry is eliminated, and but too much of the filthy talk of Parolles to Helena in the first scene and of the Clown to the Countess throughout is suffered to remain. In Scene one Helena's fine soliloquy, beginning "Our remedies oft in ourselves do lie, Which we ascribe to heaven" is omitted. The entire first act is much curtailed; "there is," says Gentleman's footnote, "about one third . . . reduced, and yet it lies heavy on attention." Though the play is carried on, according to Shakespeare's theatric idea (with transposition of scenes to be sure), one feels that it is but a mere skeleton. Without Shakespeare's poetry, this play is hardly worth saving. Bell's edition makes the Countess the leading character, but really seems to care more for the quarrel of Lafeu and Parolles and the "fooling" of Parolles and his final unmasking than for anything else in the play. A more unlovely pair of lovers than the Bertram and Helena of this version it would be hard to imagine. In Act V, it may be said in passing, the important scene of Diana, Helena and the Widow in the streets of Marseilles is omitted.

AS YOU LIKE IT, 1773

The As You Like It here to be discussed is undoubtedly about the version that was employed throughout the Garrick period, and is the only form in which we can find that version. Though Dublin imprints of the acting-copy were published, we find none of the London copies during the

years that followed the revival in 1740 until now. In view
of the great popularity of the comedy, it will be interesting
to see what theatre-goers were given in the year 1773.
The sequence of scenes, it may be said at once, is almost
identical with Shakespeare's. All the Sir Oliver Martext
business, however, is omitted, and Jaques does not watch
and comment on the first interview of Touchstone and
Audrey. The scene in which Duke Frederic learns of the
flight of the girls and that in which he threatens Oliver are
retained; I have never seen either acted, and I have seen
the play many times. A great deal of the insipid Phebe
has been taken from the text, though Gentleman prints
some of the excised material in foot-notes, remarking that
it should be retained. The scene of cross-purposes with
the recurrent refrains of "And so am I for Ganimede,"
"And so am I for Rosalind," and "so am I for no woman,"
is shorn of much of its substance, though Gentleman's
foot-note explains "it should certainly be retained for *Silvius's* beautiful explanation of love." Hymen's song "There
is mirth in Heaven" is sung, by whom I do not know, since
Hymen does not appear. I may end by saying that the
beautiful songs of the play are either omitted altogether,
like "What shall he have that killed the deer," or cut
to one stanza, like "Under the greenwood-tree." Jaques's
"ducdame" parody is eliminated.

Two century-long customs are observed in this version.
To Jaques, not to the First Lord, are assigned the lines on
the dying deer and Jaques's moralising thereon. This
practice began in 1723 in Johnson's Love in a Forest. Colley Cibber, as we have seen, in that alteration played the
part of Jaques, and could, as manager, fatten his slender
part with these good lines, even though they make of
Jaques a vain coxcomb, thus publicly to admire his own
thoughts in the description he gives of his "similes" on the
fate of the deer. Probably Quin and the other heroes of
the revivals of this pastoral comedy in the early '40's seized
on this device for strengthening the character (in number
of lines at least) and sent on even to our own day, almost,

a very bad custom of the theatre. The second trick I refer to is that of assigning to Rosalind the altogether too suggestive Cuckoo Song which a century of Rosalinds has warbled. This practice is followed in Bell's version. In Act IV, Scene 1, Rosalind, after her speech to Orlando, "O that woman that cannot make her fault her husband's accusation, let her never nurse her child, for she will breed it like a fool," begins the song "When daisies pied, and violets blue." Gentleman observes, "This song is taken from Love's Labour [sic] Lost, and is well introduced here." Later critics have not agreed, though many actresses have continued to sing the song. Mrs. Clive, as Celia, we saw, originally sang it; indeed, fifteen years after Bell's edition —in October, 1788, to be exact—Genest records that Mrs. Wilson as Celia still followed the early practice of Mrs. Clive. Perhaps the ditty was apportioned to either Rosalind or Celia, according to the vocal ability of the performers.

MEASURE FOR MEASURE, 1773

Exigencies of arranging by alphabetical order bring on that second of Shakespeare's bitter comedies—Measure for Measure. This like the other—All's Well that Ends Well —has a revolting plot, and its sub-plot is even more indecent than that of its fellow play. Both comedies really deserve the stage-oblivion into which they have fallen, though Measure for Measure held a fair degree of popular acclaim during the regency of Garrick and of Kemble. This vogue I take to be attributable entirely to the assumption of the part of Isabella by several very great actresses, the most notable being Mrs. Yates, Mrs. Barry and Mrs. Siddons. The Bell version, in which the first two probably appeared, strikes me as more satisfactory than Kemble's by just so far as it eliminates more of the offensive underworld matter of bawds and pandars and gentlemen of loose living. I believe that this subplot was necessary to round out Shakespeare's scheme, but I cannot alter my opinion that on the stage it is exceedingly offensive. In fact, I am

not sure that Measure for Measure should be acted, if its
rendition necessitates the retention of much, or indeed any
of the Froth, Pompey, Elbow, Mrs. Overdone material.

If I am correct in this view, Bell's version of Measure for
Measure is almost ideal; the character of Mrs. Overdone is
entirely eliminated. The second scene of the second act
omits the loose talk of Lucio and the two gentlemen, and
of course the Overdone business; it starts with the entrance
of the Provost, Claudio and Juliet, with Claudio's "Fellow,
why dost thou show me thus to th' world?" After this, to
the close, the editor follows the original. Gentleman's
foot-note is, as usual, very charming: "There are three very
slight, unworthy pages of the original most properly rejected." A very little of the Elbow-Froth-Pompey episode,
wherein they meet the Duke in the Street, is retained in
Act III, Scene 2, but of the first of these scenes omitted
Gentleman writes: "Here follows no less than seven pages
of absolute ribaldry, . . . the annihilation of them does
credit to our author and the stage." Otherwise the stage
is fumigated free of these people, except for the necessary
retention of Pompey (here called *Clown*) in the late prison
scenes. It would have been well if Kemble had continued
the same practice, though candour elicits the statement
that he has rendered the group as little maladorous as their
retention at all in the *dramatis personæ* would admit. Of
course the amusing scenes involving Lucio and the Duke
are retained. The main plot is very well handled in Bell's
edition, more of Juliet being retained than was usual in
later versions. The first of the scene of Mariana in the
Moated Grange, is excised, including the song, "Take, oh
take those lips away"; the rest is given entire. The last
two scenes of Act IV, the first involving the Duke's instruc-
tions to Peter and Varrius, and the second showing Isabella
and Mariana preparing for the great scene of accusation,
are likewise omitted, somewhat to the detriment of a complete understanding of the plot. In general, this is an
excellent acting version—its being disinfected of the gross
underworld folk makes it unusually pleasing. I am glad

to think that Mrs. Yates appeared in such good company.

Throughout the Eighteenth Century we find grandiloquent tags affixed for star actors to last bits of scenes and acts. Garrick wrote, as we saw, a "fine" bombastic death speech for Macbeth; Tate gave Cordelia some ranting lines invoking revenge on her wicked sisters. Sometimes the authors of these lines are buried in oblivion. Measure for Measure ends with five such lines, of which Gentleman heroically writes: "The five distinguished lines which conclude, are an addition, by whom we know not; however, they afford a better finishing than that supplied by *Shakespeare*; upon the whole of this play, for we cannot stile it either Tragedy or Comedy, there are several great beauties, clouded with much trifling and indecent dialogue; it must always be heavy to the majority of an audience; yet, purged of impurities and superfluities, as we hope the readers will find it in this edition, it may be entertaining and instructive in the closet." The concluding lines he admired are these, spoken by the Duke:

> Dear Isabel, I have a motion much imports your good,
> Shade not, sweet saint, those graces with a veil,
> Nor in a nunnery hide thee; say thou'rt mine;
> Thy Duke, thy Friar, tempts thee from thy vows.
> Let thy clear spirit shine in Publick life;
> No cloister'd sister, but thy Prince's wife.

THE MERCHANT OF VENICE, 1773

The Merchant of Venice in the Bell edition is an exceedingly interesting relic; if it was anything like the Jew that Shakespeare drew—in other words, Macklin's edition—it merits special study. The first act varies but little from Shakespeare; only a few "cuts" occur, notably Portia's gibes at the English and the Scotch. The omitted parts in this, as in several other plays, are supplied in foot-notes by Gentleman's delicate literary conscience.

The second act begins with the Gobbo scene, and the

transference of Launcelot's allegiance from Shylock to Bassanio. Neither the Morocco nor the Arragon scenes are given (though, as we saw, Macklin retained them), but, as usual, they occur in foot-notes. Gentleman regrets their omission. The unimportant scene between Jessica and Launcelot is kept, and Jessica, at the end, sings a ridiculous song,

> Haste, Lorenzo, haste away,
> To my longing arms repair.
> With impatience I shall die,
> Come and ease thy Jessy's care.
> Let me then in wanton play,
> Sigh and gaze my soul away.

Jessica and Lorenzo in fact perpetrate several equally precious "lyrics" in the course of the action. Before the elopement, Lorenzo, in spite of every inducement to be quiet, sings a serenade beginning "My bliss too long my bride denies," and violates privacy to the extent of three stanzas. In the last act—to close a painful subject—he sings to the wildered moon overlooking the gardens at Belmont a vapid stanza or two:

> To keep my gentle Jesse,
> What labour would seem hard, etc.

The custom began, we saw, in 1742.

To leave this Jewess and her Christian lord, I may say that Bassanio's choice of the casket is curtailed beyond recognition, almost beyond the point of clarity. Portia's and Bassanio's earlier speeches are the greatest sufferers. To compensate for this loss, however, all the lovely poetry of the opening of the fifth act between Jessica and Lorenzo is retained; Mrs. Inchbald, later, omits it nearly entirely.

The above account fairly well describes the Eighteenth-Century Merchant of Venice. It was not a very good version—it omits much that is beautiful and essential, and retains at least two unessential scenes, the first bit between Launcelot and Jessica, and that of Launcelot and Jessica at Belmont—to say nothing of the songs indulged in by the eloping pair. The Morocco episodes should have been retained. But compared with Lansdowne's Jew of Venice this is a masterpiece of adaptation.

OTHER COMEDIES, 1773

Alphabetically it is but a step from The Merchant of Venice to The Merry Wives of Windsor. I can dismiss the latter play very quickly. It is impossible, apparently, to give it without most of its Shakespearian matter. Managers may shift scenes and cut out passages, but they are forced to keep most of the material originally supplied. Bell omits "that ridiculous excrescence of a scene in the original, which begins the fourth Act with an examination of Young Page in grammar." In the same act he leaves out the plan about the fairies, the disguise of Nan, etc., the last-named to the loss of clearness of plotting. "The fourth Act," runs the foot-note, "though much reduced in the performance, is still long enough for any matter it contains, and its conclusion is rendered more agreeable, by getting rid of that insipid scene which *Shakespeare* tacked to it" (i. e., the scene between Fenton and Mine Host of the Garter). In the last act several bits are sacrificed, including most of the rhymes of Quickly and Evans about the Oak. It would seem as if the later scenes were a grab-bag, from which the editor selected whatever his hand lighted on.

I can dismiss the Bell Much Ado about Nothing with a very few words. It is an admirable acting copy, "cutting" some speeches in whole or in part, but omitting no important scene. The episode of Claudio at the tomb (supposed of Hero) is justly eliminated; it savours of the ludicrous at best. Knowing the fair one is not interred therein, we can take but little interest in the woes of her guilty lover. This play, like the one discussed immediately before, is given in a way to satisfy almost the most exacting; scenes now usually omitted, like that between Hero and Beatrice just before the wedding, are retained, I think unnecessarily. It might be called a reverent treatment of the bard.

THE TEMPEST, TWELFTH NIGHT, THE WINTER'S TALE, 1773

The reader who has followed the fortunes of The Tempest from the days in which Davenant and Dryden rifled it of its sweets to plant in their own Restoration parterre will be surprised to learn that almost every word of Bell's edition of the play is Shakespeare's. We have seen that during the Garrick period the fantasy had been acted *à la* Dryden and Davenant, in its Shakespearian guise, and as an opera. Bell had the taste to present it to his readers free of the desecrating touch of successive adapters. His version is really all that one could ask. It opens with the storm at sea, though Gentleman's conscience forces him to say quaintly in a foot-note, "the name, and first material incident of this piece are exceedingly contrastic to comedy; however, there is a good opportunity afforded for pleasing scenery and curious mechanism." The rest of the play to all intents and purposes follows Shakespeare's arrangement, every vestige of the Dryden-Davenant stuff being eliminated. In the first long expository scene, Prospero's speeches are considerably curtailed. In Act II we are spared a great deal of the miserable verbosity of the scene between Gonzalo, Antonio, Sebastian, etc. Gentleman admits that there are nearly three pages of the original "very properly left out." So much has been "cut" that several transition-lines are enforcedly introduced by the adapter. All the Stephano-Trinculo-Caliban material is given practically intact. The lovely scenes between Miranda and Ferdinand are blessedly spared to us. All goes as in Shakespeare except in the scene of the disappearing banquet, here manipulated by "devils." Again, the masque is shorn of many lines—even of Iris. The dance of reapers ends the scene. The last act is almost entirely Shakespeare's, with only a few lines missing. Is not this a surprise? It seems a great pity that in 1789 Kemble felt called upon to lay hands on this very satisfactory version, and restore all the silly Hippolyto-Dorinda stuff that Bell had cleansed out of it. But Kemble seems to have cared

MISS BROWN AND MR. MATTOCKS IN THE TEMPEST
Engraved for the *Universal Magazine*, 1777

but little what elements he might mingle, so long as he could stand up and say to all the world "This is a play." Witness his Coriolanus and his Antony and Cleopatra!

Our course through the comedies is nearly run. Twelfth Night, beloved of all actors, now calls us. In the Bell version all is semblative of Shakespeare to a degree; both the Clown's songs, "O Mistress mine," and "Come away, come away, Death," with their surrounding context are omitted, more's the pity, but nothing of importance, otherwise, is cast aside. The first scene of Act II at the beginning is the same as Shakespeare's, introducing Sebastian and Antonio; to it Bell tacks on the episode of Malvolio bringing the ring to Viola. Otherwise, throughout the play the scene divisions are exactly as in the original. This, again, is a reverent dealing with Shakespeare.

As to The Winter's Tale, it will be sufficient to refer the reader to the discussion given in its proper place, at the time of its production in 1771 (Vol. I, 382); more is unnecessary here. Let me end with a snatch from Gentleman anent Hull's treatment of Act IV: "Mr. Hull has taken uncommon pains, by slicing, transposing, &c. to give its beauties fair play by ridding them of dull company."

In looking back over these acting versions of the comedies, we find but little to condemn and much to praise. Most of the material was Shakespeare's and whatever sins were visible were sins of omission, not of commission. Some poetry was wantonly sacrificed, as in Measure for Measure and All's Well that Ends Well; on the other hand, more poetry was retained in The Tempest and in the last act of The Merchant of Venice than Kemble later saw his way to preserving. Twelfth Night, Much Ado about Nothing, The Merry Wives of Windsor and The Winter's Tale were not changed enough to hurt any but the most delicate and exigent susceptibilities. As You Like It, with the assigning to Jaques of the speeches of the First Lord, suffered the most marked change. We may say in conclusion that these standard comedies were reasonably well freed from the vandals. In 1773 theatre-goers saw

something appreciably like Shakespeare, when they elected
to attend a performance of one of his comedies. Not quite
so much could be said of the tragedies.

THE TRAGEDIES, 1773

The tragic plays may be dismissed with a far more cursory glance. It will be remembered, of course, that it was
not until the last years of the decade 1730–40 that the
comedies began to be revived in anything approximating
their original form; most of them, therefore, escaped the
process of tinkering to which they had been subjected in
earlier days, and to which the tragedies were still somewhat
liable. Being produced largely as Shakespeare left them,
they were not published to gratify the vanity of some wit-
ling improver; we were, therefore, usually forced to wait
for Bell's Shakespeare to find out what versions of the
comedies were handed on by the age of Garrick to the age
of Kemble. With the tragedies it is different; most of
Bell's versions had been published in the decades preceding, and as they have already been treated in the foregoing
narrative, they demand, in general, but scant description
here.

For instance, the Macbeth, the Romeo and Juliet and
the Cymbeline edited by Bell are almost precisely the versions used by Garrick; they may be dismissed now without
further comment. The King Lear I have discussed in its
proper place, in the history of its revival by Garrick in
1756, with restorations from Shakespeare. Two more of
Bell's tragedies may be included in the list of dismissals.
Coriolanus I have reviewed with sufficient detail in a previous chapter. The Timon of Athens is a bit more uncertain. The play was acted at Covent Garden during the
season of 1745–46, but not again at either house till the
Cumberland version was produced in 1771 at Drury Lane.
Gentleman, himself, says in a foot-note: "It is so long
since this play has been acted in its original state, that it
was thought needless to collect performers' names." Yet

earlier, he says, "we have seen three alterations of this play; the last, Mr. *Cumberland's* is much the best, but we think *Shakespeare,* properly pared, better than any of them. . . . We give the piece to perusal [mark the word] greatly and properly reduced from the original." As I can find no record of a performance of the play thus "properly pared" from Shakespeare, I see no reason for discussing it in this history of the acting of Shakespeare. Yet I confess that in similar cases, Bell prints the entire play, with lines that his editor thinks should be omitted on the stage enclosed in inverted commas. The question remains, what were the three versions Gentleman had seen acted? Love's (or Dance's) and Cumberland's we know; what was the third? For fear it may be this, let me hasten to say that it is all Shakespeare, scene by scene, only considerably cut; that admission frees our literary conscience.

HAMLET, 1773

The Bell Hamlet invites more detailed comment. This noble masterpiece had suffered as little as any of the plays by the hand of the violator. The quartos of Betterton's time print the play entire, merely indicating by inverted commas the lines omitted in representation. The Bell version differs but slightly from those early editions. The most notable "cut" is all the material involving those uninteresting ambassadors, Cornelius and Voltimand, though a few words are retained in the opening scene about the relations between Denmark and Norway. This elimination includes, of course, the scene of Hamlet's observing Fortinbras and his army on the plains of Denmark, and the episode of Fortinbras's soldier-like entry at the close of the play. To Horatio, at the very end, are assigned some of the lines of Fortinbras.

Throughout, minor curtailments (minor in size, at least) involve the abandonment of much of the best poetry of the play. In the first scene, the passages about the ghosts in the Roman sheets, and "Some say that ever 'gainst that season comes," etc., go as by a *fors clavigera;* the pretty scene between Ophelia and Laertes is much curtailed, though the bit about "the violet in the youth of primy nature" is permitted to shed a gentle fragrance over what remains. Laertes is deprived of Polonius's long speech of fatherly advice; Gentleman, who thinks it should certainly be retained, prints it in a foot-note. Dramatic criticism of the time complains that the low comedians, to whom the part of Polonius was given as a rule, always made the old chamberlain a buffoon; perhaps the omission of his sententious speech encouraged the actors to that view of the character. At the end of Act I, Hamlet's far from respectful references to the ghost of his father as "the fellow in the cellarage," "true penny," "old mole," etc., are omitted. Some of Hamlet's soliloquies—the "O that this too, too solid flesh would melt," and "O what a rogue and peasant slave am I," are shorn of many lines.

The scene between Polonius and Reynaldo is missing, as usual, and not missed. The advice of Hamlet to the Players, though omitted by Betterton, had been restored by Wilks, and is found in this version of 1773; the play scene is much "cut." The scene which neo-Græco-dramatic scholarship has assigned as the "climax" of Hamlet, the scene where the Prince discovers the King praying in his closet, is given, shorn of the crucial touch. The prayer and soliloquy of the guilty monarch occur, but not Hamlet's hair-splitting soliloquy giving his reasons for not killing the murderer. So little did Gentleman anticipate modern criticism, that he prints a foot-note saying that Hamlet's speech "is here commendably thrown aside, first as being unnecessary [!], and next, as tending to vitiate and degrade his character." So easily did the Eighteenth Century brush away cobwebs in which our modern scholarship has entangled itself!

Both the scene of the Gravediggers and that of Osric are retained (one year after Garrick had abolished them). In face of the great Roscius, Gentleman timidly but firmly waves two flags of truce. Of the Gravediggers: "These

gentry, and their quibbling humour, certainly trespass upon
decorum; but the moral reflections occasioned by the grave,
&c. make ample amends; and though their dialogue is often
stigmatised as mere gallery stuff, yet we think that sensible
boxes may be pleased and instructed by it; for which reason
it is cause of concern to think that Mr. *Garrick* has politely
frenchified his alteration by endeavouring to annihilate
what, though Mr. *Voltaire* could not like it, has indubitable
merit." Of Osric, "This fopling: Mr. *Garrick* has rejected
him indeed, as *Shakespeare* says . . . 'he speaks an infinite
deal of nothing.'"

But Gentleman kept on the shadow of his age in this last
general remark: "We think the last scene of this play very
reprehensible; it teems with slaughter, and, though the plot
in many places is disgustful to criticism, even with latitude,
we have no scruple to pronounce its catastrophe the worst
part of it. . . . . The fifth Act of this play is by no means
so good as we could wish; yet it engages the attention in
public, by having a good deal of bustle, and, what English
audiences love, many deaths."

I may leave this play by repeating that it was handed
from Betterton to Wilks, by him to Garrick, and by Bell to
Kemble, almost unchanged in its acting estate. The
"frenchifying" of it by Garrick was the only break in the
inheritance. One can only wish, for curiosity's sake, that
Bell had been enabled to print the "frenchified" Hamlet of
Garrick.

OTHELLO, 1773

Another tragedy that Bell gives us opportunity to discuss
is Othello. Like Hamlet, it has not suffered through the
centuries from the passion for alteration that has invaded
the holy places of others of the great dramas. This edition
is a landmark, then, in showing how the work had come
through from Betterton's time to Garrick's. It may be
said at once that the play follows accurately Shakespeare's
original until we reach the address of Othello to the senate;
at that point, oddly enough, the great warrior gives up his

references to "anthropophagi and cannibals and antres vast," and irons out his narration of the wooing of Desdemona into these commonplace lines—origin unknown to me:

Of battles bravely, hardly fought; of victories
For which the conquerors mourn'd, so many fell:
Sometimes I told the story of a siege,
Wherein I had to combat plagues and famine;
Soldiers unpaid; fearful to fight,
Yet bold in dangerous mutiny.

In Act II, all the tumult of the storm is omitted, the scene beginning with Cassio's entrance: "Thanks to the valiant of this warlike isle." Gentleman thinks the earlier scene should be retained, as "it . . . raises a pleasing, proper anxiety for Othello's safety." The scene of the Herald is deleted. The third act omits the Clown, and Bianca is not allowed to appear throughout the play. This is an important change and subtly affects many episodes, involving the working up of the jealousy of Othello. The last-named, be it noted, is deprived by the stage-manager of the fit which so aptly summarises his woe. These last-cited elisions were, I have discovered, of ancient usage. In 1725 were published Original and Genuine Letters sent to the Tatler and Spectator, "none of which have been before Printed." And the ninety-sixth rejected epistle says, "Being at the play of Othello, I was surprized to find whole scenes left out, and others barbarously mangled; among the rest, that which confirms Othello's jealousy, when he sees the handkerchief in Cassio's hands, and misapplies the expressions by him spoke of Bianca . . . Othello's trance . . . how that comes to be omitted, I know not." In the very early days of Cibber, then, these omissions were usual; there is nothing, however, in the letter to impugn our theory that only Shakespeare spoke in the words the stage-director left in the Venetian tragedy.

At the end of the play the pathetic scene between Desdemona and Emilia, as the former prepares for bed, is very grievously missed; and the death of Desdemona is hastened by a dagger, apparently. The foot-note says: "It has been justly remarked, that, *stabbing Desdemona* here, reconciles her recovering speech, yet dying afterwards; which is, otherwise, highly unnatural." Later acting versions, Inchbald's and Kemble's, blandly give stage-directions for this stabbing.

On the whole, Bell's acting version is effective. One could wish certain omitted episodes were retained, but the tragedy moves tensely to its catastrophe. Of course many of the long speeches, especially Iago's, are severely cut; but of Iago, as our trustworthy writer of foot-notes says, "this part, though much curtailed in the acting, is still so long, and had so many soliloquies, that, without capital abilities and strict attention, it must pall an audience." Of the omission of Bianca, the same honest critic remarks: "The third act ends better here, without introducing Cassio and his female cypher." Of the excision of much at the beginning of Act IV, including the important scene of Bianca, Cassio and the handkerchief, with Othello watching, Gentleman says, debonairly, "It does *Shakespeare* great service to begin the Fourth Act here, as the six original pages which precede, are tedious, confused, trifling, and often indecent: the Moor has already been sufficiently wrought on; besides, the character of *Othello,* as it now stands, is as much as any great spirit and acting powers can go through; more, must sink the ablest performer."

JULIUS CÆSAR, 1773

Julius Cæsar—the last of Bell's editions of the tragedies that we need to discuss—is an exceedingly interesting study. In the first place, it is the only authentic acting version we possess since the anomalous 1719 affair, and it may well be regarded as the real version represented in the theatres during the better part of a century. At any rate, it is the accumulated wisdom of many stage-managers. We saw that the first quartos published after the Restoration gave to "Caska" the speeches of Marullus in the first scene of

the play; this custom continued in 1719 and down to the
days of Edwin Booth. In Bell, some of Flavius's speeches
are given to Decius Brutus. Yet, later, Casca tells Brutus
and Cassius that Marullus and Flavius, "for pulling scarfs
off Cæsar's images are put to death." To close this confusing account, I may say that Casca and Trebonius do an
amazing amount of doubling or trebling before the play
ends. In the scene of night-prodigies, Cicero's part is
given to Trebonius, who at the end of Scene 3 in Act II
(in which Cæsar is persuaded to go to the Senate) takes
the place of Publius. In the bit preliminary to the quarrel
scene, in Act IV, "Lucilius, Titinius, &c.," as Gentleman
says, "are advantageously blended into Casca and Trebonius." Nay, more, Casca (not Pindarus) is told by Cassius "to bid the commanders lead their charges off," Trebonius (not Lucilius) being told by Brutus to "do the like."
The counsel scene, following the quarrel, includes Casca
and Trebonius, not Titinius and Messala, as in Shakespeare;
Casca is now Shakespeare's Titinius, and Trebonius is
Messala. Unless I have counted wrongly, Casca has now
obligingly been four gentlemen in one, and Trebonius also
has been content to quadruple his single entity. They continue to be these characters—Titinius and Messala—at the
end of the play. The part about Cassius's birthday is not
given in the main text in Bell, but printed in a foot-note;
Messala's share in it is assigned to Casca, who thus enters
upon his fifth character. Gentleman says, "this short
conversation between *Cassius* and *Casca* is sometimes, but
very improperly rejected by the stage." Except for this
scene, however, Casca, as in the 1719 version, is Shakespeare's Titinius to the close, killing himself on Cæsar's
body. Trebonius, having obligingly surrendered the part
of Messala in the scene just mentioned, resumes it for the
rest of the play. He is told by Brutus, to "haste, haste,
Trebonius, and give those bills," wearing his *haste* (not
Shakespeare's *ride*) with a difference due to his change of
name. The scene of the death of Brutus is also changed
as to personnel. Brutus begs not Clitus, Dardanius and

Strato to hold his sword while he runs on it, but Decius and Metellus. So much for the doubling of parts, which was occasioned possibly by shortage of players, but probably by a desire to make certain characters "fatter" for the acceptance of second-rate and pretentious actors. The fact that Marullus, Casca and Titinius are poles apart in character, and when combined, literally, like Cerberus, three gentlemen in one, would have no bearing with a vain actor who saw a chance to appear before an audience for an entire play, rather than for half its course. A foot-note in Bell's Macbeth shows the justice of my contention as to the cause of this "doubling": "The characters of *Rosse* and *Angus*," it states, "have been judiciously blended at *Covent-Garden* Theatre, into those of *Macduff* and *Lennox*, to make them more worthy the attention of good performers and the audience."

Having thus disposed of changes in the *dramatis personæ*, let us see about changes in the scenes. At the close of the great scene in Brutus's orchard, the bit with the sick Caius Ligarius is left out. Act III runs together the characters of Artemidorus and the Soothsayer, and consequently the scenes in which they occur. The Soothsayer does not appear at the beginning of the Senate scene. The great body of the play remains intact, but the minor episodes are sacrificed. Thus, the episode of the killing of Cinna, the poet, artistically, but not dramatically significant, is deleted.

Several speeches of Brutus demand consideration. The first occurs in his first scene. Four or more lines are cut bodily from one of his speeches and saved for his exit:

> Till then, my noble friend, chew upon this:
> *Brutus* had rather be a villager
> Than to repute himself a son of *Rome*,
> Under such hard conditions as this time
> Is like to lay upon us.

The foot-note quaintly says: "Here the transposed lines come in advantageously for the actor's going off." Could anything be simpler? His advice to Lucius about enjoying "the honey-heavy dew of slumber" is omitted in representation, though printed for perusal. The fine speeches beginning

Cassius.   Stoop, then, and wash,—how many ages hence, etc.
Brutus.   How many times shall Cæsar bleed in sport, etc.
Cassius.   So oft as that shall be, etc.,

are printed in italics, with this note: "This, and the two following speeches, though seldom delivered on the stage, certainly deserve preservation."

At the vanishing of the Ghost of Cæsar, Brutus, to "send him off with a flourish," is given these lines from the 1719 edition of the play:

> Sure they have rais'd some devil to their aid,
> And think to frighten *Brutus* with a shade;
> But ere the night closes this fatal day,
> I'll send more ghosts, this visit to repay.

At the death of Brutus he utters more interpolated lines, "not Shakespeare's, but properly added," says Gentleman:

> Scorning to view his country's wrongs,
> Thus Brutus always strikes for liberty.
> Poor, slavish Rome, now farewell.

This wretched interpolation is found in 1719, and also in Inchbald, and, with variations, in Kemble.

The various acting editions of Julius Cæsar are among the hardest problems of the task I have undertaken. The Bell version is far from satisfactory, but we must remember that this tragedy, after having been a mainstay of Hart and Mohun, and later of Wilks and Booth, had sunk into desuetude during the age of Garrick, and was hardly played until the very last days of Kemble. Probably there was no good acting version in 1773, when Bell desired to publish the play.

Of the nine tragedies, so-called, included in Bell's Shakespeare, but six really represent stage-versions generally accepted by theatre-goers. There is strong reason to

believe that Cymbeline, Hamlet, King Lear, Macbeth,
Othello and Romeo and Juliet, as he prints them, were
exactly what was presented on the stage of the theatres.
Julius Cæsar was probably presented—when presented at
all—in some such way as his publication would indicate.
As for Timon of Athens and Coriolanus, when had they
been presented, except in the versions of Cumberland and
Sheridan respectively? They are negligible, I believe, in
the history I am trying to write.

THE HISTORIES: KING JOHN, 1773

I shall take up in the chronological order of their subjects the historical plays included among the acting versions
in Bell's Shakespeare. These are six in number, and King
John heads the list.

The changes from the original in this play are merely
matters of curtailment, and therefore, fortunately, need
detain us but a minute. Hardly a scene is eliminated in
its entirety, the short parley in the Dauphin's camp—Scene
5 of Act V—being an exception; but long speeches are mercilessly (or mercifully) cut, and sometimes wholly sacrificed.
Act I suffers least of all, but in Act II the speech of recrimination between Constance and Elinor is cast out, as well
as much from the scene of the marriage compact. Gentleman advocates giving up all about the fight between the
French and English behind the scenes; it is absurd, he
thinks, to have a fight so decisive and so ridiculously brief
fought outside, while the stage waits. In the first scene of
Act III the twelve lines from The Troublesome Reign of
King John, incorporated by Pope, are, curiously enough,
retained. They occur after one of the Bastard's repetitions
of "And hang a calf's skin on those recreant limbs."

Austria. Methinks that *Richard*'s pride and *Richard*'s fall
    Should be a precedent to fright you, Sir.
Faul. What words are these! How do my sinews shake!
    My father's foe clad in my father's spoil!
    How doth *Alecto* whisper in my ears,

"Delay not, *Richard ;* kill the villain strait;
Disrobe him of the matchless monument,
Thy father's triumph o'er the savages"—
Now by his soul I swear, my father's soul,
Twice will I not review the morning's rise,
'Till I have torn that trophy from thy back,
And split thy heart, for wearing it so long.

This may be all right for a prompt-copy; but what about the correct Mr. Pope? To the end of the play nothing essential is eliminated except some of the poetry, notably some lines in the "to paint the lily" speech, and above all the magnificently imaginative line, "How easy dost thou take all England up." All in all, this is a very admirable acting version.

HENRY IV, PART I, 1773

Henry IV, Part I is equally near the original. It cuts from every scene parts of speeches, owing, I suppose, to the exigency of finishing a performance in reasonable time. The long speeches of the King in the first scene and in the touching rebuke to his son are almost barbarously curtailed; Lady Percy's first remonstrance to her lord is also shorn of nineteen lines. But in general the play is given in Shakespeare's order, and with a quickened dramatic pace. Concerning "cuts," Gentleman's note says of the first, "As the author wrote the part of the King, in this conference with his son, it bore too hard on the powers of the actor, and patience of the audience; two speeches only produced an hundred lines; as they are at present reduced, they work a good effect, both in utterance and perusal." Again, after giving in a foot-note the lines omitted from Lady Percy's speech, he says they "well merit preservation, and we believe are only rejected by the stage, because Lady *Percy* is seldom personated by a principal actress." Verily, in this business, we cannot afford, like the closet-student of the closet-drama, to overlook the actor. Gentleman knew more about this than did Johnson or Steevens.

Scenes entirely omitted are best indicated in Gentleman's charming notes. "This scene [i. e., the Tavern scene of Act II] in the original is vastly too long: therefore it is curtailed of a mock trial the author introduced; which rather checked and loaded the main business, notwithstanding a vein of pure comedy runs through it." Of the earlier tavern scene he writes, "This scene, throughout, especially the latter part, is totally in the *bamming* stile; we are to look for no meaning, but amuse ourselves with the idleness of the sport"—a very wise sop to conscience. Of Act III: "*Shakespeare* wrote, to begin this third Act, a wild scene, of seven pages, between Hotspur, Glendower, &c. which is properly rejected in representation." This also dismisses Lady Percy and the Welsh lady. The scene in Act IV at the Palace of the Archbishop of York is gone. Gentleman concludes by saying that "the play, as it now stands, is free from superfluities, and possesses much strength of character and sentiment; yet we are sorry to say, that the want of ladies, and matter to interest female auditors, lies so heavy on it, that through an excellent *Falstaff* only, can it enjoy occasional life."

This version of the first part of Henry IV is very similar to Betterton's, noted earlier in the history. In fact, Betterton had done his work so well as regards omission and retention, that no subsequent producer ventured to disturb the main outlines of his scheme. Kemble's version hardly differs from Bell's. It is an almost perfect acting copy.

HENRY IV, PART II, 1773

As regards the second part of the same play, the Bell edition varies considerably from the "Sequel" to Henry IV produced in 1719. That, it will be remembered, affixed to material of the original much from the first and second acts of Henry V. The arrangement we are about to study is made up entirely of matter from the original play, and, like the first part, offered so little ground for improvement that even the facile Kemble found little to alter or destroy. Of his own version, the editor of Bell says, "in the original it is loaded with superfluities; the Reader has it here considerably and very well, purged; but, however well reformed, it will never be a popular play on the stage."

The prompt-book omits the Induction (by Rumour) and Shakespeare's opening scene at Warkworth Castle, in which Northumberland learns of the death of his son. The play begins with the entrance of Falstaff and his page, soon followed by the Chief Justice. Between this and the second scene involving the same characters and Quickly, is interjected a shortened version of the scene in the Archbishop of York's palace. The second act is devoted to the scenes with the Prince and Poins, then to the tavern scene, somewhat fumigated. The intermediary scene at Warkworth involving the Northumberlands and Lady Percy is deleted. The third act belongs to Falstaff and Shallow, with the addition of the tiresome parleys between York and Mowbray, on the one side, and John of Lancaster, on the other, ending in the treachery of the latter. Of the omitted scene at court, the interesting foot-note tells us, "There is a scene of the original, between King *Henry* and some of his Peers, which begins the third act, omitted, and we think properly, in representation; the King's excellent soliloquy [on sleep] is well transposed to the beginning of the fourth act." Kemble's version follows the same practice.

Act IV begins with the King's apostrophe to sleep, and is given entirely to the touching episode of the crown. This is the perfect gem in the play. Says the guiding foot-note, "There are several judicious transpositions in the last act, which, however, is still laboured and heavy." Bell gives in order all the matter pertaining to Falstaff's learning of the death of the King, and his starting for London, the arrest of Doll and Quickly (omitted by later versions), the reconciliation between the King and the Chief Justice, the coronation and the casting out of Falstaff. This last act differs decidedly from Kemble's, but I believe to the disadvantage of the latter. It does not vary much from the original. In general, it is a good acting version.

HENRY V AND RICHARD III, 1773

The Henry V of our series may be passed over with a word; it is very close to the original in order of scenes, and its cutting is on the whole judicious; it omits the Chorus, much to Gentleman's distress—he laments the habit of neglecting such noble lines. Of the lesson scene between Katharine and Alice he says, with unusual asperity, "After this [the preceding] scene, we meet in the original, to wound our patience, a French one, of the most trifling, childish nature; disgraceful to the author, and the piece." Of course the long speeches throughout are considerably lessened in extent, including the numerous prayers, exhortations and soliloquies of the King. None of the comic characters are omitted, not even MacMorris and Jamy and Bates; we are not spared one of them. On the whole, this is a good acting version, but, as too often with Bell, some of the best poetry is gone.

Of Richard III we shall have practically no need to speak; it is Cibber's version, and we dismiss it with Gentleman's commendation: "This Tragedy being admirably altered from the original, by that excellent judge and ornament of the stage, *Colley Cibber*, we shall have few observations to make. . . . The alterations have been produced from a very extensive and settled knowledge of stage effect: we have been studious to find error, but could not materially." Shakespearians to the contrary, notwithstanding, subsequent students of the stage have borne witness to the truth of Gentleman's verdict.

HENRY VIII, 1773

The trouble with Henry VIII is that it is impossible to maintain interest in its story after the fall of Wolsey and the death of Katharine; the bits about the christening of Elizabeth and the trial of Cranmer are actually glued on the first part in order to eke out the necessary five acts. Irving and Tree realised this fact, and cut away most of the unnecessary appendages, filling up the deficiency with scenery, spectacle, dance, music and procession. Bell's edition was not so wise in its day and generation. It gives us in Act I the scenes of the arrest of Buckingham, the accusation of his surveyor, the unnecessary episode of Sands and the Chamberlain preparing to go to the palace of York, and the dance and feast at the Cardinal's with the meeting of Anne Bullen and the King. Act II shows, in its four scenes, the execution of Buckingham, the introduction of Campeius to the King, the interesting talk between Anne and the old lady, and the trial of Queen Katharine. The third act opens with the strong scene between Katharine and the two Cardinals, followed by the scene of Wolsey's fall. Bell curtails this, especially in the talk between Cromwell and Wolsey. He even omits the last four lines of Wolsey's farewell to his greatness. The fourth act is composed of the material of the death of Katharine at Kimbolton, continuing to the end with all the final directions to Capucius. In this scene (probably to satisfy the actor) Griffith's part is assigned, ridiculously enough, to Cromwell. The last act, with all its Elizabethan christening and Cranmerian "heresy," drags its weary length along, much as in the original, to something of a spectacle in the way of a christening described with some accuracy in the text; of that, more anon.

These, of course, are the only historical plays of Shakespeare deemed feasible for the stage by Eighteenth-Century playgoers; Richard II and the three parts of Henry VI slumbered peacefully on library shelves. The six plays I have discussed seem to me to have been, with the exception of Henry VIII, and granting the Cibberism of Richard III, admirably prepared for the stage. I can say no more.

CHAPTER XIX

THE PLAYS: THE ACTIVITIES OF KEMBLE

JOHN KEMBLE AND THOMAS HULL

FROM 1788, when he became acting director of the stage at Drury Lane, until 1817, when he retired, laden with honours, from public life, John Kemble is to be reckoned with as the leading man in English theatricals, the brains, as Mrs. Siddons was the heart, of the machine. From that date, his stage adaptations dominated, and set the pace for other producers; furthermore, he passed on to the next age, that of Kean, the versions it was, in great part, to employ. Hereafter, in the present chapter, therefore, we shall deal largely with his attempts to make Shakespeare palatable to his audiences.

Before we come to him, however, we must pause for a moment to introduce Thomas Hull, actor, writer, and general utility man at Covent Garden. His adaptation of The Winter's Tale, as printed in Bell's Shakespeare, we have already examined; his Comedy of Errors, brought out at Covent Garden on January 22, 1779, was destined to have considerable life on the stage. After a few years it was superseded by a three-act version, but when Kemble revived the piece at Covent Garden on January 9, 1808, he availed himself of practically all of Hull's additions and alterations. According to the purpose announced in his preface to the 1793 edition of his work, Hull has sentimentalised the rather brittle mechanism of the original, not only in the fifth act, but in all the scenes involving the Antipholis (as he spells the name) of Syracuse, Luciana and Adriana. He has also strengthened the character of the Dromio of Syracuse, by enlarging at least two scenes to be indicated immediately. All in all, the new matter is considerable in quantity, but its effect on an audience could be seen with-

out the proof of the readiness with which John Kemble
retained it many years after.

In Act I, Scene 2, note the addition to Shakespeare's
scene for Dromio, ending with only the two lines,

> Many a man would take you at your word,
> And go indeed, having so good a mean.

Observe what Hull makes of it:

Antiph. of S.   Get thee away!
Dr. of S.   Many a man would take you at your word,
> And go away indeed, having so great
> A treasure in his charge.—Of what strength do
> You conceive my honesty, good master,
> That you dare put it to such temptation?
An. of S.   Of proof against a greater charge than this;
> Were it remiss, thy love would strengthen it:
> I think thou would'st not wrong me if thou could'st.
Dr. of S.   I hope I should not, sir; but there is such
> A thing as trusting too far.—Odds, heart, 'tis
> A weighty matter, and, if ballanc'd in
> A stilliard against my honesty
> I doubt—
An. of Syr.   That very doubt is my security.—
> No further argument, but speed away.

As, at the end of Act II, this same Dromio of Syracuse
follows Adriana, Antipholis of Syracuse and Luciana to
dinner, he indulges in an expository speech of sixteen lines
—Hull undiluted by a word of Shakespeare.

At the beginning of the first scene between Adriana and
Luciana, there is a great deal of extra stuff, which I cannot
here reproduce. Let me quote directly from an entire
scene of Hull:

ACT III—SCENE 2

*A Garden. Antipholis of Syracuse, Adriana, Luciana, and Hermia
discovered.*

Ad.   Why was I to this keen mockery born?
> How at your hands have I deserv'd this coldness?
> In sooth, you do me wrong.   There was a time
> When I believ'd (so fond was my credulity)
> The sun was scarce so true unto the day,
> As you to me.

An. of S. I would some friendly light
    Might chase away the mist that clouds our fancies,
    And give this dream a meaning!—True, I see,
    These beauteous bowers, in nature's fragrance rich;
    Behold the painted children of her hand,
    Flaunting in gay luxuriance all around.
    I see imperial Phœbus' trembling beam
    Dance on the curly brook; whose gentle current
    Glides imperceptibly away, scarce staying
    To kiss the embracing bank.
Ad.   So glides away
    Thy hasty love—(O apt allusion!)
    And mocks my constant and attentive care,
    That seeks in vain to keep it.
Luc.   Dearest brother,
    Why turn on me your eyes?—regard my sister
    Who with such earnest suit solicits you
    To heal her wounded peace.
Ad. It cannot be
    But that some phrenzy hath possest his mind,
    Else could he not with cold indifference hear
    His Adriana pleading.—Music's voice
    O'er such entranced dispositions
    Hath oft a magic power, and can recall
    The wand'ring faculties. Good cousin Hermia,
    Assay those melting strains, wherewith, thou told'st me,
    Forsaken Julia labour'd to retrieve
    Lysander's truant heart.

[SONG]

Ad. Sister, there is some magic in thine eye
    That hath infected his—Perchance to thee
    He may unfold the source of his distemp'rature:
    For me, no longer will I sue for that
    My right may claim: loose infidelity
    And lawless passion have estrang'd his soul.

After fifteen more such lines she departs, and Luciana and Antipholis of Syracuse then begin something like Shakespeare's scene, but much curtailed.

The additions of Hull to Act V, to strengthen the recognition of the long-separated family of Ægeon, I consider, in spite of Hull's pluming himself on them, so slight and unimportant that I pay no attention to them. He omits the

final scene between the two Dromios.   If I were a getter-up
of shows, I should approve of Hull's adaptation; as ardent
a Shakespearian as I maintain myself to be, I shall not
shed tears over any milk spilled in connection with this
early, mechanical performance of the bard.   Looking fur-
tively over my shoulder lest the irate spirit of the Rev.
John Genest should be behind me, I wish to state that I
believe an audience would get more enjoyment from Hull's
(and Kemble's) Comedy of Errors than from Shakespeare's.

WOODS'S THE TWINS, 1780

The reasons for my saying this are very well stated by
W. Woods, whose three-act farce of The Twins, or Which
is Which? altered from The Comedy of Errors, was performed at the Theatre-Royal, Edinburgh, and published in
London in 1780.   This farce must be very like—and is
assumed to be very like—the three-act Comedy of Errors
which superseded Hull's alteration at Covent Garden on
April 3, 1790, and continued to be acted for some years
thereafter.   In fact, for several years, this artificial comedy,
either in Hull's version or as a three-act farce, held the
stage at Covent Garden with astonishing tenacity.   But
let us see why Woods made of it a farce, and why a farce
such as his was probably deemed better than Hull's attempt
to sentimentalise the unsentimentalisable.   I will quote
from the author's apology for his labours: ". . . That the
Characters and Incidents in general of this entertaining
Piece would rank with much more Propriety under the
Title of *Farce* . . .   It would also, he thought, obtain a
great Advantage in Representation by being shortened:
For the similarity of Character, and quick Succession of
Mistakes, must render the Subject very liable to pall upon
an Audience during the Exhibition of Five Acts; whereas,
by being reduced to Three, the Judgment will not be so
much offended, having less Time to reflect on the Improb-
ability of the Events. . . .   He has added little of his own,
except where it was necessary in transposing or altering

Speeches for better effect, in ridding others of the Incumbrance of Jingle, or in connecting Passages rendered distant by proper Omissions." This really describes accurately what has been done in The Twins. Much of the stupid witty (?) dialogue between each of the Antipholuses and his servant is omitted. The heroes are called Antipholis of Syracuse, &c.

Hull is responsible, also, for a new attempt on the tantalising Timon of Athens (which was a veritable Jack-o'-lantern to these adapters), produced at Covent Garden on May 13, 1786. This is merely a revival of Shadwell's ill-starred venture, and brings back to the stage the impossible Evandra-Melissa stuff. *Requiescat in pace;* it did not survive its birth-pains.

JOHN KEMBLE

Enter John Philip Kemble, acting director of Drury Lane Theatre, 1788–89. I have previously stated that there were four periods in his active and interesting career in which he had a chance to revive Shakespeare, and produce his plays with something of the dignity, the reverence and the pomp to which they were entitled. These periods were, first, the few years following his assumption of the stage direction of Drury Lane in the autumn of 1788; second, the few years following the opening of the enlarged, remodelled, refurbished Drury Lane, a highly important event which occurred in the spring of 1794; third, the early years of his control of Covent Garden Theatre, beginning in the autumn of 1803; and, fourth, the few years following the opening of the new Covent Garden in 1809–10. After the distressing weeks of the riots for the renewal of old prices of admission, this theatre settled down to a few years of splendour such as no other English playhouse had ever before enjoyed.

In each of the four periods indicated above, John Kemble showed by his performance how seriously he took his responsibilities and how earnestly he strove to meet them. The list of his printed revisions of Shakespeare starts in 1789 and continues until 1815, when the series was published complete in a handsome set of volumes that any one interested in Shakespeare on the stage would be happy to possess. The dates of these successive editions are likely to confuse the student unless he anchors them in the four periods I have indicated. It will then at once be apparent that Kemble produced several of the less frequently acted works at each of these times, and possibly brought out reprints of the familiar plays more regularly issued hitherto. Of course, the standard comedies, tragedies and histories as acted are printed almost throughout his career, but we learn to track his activities by the publications following each of these four important new changes in his artistic life.

With this clue, we discover that on November 25, 1788, only about a month after Kemble assumed the management of Drury Lane, Henry VIII (not acted twenty years) was revived; on February 7, 1789, Coriolanus, or the Roman Matron was brought out. On October 1, 1789 (not acted twenty years) Henry V, and on October 13, 1789, Kemble's amalgamation of Dryden's and Shakespeare's Tempest were produced; on January 15, 1790, The Two Gentlemen of Verona (not acted twenty years). One becomes a bit nervous about the glibness of this invariable "twenty years," but we know that a considerable period had elapsed since any of these pieces had been produced at Drury Lane. The five revivals listed here prove the sincerity of Kemble's purpose, and make, I think, a record he might be proud of. They were not—the printed copies will show—brought out with that splendour of setting and accessories that distinguished the three later periods, but Kemble was doing his best with the handicap of the spendthrift Sheridan always in the near view. Kemble gave full measure, too, by reviving—after shorter intervals of disuse—both Henry IV, Part I, and King John, in the season of 1791–92.

The glories of the remodelled Drury Lane of 1794 have been sung by Boaden. Suffice it here to say that Kemble signalised the occasion by two new oblations to the memory

SCENE FROM RICHARD CŒUR DE LION WITH JOHN KEMBLE AND DORA JORDAN

From a contemporary print, 1787

of Shakespeare: On December 12, 1794, he brought back
All's Well that Ends Well, and on December 30th, Measure
for Measure.

The two periods at Covent Garden, from 1803 to the
burning of the house in 1808, and the days of glory from
1809 to 1817, might almost be catalogued as one unbroken
lapse of time. During those years most of the 8vo Kemble
editions appeared, and one can date his revivals and his
recensions by successive title-pages. His Shakespearian
productions for the first year of his management of Covent
Garden, 1803–4, were, in the order of their first performance, Romeo and Juliet, Hamlet, Richard III, Henry V,
Much Ado about Nothing, Henry IV, Part I, The Merchant of Venice, Measure for Measure, Macbeth, Henry IV,
Part II, Othello, King John, The Merry Wives of Windsor.
This strikes me as a test of John Kemble's sincerity as to
Shakespeare; it is an imposing array. The strength of the
casts can be ascertained from that of The Merchant of
Venice: George Frederick Cooke (Shylock), Kemble (Antonio), Charles Kemble (Bassanio), Mrs. Siddons (Portia),
Munden (Launcelot), Emery (Old Gobbo). Cooke's presence in the company accounts for the revival of the Falstaff plays; Mrs. Siddons, of course, was a tower of strength
as Lady Macbeth, Queen Katharine and Isabella. During
the year all of these plays were newly imprinted according
to Kemble's stage versions. Let me repeat, we can always
trail him by these dates.

Unfortunately, the Master Betty furore came, in 1804–5,
to interrupt this tide of splendid accomplishment. Mrs.
Siddons, disgusted, appeared but once during the season.
But by 1806, the nuisance was brushed aside, and Kemble
was once more started on his triumphant way. As You
Like It, with Charles and John Kemble as Orlando and
Jaques, and Cymbeline were added to the current repertoire. Katharine and Petruchio, I suppose, hardly counts.
On November 3, 1806, Kemble magnificently revived his
own version of Coriolanus, but slightly differing from that
of 1789, and on December 8th of the same year, his own

recension of The Tempest (greatly different from that of
1789). These two versions will demand our attention later
on. The next season, on January 9, 1808, came a revival
of The Comedy of Errors, and on April 21st, one of The
Two Gentlemen of Verona. On May 18th, Kemble acted
King Lear for the first time in eight years. Nearly a year
later (February 27, 1809) at the Opera House in the Haymarket (Covent Garden having been reduced to ashes) he
took from the play much of Shakespeare that Garrick had
returned, and put back a corresponding amount of Tate.
All these important revivals, implying important changes
from Kemble's previous acting versions, were accompanied
by printed copies now (once more let me say) standing as
landmarks in the history of Kemble's career.

The last great period, following the opening of the new
theatre in 1809, is signalised by a new study of Twelfth
Night on January 5, 1811, and by Kemble's revision of
Cibber's Richard III, on April 1st of the same year. The
next season, 1811–12, saddened at its close by the retirement of Mrs. Siddons, was, nevertheless, for Shakespeare
a banner-year. The Winter's Tale was newly staged with
Kemble as Leontes and Mrs. Siddons as Hermione; Coriolanus had a new setting, and Julius Cæsar, after years of
neglect, was magnificently mounted. Practically the last
effort of Kemble in this direction was a revival on November 15, 1813, of Antony and Cleopatra, with additions from
Dryden. Last stage of all came, on January 17, 1816, a
new operatic treatment of A Midsummer Night's Dream,
long left in peace by desecrators, and now re-edited by
Frederick Reynolds, as the first of his attempts to popularise Shakespeare's more romantic and fragile comedies by
the infusion into them of much song, spectacle and dance.
Kemble's share in this first offence was probably but slight.
In the following season Kemble retired, his departure perhaps hurried by the tremendous success of Edmund Kean
at Drury Lane.

It will now be my pleasing task to review the more
notable of these stage versions of Kemble.

JOHN KEMBLE'S METHODS

Twenty-six plays are included in the 1815 collected edition of Kemble; to these we must add Antony and Cleopatra, issued in 1813, without Kemble's name, but as produced at his theatre. Successive editions of these versions,
some of them dating back as far as 1789 (though in that
year, again, Kemble's name is not printed on the title-
pages) show the extreme care bestowed by Kemble on his
work, and a progressive tendency toward crispness of action,
clearness of plot-outline, in most cases care for the Shakespearian text, and a just combination of all the elements
that might be characterised as dramatic. The excellence
of these versions is shown by the long vogue they enjoyed;
the Shakespeare in Oxberry's English Drama (1818-23),
in Cumberland's (1828-30), and in Taylor's (later French's)
in this country, is to a great extent regulated by Kemble's
copies. Boaden, in speaking of one of the earliest of Kemble's revivals, Henry V, in 1789-90, says, "He therefore set
himself seriously to prepare the play for representation.
Now this, in Mr. Kemble's notion of the business, was, not
to order the prompter to write out the parts from some old
mutilated prompt copy lingering on the shelves; but himself to consider it attentively in the author's genuine book:
then to examine what corrections could be properly admitted into his text; and, finally, what could be cut out in
the representation, not as disputing the judgment of the
author, but as suiting the time of representation to the
habits of his audience, or a little favouring the powers of
his actors, in order that the performance might be as
uniformly good as it was practicable to make it. The
stage arrangements throughout the play were all distinctly
marked by him in his own clear, exact penmanship, and
when he had done his work his theatre received, in that
perfected copy, a principle of exactness, which was of itself
sufficient to keep its stage unrivalled for truth of scenic
exhibition." This practice became a custom with Kemble,
and accounts for the effectiveness of his efforts.

It would be very tedious for the reader, and unnecessary as well, to go through the twenty-seven versions of Shakespearian plays by this master-craftsman, from their first stage to the last in 1815. Most of the changes made in the plays during that long period were minor, and incorporated for the purpose of securing greater polish and greater articulation in dramatic effect. In the case of certain plays, however, Kemble's experience led him to restorations or interpolations that merit all the comment I can reasonably afford to bestow upon them. I have therefore decided to brush aside non-essentials, in order to render more clear what is really pertinent.

MANY PLAYS NOT TO BE DISCUSSED HERE

In pursuance of this policy, therefore, I shall say nothing of Kemble's recensions—early or late—of All's Well that Ends Well, As You Like It, both parts of Henry IV, Henry V, Henry VIII, King John, Macbeth, The Merry Wives of Windsor, Much Ado about Nothing, Othello or The Winter's Tale. They are really enough like Bell's edition to pass muster as copies eased of a few incumbrances, and more highly finished throughout their full extent. The Comedy of Errors, as we have seen, is Hull's version, additions and all. Cymbeline (if the so-called Roach edition of 1806 be Kemble's, as Mr. Jaggard and most librarians think), the Katharine and Petruchio, and the Romeo and Juliet are, to all intents and purposes, Garrick's versions, as found in Bell; it would be idle to deny that minor changes, verbal and by way of curtailment, occur; it would be equally idle to burden the already over-wearied reader with all the forgettable minuteness thereof, except to say that Cymbeline restores the passionate soliloquy of Posthumus concerning the faithfulness of women. In As You Like It, Jaques, of course, has the important speeches of the First Lord, and Rosalind sings the Cuckoo song.

Hamlet may detain us for a second to reiterate that Kemble has made of it a polished gem of dramatic intensity; much of the fine poetry is gone; also, as usual, all the

Norweyan business, Polonius's advice to Laertes, etc.; but the whole thing moves with splendid vigour to its conclusion. Perhaps, after all, poetry is better in the ear of the student than in the mouths of ordinary actors. And just a word as to two other tragedies. Having, apparently, used something like Garrick's version of King Lear, in its infrequent revivals during the reign of the imbecility of George III, Kemble in 1809 restored almost all of the Tate material, except that he did not have Gloster blinded in sight of the audience—his speeches being heard from the wings—and he gave up the "fall" of Gloster from the cliff, Lear in his madness entering before the consummation of that "ridiculous" act. In some places, Shakespeare's text replaces Tate's, but not enough to impair its general commonplaceness. Why did Kemble perform this act of vandalism? Who knows? It is at least to be said in his favour, that Lear as popular stage entertainment has gone down since the Shakespeare play was restored by actors; in one sense King Lear is too good for the stage, and perhaps in another not good enough. At any rate, who has succeeded greatly in Lear, who did not use the Tate version? This seems an irreverent thing to say, but facts are facts. The same observation may be made of the Cibber Richard III. Whatever we think of that master-craftsman's hatchet work and carpentry on several of the historical pieces, the fact remains that his Richard III was a magnificent bit of theatrical effectiveness; all who have given it up in favour of the original, have regretted their choice. Richard III, as acted to-day, is still Cibber's, not Shakespeare's. The solution, of course, is that Cibber is to Shakespeare as nervous tensity is to sprawling leisure; which is the more effective? Of course, I am not considering poetry here; I am talking of plays to be acted in a theatre before an audience, as Professor Brander Matthews would say. In all probability, something like this consideration moved Kemble to restore Tate and retain Cibber. In 1811, Kemble "revised" Cibber's play, but his changes in no way affect the ordering of the scenes. He restored some of Shakespeare's language, and gave different names to some of the characters; the

Lieutenant of the Tower becomes Sir Robert Brakenbury, and Brandon takes the place of Tressel in the soliloquy with Stanley, and throughout the play.

KEMBLE'S NAMING OF UNNAMED CHARACTERS

Let me dismiss that particular phase of Kemble's activities by saying that he showed an increasing predilection, as time went on, for giving definite names to Shakespeare's nameless lords, servants, captains, senators, etc. In Cymbeline not only does he retain the elder practice of giving, in the first scene, the First Lord's speeches to Pisanio, but the other lords acquire the fine British names of Madan, Locrine, etc. The Second Merchant in The Comedy of Errors becomes Chares; in Macbeth, the Servant is called Seyton (one of Shakespeare's names, to be sure). Seyton is general errand-boy and consoler to the Macbeth pair in the Kemble version. In Othello, Act I, Scene 3, Kemble has a fine chance to bestow on stray senators and messengers such unobjectionable appellations as Marco, Paulo, Giovanni, etc. In Twelfth Night, Viola's captain is effeminated to Saxon ears by the name of Roberto; why Roberto? Finally—though there are many other such cases—the lawless gang of foresters in The Two Gentlemen of Verona, rattle away to the resounding artillery of such names as Ubaldo, Luigi, Carlos, Stephano, Giacomo, Rodolfo, Valerio, &c. Kemble never laughed, I suppose (how could he with that classic aquiline face?), but I wonder whether he did not nearly smile as he wrote down that fine lot of comic opera outlaws.

KEMBLE'S CORIOLANUS

To begin, then, with Kemble versions demanding attention, the edition of Coriolanus, published in 1789, "exactly conformable to the Representation at Drury Lane, by permission of the Managers, under the Insepection [sic] of James Wrighten, Prompter," as well as that of The Tempest, "with additions from Dryden, as compiled by J. P.

MRS. ABINGTON AS BEATRICE
From a contemporary print,
1776

JOHN PHILIP KEMBLE AS HOTSPUR
From a painting by J. Boaden, engraved and published in
1820

Kemble, 1789," we may take as authentic versions of the Drury Lane offerings following so soon on the accession of Kemble to the acting management.

The Coriolanus differs but slightly from the version printed in 1806, at the time of Kemble's great production at Covent Garden. It is all Shakespeare to the end of the third act. Of the ten scenes of Shakespeare's first act but four are given here, the first, third, sixth and ninth, with some curtailment, at that. Thereafter, until the beginning of Act III, all of Shakespeare's scenes are represented by fragments, at least. Seldom has a play been so bountifully, so lavishly cut to the quick; the kernel is retained with intensity supreme, but a large part of Shakespeare's enveloping speeches and comments has been shelled away. Coriolanus's farewell to his women and to Menenius—Shakespeare's first scene of Act IV—is omitted, and its place supplied by the first scene of the first act of Thomson's play, that between Tullus Aufidius and Volusius. It is clear that Kemble brought in the fragments from Thomson to strengthen the jealousy *motif* between Coriolanus and Aufidius. Thereafter, to the close, much is introduced from the gentle author of The Seasons—the conspiracy of Aufidius and Volusius, until the final scene of the assassination of Coriolanus by Volusius and the other conspirators. The great scene of the supplication is spoiled by this admixture of the two poets. All the first half is Shakespeare; at the close Volumnia loses all dignity by drawing her Thomsonian dagger and threatening dire things:

> Hear me, proud man! I have
> A heart as stout as thine; I came not hither,
> To be sent back rejected, baffled, sham'd,
> Hateful to Rome, because I am thy mother:
> A Roman matron knows, in such extremes,
> What part to take.—
> Go, barb'rous son; go, double parricide;
> Rush o'er my corse-to thy belov'd revenge!
> Tread on the bleeding breast of her, to whom
> Thou ow'st thy life! Lo, thy first victim.
> [*She draws a dagger.*

Cor. [*Seizing her hand*]. Ha!—
                 What dost thou mean?
Vol. To die, while Rome is free.

Much more is borrowed from Thomson.   One hates to think
that the great Siddons was forced to rant herself down to
posterity in this part with fustian of that sort.   The following quarrel between Aufidius and Coriolanus is a clever
mosaic of Shakespeare and Thomson.

It is easy to see why Kemble introduced such passages.
Coriolanus becomes thereby a more understandable play
to the gallery; the jealousy of Aufidius is motivated and
explained, and the resulting assassination of Coriolanus
becomes more reasonable.   As for the dagger of Volumnia,
tragedy queens from time immemorial have found such adornment more profitable than the jewelled crown or the jewelled
tear of pity.

KEMBLE'S TEMPEST

Kemble's version of Coriolanus remained practically
static from 1789 to 1815.   The 1789 Tempest, on the other
hand, is but a feeble effort as compared with that of 1806
and later.   The chief features of all Kemble's versions of
this play are, of course, the restoration of the Hippolyto-
Dorinda plot from Dryden and Davenant, with its tiresome
accompaniments of the duel, the wrath and judgment of
Prospero, etc., and the rejection of all the rest of the stuff
introduced by those two powerful admirers of Shakespeare.
To atone for the new ingredients, Shakespeare's long con-
versations between Antonio, Alonzo, Gonzalo and the rest
are reduced to almost nothing.   Milcha and Sycorax are
gone, and Trinculo (here spelled Trincalo as in Dryden)
and Stephano take the place of Trincalo, Ventoso, Mustacho,
etc.   Speaking of spelling, Antonio, according to invariable
Eighteenth-Century usage, appears as Anthonio, like the
gentleman who knew not why he was so sad, in The Merchant of Venice.   The scenic directions in 1789 also indicate a continuance of early habits, the book calling twice
for "three vistos, each terminating in a cave."

The main distinction, however, between early and late
Kemble versions is the greater or smaller amount of operatic
song therein found. In 1789 the piece bristles with music.
Both Ferdinand and Miranda have a great deal to sing. In
the log-bearing scene, before Ferdinand enters, Miranda
anapestically warbles

> To see thee, so gentle a creature distrest,
> With tears fills my eyes, and with sorrow my breast.
> Oh, would I, possess'd of my father the art,
> Or had I his power, or he had my heart!
> With tears I'll beseech him, with sighs I'll assail,
> Can the sigh of my soul with my father e'er fail?

In course of the scene, Ferdinand and Miranda sing a duet:

> What new delights invade my bosom;
> In every vein what rapture plays;
> What new delights invade my bosom;
> Whilst on thee I fondly gaze.
> Oh, thou art source of all my pleasure,
> Treasure of my soul art thou.
> > Without measure
> > Am'rous pleasure
> Crowns my nights and wings my days.

If the reader's taste sickens at all this, let him console
himself with the reflection that, in 1806, Kemble gave it
up, and restored much more of Shakespeare's poetry in its
stead. Poetry is exactly what was missing in 1789. The
lovely first meeting of Ferdinand and Miranda is reduced
to a mere scenario of what Shakespeare wrote, whereas
Dryden's Hippolyto and Dorinda prattle away to a revolting degree in their original not very decent Restoration
language. In 1806 the proportion between the two pairs
of lovers is a little more evenly maintained. The part of
Miranda, in 1789, was given to the "lovely Crouch," who
has come down in history as the actress who persisted in
dressing one of the singing witches in Macbeth in powdered
wig, stomacher, hoop-skirts, laces and gloves. Poor Miranda! I pause here to remark that, throughout the Kem-

ble period, Dorinda was regarded as the better part of the
two sisters for an actress. Miss Farren played it in 1789,
and, in 1806, Dora Jordan. Later on Miss Booth essayed
it. Hippolyto was always impersonated by a woman. The
reason for the popularity of Dorinda with actresses is due
to her close kinship with the Miss Prues and Miss Hoydens,
in which players like Mrs. Jordan excelled, and which
mightily pleased play-goers of the time. Dorinda is really
a minx, who knows more by nature of the workings of
nature, than most girls ever learn by association with the
world. She is a blot on the purity of The Tempest, and
Kemble should be reprobated for restoring her.

The scene-arrangement of the play in 1789 is not quite
the same as in 1806. I shall dismiss the discussion by
saying that at the earlier date the outlines are blurred; in
the later years, they become exceedingly clear. Kemble's
Tempest at the end is as good a union as can be made of
the discordant elements of Dryden and Shakespeare; the
question is, why mingle them after a lapse of so many
years? Before deciding, let us remember that this version,
when finally perfected by Kemble, had a steadier and a
longer stage life than Shakespeare's own work has ever
since enjoyed. Perhaps we should remember that in judging a man who strives to attract audiences.

Without some such tempering mercy, we shall hardly
know how to deal with a manager whose King Lear is
Tate's, whose Richard III is Cibber's, whose Comedy of
Errors is Hull's, who uses Garrick's Romeo and Juliet, and
goes out of his way to engraft on Coriolanus large bits of
Thomson, and on The Tempest larger masses of Dryden
and Davenant. Meantime, it is something to be able to
admit that Measure for Measure as performed by Mrs.
Siddons was all Shakespeare—with much cut out from the
text. Kemble restored, rather questionably, a great deal
of the Overdone-Froth-Elbow-Pompey nastiness which the
Bell edition rejected; but barring this, I do not see how a
better stage version of the play could be desired. His
Merchant of Venice differs but slightly from the Inchbald;

only it restores far more of the poetry of the first of Act V to the stage. All of Lorenzo's speech about the floor of heaven inlaid with patines of bright gold is put back; also the bits about Orpheus and the wanton herd. Unfortunately Lorenzo and "Jessy," as the songs persist in naming her, sing too many duets and solos for the auditor who would persist in the vein of comedy, not in that of music.

THE TWO GENTLEMEN OF VERONA

The Two Gentlemen of Verona has never been a popular play on the stage, and probably never can be; it is too evanescent, too unreal to satisfy an audience that looks in Shakespeare for something as weighty as the great tragedies or as truly poetic as the real comedies. Kemble tried it, however, on several occasions. His version made use of Victor's (1763), though not slavishly. Obsessed with the idea of getting all the Verona episodes in the first act, he crowded the incidents rather unduly. Victor by running together all the Lucetta-Julia-Proteus scenes, made Proteus receive Julia's letter before it was written; Kemble avoids this by following Julia's tearing of Proteus's letter by the scene of Panthino, Antonio and Proteus, and ending the act with the farewell of Proteus and Julia, his departure, and her determination to follow to Milan. A bit of Launce's weeping at leaving home is given in a penultimate scene, but the long monologue on the sour dog Crab comes in the second act, as in Victor, where it is strangely out of place, Launce and Crab both having been so long from home and past occasion for weeping at departure therefrom. Kemble crowds all this Verona material in five scenes (Victor used only three), and having thus removed from the second act all foreign matter, he is ready to start his version of that act at Milan, and run along regularly on Shakespeare's tracks until the close of the play. Victor's two original scenes of Launce and Speed in the forest, frightened by the outlaws, Kemble runs into one, largely of his own wording; I must say it is not very funny. He also, for purposes of frightfulness, writes up an entrance scene for the bandits, to whom he gives the string of names heretofore noted. The moral of the events in the catastrophe-scene he considerably changes; he omits Proteus's attempted violation of Silvia, and writes in a good deal of stilted stuff about Valentine's sending off Proteus to await sentence.

TWELFTH NIGHT, 1811

Kemble, who had not hitherto done much with Twelfth Night, in 1811 made a careful revision of the play, adding to it a number of names undreamt of by Shakespeare, as Genest says. It gives practically all of the Shakespearian matter necessary to retain, and on the whole is a straightforward production. The first two scenes are transposed, and in the first we find three unusual lines, spoken by Viola:

> I'll serve this duke;
> Thou shalt present me as a page unto him,
> *Of gentle breeding, and my name Cesario:*
> *That trunk, the reliques of my sea-drown'd brother,*
> *Will furnish man's apparel to my need.*
> It may become thy pains, etc.

Evidently Kemble feared an audience might wonder where Viola's page-dress came from; it did not occur to him to think they might have wondered more, how Viola had saved her brother's trunk, while he was lost. This version varies in some degree in arrangement of scenes, retention or omission of speeches, etc., from the Inchbald version (1808). In general Mrs. Inchbald corresponds very accurately to Kemble in the Shakespearian plays given by both around 1808; but Twelfth Night was really a later arrangement of Kemble's (1811), and curiously enough, the second edition of Mrs. Inchbald in 1811 or thereabouts is exactly like it; moreover, the title-page of her second edition says the play is revised by J. P. Kemble. So closely did the two editions in general run together; by this time the publishers of both were the same. Let me say here that those who find difficulty of access to the Kemble versions will find a reasonably close replica of his editions in the Inchbald text. This does not apply to all the plays with equal certainty, but it is a close guide. Perhaps Julius Cæsar and Twelfth Night are least like the 1808 Inchbald, but in both cases Kemble's version came later.

JULIUS CÆSAR, 1812

I now come to Kemble's Julius Cæsar, printed in 1812, the year of its great revival at Covent Garden. Mrs. Inchbald's version of 1808, also from the Covent Garden copy of that date, and undoubtedly representing an earlier acting edition, may well be examined in connection with Kemble's. The change of names among minor characters, mentioned in the discussion of the 1719 edition and of Bell's, again will arrest our attention. In Kemble, the two chiders of the mob, in Scene I, are Casca and Trebonius; in Inchbald, Casca and Decius Brutus, Kemble preserving more of the scene, even to the very last speeches. The second scene varies but little in both, and each is close to the original; Kemble gives many stage directions for processions, etc. In both versions the act ends with this scene.

Shakespeare's third scene becomes thus the first in Act II. In Inchbald Trebonius takes the place of Cicero at the beginning, but all this early part is omitted by Kemble, who starts with Cassius's demand, "Who's there?" with Casca's answer, "A Roman." At first Kemble cuts this scene more than Mrs. Inchbald; at the end, less than she. Both retain Cinna, the poet. In the second scene—in Brutus's orchard—the episode, at the end, with Caius Ligarius, is expunged by both, as in Bell. Of course, in Scene III—the inducing of Cæsar to go to the Senate—Kemble must needs find the Servant a name—Flavius.

In the confused opening of Act III, Kemble gives to the Soothsayer the scene of the letter of Artemidorus, omitted by Inchbald; the Soothsayer has the following scene with Portia, though Inchbald has Artemidorus become the

Soothsayer in the same episode. I hope the reader follows
this clearly. The opening scene of the Soothsayer in the
capitol Kemble retains and Inchbald rejects. The introductory part about Popilius Lenas Kemble retains, but
Inchbald begins her scene with Cassius's "Trebonius knows
his time." In both, all goes about as in Shakespeare, Inchbald, however, discarding much more of the original than
does Kemble. Inchbald ends the scene with Antony's
stirring rant, "Let slip the dogs of war," etc.; Kemble goes
on with the entrance of a servant, who, to allow of carrying
off Cæsar's body, is multiplied into Flavius, Clitus and
attendants. Kemble gives Scene 3, "a street," with the
mob's shouting, "we will be satisfied," etc. All this Inchbald omits. The scene of the great orations of Brutus
and Antony follows. Inchbald ends with Antony's

> Mischief thou art afoot
> Take thou what course thou wilt.

But Kemble goes on with the scene between Antony and
the servant, whom he particularises by the name of Flavius.
Both revisers omit the logical scene of the killing of Cinna
the Poet by the mob.

Kemble, but not Inchbald, omits the first scene of Act IV,
the council of Antony, Octavius and Lepidus. Kemble
does not again bring in Casca, but Inchbald follows the
earlier use of Bell in this regard. It is almost useless to
try to disentangle the confusion in the naming of minor
characters, as between Shakespeare, Inchbald and Kemble.

The first scene in Act V in both the adapters is Shakespeare's first—the parley between the opposing forces.
Inchbald, like Bell, changes Brutus's charge, "Ride, ride,
Messala," to "haste, haste Trebonius"; Kemble omits it
entirely, beginning the scene with

> O look, Trebonius, look the villains fly.

In Shakespeare, it is Titinius who is told to look; in Inchbald, it is Casca. What a mix-up between these two revisers

and the original! Once more, to illustrate, Brutus's speech
in entering after the death of Cassius, and the answer
thereto, runs in Shakespeare:

Bru. Where, where, Messala, doth his body lie?
Mes. Lo, yonder, and Titinius mourning over it.

In Inchbald (and in Bell, I may add):

Bru. Where, where, Trebonius, doth his body lie?
Treb. Lo, yonder, and Casca mourning over it.

In Kemble:

Bru. Where, where, Titinius, doth his body lie?
Tit. Lo, yonder, and Trebonius mourning over it.

It seems almost cruel to burden the reader further by
saying that those whom Brutus urges to hold his sword
while he runs on it are, in Shakespeare, Clitus, Dardanius,
Volumnius and Strato; in Inchbald, Decius and Metellus;
in Kemble, Lucius, the boy (!), Metellus, Volumnius.
Inchbald, to go back a minute, gives at the end of the
Ghost scene the four "uncharacteristic, bouncing lines" for
Brutus. Both she and Kemble print, to conclude Brutus's
death scene, variants of the unidentified lines found in 1719
and in Bell:

INCHBALD	KEMBLE
Now one last look and then farewell to all.	This was the justest cause that ever men
Scorning to view his country's wrongs,	Did draw their swords for; and the gods renounce it.
Thus Brutus always strikes for liberty.	Disdaining life, to live a slave in Rome,
Poor slavish Rome, farewell.	Thus Brutus strikes his last for liberty!
Cæsar, now be still;	*(He stabs himself.*
I kill'd not thee with half so good a will.	Farewell,
[Runs on his Sword, and dies.	Beloved country!—Cæsar now be still,
	I kill'd not thee with half so good a will. *[Dies.*

I cannot call either of these a perfect stage-copy; there is
no reason, that I can see, for so doubling and confusing the
minor parts. The main issues are given, but the lesser
details are blurred. In conclusion, I draw attention to the
fact that Mrs. Inchbald's Julius Cæsar is much more like
Bell's than Kemble's.

ANTONY AND CLEOPATRA, 1813

Practically the last attempt of Kemble to do something
for Shakespeare was the Antony and Cleopatra, with alterations, and with additions from Dryden, produced in 1813.
Kemble's name does not appear on the title-page; and the
work is not included in his collection of plays in 1815; there
is no certainty, therefore, that he had a hand in the con-
coction.

The first act of the play is made up wholly from Shakespeare, the first scene having fragments of the conversation
between Mæcenas and Enobarbus from Act II, Scene 2,
though those characters here become for the nonce Philo
and Canidius. The beautiful and famous description of
Cleopatra on the barge, due in this second act scene, is
deferred to a later place. The five scenes are Shakespeare's
five, involving the enslavement of Antony, Enobarbus's
sorrow thereat, Antony's learning of the death of his wife,
Fulvia, his departure from Alexandria, and Cleopatra's
grief. Scene 4 involves Octavius, Lepidus, etc. In the
scene-divisions of Shakespeare's tragedy, I follow the
scheme of the Cambridge text. The Folio of 1623 has no
scenes specifically marked. Indeed, this reservation applies to Coriolanus and some of the other plays mentioned
in my discussion.

Act II begins with Shakespeare's Scene 2, a room in
Lepidus's house. Antony and Cæsar are reconciled by
Agrippa's plan for the marriage of Antony and Octavia.
All the last of this scene between Enobarbus, Agrippa and
Mæcenas is omitted, part of it having been incorporated,
as we saw, in the first scene of Act I. The second scene is

Shakespeare's fifth, a room in the palace at Alexandria, much "cut." Cleopatra learns of the marriage, smites the messenger, etc. The third scene is Shakespeare's Act III, Scene 4, at Athens—a room in Antony's house, a scene between Antony and Octavia, with her offer to intercede with her brother. At the end, part of Act III, Scene 2 is tacked on. Scene 4 returns to Alexandria, and after a few lines of Shakespeare brings in Dryden's (All for Love) Act II, Scene 1, a messenger taking the place of Charmion in telling how Antony received Cleopatra's messages. Then follows more Shakespeare, with the Messenger's description of Octavia. Now, oddly enough, Antony enters, and we have much Dryden, the scene after his entrance in Act II, Scene 1. As Genest says, he seems to have come to Alexandria expressly for this interview! Enobarbus takes the place of Dryden's Ventidius, as he well might do, considering the sameness of their character and function. This ends the 1813 second act as it ends Dryden's second. Cleopatra wins back Antony, despite Enobarbus (Ventidius).

Act III begins with Shakespeare's Act III, Scene 6, a room in Cæsar's palace. Octavia learns that Antony has gone back to Cleopatra. The second scene is again all Shakespeare (his seventh of this act). Antony decides to fight by sea, against the advice of Enobarbus. Scene 3 is a short bit from Shakespeare, with these added lines, probably original with the 1813 adapter:

> The fleets
> Draw near each other; Roman strains of war,
> With Ægypt's timbrels mingling, on the sea,
> Proclaim immediate action,—To the heights;
> Steadily, soldiers.—March!

These high lines introduce a wordless tableau of a grand seafight, which ends in the defeat of Antony and Cleopatra—a fine bit of spectacle, we learn. Scene 5 shows Enobarbus and others lamenting, in Shakespeare's words (Scene 10), the loss of the day. In Scene 6, Cæsar receives Antony's

ambassador, and refuses to treat with Antony—this also is
Shakespeare. Scene 7 is Shakespeare Scene 11—at Alexandria; part of Shakespeare's Scene 13 is run on, permitting
of the whipping of Thyreus. The act ends with the reconciliation of Antony and Cleopatra; it is her birthday, and
they will have one more grand feast to-night.

Act IV, by all that's wonderful, opens with Dryden's
Act I, Scene 1, Alexas and Enobarbus taking the places of
the Serapion and Alexas of Dryden, respectively. Ventidius
now enters, bluff old soldier, and puts Enobarbus, his pro-
totype, out of business, for the rest of the play; they both
figure for a moment in this scene. All of Dryden's best
poetry is retained, though the part about the prodigies is
sacrificed. But we still have the great soliloquy beginning,
"Lie there, thou shadow of an emperor." This and the
scene are "cut," but all is semblative of Dryden. As
Genest truly says, the former scene incorporated from Dryden, follows as a direct consequence of this, and yet it is
given first—effect before cause. As, however, the situation
is so general with Antony and Ventidius, the latter's trying
to urge the former not to see Cleopatra, I do not see that
much harm has been done. Scene 2 is in Cæsar's camp,
equivalent to Shakespeare's Scene 6, in little. Scene 3 is
an interesting mixture, made up partly at the beginning of
a few lines from Shakespeare's Scene 8, followed by a few
lines for Ventidius, written in, the rest all Shakespeare.
Then follows a long scene from Dryden (Act III, Scene 1);
in this, Ventidius tries once more to win Antony from Cleopatra. During the course of the episode, Antony (O these
star actors!) delivers to Dolabella, Enobarbus's splendid
description of Cleopatra on the barge; or, to be perfectly
fair, he delivers the first half of Shakespeare's and the
second (and worse) half of Dryden's. Could anything be
more equitable? Ventidius brings in Octavia (without the
children) to meet Antony. The scene, though somewhat
curtailed, adheres closely to Dryden.

I shall not attempt to disentangle the threads of Dryden
and Shakespeare in the last act; they are mingled in pro-

fusion throughout. The killing of Ventidius is, of course, pure Dryden. The sixth scene is written in wholly for theatrical and spectacular effect. Let me quote it entire. If such a funeral procession pleased in Romeo and Juliet, why not here? Fitness probably did not enter into the calculations of the stage-manager.

The scene is a street in Alexandria, and introduces Proculeius and Dolabella, who discuss the funeral procession. Then Dolabella gives a few of Cleopatra's lines:

> His legs bestrid the Ocean;—his rear'd arm
> Crested the world;—his voice was propertied
> As all the tuned spheres, unto his friends;
> But when he meant to quail, and strike the orb,
> He was a rattling thunder.
> *Proculeius.* How stands the order of the march? etc.

The play ends with

> Scene Alexandria
> A Grand Funeral Procession
> During which is sung the following
> Epicedium.
>
> Chorus
> Cold in death the Hero lies;
> Nerveless now, the Victor's arm;
> Quench'd the lightning of his eyes, &c.
>
> Solo.
> Oh, Comrades, many a time has he
> Led us to glorious victory, etc.
>
> Trio or Quartette
> A constant Fire his Courage glow'd,
> A ceaseless stream his bounty flowed, &c.
>
> Solo
> When Mars no longer settled on his side
> And Neptune, weary of his prowess grown, &c.
>
> Grand Chorus
> Nor monument, till now, could boast a pair
> So fam'd, yet, ah! so luckless in their doom;
> Long will the doves of Venus murmur there,
> And shouts of Warriors thunder o'er the tomb.

Verily the play, in its entirety, was not a pretty dish to set before the king. It met—in spite of its spectacle—with exactly the success it deserved. Of course Young and Mrs. Faucit were rather prosaic actors to select for Antony and the Nile-serpent.

I have finished with Kemble's so-called versions of Shakespeare. In closing I refer again to their long vogue, and their general neatness and compactness—their actableness —apparent in a reading to-day. It is rather late now to become indignant over their admixture in notable cases of unworthy selections from Dryden, Davenant, Tate, Cibber, Thomson, &c. We must admit that Shakespeare is gold and they alloy; but, after all, acting is acting, and audiences are audiences, two weighty facts that Kemble had to face all his life. I am not defending; I am explaining.

VALPY'S KING JOHN, 1803

Four productions, three at least outside the Kemble influence, remain to be recorded for the period under discussion. On May 20, 1803—the spring before Kemble began as manager of the house—King John was produced at Covent Garden. The ostentatious title-page of the printed play tells much of the story of the venture. "King John," it runs, "an Historical Tragedy (altered from Shakespeare), as it was acted at Reading School, for the Subscription to the Naval Pillar, to be Erected in Honor of the Naval Victories of the War; and as it is now performing at the Theatre-Royal, Covent Garden, with Distinguished Applause. Reading, 1803." This was one of the numerous adaptations from Shakespeare by the Rev. John Valpy, Headmaster of Reading School, and played by the Reading schoolboys with some acclaim. The present is the first of these to come under the necessity of our subject, and may be the last. Most of these alterations were published separately, and were issued finally in a collected edition, no doubt to the satisfaction of all concerned—the headmaster, the boys and their mammas, and, let us hope, the pub-

MRS. SIDDONS AS LADY MACBETH
From an engraving by Cooper, after a painting by Harlowe, 1822

lishers. How Valpy's King John came to the dignity of
production at Covent Garden, I do not know. Mine not
to reason why, but simply to wonder. The first act of
Shakespeare's play is entirely cut away, properly enough if
to be acted by innocent schoolboys; but Cibber had done
the same thing in his Papal Tyranny, in 1745. Thereafter,
the play goes on in Shakespeare's order of scene, but with a
modernising and "refining" of the language quite natural
for a headmaster used to correcting themes and Latin
verses. In Valpy's Act II, Scene 1 (Shakespeare's Act III)
observe the difference:

SHAKESPEARE	VALPY
Constance.	
If thou, that bid'st me be content, wert grim,	If thou, that bid'st me be content, wert grim,
Ugly, and slanderous to thy mother's womb,	Ugly, deformed, offensive to the sight,
Full of unpleasing blots and sightless stains,	
Lame, foolish, crooked, swart, prodigious,	
Patch'd with foul moles, and eye-offending marks,	
I would not care, I then would be content,	
For then I should not love thee, no, nor thou	Still, as my child, my heart would feel thy wrongs.
Become thy great birth, nor deserve a crown.	
But thou art fair, and at thy birth, dear boy,	But thou are fair, and at thy birth, dear boy,
Nature and fortune join'd to make thee great.	Nature and fortune join'd to make thee great.
. . . .	
I will instruct my sorrows to be proud,	I will instruct my sorrows to be proud,
For grief is proud, and makes his owner stoop.	For grief is proud and dignifies the mourner.
To me and to the state of my great grief,	To me, and to my venerable grief,
Let kings assemble, etc.	Let kings assemble, etc.

Valpy's entire play is laden with such blurring; yet some-
time in his march through it he must have noted the lines
about painting the lily, and gilding refined gold. The
play had a few performances in the season of 1802–3, and
was heard of no more. Kemble's and Siddons's King John
in their first year at the same theatre, in the following season, simply snuffed it out. To my surprise, I found a note
in Lacy's Merchant of Venice, stating that the often-per-
formed four-act version of the comedy concludes the trial
scene with a scene of recognition between Portia and Bassanio, usually supplied from Valpy's edition of the play.
These lines Lacy gives in a foot-note, and Valpy enjoys
thereby a sort of posthumous glory that he little anticipated.

WROUGHTON'S RICHARD II

Drury Lane, reduced to innocuous desuetude, since the
secession of the Kembles, had its days of returning glory
with the first appearance of Edmund Kean on January 26,
1814. During the second season of this marvellous genius,
he appeared in a revision of Richard II, made by Richard
Wroughton, an actor of respectable parts, who retired from
the stage at just this time. This version was a great success, and probably deserved to be. It was acted thirteen
times during the season, and was revived frequently during
the next five years. It is really a good bit of dramatic
workmanship, an effective acting medium. Like Cibber, in
Richard III, Wroughton helps himself rather liberally to
passages from other Shakespearian plays, introducing, however, for articulation, several lines of his own. The play
was published in 1815, and gives, in its Advertisement, the
purpose of the reviser to rescue the play from neglect, by
making it presentable, with interpolations from others of
the plays, with lines of transition, etc.

This version runs together, in Scene I, all the material of
the quarrel between Bolingbroke and Mowbray, and their
banishment. The Tournament is omitted. The King ban-
ishes them just after their wrangling at court. Gaunt con-

soles his son before he starts into exile. The second scene shows Aumerle questioned as to how far he saw Bolingbroke on his way. Bushy brings news of Gaunt's illness. The King charitably hopes he may die, so that the crown may become possessed of his revenues.

The first scene of Act II is at John of Gaunt's castle. The sick man rebukes the King (the Queen is not present in Wroughton's version). Gaunt dies, and the King seizes his treasures, York remonstrating in vain. Willoughby, Ross and Northumberland resolve to join, at Ravenspurg, the wronged Bolingbroke, thus violently deprived of his patrimony. The second scene of the act shows the Queen in her palace, sad over the news of the rebellion of Boling-broke. York takes charge of all the affairs of the kingdom, the King being on his Irish expedition, and Worcester away.

Scene I of Act III gives the wilds of Gloucestershire, with the compact formed between Bolingbroke and Harry Percy. York enters and reviles Bolingbroke, but finally invites him into the castle. The second scene is that in Wales, between Salisbury and the Captain, showing the weakness of the King's cause. Scene 3 is at the camp at Bristol, the King's minions, Bushy and Green, being sent to death. The fourth scene brings the effective climax in Richard's landing on the coast of Wales, and learning the worst from Salisbury and Scroop.

In Act IV, the first scene, "before Flint Castle," shows Richard practically yielding to Bolingbroke, and agreeing to go with him to London. The second scene is that pathetic little interlude of the Queen in the garden, learning from the gardeners of the fate of her husband. The last big scene of the act is Richard's resignation of the crown, ending in his being sent to the Tower. The last act begins with a scene in the Duke of York's palace, in which the Duke tells his son, Aumerle (not the Duchess, as in Shake-speare), the story of the pitiful entrance of Richard into London. The episode of the plot of Aumerle is omitted, along with the character of his mother. Scene 2 is the street leading to the Tower, with the meeting of the King and the Queen; Northumberland tells her of her banishment to France.   In the next scene, the Queen demands of Bolingbroke the right to see her King-husband in prison. The play ends with the death of Richard, and the Queen's lament over his body.

It will be seen that the changes made by Wroughton led to increase in the elements of pity and terror.   The Queen's part is greatly amplified, and must have wrung tears from susceptible auditors.   The Aumerle plot, no doubt, was excised, in order to allow for the many new scenes of the Queen, especially her plea to Bolingbroke for mercy, not unlike that of the Duchess of York for her son, Aumerle. In this scene of beseeching, Wroughton gives to Isabel some lines of Elizabeth in Richard III:

> O quickly then—my Richard dies this moment.
> Lend me ten thousand eyes, and I will fill them
> With prophetic tears—O my ever-lov'd!
> If yet thy gentle soul fly in the air,
> And be not fix'd in doom perpetual,
> Hover about me with your airy wings,
> Till I have printed on thy clay-cold lips
> A dying kiss, etc.

But ere she could arrive at the point proposed, Richard had been murdered, and she could do nothing but lament over his body, in terms almost wholly extracted from Lear's lament over the body of Cordelia.   This pilfering from one play to help another was possible in this case because Tate's Lear, so long in possession of the stage, had banished for upwards of a hundred and forty years the very words now assigned to a speaker of different sex, age, and relationship to the person mourned.

> Queen.   Never will we part!   O, you are men of stone,
>   Had I your tongues and eyes, I'd use them so,
>   That heav'n's vault should crack!   O he is gone forever.
>   A plague upon you!   Murderers—Traitors all!
>   [To Bol.]   You might have saved him—now he is lost forever.
> Bol.   What words can soothe such aggravated woes!

Queen. O dearest Richard, dearer than my soul,
  Had I but seen thy picture in this plight,
  It would have madded me—what shall I do,
  Now I behold thy lovely body thus?—
  Plot some device of further misery,
  To make us wonder'd at in time to come.
Bol. Be comforted, and leave this fatal place.
Queen. Why should a dog, a horse, a rat, have life,
  And thou no breath at all? O, thou wilt come no more,
  Never, never, never!
  Pray you undo my lace—Thank you.
  Do you see this, look on him, look on his lips,
  Look there, look there. [*Falls.*

All this increases the pathos of the King's part, as well as that of the Queen's. In fact, we must admit that, for purposes of Kean, and acting in general, this version was very effective. It is compact, and the interest is heightened just where it needed heightening—on the female side of the cast.

REYNOLDS'S MIDSUMMER NIGHT'S DREAM, 1816

On January 17, 1816, was produced at Covent Garden (still in the consulship of Kemble, though absence and inertia were weakening his grasp, until the last outburst in 1816–17, the season of his farewell) the first of Frederick Reynolds's operatising of Shakespeare's comedies, and the only one that we shall consider in this chapter. The play selected for this process was that ancient victim of adapters' ruthlessness—A Midsummer Night's Dream. Reynolds, in his Life and Recollections, takes a rather braggadocio attitude toward this and his similar subsequent acts of vandalism; Genest can hardly be severe and satirical enough in his condemnation. But I rather suspect Genest had no ear for music. Reynolds says that at the second rehearsal of his version Miller, the theatrical bookseller, offered him £1,000 for the copyright of the work. The play was produced, as usual, with many songs, some of them to music by Arne and Smith, and partly in words, as well, selected from Garrick's Fairies of 1755, and the unfortunate Midsummer Night's Dream of one performance only, in 1763. The major part of the music was by Bishop, who performed a similar service for Reynolds's later tamperings with Shakespeare's comedies. Reynolds, in his preface, prides himself on bringing back Shakespeare's fairy-play to the stage; compared with previous attempts, he might, in some sort, be said to have done so. On the whole, his version is poor indeed, and was but a framework for spectacle and dance and song, all, I suspect, of an unusual degree of excellence.

But the greatest liberties were taken with the text. I shall cite the most notable. (1) The entire scene with Helena is omitted in Act I, making it rather difficult for the audience to know how Demetrius has come (in Act II) into the knowledge of the proposed flight of Lysander and Hermia. Against this excision Hazlitt and Genest both inveigh. (2) Much of the dialogue of the four lovers is mercilessly curtailed throughout the play. (3) The scene of the acting of Pyramus and Thisbe is transferred to the wood, Theseus and Philostrate observing from behind a tree. On being recognised, Theseus is greeted by Bottom-Pyramus with this pre-Adamite operetta speech:

> Mercy! the King! dead! dead in earnest!
>   (*Falls on the stage, at the King's feet*).

This transposition is effected in order to allow, at the end of the play, of the grand pageant of Theseus's triumphs. Shakespeare's final scene with the fairies is omitted. All these changes were made necessary by the great number of musical numbers interspersed wherever possible. All the opportunities for singing offered by Shakespeare are seized upon; but everywhere we get "gems" like this, set to music by Bishop and sung by Demetrius just as he flies Helena to hide in the brake:

> Recall the minutes that are fled,
> Forbid fleet time to move;
> To new life wake the sleeping dead,
> But ne'er recall my love.

> Forbid the stormy waves to **roar,**
> The playful winds to rove,
> Revive the sun at midnight hour,
> But ne'er recall my love.

And while at the close Theseus, with the rest, modestly reviews his own deeds, Hermia sings, having been royally bidden thereto by these interpolated lines:

> Hark! they approach!
> My hardy veterans!
> My brave companions in the toils of war!
> And since ourselves, we boast not of the pow'r
> To welcome them in aught, save the plain
> Rough language of a soldier,
> Hermia, stand forth, and with thy dulcet tones,
> Give, give to all, harmonious greeting.

Hermia, apparently nothing loth, warbles a martial lay by Bishop, beginning (after recitative),

> Now Pleasure's voice be heard around!
> And sweetly lute and lyre resound!

GEORGE LAMB'S TIMON OF ATHENS

This kind of thing was to burden the early years of the next period we shall be called upon to discuss; meantime, I close the present record with an account of yet another attempt to make palatable for an audience that elusive thing, Timon of Athens. This time an elegant young man, the Honorable George Lamb, was the aggressor and the victim. The work was produced at Drury Lane, October 28, 1816, with Kean as Timon, and J. W. Wallack, founder of the American house of Wallack, as Alcibiades. Lamb's own airy Advertisement informs us of his purpose in thus venturing into the arts:

The play of Timon of Athens has at times, within the last fifty years, been presented to the public with considerable alterations. The present attempt has been to restore Shakspeare to the stage, with no other omissions than such as the refinement of manners has rendered necessary.

The short interpolation in the last scene has been chiefly compiled from Mr. Cumberland's alteration, acted in the year 1771.

Most of this version is really Shakespeare. Lamb fairly outdoes Kemble in assigning names to first and second gentlemen, servants, senators, &c. Desiring to raise in importance the characters of Lucius and Lucullus, the chief figures in the scene interpolated from Cumberland, he gives to Lucius the speeches of the First Lord in Scene I, and later in the play, and to Lucullus the speeches of the Second Lord. With the parts these two play in the refusal to lend Timon money, and the inclusion of Lucullus in Timon's barmecide feast, two rather lengthy and interesting characters are patched together, and, I must say, a certain personal interest, sadly lacking to Shakespeare's play, is provided. The only bit from Cumberland concerns these two worthies; in Scene 2 they are brought in, as in Cumberland, by the angry mob, and stripped of their most cherished treasures, paying a sort of poetic justice to the *manes* of Timon. The entire help from the earlier dramatist does not exceed thirty-five lines, complete or in part. It goes thus:

> *Alcibiades.*   Yet all's not done:
>   Vengeance must work. Where is that loathsome crew,
>   Whose black ingratitude corrodes the heart
>   Of Athens' noblest son?
>   [*Lucius, Lucullus, Sempronius, and other of Timon's former
>   friends, brought in bound.*]

Vengeance is wreaked. Lucius loses all. "What," he cries,

> What all my wealth, my pictures, statues, coin,
> Plate—jewels—gems . . . . .
>
> . . . . . . All swept away—
> My hangings, couches, vestments wrought with gold.
> Oh what a luckless piece of work is man!

Lucullus says,

> I've a mine of gold
> A magazine to sack or save a city.

Alcibiades answers,

> And it shall buy you banishment, &c.

It does not appear that this gold is that which Timon found (as it was in Cumberland).

The only other part of this forgotten play that I shall speak of is that long episode in the wood between the mad Timon and his quondam friends. The scene between Alcibiades and the misanthrope is retained, but the two mistresses of the former do not appear. The two thieves are, however, brought on the scene, followed by Apemantus. The long, the vast array of speeches between Apemantus and Timon is mercifully cut, especially toward the end of the scene, and Timon's soliloquy at the close is almost gone. Lamb's fourth act ends with the departure of the thieves, and his fifth act begins with the entrance of the faithful Flavius. The poet and the painter are also mercifully eliminated, and Lamb's scene goes right forward with the Senators and Flavius. Some bits are transposed from another scene in the play. The episode ends with Timon's farewell,

> Come not to me again; but say to Athens, etc.

This is not a bad version of Shakespeare's play; it fails, as does the original, in female interest, but possibly that did not so much matter when a Kean could play the leading role. Shadwell and Cumberland, with their Evandras and Evanthes, hit on the essential weakness, dramaturgically, of this play of Shakespeare's; but what they indicated, they could not perform. Lamb's version has no woman-character throughout its entire five acts.

The long period we have now closed might be described as static; it was formulating the standard acting texts for the twenty-five plays, more or less, of Shakespeare that

were constantly acted. Kemble brought this task to perfection. At the close there was some light skirmishing with
efforts such as those just described, but by 1817 actors and
audiences knew just about what of Shakespeare could and
could not be played. The next periods will see the gradual
restoration of Shakespearian texts to some pieces heretofore
sullied with the alloy of lesser geniuses; but, alas! just as
this purifying process began, the race of the greater actors
ceased. Taste changed, and Shakespeare was relegated
more and more to the rear. The age of Macready is not a
brilliant one; like Tennyson's waterfall, its broken purpose
wasted in air.

CHAPTER XX

SCENERY AND COSTUMES

THE BEGINNING OF LIGHT

WE have at last arrived at a period in connection with which perfectly authenticable statements may be made concerning the staging of plays. Furthermore there is sufficient Shakespearian material to enable us to dispense with the mounting of extra-Shakespearian productions. This is indeed a relief after a century and more of groping in half-lights and visible gloom. For our instruction we are indebted to the innumerable prints of actors and actresses published in such collections as Bell's British Theatre, as well as Oxberry's and Cumberland's; to the increasingly numerous plates appearing in magazines—the Universal, the Westminster and the European—as well as more specialised periodicals like the Lady's Magazine, and a large host of papers purely theatrical—these latter especially common in the first decade of the Nineteenth Century. Dramatic criticism, also, particularly in the latter brilliant days of Kemble, devoted more and more attention to the discussion of stage effect. Biographies of actors likewise throw powerful, if fitful, gleams on the subject. Stage books of the plays will sometimes describe sets desired, if not actually attained, and are rich in details of processions, etc. And finally, play-bills, which had heretofore confined such information to the programme of pantomimes, begin by 1815 to print schedules of scenery for the more elaborate productions of Shakespeare's works. These various sources of knowledge make, for the first time in the history, an almost infallible guide to our subject. We could wish for more details, but the harvest is rich compared with that of preceding ages.

The theatres, at the beginning of the period upon which

we are now entering, might be said to be passing through an interregnum bounded on the one hand by the retirement of Garrick in 1776, and on the other by the rise of John Kemble to managerial dignity, in the season of 1788–89. This little gap of time saw the passing of De Loutherbourg, and the prodigal personal expenditure of Richard Brinsley Sheridan. In 1782–83 Mrs. Siddons appeared in full glory, and the next year her brother, John Kemble. Their influence increased mightily from that time until Kemble took up the reins of management in 1788. Practically all the great staging of Shakespeare from that time until 1817 was due to Kemble, and the annals of his activities therein will serve as material for almost our entire chapter.

EVIDENCE FROM PICTURES

Nevertheless, before we come to that, I should like to introduce to the reader certain illustrations of the years 1777–88 that will show something of the manner of producing plays in the time immediately anterior to Kemble's full control. The first that I shall offer is a plate from the Westminster Magazine, of February, 1777, representing Miss Catley, the erratic vocal genius, in the character of Euphrosyne in Comus. This, of course, was made in the first year of Sheridan's consulate at Drury Lane, and the reader will note the scenery, professedly a reproduction of that used in the theatre. There is a back-drop, or, more probably, there are "flats" with a cut arch, through which an outer room is discovered; but what specially interests us is the wings, representing the sides of the room in which the characters are discovered, and through which they make their exits and their entrances, sublimely oblivious to the fact that human beings do not ordinarily walk through plaster and wainscoting. The absurdity of the dress of Miss Catley and her attendant spirit needs no comment; Milton might have said to her, "Ay, you can tag-rag my verses if you will."

A better-known example of the same custom of setting

MISS CATLEY AS EUPHROSYNE
IN COMUS

From an engraving by Walker after a drawing by
Dighton, 1777

MRS. HARTLEY AS
HERMIONE

Published by Fielding and Walker,
1780

MRS. HARTLEY AS CLEOPATRA
Published by Wenman, 1778

the stage, with back drop or flats and with "wings" representing walls, through which the "dramatis personæ" walked, is the frequently reproduced plate of the screen scene from the original production of The School for Scandal, published in 1778. Joseph Surface's library is painted on the back scene; also the window. The rest of the room is really non-existent, but the audience took the pillared wings for two of the remaining three walls of the room. Possibly the characters entered through the stage-doors, sometimes, if not always. This print, with the stage-doors and stage-boxes, and with the actors far out of the scene on the "apron," is one of the most interesting and valuable in existence.

Much less common is the print I found in the Lady's Magazine for 1786, illustrating a scene in Burgoyne's comedy of The Heiress. This seems to me absolutely authentic. The walls as wings were never more effectively or unmistakably represented; the stage-door is obviously used as a door in the room represented, and altogether the thing seems exactly what was put on the stage of Drury Lane Theatre on January 14, 1786, when Burgoyne's play had its first performance. A mere illustrator, drawing a room, would never have put in those wings; a man desirous of reproducing a stage-set would. This print seems to me a genuine "find."

More directly bearing on our subject are two prints of the same time representing scenes from Shakespeare's plays. The first, from the Westminster Magazine of March, 1777, represents what I believe to be a fairly accurate drawing of a stage picture of The Tempest (page 28). The cave of Prospero, the back sea-drop with the foundered ship, the logs of Ferdinand, are as good as one could expect at that time; was the scene De Loutherbourg's of 1777? The dress of the two most ideal of Shakespeare's lovers is enough to appal the imagination that would try to grasp the point of view of the Eighteenth Century. Ferdinand's powdered George III wig and the gentle Miranda's towering coiffure show how much was yet to be done before historic accuracy could obtain on the stage. This plate, also, has been seldom reproduced, and stands as a landmark in the chronicle of Shakespearian staging.

I confess to a great fondness for the picture of Mrs. Hartley, as Hermione, also culled from the Westminster Magazine for 1780. This beautiful actress seems to have had some faint idea of propriety in dressing; to be sure, there is nothing sculpturesque about the costume, and her coiffure might be justly described as exaggerated, but, on the whole, one could say her mind was less on her personal adornment than on the character portrayed. There is a fine dignity about the pose, though it fails in grandeur. The arch I admit is finicky; I also admit my belief in it as a representation of the setting at Drury Lane Theatre. Compared with Pine's portrait of Mrs. Pritchard as Hermione, Mrs. Hartley's is merely pretty.

Two pictures that remain to be treated are better than many chapters of description. They belong to the same year, 1787, that preceding John Kemble's entrance on the arduous duties of general stage-director at Drury Lane. The first is an old print representing the interior of the Royalty Theatre—John Palmer's unfortunate venture— with the stage set, apparently for the opening scene of The Tempest. The figures of Prospero and Miranda seem to be faintly outlined on the left. Palmer tried to open this theatre, in opposition to the two patent houses, for the production of legitimate plays. He was prevented by law, in the very year—1787—that is printed on the picture I reproduce. Perhaps the picture was issued before the fiasco, and in anticipation of the production of The Tempest. Why may not conjecture go to the length of supposing that the artist worked from an actual scene set up for his convenience? Note that the theatre is empty—an unusual circumstance in such pictures. In any case, I must say that I cannot imagine a more effective storm-scene in any theatre, even to-day—the composition is admirable, the cloud-effects superb, the imagination free and untrammelled. Whether meant for The Tempest or not, it is good enough for The Tempest. I doubt if Drury Lane or Covent Garden could set the first scene as well.

The last illustration is for Richard Cœur de Lion at Drury Lane in 1787 (page 50). There is fine massing and spaciousness, but somehow, to me, the whole thing is unsimple; there are too many projections and too many "cutouts." I do not like the fortified place on the left, nor do I see its relationship to the rest of the scene. Yet it is so satisfactory a reproduction of a set of the time that my delight was unbounded when I first came upon it.

A glance at several of the studies reproduced in this, the beginning of our scenic journey through the age of Kemble, will, I think, open the eyes of many who have hitherto thought but slightly of what the stage of 1780 or thereabouts could offer in the way of embellishment. It is always unnecessary to pity our forefathers; they generally had the best there was, and frequently their best is far from being as bad as our worst. Sometimes it is better than our best. A moment's thought will convince us that the most crying need of the stage, as represented by the pictures just presented, was a reform in matters of costume. This was to come with Kemble and Mrs. Siddons, and will occupy us at the proper time.

JOHN KEMBLE

It is with something like reverence that one approaches the name of John Kemble, certainly the first great "producer" of Shakespeare on the English stage. Whatever we may be taught to believe of his talents as an actor as opposed to those of Kean, as a man and as a shaper of dramatic forms he stands immeasurably above Kean. In the present chapter we shall deal almost entirely with his efforts as a manager in the four great periods of his career— the beginning of his directorate at Drury Lane in 1788–89, the opening of the altered and enlarged Drury Lane in 1794, the commencement of his tenure of Covent Garden in 1803, and his work at the new Covent Garden, starting in September, 1809.

James Boaden's delightful Life of Kemble is almost the first dramatic biography that devotes anything like satisfactory space to questions of staging and kindred subjects, and from it I shall quote liberally in the course of the present essay.   Garrick, as the reader may remember, had produced a number of frigid tragedies, of impeccable "regularity," on subjects of classic antiquity or Oriental luxury and despair.   Sheridan fought shy of this avalanche of frozen dulness and was ably encouraged by Kemble, who, as early as 1784–85, urged him to give up the production of such ephemeral respectabilities, and "encrease the power of Shakespeare."

This he proposed to effect by a more stately and perfect representation of his plays—to attend to all the details as well as the grand features, and by the aids of scenery and dress to perfect the dramatic illusion. . . .

Upon the London stage, nearly everything, as to correctness was to be done.   The ancient kings of England, or Scotland, or Denmark, wore the court dress of our own times, as to shape; and as to color, rival monarchs of England and France opposed their persons to each other in scarlet and gold lace, and white and silver. . . . . .   The old scenery exhibited architecture of no period and excited little attention.   The powers of De Loutherberg's pencil were devoted to the decoration of some catching novelty of the time . . . . but nothing could be less accurate or more dirty than the usual pairs of low flats that were hurried together, to denote the locality of the finest dialogue that human genius ever composed.   The error was too universal to admit of a speedy or radical corrective.   The vast old stock could not be entirely condemned and the treasury could seldom bear the expense of any very considerable novelties. . . . .   But the great reform was to take place in those parts of representation, which nothing but propriety can raise above derision or disgust—the whole tribe of mobs, whether civil or military plebeians, and their pasteboard and leathern properties.   Whatever credit might be taken by managers, and the newspapers and playbills gave them much, for liberality in their expenditure, the fact is certain, that the expense which attended one of Mr. Kemble's revivals would have defrayed the demands during a whole season of any former management. . . .   He carried his design into complete effect during his influence as a proprietor in Covent Garden Theatre.

SCENE FROM BURGOYNE'S PLAY OF THE
HEIRESS
Engraved for the *Lady's Magazine*, 1786

SCENE FROM THE SCHOOL FOR SCANDAL
From a print, 1778

That everything was not accomplished at once, however, is proved by a paragraph concerning the Witches in Macbeth. Smith had retired, and Kemble now fell heir to the part of Macbeth; Mrs. Siddons was exhausting superlatives of all the writers in these the earlier days of her triumphs as the iron Lady Macbeth. In Kemble's first season as manager, a new reading of Macbeth was given by this worthy pair of actors. Of course, neither dreamed of cutting away the Davenant nonsense from the Witch scenes, the music, dancing and spectacle of which combined to preserve it for many years to come. Listen to Boaden:

The music of Matthew Locke in this tragedy has crowded the stage with people to sing it; and in the crowd beauty, formerly and since, forced its way into notice. The Witch of the lovely Crouch wore a fancy hat, powdered hair, rouge, point lace, and fine linen enough to enchant the spectator. Perhaps in her vindication it may be allowed, that in so enormous a rabble, one invariable squalidness of attire would be merely disgusting. Among mingling black, white, red and grey spirits some may be imagined fantastic to assume the garb of beauty, as in all probability many must possess the features . . . . . . The group did not consist entirely of witches—spirits of the four elements mingled in the incantations.

KEMBLE'S CORIOLANUS, 1789

Kemble never quite abandoned the great horde of singers and dancers in these witch scenes—nor did Macready many years after; but, in others of these early revivals, he did far better. As to Coriolanus, Boaden says:

But he turned to Shakspeare once more this season for striking effect, and produced Coriolanus, with a few additions from Thomson. . . . . I do not pretend that at the first production, either Kemble or Mrs. Siddons achieved the fame subsequently attached to their performance of Coriolanus and Volumnia. By a course of peculiar study, antiquity became better known to Mrs. Siddons; and Mr. Kemble also grew more completely Roman. Mrs. Damer had led her friends into admiration of the forms which she had modelled; and I presume it was from the display of that lady's talent, that the great

actress became attached to the same pursuit. The application to
statuary is always the study of the antique. It soon became apparent, that Mrs. Siddons was conversant with drapery more dignified
than the shifting robes of fashion; and in truth her action also occasionally reminded the spectator of classic models. She had not
derived this from any foreign theatres, for she had then seen none.
Her attention to sculpture accounts for it satisfactorily.

Mr. Kemble this season fully developed his system as a manager:
it was that of good sense and fine taste. . . . . The earth-born
spirits, therefore, were kept at proper distance and in due subordina-
tion; and imitating the wisdom of Copernicus, he placed our dramatic
sun in the centre of the system.

By this last magniloquent sentence, I take Boaden to
mean that new tragedies were not produced, and that
Shakspere was "given a great chance."

KEMBLE'S HENRY VIII, 1789

Henry the Eighth, in which Kemble at first combined the
characters of Cromwell and Griffith into one, and acted the
part himself, was also produced during Kemble's first season as director. Having but little acting to do, the manager
could devote much time to spectacle. According to Boaden,
"The processions, in which this play particularly abounds,
afforded great scope for the knowledge of ancient habits
and manners which Mr. Kemble had acquired; and that
study of the picturesque, by which Shakespeare himself
quite as much as by any other quality, transcended all
other writers for the stage. Mr. Kemble arranged these
exhibitions with punctilious exactness; and having himself
to sustain a character not very much in the play, he gave
his attention . . . throughout; until all the raw material
was worked into the smoothness of a graceful habit."

Another play that he prepared, and rendered prodigiously attractive [says his faithful and admiring chronicler] was the Tempest,
admitting in a temperate way some of the additions of D'Avenant
and Dryden. These rendered it fuller as a stage spectacle, and
secured the assistance of Miss Farren in Dorinda and Mrs. Goodall
in Hippolyto. It gave a terrible dance of Furies in one place, and a
masque of Neptune and Amphitrite in another; and a beautiful acces-

sion indeed in the occasional Epilogue, written by the elegant Burgoyne, and spoken by Miss Farren.

KEMBLE AT DRURY LANE, 1794

All this display concerns itself, the reader observes, not so much with scenery, as with dance, music, processions, masque.   Indeed, until the new Drury Lane was opened in 1794, Kemble was probably forced to content himself with these adjuncts to spectacular splendour.   With the difference in size, the old scenery of the little old Drury would not fit the new stage, and Kemble set to work to provide settings commensurate with what he conceived to be the glories of Drury Lane as a great national theatre.   Boaden's account of this is particularly valuable.   "As the dimensions of the new theatre were calculated for an audience, the price of whose admission would amount, even at 6s. in the boxes, to more than £700, it was quite clear that for all grand occasions they would want scenery of greater height and width than had been exhibited at old Drury; and that in fact but little of the old stock could be used at all.   On this occasion it gives me sincere pleasure to mention the very great acquisition Mr. Kemble had met with in an old friend of mine, who really seemed expressly fashioned, as a scene-painter, to carry into effect the true and perfect decorations which he meditated for the plays of Shakespeare: the artist to whom I allude is Mr. William Capon . . . . his passion was, and is, the ancient architecture of this country.   With all the zeal of an antiquary, therefore, the painter worked as if he had been upon oath; and as all that he painted for the new theatre perished in the miserable conflagration of it a few years after, I indulge myself in some description of the scenery, which so much interested Mr. Kemble.   The artist had a private painting room."

This scenery consisted of:

A chapel of the pointed architecture, which occupied the whole stage, for the performance of the Oratorios, with which the new theatre opened in 1794.

Six chamber wings of the same order, for general use in our old English plays—very elaborately studied from actual remains.

A view of New Palace Yard, Westminster, as it was in 1793—41 feet wide, with corresponding wings.

The ancient palace of Westminster, as it was about 300 years back; from partial remains, and authentic sources of information—put together with the greatest diligence and accuracy—the point of view the S. W. corner of old Palace Yard. About 42 feet wide and 34 feet to the top of the drop.

Two very large wings, containing portions of the old palace, which the artist made out from an ancient draught met with in looking over some records of the augmentation office in Westminster.

Six wings representing ancient English streets; combinations of genuine remains, selected on account of their picturesque beauty.

The Tower of London, restored to its earlier state, for the play of King Richard III.

. . . Capon, among the other able artists of the theatre, formed a distinct feature, like the *black letter* class of a library. Such, with some modern views, were the first works he executed for the new theatre.

This new scenery was undoubtedly very fine; except for the last item enumerated—the Tower setting for Richard III restored to earlier state (a first touch of archæological accuracy, note), all these pictures were doubtless meant to serve as backgrounds for all the histories and probably many of the other plays of Shakespeare. The scenes were good, and audiences were expected to feel that they could not get too much of a good thing. I can discern in all the account of Boaden nothing approximating a complete production for any play. Unexpected testimony corroborates. The reader may remember "Harvey's palace," so ostentatiously listed in the Schedule of scenes at Covent Garden in 1744; does he also remember my mention of Nicholas Dall as chief scene-painter of that house from early in the '60's till 1777? If so, his historic imagination will be fired by some manuscript notes in a prompter's copy of Bell's Shakespeare, in the New York Public Library. One of these notes calls, in Act I, Scene 1, for "Dall's Hall"; another, in the very next scene, for "Dall's Town." This clearly shows a stock use of scenes considered important enough to be indicated merely by the name of the artist. The manuscript demand for Act V is very interesting: "Arch and *Perseus'* Town." Obviously the remains of some pantomime were used, to deck out Measure for Measure. To such base uses, Rich might have said, do we return! No doubt, however, Capon's scenes at Drury Lane, like Dall's at Covent Garden, adorned many and various plays.

OPENING OF THE NEW THEATRE, 1794

Drury Lane, the new and beautiful, the almost perfect playhouse, was opened on March 12, 1794, with sacred music. The stage was set with a scene which deserves considerable notice. Perhaps for the first time something approaching (in looks) a real roof was attempted, and obviously wings gave place to solid flats representing the sides of a room. This we learn from unmistakable testimony in the Thespian Magazine of March, 1794:

The stage for the oratorios resembles a Gothic Cathedral, with illuminated stained glass windows, &c. in exact *costome*. The *flies*, as the players call those shreds and patches which hang like so many tattered remnants in a shop at Monmouth Street, no longer wear that miserable habit, being carved like the fretted roof on an antique pile, and the *wings* to the side scenes, are removed for a complete screen, like those in use at the foreign theatres, thereby perfecting the deception of the scene.

This notice I consider a valuable "find," both in its reference to foreign custom as to side scenes, and in its implied statement of the novelty of such usage on the English stage. It renders more credible the print of the stage of the Haymarket Theatre, in 1795, reproduced in Mr. Cyril Maude's history of that famous playhouse, and unmistakably representing such arrangement—almost a box set, in fact. May we, then, assign 1794 as the date on which such a setting first emerged in the English theatre? Yet we must not forget what Aaron Hill said of the "slanting" scenes for Merope, in 1749.

The first dramatic offering of the new house was Macbeth.   W. C. Oulton, in his Continuation of Victor's Theatres of London, speaks thus of the staging of the tragedy:

On April the 21st, the house opened for the performance of dramatic pieces. . . .   The first . . . was Macbeth . . . which . . was now attended with much novelty; the scenes were all new, and the witches no longer wore mittens, plaited caps, laced aprons, red stomachers, ruffs, &c, (which was the dress of those *weird sisters,* when Mess. Beard, Champness, &c. represented them with Garrick's Macbeth) or any human garb, but appeared as preternatural beings, distinguished only by the fellness of their purposes, and the fatality of their delusions.   Hecate's companion spirit descended on the cloud, and rose again with him [*sic*].   In the Cauldron-scene, new groups were introduced to personify the black spirits and white, blue spirits and grey.   The evil spirits had serpents writhing round them, which had a striking effect.

It has been observed that these imaginary beings have been sometimes dressed above their rank, and as often beneath it; they were elevated into majestic Sibylls [*sic*] by the late Mr. Colman, and by Mr. Garrick sunk down into beggarly Gammers, though intended by Shakespeare as terrific hags. . . .   The present attempt of the managers of Drury-lane was to strike the eye with a picture of supernatural power, by such appropriate vestures, as marked neither mortal grandeur nor earthly insignificance, and likewise to avoid all buffoonery in those parts, that *Macbeth* might no longer be deemed a *Tragi-comedy.*

Oulton then proceeds to discuss Kemble's omission of the visible ghost of Banquo at the banquet; all chroniclers and scribblers were greatly exercised over this innovation, concerning which every man about town felt it incumbent upon him to express some opinion.   When, years later, Kemble gave back the Ghost to bodily vision, he was criticised with equal severity by those who would be different.

MRS. SIDDONS REFORMS COSTUME

Mrs. Siddons seems to have been accelerated, meantime, in her purpose to reform the dress of the actresses.   While the new Drury was building, the company had occupied the vast spaces of the King's Theatre, or the Opera, in the

Haymarket. The size of the building induced Mrs. Siddons to alter her style of acting, adapting it to grander, nobler and simpler lines, and something of this same feeling led her to a reform of the costume for tragedy, which still maintained the enormous head-gear, the hoops and flounces and train of a previous day.

Conspiring [says Boaden, in his well-known Life of the actress], with the larger stage to produce some change in her style was her delight in statuary, which directed her attention to the antique, and made a remarkable impression upon her as to simplicity of style and severity of attitude. The actress had formerly complied with fashion, and deemed the prevalent becoming; she now saw that tragedy was debased by the flutter of light materials, and that the head, and all its powerful action from the shoulder, should never be encumbered by the monstrous inventions of the hair-dresser and the milliner. She was now, therefore, prepared to introduce a mode of stage decoration and of deportment, parting from one common principle, itself originating with a people qualified to legislate even in taste itself. . . . . What Mrs. Siddons had chosen remains in a great degree the standard of female costume to the present hour . . . . and left our ladies the heirs of her taste and its inseparable modesty.

Let me quote again from Boaden (Life of Kemble) concerning the revival of The Winter's Tale at Drury Lane in 1801–2, during Kemble's last season there; the piece was produced "in all the splendor of decoration, and power of acting that he could impress upon it. I have already remarked the studies of Mrs. Siddons after the antique; in Paulina's chapel, she now stood one of the noblest statues, that even Grecian taste ever invented. The figure composed something like one of the muses in profile. The drapery was ample in its folds, and seemingly stony in texture. Upon the magical words, pronounced by Paulina, 'Musick; awake her: strike'; the sudden action of the head absolutely *startled*, as though such a miracle had really vivified the marble; and the descent from the pedestal was equally graceful and affecting."

THE DRESS OF THE ACTORS

What Mrs. Siddons effected in reforming the dress of female players was somewhat more tardily carried out by the men of the company. At his début in London in 1783, Kemble played Hamlet in a dress as inappropriate as Garrick's. Says the interesting Boaden of that occasion: "We have for so many years been accustomed to see Hamlet dressed in the Vandyke costume, that it may be material to state that Mr. Kemble played the part in a modern court dress of rich black velvet, with a star on the breast, the garter and pendant ribband of an order—mourning sword and buckles, with deep ruffles; the hair in powder; which, in the scenes of feigned distraction, flowed dishevelled in front and over the shoulders." Dr. Doran is especially severe on Kemble for wearing in Hamlet the order of the Garter and the order of the Elephant. We are told, also, that Kemble at one time dressed Othello in the uniform— scarlet coat and all—of a British general. If any doubt of this remains, one need but glance at his portrait as Hotspur (opposite page 56). This, in itself as ridiculous as Barry's court-costume in the same character, will cause one to marvel at the vagaries of actors' taste, even when they are on the upward path. Kemble, it will be seen, had far to go, before he reached the beauty of his performances at Covent Garden, beginning in 1810.

As far as the generality of Shakespearian productions is concerned, I rather fear that they were forced, all and sundry, to make use, during Kemble's *régime* at Drury Lane, of the fine stock of scenery provided by Capon; there was probably but little individualisation. Nevertheless, we learn from Boaden that the scenery for Cymbeline, revived during the season of 1800–1, "with some bearing upon the confusion of the manners, was a beautiful *mélange*"—whatever that may mean. The critic of the Dramatic Censor, February 12, 1801, is not so completely satisfied. Cymbeline, he tells us, "was this evening revived, with considerable costliness and splendor. . . .   Yet he [Kemble] . .

compromises the interests of the theatre, and saddles the firm with a debt of nearly One Thousand Pounds. The scenery and decorations were got up in the most superb and costly style—and we may add, with more magnificence, in many instances, than propriety. The bed, on which *Imogen* reclines was out of all proportion; so much so, that even Barrymore himself, though of the order of tall proportions, stood almost in need of a ladder to take a view of *Imogen's* person. The introduction of a Dance in the scene, where *Cloten* serenades his mistress, added to the artificial attractions of the Piece."

The years of Kemble's greatest activity at this theatre were the times of enormous popularity for adaptations from German melodramas of "wonder and terror," to use "Monk" Lewis's expression; The Castle Spectre came on December 14, 1797, and Sheridan's re-working of Kotzebue's Pizarro on May 24, 1799. These and others of their kind required much special scenery and got it. The famous bridge spanning the gorge, across which Rolla had to flee with the child, was one of the earliest trick-effects of melodrama. In the rage for this kind of thing Shakespeare suffered. He not only was forced to do without special scenery; he was reduced to a beggarly number of performances.

KEMBLE AT COVENT GARDEN, 1803

With the beginning of Kemble's occupancy of Covent Garden in the autumn of 1803, a new order prevails. For the first time, a deliberate attempt is made to produce the Shakespearian plays with proper surroundings. Kemble started at once to show the mettle of his pasture. As I have stated in the preceding chapter, a number of plays, seldom acted, were revived with revised texts and with some pretence of appropriate scenery. The records of these early performances are rather scant, but what was accomplished in general may be ascertained from an extract from Bell's Weekly Messenger, of February 19, 1804. This paper, published as usual with weeklies of its class in

London, on Sundays, was started by the John Bell whose Shakespeare we have examined; and from its later issues we glean many serviceable criticisms. The general tone of Shakespearian productions in the first year of Kemble's management may be imagined from this criticism in 1804:

COVENT GARDEN:

King John has been revived at this theatre. It seems the purpose of the Managers at this house to bring out all the noble productions of our great writers, with every advantage of the mimic art, and certainly no expense in dresses and decorations is spared in whatever is revived at this theatre. The painters and dressers, we conceive, have not had such a season of it a long time. . . . In the exhibition of one of the plays of *Shakspeare*, the meanest . . . of the house that nails one board to another, has his part in the reputation of producing the grand *tout ensemble* of the scene.

The liberality of the Managers is certainly great. Their theatrical stock is extremely rich; their wardrobe is curious, extensive, and well assorted; their armoury is polished, and plentiful, and their scenery is descriptive of every thing remarkable on land or water. We are much pleased, however, with the care Mr. Kemble extends to the upholstery of this house. A ricketty chair, a tattered sopha, or a broken table, seldom occur; notwithstanding there are many of the stock plays in which the destruction of the furniture is a principal joke. *Macbeth* and *King Harry* do not sit upon the same throne. *Juliet* has her own bier, and her plumes are as decent as though just out of an undertaker's shop, while *Desdemona* has her own bed and damask curtains.

These things are not ridiculous because they are minute; they are very necessary, and we wish the other house would not content itself so much with the grand sublime, but take a lesson of tidyness, snugness, and elegance, from the Managers of Covent Garden.

Even more valuable is the testimony of Gilliland, in his cumbrously named Dramatic Synopsis of the Theatre, Containing an Essay on the Political and Moral Uses of a Theatre, etc. (1804); this evidence is notable for its general scope and its particular bearing on what Kemble was accomplishing. It shows, too, that the best critical taste was no longer oblivious to gross violations of scenic propriety; veritably the appetite grew with what it fed on.

It gives us infinite pleasure [says Gilliland] that the Stage of the Present day, does not exhibit those grotesque and uncharacteristic

dresses which even lived with the immortal Garrick, such as Playing
a Roman or an early English character in a large *perri-wig*, or a full
dress suit of Charles the II's day. Mr. Kemble has done much in
the reform of stage attire. . . .

It has been said that Garrick in assuming the sick King in the
second part of King Henry the Fourth, was extremely happy in giving
Shakespeare's portrait every embellishment that fine acting could
possibly add to the poet's picture. If we do not presume too much,
we think it impossible that greater justice could have been done to
the aged and infirm Monarch, than Mr. Kemble has performed in
this character. . . . . His attention to the dignity of his situation,
as a King, in giving the scene all the splendor the chamber of a
Monarch requires, and his person all the elegance of costume, shews
a desire on his part to render Stage exhibitions as perfect as possible
for public gratification. There was not an article of the most trivial
description connected with his scenes, but what was necessary to
impress on the imagination the reality of his character, and the dignity of the Monarch; his dress in this part displays the taste of a very
refined actor.

All this "decoration," however, was probably trifling in
splendour, compared with the effort of Fawcett at the
Haymarket, in June, 1804, to stage a ballet of The Enchanted Island, founded on incidents "which the Muse of
Shakespeare has traced in narrative"; the incidents, in
other words, of the long-abused Tempest. The scene-plot
of this spectacle calls for astounding effects—quite beyond
what Kemble gave his own Tempest at either of the royal
theatres—but, after all, it has but slight relationship to
Shakespeare, and may be omitted from our discussion.
The curious may turn to it for a study of staging at the
beginning of the last century.

To close the record for the time of Kemble's first venture,
I call to the attention of the reader an interesting print of
the interior of Covent Garden, during a performance of
Pizarro, in 1804—actually in the initial season of Kemble's
management. The practicable bridge, which was so prominent a character (I speak advisedly) in the play, and the
child, about whose baby head so much of the plot was
twined, are conspicuously represented. The scene strikes
me as very good, and I am not sure we could do much
better with it to-day.

Another important picture is Ackerman's charming aquatint of the interior of Drury Lane, in 1808, just before the great fire. If the stage is not set for Coriolanus, for what play is it ready? The simplicity and dignity of the scenery and of the grouping of the characters seem to me to be beyond all praise. We should expect a greater army in this scene of Volumnia's pleading with her son, but perhaps the artist crowded his stage less than did the actual stage-manager. These two early-century plates, depicting scenes for Pizarro and for Coriolanus, seem to me to be valuable evidence in the case we are presenting.

THE NEW COVENT GARDEN THEATRE, 1809

By the time of the opening of the new Covent Garden Theatre in 1809, we arrive at what to us appears a rich supply of evidence concerning theatrical affairs. Weekly papers, like Bell's Weekly Messenger, and John and Leigh Hunt's Examiner (published on Sundays) and dailies, the Times especially, furnish regular dramatic criticisms, and devote more and more attention to the very subject, that of staging, which at present occupies our thought. Their remarks on this feature are very valuable, and are elicited by the efforts of John Kemble to make this last of his theatres a great national institution. That he succeeded, at least in the estimation of his contemporaries, is amply certified by the criticisms from which I shall quote. Drury Lane had sunk into the position of a negligible factor. The company had, since the fire, inhabited the Lyceum—a minor theatre—and had been none too successful. The new Drury Lane did not open till 1812. It was not until Edmund Kean appeared, early in 1814, that old Drury—or, rather, new Drury—could be said to have lifted its head above the waters. And it was in precisely those very years, 1809–13, that John Kemble set his mark broadly and definitely on the history of Shakespearian productions and established a practice that no future manager could ignore. From him the torch was handed on to various suc-

INTERIOR OF THE ROYALTY THEATRE, 1787
From a contemporary print

THE ROYAL FAMILY AT COVENT GARDEN THEATRE
From an engraving by J. Fittler, 1804

cessors until it burned brightest yet was finally almost extinguished in the great career of Henry Irving. Sir Herbert Tree exemplifies the truth of the lines about the little more and the little less, but must be counted in the history.

It is, fortunately, in connection with the very years I have just mentioned that playbills and critical reviews combine to illuminate our discussion. The reader may remember that, during these years, Kemble revived many of the less-frequently acted plays of Shakespeare—The Winter's Tale, Henry VIII, Julius Cæsar, Coriolanus, Antony and Cleopatra; the acting versions of all were considered in the last chapter. Let us see what were the more material adjuncts of the performances. A previous account of the O. P. riots which disgraced the first season releases me from the necessity of rehearsing them here; suffice it to say that at the end affairs settled down to a long reign of glory for Kemble and the English stage.

Bell's Weekly Messenger for September 24, 1809, gives an account of the opening performance: Macbeth, with Kemble and Mrs. Siddons. Of course, the disturbance in the audience prevented the hearing of a single word spoken by the actors. The critic, then, can vouch only for the visible part of the production, but what he has to say of the scenery is of interest:

The drop is peculiarly grand. It represents a temple dedicated to Shakspeare, in the back of which is seen his statue, from Westminster Abbey, supported by Tragedy and Comedy; and between pillars on each side are statues of Æschylus, Plautus, Lope de Vega, Ben Jonson, Molière, &c. &c.

Although we are unable to speak of the merits of the performers . . . . yet of the dresses, the decorations, and the scenery, we cannot speak with too warm an eulogium. They are in every respect suited to the magnificence of the Theatre, the grand scale of the whole establishment, and the liberality and taste of a British audience. The scenery in particular excels in general effect and appropriate detail all we have yet witnessed; and the pencils of Phillips, Whitmore, Grieve, and Lupino, have never been more happily employed. To the mechanists in the management of the scenry much praise is due.

Just after the cessation of the riots, Kemble produced
King Lear, which George III's recurrent mental states had
kept from the stage, and apparently gave to it not the rude
barbarism of Macready's later setting, but a conventionalised dress of a somewhat Saxon tendency, elegant enough
for the taste of 1809. Bell's Weekly Messenger for December 24th of that year is rather definite on this point. One
could wish for further details.

With respect to the manner in which the play was gotten up, it
may generally be said, that the magnificence of the scenery was not
inferior to the dignity of the Tragedy. Propriety of age and time
would have here perhaps destroyed the effects of the piece—If Lear
ever lived at all, it was in an age before British Kings wore purple
and gold,—before there were Earls and Dukes,—before there were
Palaces, and almost houses.—A manager is not to be pinned down to
this rigid propriety.—The times were Saxon, and the scenery and
appendages were generally of the Saxon character. This was enough
—More would have hurt the effect of the scene.

All this attention to appropriateness or uniformity of
attire, it may be assumed, was a special feature of the productions at the new theatre. Before this, there seems to
have been, at times, a confusion that recalls the famous or
infamous days of Quin and Henderson, and—why not say
it?—the early Kemble. A disgruntled correspondent gives
us some clue to the state of affairs in the last days at Covent
Garden before the fire. He writes in the Examiner of
January 21, 1810:

I saw "Much Ado about Nothing" at the late Covent-Garden
Theatre, about two years since, in which, notwithstanding the scene
is laid in Messina above two hundred years ago, and the characters
are Sicilians, I had the pleasure to see *Benedict* in the full uniform of
a *British Infantry Officer* of the present day, *Leonato* in the dress of
an *English Gentleman* of the year 1750, and most of the other characters dressed in the same appropriate manner; but it must be all
right, for it is under the superintendence of that man of classic lore,
Mr. J. P. Kemble! !

Mangin's Parlour Windows (1841) shows, indeed, that
everything was not right in Kemble's dressing, I take it, to

the very end of his career; here we learn that "Some yet survive who witnessed the renowned actor, John Kemble, learned and judicious as he was, marching to the fatal field, and fighting the battle of Bosworth, as *King Richard the Third*, arrayed in spotless silk stockings and long-quartered dancing shoes, adorned with the Rose of York; or rushing forth as mad *Lear* or the murderous *Macbeth* with a flowered satin night gown, which might have been, and possibly was, the lounging robe of one of Louis XV's coxcomb courtiers; and wearing, as Lear, a straw crown as large, massive and elaborately constructed as a beehive. . . . . These and similar absurdities continued, indeed, till Kean's discernment taught the boards, and the public, a purer lesson." Kean, according to this writer, was the first to go to the field of battle attired something like a warrior.

That this helter-skelter method, however, did not generally prevail in the new house, I gather from the review of Kemble's first season, published in the Examiner of June 3, 1810:

If Mr. Kemble nas not succeeded Garrick in all tragic excellence, as some of his admirers pretend, he has worthily succeeded him in one important respect, that of loving *Shakspeare* and keeping him before the public. The other managers of the present day have so little taste, with the exception of Sheridan, who cares for no taste but that of port, that were it not for Mr. Kemble's exertions, the tragedies of our glorious bard would almost be in danger of dismissal from the stage; and it does him infinite credit to have persevered in his exertions in spite of comparatively thin houses; to have added to the attractions of the poet by a splendour of scene as seasonable as well-deserved; and to have evinced so noble an attachment, and helped to keep up so noble a taste, in an age of mawkishness and buffoonery. —It is in this spirit that Mr. Kemble continues to draw from *Shakspeare* a kind of stock play for the season, which is performed regularly once a week, as he has done with *Macbeth*, *Hamlet*, and *K. Henry the Eighth*, and is now again doing with *King John*.

HENRY VIII AND THE WINTER'S TALE

I take the expression "splendour of scene as seasonable as well-deserved," to refer to appropriateness and richness

of detail; perhaps I am wrong, since the wording is triumphantly vague. As to the criticisms about to be adduced
there can be no doubt. The season 1811–12 was a banner
period for Shakespeare and Kemble. With the O. P. riots
behind them, and Drury Lane feebly struggling at the
Lyceum, Covent Garden had everything its own way. In
that year elaborate revivals of eight Shakespearian plays
were effected—Henry VIII, Measure for Measure, Twelfth
Night, The Merry Wives, Much Ado, Comedy of Errors,
The Winter's Tale and Coriolanus. This is doing late but
plentiful justice to the poet. Of Henry VIII the London
Times, on October 21, 1811, speaks with glowing eulogy,
and is, at the same time, remarkably illuminating as to
details:

Processions and banquets, find their natural place in a work of this
kind; and without the occasional display of well-spread tables, well-
lighted chandeliers, and well-rouged maids of honour, the audience
could not possibly sustain the accumulated *ennui* of *Henry the Eighth*.
In its five acts it has, as distinctly as we can remember, three processions, two trials before the king, a banquet, and a royal christening.
The banquet deserved all the praise that can be given to costly elegance. It was the most dazzling stage exhibition that we have ever
seen. The tables were continued round the stage, covered with
golden ornaments, and the whole pomp of princely feasting. As the
scene receded, it was filled with attendants and guards in their glittering "coats of livery." The Gothic pillars,—the rich tracery of the
architecture,—the various and shifting splendour that fell from the
chandeliers,—the glittering company of "courtly dames and barons
bold" . . . . . gave as many images to the eye and the mind, as
perhaps could be given by the highest combination of theatric ornament and theatric taste.

All playbills of this (as of earlier and later) date stress
the scenes of Wolsey's banquet, the trial of Queen Katharine and the christening of the Princess Elizabeth. Nothing was done with the vision of Queen Katharine; nothing
was visible—Patience merely sang Handel's "Angels ever
bright and fair," while the Queen slept. The critics who
objected to the visible representation of the ghost of Banquo
in Macbeth, also objected to the vision of Katharine's

THE KEMBLE FAMILY IN HENRY VIII
From a painting by Harlowe

angelic visitants.   By the way, I should like to insert here
a statement to the effect that at the new Covent Garden
Kemble had evidently restored the ghost of Banquo.   A
writer in the Times of September 19, 1811, inveighs against
the appearance as "a mere trick for the galleries.   An
actor might make the presence of the *perturbed spirit* visible by his action,—by the eye of terror,—the agitation,—
the changed countenance,—the sunk voice . . . . Banquo's
ghost ought to be laid, and laid forever."   Poor Kemble!
he must have grown weary of trying to please.   In the playbills of Macbeth, Romeo and Juliet and Henry VIII, at
this time, long lists of names of singers and dancers were
printed in connection with the scenes in which they figured.

I wish the writer in Bell's Weekly Messenger had been
a little more explicit in his account on December 1, 1811,
of The Winter's Tale at Covent Garden.   One strains one's
eyes in trying through the mist of generalities to get some
definite impression or vision of the actual production:

On Thursday was revived at this Theatre the Comedy of *The
Winter's Tale.*—The taste and refinement of the Managers are well
displayed in the elegance of the decorations, and the purity of the
whole suite of appendages, belonging to this Revival.—This species
of magnificence is a just tribute to our great Bard; it is a kind of
nightly monument to his fame.—The only suitable patronage which
a people can bestow upon his deceased Muse, is by decking her from
the wardrobe of a moral taste, and giving her that chaste pomp, and
matronly attire, which embellishes all her charms, and serves to
excuse many of her defects.—The Managers of this Theatre are
lavish upon right principles, and prodigal for the purpose of furnishing the most refined amusement to the town.

On the other hand, the Times of November 29th questions the utility of the production: "Upon the whole," it
says, "we think that the theatre might have bestowed its
splendid trappings [so then they were splendid] upon a
more vivifying play than the Winter's Tale."   For lack of
information more specific, we fall back on the playbill of
November 28th (the first night of the revival) and learn
only that "the Decorations (and the greater part of the

Scenes and Dresses) are entirely new," and that "the overture and symphonies between the acts are composed by
Mr. Bishop." The habit of printing synopses of scenes for
Shakespeare was still a year or two in the future. But an
examination of this playbill causes the casual reader to
lose all interest in scenery when he learns that the cast
included Kemble as Leontes, Charles Kemble as Florizel,
Fawcett as Autolycus, Liston as the Clown, Mrs. Siddons
as Hermione and Mrs. H. Johnston as Perdita.

KEMBLE'S CORIOLANUS, 1811

Coriolanus has come down in theatrical history as that
part in Shakespeare which most exactly fitted the style and
personality of John Kemble. What of his production of
the play in 1811? I gather that it embodied all his best
ideas on the subject of Roman architecture, dress, habits
and manners, and that it was presented on a scale of great
sculpturesque beauty. The Rome of his Coriolanus was
of marble—the Rome of the Cæsars—but granting the
anachronism, it was very fine. Much spectacular splendour
was successfully accomplished. The Times, which is usually
more exact than its contemporaries in giving detail, is, on
December 16, 1811, very enthusiastic in praise of the production:

The decorations of the play are prepared with great appropriate
skill and magnificence. The scenery, which is, we believe, altogether
new, exhibits a succession of Roman architecture, which exceeds any
we have witnessed: the triumphal arch scene in particular. The
dresses are in general excellent; and the costume, for attention to
which the manager has long deserved credit, is here better preserved,
upon the whole, than in any other play. The ceremony of the ovation on *Caius Marcius's* triumphant return from *Corioli* is superb;
and we think the pains and cost bestowed upon it, much better bestowed than on the ballets we have seen, or those which, we hear, are
forthcoming.

Bell's Messenger of December 22 is equally enthusiastic,
but, as usual, unfortunately vague and magniloquent.

Evidently, then, both the daily and the weekly press considered that things were going very well with Shakespeare at Covent Garden. Encouraged by such praise and, I hope, by public support, Kemble threw himself with great zeal into a revival of Julius Cæsar, on February 29, 1812. As usual, the playbill states that "the overture and act-symphonies are composed," this time, "by Mr. Ware, and . . . the Dresses, Scenes, and Decorations are, for the greater part, new." The lesser part that was old was doubtless adapted from the Coriolanus equipment. The cast was remarkably strong, Kemble playing Brutus, his brother, Antony, and Young, Cassius. All three were excellent, Young probably being the best. The Times of March 2 is more than usually informing:

We are not peculiarly inclined to panegyrise either the managers or performers of our theatres; but we are always inclined to do justice; and justice certainly will allow of some praise to the managers of the performances at Covent-garden. . . . . . . They have given us the most celebrated dramas of our great national Poet in a style of tastefulness and beauty, so far as the stage equipment was concerned, to which scarcely any addition could be required. The play of *Julius Cæsar* was revived on Saturday, in the spirit of this taste; and we have to congratulate the public on the exhibition of this noble drama, with every attention to scenic splendour, and classical costume, which could represent the dignity of "the old heroic time."

. . . . In a stage which professes a strict adherence to classic models, we cannot in the first instance pass over the *form* of the rostrum without some disapprobation. It appeared to us merely made for the exhibition of the actor, and quite unlike the form of the ancient rostrum, as it appears on bas-reliefs and medals; the beaks of the ships might be mistaken for anything else, and the whole erection was coarse and unsuitable to the scene.

. . . . The effect of this fine display was much diminished by the small number . . . on the stage: the populace were noisy, but certainly not numerous enough to give an idea, even with all stage allowances, of that turbulent and overwhelming concourse that would have poured round a rostrum where a Brutus was to vindicate the death of a Cæsar.

Bell's Weekly Messenger of March 8, 1812, speaks of the success of the play, and dwells with equal insistence on the paucity of representation in the mob-scenes. The Examiner of March 29, 1812, bears witness to the continued vogue of the production:

It is highly creditable to the taste of the public, that in spite of the largeness of this theatre, which at certain distances sets the ear and almost the eye at nought, the revival of *Julius Cæsar* continues to fill the house twice every week. The play is, indeed, to use a theatrical phrase, excellently *got up ;* and on the part of two of the principal actors, most excellently performed; so that what with the propriety of the costumes, the splendour of the decorations, and the intellectual treat always to be found in *Shakspeare*, the piece goes off in a very satisfactory manner; and an impression is left upon us of Roman manners and greatness,—of the appearance as well as intellect of Romans,—which to a young mind in particular must furnish an indelible picture for the assistance of his studies, resembling perhaps the clearness of local conception which is afforded by a panorama.

This is approaching pretty closely to the domains of modern criticism. The playbill of a revival of The Tempest on October 26, 1812, gives the names of the staff that was producing these splendours at Covent Garden. The scenery, it says, is designed and executed by Messrs. Phillips, Whitmore and Grieve, the second of whom painted Fawcett's ballet of The Tempest, and the third of whom was to become one of the most celebrated of English scene-painters. The playbill gives credit for the machinery and decorations to Messrs. Bradwell and Saul—the latter the designer of the stage—whose names constantly reappear, thereafter, on Covent Garden bills; and the dresses are by Mr. Flower and Miss Egan, whose names will also come again to our notice. Veritably the art of production had advanced with tremendous strides, when the host of decorators thus were celebrated in the bills along with the actors.

Kemble's texts of The Tempest from 1806 to 1815 bear direct testimony to the sort of spectacle he was striving for. Transferring the scene of the shipwreck to the beginning of Act II, his directions are: "The Sea. A Ship in a Tempest. Spirits of the Wind dancing. Chorus by Spirits of the Storm. The ship seems to founder. Ariel and all the other spirits disappear." Thunder and lightning accompany. The play ends by Prospero's waving of his wand: "The scene vanishes, and discovers a view of a calm sea, and the King's ship riding at anchor. . . . . Ariel and the Spirits re-ascend into the Sky." Mummery and trick scenes drive Caliban and his two mates, and Antonio and Alonzo to "distraction." Evidently The Tempest was regarded as fair game by the masters of pantomime.

ANTONY AND CLEOPATRA, 1813

The revivals just described in so much detail were to constitute a staple part of Kemble's repertoire during the remaining years of his life on the stage. The revival of Antony and Cleopatra, effected with great splendour, on November 15, 1813, had its day and ceased to be in the season that produced it. The bill of the play is more than usually specific. The overture, marches, and act symphonies are by Mr. Ware; the Egyptian scenery is by Messrs. Phillips, Pugh, Hollogan and Whitmore; the machinery, dresses and decorations are entirely new, and the machinery and decorations are by Mess. Bradwell and Saul, the dresses by Mr. Flower and Miss Egan. These people were on the regular staff of the house, and most of them had participated in the revivals preceding. The two features specially stressed by the bill are, in Act III, the sea-fight at Actium, and at the end of Act V, "the grand funeral of Antony and Cleopatra, with an Epicedium, the musick new, composed by Mr. Bishop." This is a good deal of information to find on a playbill for a "legitimate" drama, at that period. The first of these is described succinctly in the prompt-book: "Scene.—Sea-Shore.—Open Sea beyond it. A grand sea-fight, which ends in the defeat of Antony and Cleopatra." The second has been described in my analysis of the elements composing the play. The Times of November 16, 1813, has several interesting remarks on the performance:

The play is equipped in a very handsome manner. The costume expensive, and the scenery accurate. The sea-fight, on which, however, a very disproportionate expenditure was wasted, appeared to us unfortunately contrived. The encounter of real combatants required gallies of a size that impeded all their movements, and the whole, scene gave us the idea of unwieldy and unpicturesque confusion. The last scene, in which the bodies of *Antony* and *Cleopatra* were brought in to the mausoleum, was well conceived. By ranging the chorus and attendants on the steps of the sarcophagus, a fine depth was given to the view; and, excepting the biers, which were narrow gaudy fabrications, like children's cradles, there was nothing which we would wish to see removed. The funeral song had no peculiar merit. The choruses were not worse than the usual choruses of the stage. The solos feeble; and the poetry only worthy of laureatship.

The Examiner of December 5th observes that "it is not a matter of much surprise that the play of *Antony and Cleopatra* has proved such an object of attraction. Independently of the magnificent raree-show so usual at this theatre——." By December 19th, it was ready for a longer review, and the critic puffs out his chest to show his scorn and contempt for the methods of Kemble. Critical acerbity was beginning to grow with what it fed on:

The Managers of this Theatre, who occasionally affect to be classical, regale us now and then, to prevent a satiety of farce and pantomime, with a fragment of *Shakspeare;* they strip it indeed of many of its chief beauties; but then to make amends, they supply its mutilations by gorgeous ornaments and pompous shows. . . . . . Thus *Antony and Cleopatra* is acted for the sake of the sea-fight and the funeral procession; and *Coriolanus* is suffered to live on the boards of Covent Garden, because it offers a vehicle for a paltry imitation of a Roman Triumph, though as much like one, as it is like a Lord Mayor's shew.

Remember the Examiner is the paper of the Hunts, and that first Leigh Hunt, and then Hazlitt, wrote its dramatic criticisms. Let me dismiss this phase of my subject by quoting from the more easy and tractable critic of Bell's Weekly Messenger, under date of December 19th:

The Managers of this Theatre are laudably ambitious to gratify the public by every novelty in their power, without any check from expence or impediment from trouble. Their revival of *Anthony and*

Cleopatra, of *Henry the Fifth*, and *Coriolanus*, has been accompanied with a peculiar pomp and taste in the scenery and decorations. We question, whether Greece, in all her elegance, and Rome, in all her luxury, possessed a stage which could rival Covent-Garden, in pure refinement, and classical splendour. It is very creditable to have dramatic entertainments carried to their present point of excellence.

Evidently Kemble received much attention from the press, and it is very possible the shade of Garrick observed these modern proceedings with a considerable degree of envy.

EDMUND KEAN AT DRURY LANE, 1814

Edmund Kean appeared first in London, at Drury Lane Theatre, on January 26, 1814. The younger critics, like Hunt and Hazlitt, felt that a new star of intense brilliancy had arisen; with them Kemble's glory withered. We can read, in Hazlitt's Short View of the English Stage, long criticisms of the first performances of the new genius. It is apparent that the management of Drury Lane, when once they realised the value of their "find," did everything to further Kean's success. They even provided new scenery for his productions, especially the later ones. Hazlitt, reviewing his Richard III for the Morning Chronicle of February 15, 1814, announces that "the play was got up with great skill. The scenes were all painted with strict regard to historic truth. There had evidently been research as to identity of place, for the views of the Tower, of Crosby House, etc., were, in the eye of the best judges, considered as faithful representations according to the descriptions handed down to us." These things must have been indeed fine to elicit thus much praise from the sullen Sir Hubert. Doubtless Drury Lane felt that with Kean it could at last afford to meet Covent Garden on its own special ground of correct historic setting. The bill of Richard III for Monday, February 28, 1814, states that "the following Scenes will be exhibited in the Course of the Tragedy: State Chamber of King Edward III.—Vaulted Chamber of King Henry VI.—Crosby Council Chamber.—Baronial Hall.—

Tudor Hall. By Mr. *Capon*. Old English Market Cross.—Exterior of the Tower.—King Richard's Camp. And the Camp of the Earl of Richmond. By Mr. *Greenwood*. The Dresses by Mr. Banks, Miss Rein, and Miss Robinson." On the contrary, there are no synopses of scenes for Hamlet or Othello. It will be observed that some of the settings for Richard III were painted by Capon, Kemble's great "find" at the opening of Drury Lane in 1794; were they the same, I wonder, or new? Boaden tells us the old were consumed in the fire.

The great effort was directed to Macbeth, presented in the following season—to be exact, on the 5th of November, 1814. The playbill announces "the original Musick by Matthew Locke, with a new Overture and Act Symphonies, composed and arranged by Mr. Horn." Then, to our delight, it proceeds thus—an entirely new way of doing things:

> The following new Scenes, designed and painted by Mr. Greenwood and Assistants.
>
> Romantic Landscape—Rocky Pass and Bridge—Gothic Screen —Gallery in Macbeth's Castle—Banquet Hall—Cavern and Car of Clouds—Hecate's Cave—Castle Gate and Courtyard— Exterior of the Castle.
>
> The other Scenery by Mr. Capon and Mr. Greenwood. The Machinery by Messrs. Underwood and Drory.
>
> The Armour and Decorations by Mr. Morris. The Dresses by Mr. Banks and Miss Rein.

This all sounds very attractive. Hazlitt, in his fine criticism from the Champion, included in his Short View, does not deign to speak of the scenery, but other critics were less superior. Bell's Weekly Messenger of November 6th is excessively polite:

> Last night Kean made his first appearance in the character of *Macbeth*, which the Managers have brought out with a profusion of magnificence, and a propriety of decoration and pomp highly creditable to their taste and liberality.—Our Stage seems, indeed, to have reached its highest point of refinement, and we much question whether Rome, in all her luxury, and Greece, in all her elegance, could rival a British Theatre.

The whole play was well supported, and the scenes of witchcraft, and the sublime horrors of the incantations, were admirably exhibited by the respective performers, and produced with all their suitable equipage by the Managers.

A week later, it resumes:

We never recollect seeing the parts of the Witches better filled than by Dowton, Lovegrove, and Knight. The proper character of these malignant beings is well preserved, and they are not rendered, as they used to be, elaborately ridiculous. The Incantations, too, are remarkably well managed. The Cauldron is such a kind of magical utensil as it ought to be, and not as we recollect it, degraded to a mere carpenter's pitch kettle. The ascent of *Hecate* in her car is likewise well contrived. Upon the whole, we never recollect seeing Macbeth so well arranged in all its externals, or more suitably adorned, than it now is at Drury-Lane.

It will be observed that every management of the witch episode seems to Mr. Critic to be better than the last; and probably it was.

Kean's appearance as Richard II, in that *mélange* of Richard Wroughton, was also announced with the extra grandiloquence only the biggest happenings received. The playbills assert in the familiar language that there are "new Scenes, Dresses, and Decorations, and a new Overture, Act Symphonies, and Marches, incidental to the Tragedy, composed by J. F. Burrowes; the Scenery designed by Mr. Greenwood, and executed by him and his Assistants. The Dresses by Mr. Banks and Miss Rein; Embroideries by Miss Robinson; the Armour and Decorations by Mr. Morris." This imposing list of designers and executants we are now able to set off against Kemble's similar array, already familiar to us from previous records.

I hate to end the chapter with Frederick Reynolds, but chronologically his Midsummer Night's Dream just about closes it. This operatic spectacle was brought out at Covent Garden, on January 17, 1816. Hazlitt was completely disgusted with the result. "We hope," he exclaims, in the Examiner of January 21st, "we hope we have not been accessory to murder, in recommending a delightful

poem to be converted into a dull pantomime; for such is the
fate of the *Midsummer Night's Dream*. We have found to
our cost, once for all, that the regions of fancy, and the
boards of Covent-Garden are not the same thing. All that
is fine in the play, was lost in the representation. The
spirit was evaporated, the genius was fled; but the spectacle
was fine: it was that which saved the play. Oh, ye scene-
shifters, ye scene-painters, ye machinists and dress-makers,
ye manufacturers of moon and stars that give no light, ye
musical composers, ye men in the orchestra, fiddlers and
trumpeters and players on the double drum and loud bas-
soon, rejoice! This is your triumph; it is not ours; and ye
full-grown, well-fed, substantial, real fairies . . . we shall
remember you: we shall believe no more in the existence
of your fantastic tribe. Flute the bellows-mender, Snug
the joiner, Starveling the tailor, farewell! you have lost the
charm of your names; but thou, Nick Bottom, thou valiant
Bottom, what shall we say to thee? . . . . . All that was
good in this piece (except the scenery) was Mr. Liston's
Bottom, which was an admirable and judicious piece of
acting."

To show the group of artists and artisans concerned in
the "getting up" of this spectacle, I reproduce the essential
part of the playbill of the third night of representation:

THEATRE ROYAL, COVENT-GARDEN

This present Monday (3rd time these 50 years in 3 Acts)

Shakespeare's Play of

A MIDSUMMER NIGHT'S DREAM

With Alterations and Additions, to introduce the Original Musick
Composed by *Arne, Battishill,* and *Smith,* with Additions by
Handel, Dr. *Cooke, Stevens, Bishop,* &c.
The whole arranged and the Overture Composed by Mr. *Bishop*
The scenery Painted by Mess. *Phillips, Whitmore, Pugh, Grieve,*
Hollogan, Hodgins, and Their Assistants.
The Machinery by Mr. Saul. The Decorations by Mr. Bradwell,
The Dresses by Mr. Flower and Miss Egan.
The Dances composed by Mr. *Noble.*
Fairy Ballet

A catalogue of the songs, duets and choruses follows; as I have said elsewhere, much of it is culled from Eighteenth-Century versions. But the scenery chiefly allures us. The first scène is "a Grand Doric Colonnade appertaining to Duke Theseus' Palace," and is ushered into view by an heroic march. All this sounds like later representations of the play, from Madame Vestris's revival onwards. The third scene—to skip that in Quince's shop—is "A Wood—Moonlight"; in course of it, "Enter, in Procession, Oberon, . . . at one Wing, with his Train, and the Queen at another, with hers." Both the fairy royalties are in cars—no doubt very spectacular. In Act II we enter "Titania's Bower, decorated with Flowers. In the Centre, the Duke's Oak." We flit from one part of the woodland to another, and in the last scene become very pantomimic, on the approach of the Indian Boy. "Clouds descend and open," discovering a Fairy, who sings. These clouds ascend again. "Clouds having ascended, the Sea is discovered. A Fairy Palace in the distance. Titania's galley and other gallies in full sail. Dance, during which the Indian Boy is brought forward," and the act ends to a lusty chorus. In the third scene of Act II "a part of the Wood opens—a Mist is seen—the Mist gradually disperses, and Lysander is discovered asleep on a flowery Bank, Puck standing by him, with the Herb in his hand."

All these were, no doubt, very pretty pictures, and I have an idea that, if I had been a tired man in 1816, I should have found them very impressive; if I had been one of those new preachers of the perfection of Shakespeare—a Hazlitt, a Hunt or a Lamb—I fear I should have been vexed at the liberties taken with the text, and at the sacrifice of Shakespeare to spectacle and song. The playbill gives an elaborate catalogue of the triumph of Theseus, the final tableau, much talked of in its day, and frequently referred to in my work. In it are introduced "the Cretans, the Amazons, the Centaurs, the Minotaur, Ariadne in the Labyrinth, the Mysterious Peplum or Veil of Minerva, the Ship Argo, and the Golden Fleece!" This strikes me as an aggregation of races and monsters sufficient to satisfy even the most thoughtless follower of the eyes at any kind of show—Shakespearian, pantomimic or spectacular-melo-dramatic.   With it, my record closes.

BOOK V

THE LEADERLESS AGE
(1817–1837)

CHAPTER XXI

THE THEATRES AND THE MANAGERS

THE BEGINNING OF THE END OF THE PATENT-HOUSES

WITH the departure of Kemble in 1817, began what could aptly be termed the period of the decline and fall of the patent theatres, if not of the drama in general. The disaster is to be attributed partly to public taste, ever more and more desirous of novelty, of show, spectacle, dancing and clowning; partly to the lack of suitable actors—Kean excepted—for the great masterpieces of tragedy; but chiefly to the misfortune indicated by my title—the lack of a leader of commanding personality to guide playgoers, train and develop talent, and keep the theatre to its former high excellence of endeavour and accomplishment. We must also never overlook the fact that all things human progress toward their dissolution; the abuses of the patent system, after years of accumulating, gradually brought the system to its inevitable end.

Nevertheless, I believe that a Garrick or a Kemble could have deferred ineluctable fate. Kean was the only great actor so far recorded in theatrical annals who had not been able to organise the stage into a power for good and for social reputability. Betterton, Booth, Wilks, Cibber, Garrick, Kemble, had not only been respectable in themselves but the cause that respect was in other actors. By sheer force of character they had led the dramatic hosts to higher standing in the community, and had inspired them with sufficient loyalty to maintain the glories of the playhouse with which they were connected and to group themselves willingly about the leader of the particular period to which they belonged. Edmund Kean was wholly lacking in this power or, apparently, the ability to possess and wield it. Genius as he was, he lacked character not only to manage

117

others, but even himself. He was the first of several intemperate and dissipated tragedians who quickly brought back to the calling of the actor the ill-repute which had been removed from it by his great predecessors enumerated above. Charles Mayne Young, a formal actor of the Kemble school, and Charles Kemble, an incomparable exponent of elegant comedy, were incapable of carrying on the managerial policy that had been developed and handed down from the days of Betterton to those of John Kemble.

THEATRICAL SPECULATORS

In this state of affairs, the management of the two great patent-houses fell into the hands either of actors who proved to be incompetent directors, or of mere theatrical speculators, exploiting the art for personal aggrandisement. The glory that was Drury Lane and the splendour that was Covent Garden soon ceased to be, and both were thoroughly snuffed out by the Act of 1843, taking away the monopolistic privileges, nearly two centuries old, inhering in these two houses alone. Drury Lane, after seven years of well-intentioned but ill-conducted endeavour by the unfortunate Elliston (one of the most attractive and versatile of actors), passed in 1826 under the control of Stephen Price, the American, who had long directed the affairs of the famous Park Theatre in New York. Price was honest and efficient, but probably misunderstood the state of mind of the British playgoer; his tenancy was brief, and Drury Lane offered an opportunity to Captain Polhill to sink something like £50,000 in the all-devouring maw of two or three annual deficits. The last notable manager was Alfred Bunn, mortal enemy of Macready, and author of a diffuse work on The Stage, from which we glean details of the catastrophes merely stated above. He had served an apprenticeship under Elliston and Price, in some handyman capacity, and, in 1832, the bored committee of the stock-holders leased to him the temple of Garrick to wreak his will upon it; he directed its affairs from 1832 to 1839, and in the last-named year deftly steered it on the rock. A man named Hammond supervened between Bunn and Macready—Macready guiding the institution for two memorable seasons from December, 1841, to the spring of 1843.

The history of Covent Garden is but slightly different. During the glorious consulship of John Kemble from 1809 to 1817, the business management of the theatre had been vested in the very capable hands of Thomas Harris, another (and very large) shareholder. Harris died in 1820, leaving his share, but not his controlling vote, to his no less capable son, Henry Harris; in the same year John Kemble assigned his sixth share to his brother Charles—John Kemble dying not long after. Dissensions almost at once arose between these two beneficiaries. Charles Kemble was apparently somewhat difficult. In a few years he succeeded in eliminating Harris from the board of control, and thenceforth he ran the great theatre into disaster and practical bankruptcy. In 1832 he left it a wreck. A few of the later years of this decade of mismanagement were saved from utter ruin by the great success of Fanny Kemble, Charles's beautiful and talented daughter, who made the British public believe that the line of the Kembles was almost like the line of Banquo. They all inherited the Kemble nose and most of them the Kemble genius.

THE ACTIVITIES OF ALFRED BUNN

From 1833 to 1835, the indefatigable Alfred Bunn directed the affairs of both Drury Lane and Covent Garden. He conceived the brilliant idea that it would be more economical to play off one theatre against the other, devoting Covent Garden to opera, spectacle and ballet, and Drury Lane to tragedy and comedy. The beauty of the notion was further enhanced by the reflection that, one manager being in charge of both houses, actors could no longer exact exorbitant fees and would be forced to limit their desires by the will of the director. Like most perfect theories this one did not work.   The actors were intractable, and Planché tells us that Bunn did not carry out his intention of confining each theatre to a special class of entertainment.   On the same evening he balanced tragedy against tragedy, forcing the actors, sometimes, to run in their stage clothes from one theatre to the other (a short distance), and necessitating substitutions in the last act at one house, to allow performers to reach the other in time for appearance in the after-piece.   This practice, humorously recounted by Planché, is corroborated by a bit of exquisite fooling on the same subject in John Bull of December 13, 1833:

These legitimate dramas and this splendid acting are, however, confined to the boards of Drury Lane, for the edification of the two hundred and seventy-five renters, who, as they all go in free, cannot expect anything better, while at Covent Garden, "the full, true, and particular account of that most inhuman and barbarous murder committed by Captain Ankarstrom on the body of *Gustavus the Third*, King of Sweden, with the exact representation not only of the *pistol* with which he was assassinated, but of the *ball* at which he was shot," fills boxes, pit and gallery with crowds of wondering and delighted company.

What are the pathos of *Juliet*, the witchery of *Macbeth*, the madness of *Hamlet*, or the eloquence of *Portia*, to two dozen and four glass chandeliers, with six pounds and a quarter of wax candles stuck in them!   Legitimate drama, indeed!   Here we have a legitimate monarch murdered on the stage six nights in the week, for the edification of a well liberalised audience; the effect of the exhibition being considerably heightened by the consummate folly of a herd of amateur visitors of the *Coulisses* (who really ought to know better), who, for the sake of exercising the privileges which hiding the face at a public masquerade are said to confer, make their appearance nightly before the audience—

"All among the Thespians—high boy! ho boy!"

exposing themselves equally with those ladies and gentlemen to the temper of the pit and the orange-peels of the gallery.

After the experiment of the present season, we suppose, therefore, we shall hear no more of the "legitimate drama"; for it is now proved that the spectacle succeeds so well that it pays on one side of the way for all failures on the other.   As for the "patent moveable company," under the present system, the two houses incur but one expense—no matter where they are—now at the "Lane," now at the

"Garden." Cooper and Bartley—two of the most effective actors on the stage, and two of the most gentlemanly men off of it—are exactly like *Mungo* in the farce—

"Cooper here—Bartley there,"—

till, like blacky himself, we have very little doubt both of them wish

"To their hearts they were dead."

As the leaders do, so must their followers. We are told that at certain periods of the evening it is quite curious to see the actors and actresses running, hurry skurry, skimble skamble, from one house to the other—the Drury Lane *Romeo* rushing up Martlet-court in his black puffs and bugles, to act *Sir Christopher Curry* at Covent Garden, bumping himself full butt at the corner, against the Covent Garden *Jaffier*, scudding before the breeze to play *Dr. Pangloss* at Drury Lane; and then the ladies, slip-slops, spangles and sandals, rain or blow, hail or snow, away they go, Peruvian virgins, with suns at their bosoms, at full tilt, to become Witches on *Macbeth's* Heath, well secured from the weather by pattens and plaid cloaks; while a dozen dear old men, who have just doffed their robes as Venetian Senators in the "Lane," may be seen, with corked eyebrows and flaxen wigs, with pink bows in their shoes, picking their way like peacocks through the puddles, to act "Zephyrs" at the "Garden,"—their dutiful little grandchildren carrying their wings in hat-boxes, ready for fitting on as soon as they get off their great-coats.

How far this system of economy will work well, as regards the health of the "labourers," it is impossible to say, especially when the sharp weather sets in. It is quite wonderful that so few delays take place, and that so little interruption occurs to the performances thus carried on. Certain it is, that however much the overwhelming expenses of our over-built and over-encumbered play-houses may be curtailed by the experiment, the public have no right to complain: for as far as *they* are concerned the liberality of the present lessee is most particular.

OPERA AND SPECTACLE

No doubt these satirical comments are based on fact, but the reference to Gustavus the Third is nearer the general truth. Merely a cursory examination of files of play-bills for the years of Bunn's dual monarchy, and a reading of Bunn's records in his book, The Stage, would engender the idea not that there was too much tragedy, but too little. All was opera and spectacle. For instance, in 1833–34, at

Covent Garden, this very opera of Auber's, The Masked Ball, here called Gustavus the Third, was sung nearly a hundred times; the playbills stress the wonderful scenes, dances, etc. Bunn tells us that it became "the thing" to see this production, and also informs us that he has known thirty or forty noblemen to appear at one time among the maskers on the stage in the last act. Verily the nobility are great patrons of art. After Gustavus the Third, came —on John Kemble's stage!—The Revolt of the Harem, described as a grand fairy ballet. During the same season, as Bunn rather blatantly boasts, Drury Lane exhibited a pantomime of St. George and the Dragon, for which Ducrow was engaged with a stud of forty-four horses—Ducrow playing the Saint—and for which gorgeous scenery was painted by Andrews, Marinari and Stanfield, the last-named contributing a grand Egyptian diorama. The play-bill fairly loses its breath in gasping out the glories of this delectable show. No doubt each house profited vastly by its particular offering. At Drury Lane, some little concession was made to the drama. Macready struggled on in Shakespeare. Toward the end of the season, Byron's Sardanapalus was produced, splendidly staged, with Macready as the hero and Ellen Tree as Myrrha. These were, however, the great days for opera and ballet. People cared far more for Malibran (who died in 1836) and Taglioni than for Macready and Shakespeare. In justice, one has to admit that the supremacy of the great singer and dancer in their respective lines was far more incontestable than that of the actor in his. Malibran was Malibran, but Macready was no Kean or Garrick. A reading of the bills of Drury Lane and Covent Garden from 1832 to 1837 would lead one to infer that "legitimate" plays were almost extinct as far as performance was concerned; Auber's Bronze Horse, Balfe's Siege of Rochelle, and similar works would each dominate for a season the theatre at which it was produced. The rage for spectacular splendour accounted largely for this; and not until Macready transferred to Shakespeare something of the method of spectacle did the public return, late and somewhat listless, to its former loves. If Macready had been a Garrick he might have reformed public taste altogether.

To return to Bunn, we may say that he lost Covent Garden in 1835, a scared personage named Osbaldiston succeeding in the management. In 1837 Macready assumed control, and for two years he pitted his energies against Bunn, whom he hated. Bunn is very scorching in his account of the two memorable seasons, 1837–38, and 1838–39, in which he, at Drury Lane, tried to stem the tide of fate, against Macready, engaged in the same depressing occupation at Covent Garden. Macready had annoyed Bunn by knocking him down and "beating him up" in 1836; but before that Bunn had annoyed Macready by believing Bronze Horses and similar entertainment more lucrative than Shakespeare as enacted by Macready. Hence feeling ran high, and Bunn is silly enough to say that Macready "took" Covent Garden to "get even" with his late manager. After the Macready failure at Covent Garden, Charles Mathews and Madame Vestris had three wretched years trying to furnish Covent Garden with money, entertainment and audiences. In the spring of 1842 they retired, and Covent Garden as a theatre was doomed. In 1847 it became an opera-house.

CONCLUSION

It is my purpose in the present portion of my work to trace as briefly as possible the history of Shakespeare in the twenty leaderless years from the retirement of Kemble in 1817 to the assumption by Macready of the management of Covent Garden in 1837. These lean and hungry seasons were for the bard perhaps the worst that we have to encounter from 1660 to 1843. Certainly there was greater public apathy and greater scarcity of fine actors than at any previous or later time. Edmund Kean was the only great actor; Fanny Kemble and Ellen Tree the only actresses whose names are remembered. Who to-day knows of Charles Mayne Young or Robert Elliston? Who of Charles Kemble? Great comedians flourished—Munden, Liston,

Dowton, Emery, Knight, Farren—but their fame is not associated with Shakespeare. Americans will remember, with interest, that Junius Brutus Booth and James William Wallack—founders of famous American theatrical families —appeared with more or less acclaim in the first of the two decades we are considering, Wallack especially acquiring respectful hearing at Drury Lane; and that for two seasons, Edwin Forrest won rather considerable success before English audiences. These men, however, were never regarded in London as first-rate interpreters by a generation nourished on the art of Edmund Kean.

In general, then, the twenty years we are studying were spare times for Shakespeare. It must not be supposed that Shakespeare's plays were not acted frequently—it must only be stated that they were relegated more and more to the background in public and managerial estimation. At any time a Kemble might, possibly, have entirely changed the state of affairs; but what could one expect of a Price or a Bunn or an Osbaldiston, beset by the spectre of diminishing box-office returns? They were crushed between the upper millstone of the Committee of Shareholders, and the lower of the ebb and flow of financial support from the public; or the millstones may be reversed, if the reader so desire.

In the season of 1817–18, the playbills bear notice of change in the hour of beginning the performance: "In consequence of repeated applications, both from the city and the West end of the town, the Managers of the Two Patent Theatres will commence their performances at 7 o'clock, instead of half past six—and by drawing up the curtain *punctually* at the hour appointed, and by allowing the shortest possible time between the acts, this new regulation will not protract the evening's entertainment beyond the usual time." This notice came from both houses in the autumn of 1817.

CHAPTER XXII

THE PLAYS

OXBERRY AND CUMBERLAND

A KNOWLEDGE of the texts generally represented during this period may undoubtedly be obtained by an examination of the Shakespearian plays in the collection of The New English Drama, with Prefatory Remarks, etc., by W. Oxberry, Comedian (1818–23). This very attractive set of books, attractive by letterpress and charming portraits of players, is nearly the best edition of stage versions extant. The editor, a poor actor of fools and country bumpkins, and a seller of wine, issued many books on the theatre, and has secured thereby a sort of immortality denied him by his mediocre acting. It might equally well be said that a knowledge of Shakespeare as performed could be obtained by remembering what has formerly been stated of the John Kemble acting versions of 1814–15.

As a matter of fact, Oxberry so closely follows the later Kemble (as Mrs. Inchbald had followed the earlier) that I see no reason for burdening the reader with a comprehensive survey of Oxberry's labours. That he adopted Kemble's arrangements is shown (1) by his almost invariable custom of giving to Shakespeare's nameless lords, senators, officers, servants and messengers the actual names bestowed on them by Kemble; and (2) by his omission of scenes omitted in Kemble's ultimate revisions, notably in The Tempest, where both expunge much of Dryden's Dorinda-Hippolyto-Ferdinand-Miranda silliness. But Oxberry was no slavish follower. In general, his versions may be said to be shorter than Kemble's by a line or two cut here and there; occasionally, however, he restores a line. His most notable cut is the entire useless scene of Beatrice's awakening of Hero on her wedding morning (Act III, Scene 4) in

Much Ado about Nothing. Henry V is also much curtailed, in groups of lines, especially in the council scene in Act I, where twenty lines are left out before the entrance of the French Ambassador (the Constable in both versions). In the scene of the condemnation of Scroop, Cambridge and Gray, also, the King is forced to give up many lines of fine moralising. Thereafter, the two versions are identical. Macbeth is finally shorn of Garrick's ranting death-speech for the hero. The Merry Wives of Windsor and As You Like It show minor differences of omission and retention of lines that do not in the least affect the main fabric. In Measure for Measure, the second big scene between Angelo and Isabella is cut down by seventeen and one-half lines, including some very frank ones of the innocent Isabella. Finally, King Lear restores to the first scene of Act III (Lear's raving on the heath), and the first of Act V (Lear's return to reason and his recognition of Cordelia) several beautiful lines of Shakespeare, hitherto banished by Kemble; in the process, Oxberry (for those he represents) sends many lines of Nahum Tate to the limbo of forgotten things. In this his version is very like Elliston's published during the same year (1820) and to be discussed very soon in this chapter. With these exceptions, Oxberry's versions are sufficiently like Kemble's to be dismissed from further note. The twenty-two plays he edits are, of the tragedies, Coriolanus, Cymbeline, Hamlet, Julius Cæsar, King Lear, Macbeth, Othello, Romeo and Juliet; of the comedies, As You Like It, Measure for Measure, The Merchant of Venice, The Merry Wives of Windsor, Much Ado about Nothing, The Tempest, Twelfth Night, The Two Gentlemen of Verona, The Winter's Tale; of the histories, King John, the first part of Henry IV, Henry V, Richard III, Henry VIII.

How closely the publishers and editors of these dramatic collections kept their fingers on the pulse of change in the theatres may be guessed from what I have just said of the changes from Kemble to Oxberry, few though the intervening years had been; it may be better agnised by an examination of another set of books, very pleasingly "got up," as to letterpress and illustrations (this time from drawings by Robert Cruikshank, purporting to be made in the theatre). This is the charming series of plays edited by D. G. (George Daniel) and published by John Cumberland. The first volume appeared in 1826, the last, after 1840, soon before the series merged into the equally interesting collection of Thomas Hailes Lacy. In general, the differences between Oxberry and Cumberland are too slight to occupy a moment of our time, but in one or two instances —notably that of King Lear—we are indebted wholly to Cumberland for a knowledge of very important changes made in the manner of presenting Shakespeare on the stage in the years immediately following the cessation of Oxberry's activities. Except for these significant alterations, we shall here dismiss Cumberland with the remark that he is even closer to Oxberry than Oxberry is to Kemble. At the risk of being tedious in repetition, I shall again assert that—except for the few things noted or to be noted—the differences between Inchbald, Kemble, Oxberry and Cumberland are almost infinitesimal as compared with the differences between their basic prompt-books and those printed by Bell in 1773. Probably the changes from 1773 and the similarities in all later editions are attributable to the commanding personality of John Philip Kemble. He selected the plays to be given and moulded the form in which they were to be presented.

TENDENCIES IN THE LAST YEARS OF THE PATENT HOUSES

In spite of the barrenness of this period, and in spite of the general standardisation of texts, three distinct movements can now be traced in the presentation of Shakespeare in the twenty years, 1817–37. The first of these was a more or less persistent effort to "operatise" his comedies. This process began with the Midsummer Night's Dream in 1816, and originated in the fertile brain of Frederick Reynolds, abetted by the musical genius of Henry R.

Bishop, and the scenic art of an increasing group of notable scene-painters, the Grieves especially. The second movement was of more lasting benefit and finally prevailed; it was the effort, at first vague and half-hearted, at last determined and austere, to restore to the stage the actual text of Shakespeare, freed from the shackles of Tate, Dryden and their school. In the final victory, the name of William Charles Macready must stand high. He did the deed finally and forever. The third movement was the placing of Shakespearian plays on the stage, no longer as stock pieces, with stock scenes and dresses, but each play as a complete production, with appropriate setting, costume and decoration. This last phase of the subject will be properly left for discussion in the next chapter, but the first two I shall at once take up.

KEAN'S VERSION OF HENRY VI

At the very outset, however, I must record the very last effort to mutilate Shakespeare, and to make a new play out of the shattered remains of his handiwork. The piece in question is another attempt to do something with the three parts of Henry VI, none of which, so far as I know, was ever acted after the Restoration, until, in order to gratify those indefinite but serviceable "Ladies of Quality," the first part was acted (and once only) at Covent Garden Theatre in 1738. The very last milestone on the road that saw the wrecks of Crowne, Theophilus Cibber and others, was published in 1817, the year of its production, and has sometimes been attributed to Edmund Kean, who enacted the leading character. It was performed at Drury Lane, on December 22, 1817, and at once printed under the title of Richard Duke of York; or, the Contention of York and Lancaster (as altered from Shakspeare's Three Parts of Henry VI).

This play is made up, for the greater share, of Shakespeare's second part, preceded by the scene of the roses in the Temple Garden, the Lancastrians and Yorkists pluck-

EDMUND KEAN AS GLOSTER
From an engraving by Cooper after a painting by Clint, 1822

ing red or white blossoms, according to their party prejudice, and the episode of Edmund Mortimer and Plantagenet in prison. The removal of attainder against York is also represented. The King puts on the red rose—the Vernon-Bassett scene preceding in double quotation, as not given, because of the length of the play. In the fourth scene of the first act, Suffolk brings Margaret to the King, and Warwick and Gloster lament the loss of the French provinces.

The rest of the play is a frightful, unintelligible hodgepodge of material selected at random from the two later parts of Shakespeare's trilogy. The quarrel between Beaufort, Bishop of Winchester and Humphrey, Duke of Gloster (really the best part of Shakespeare's work) is amplified to some extent, the Duchess of Gloster (one of Shakespeare's best characters) being omitted. Of course York takes his due place in these proceedings. In the scene following the murder of Gloster, York (the star part, played by Kean) appropriates the words of Warwick respecting the change in the face of the slaughtered duke. Jack Cade's rebellion is given very briefly, and we hurry on to York's return to England, the consequent fight, Henry's promise to leave York the crown, if he may have it during life, with Margaret's burst of rage against this trifling cowardice. Suffolk is banished, and Margaret hears of his death, in a new and not too pleasing scene. Then follows the great battle between the Yorkists and Lancastrians, the play ending with material from the first act of Shakespeare's third part, involving the death of York. The episode is omitted of placing the paper crown on his head. He has the farewell scene with his son, Rutland, as in Cibber and indeed in Crowne; the very pretty and pathetic scene, in imitation of the manner of John Webster, not found in Shakespeare. The author of the 1817 adaptation must have read this in Crowne or Cibber, though he prides himself in the preface on this very scene so palpably "lifted" from the plays of his two predecessors mentioned above. Rutland's death is also portrayed.

This is about the worst *mélange* we have been called on to notice in the entire course of our history of Shakespearian alterations. The author states in his preface that he had incorporated passages from works of the contemporaries of Shakespeare; he has done so, and fragments of Chapman's Bussy d'Ambois and Byron's Conspiracy, Webster's White Devil and Marston's Antonio and Mellida shamefacedly peep from behind the sheltering screen of italics and footnotes. Though this same blabbing preface says that Shakespeare is unchanged, or very little changed, the author indulges in the usual tricks of shifting order, running two lines together, etc. There is not a vast amount of this, but a surprising amount for the year 1817, the heyday of Coleridge and Hazlitt in the preaching of the Shakespearian cult.

The worst thing about the production is, of course, its utter lack of dramatic unity. As the London Times, of the date following that of the production at Drury Lane, justly remarks, "There is no deficiency in quantity, could it be brought into an intelligible connexion."

THE COBLER OF PRESTON ONCE MORE

It is a great pleasure to take leave finally of this sort of attempt to improve Shakespeare. Henceforward, we shall find that the whole tendency was to improve him by restoring, or (if I may be pardoned the bull) by leaving him alone. Completeness of record, however, demands the statement that, just before Kean did this thing at Drury Lane, somebody at the same theatre was moved to bring out a revision of Charles Johnson's century-old Cobler of Preston, with musical additions, and with an added plot involving the love of Marian, daughter of Squire Jolly, for Sir Charles Briton. These three not only act, but sing in various combinations of soli, duets and finales. The curious may find it in Cumberland's British Theatre. It had some slight success, at its production, on September 29, 1817, thanks largely to the inimitable Munden as Christopher Sly, but, since its Shakespearian matter is negligible in quantity, I hardly see why it should detain us here.

FREDERICK REYNOLDS: THE COMEDY OF ERRORS

I come at last to the maulings of Frederick Reynolds, writer of many plays and entertainments, general adviser and assistant to the managers, and transformer of Shakespeare's comedies into what were loosely styled operas. We saw the beginning of this last-named activity in his successful (financially successful) production of A Midsummer Night's Dream, in 1816. Inspired, apparently, by the results of that experiment, he laid violent hands on the best and best-known of the remaining comedies.

The first to bear the attack was The Comedy of Errors, brought out at Covent Garden on December 11, 1819. The title-page of the printed copy (1819) gives most of the information required: the play is produced "in five acts with Alterations, Additions, and with Songs, Duets, Glees, and Chorusses [sic], Selected entirely from the Plays, Poems and Sonnets of Shakspeare. . . . The Overture and new Music composed, and the Glees arranged, by Mr. Bishop. The Selections from Dr. Arne, Sir J. Stevenson, Stevens, and Mozart." This is about the combination of sources in all the subsequent Reynolds concoctions; Bishop seems to have been largely a selecter, rather than a composer of the songs rendered. Note, besides, that the words are from various compositions of Shakespeare himself, not, as heretofore in all such attempts, including the 1816 Midsummer Night's Dream, an injection of anybody's poetry into the pure stream of Shakespeare's play.

Reynolds's Advertisement to The Comedy of Errors explains his motive. "The admirers of Shakspeare having long regretted, that most of his *Lyrical Compositions*, have never been sung in a Theatre, the Comedy of Errors (one of the shortest and most lively of his Comedies) has been selected as the best vehicle for their introduction,—A few additional scenes and passages were absolutely necessary for this purpose; and however deficient these may be found, it is hoped they will be readily pardoned, as having served to bring on the stage, more of the 'native wood notes wild' of our Immortal Bard!"

Some of these assertions will bear amplifying, a hundred years after they were written. A reader of to-day will be interested to learn that many of the songs scattered through Shakespeare's plays were never given during performance of the plays; for instance, none of the lovely lyrics sung by the Clown in Twelfth Night appears in any acting version of the work, the Clown being accorded only the final "When that I was and a little tiny boy." The songs interspersed throughout As You Like It were omitted or reduced in number of stanzas in representation. Of course some of the plays with lyrics were never acted. Hence, as Reynolds says, some of his "lyrical compositions" were never "sung in a theatre." To Reynolds this may have seemed sufficient justification for transplanting them in the least poetical of all the comedies—The Comedy of Errors. Unless, as hinted in the Advertisement, the shortness of this piece was the reason for its selection, I see none for its being the first in a rather long line of eminent victims.

Reynolds says, further, that "a few additional scenes and passages were absolutely necessary" for his "purpose." These scenes he has worked in with all the ingenuity of a modern librettist seeking an excuse for the introduction of a song. For instance, the last scene of Act III is a hunting scene, with a magnificent set of snow-clad mountains, the whole thing "got up" to allow of the singing of a glee— a "quartetto" and chorus, from Love's Labour's Lost— "When icicles hang by the wall." Act IV ends with a grand bacchanalian revel in the house of Balthazar, a character certainly harmless enough as Shakespeare left him. Previous to this scene, the Ephesian Antopholis (spelled so, in the Eighteenth-Century style), Cerimon and Ctesiphon (Shakespeare would not, any more than his readers, know who these last two were) have had a "roaring" night (roaring with wine and weather, and Reynolds the sole author of it), and in Act IV, the Antipholis is led, "roaring" drunk, into the aforesaid scene of revelry in the house of Balthazar. All this seems to be an excuse for singing "Bacchus, monarch of the vine," from Antony and Cleopatra. But the reader shall judge; I quote the scene entire. A magnificent dining-room "set" is described in the stage-directions. Then they enter, leading Antipholis of Ephesus:

Bal. So—look up, Antipholis—you're safe with friends,
'Tis I—Balthazar!
Ant. of Eph. Balthazar!
Bal. Hearing noise, we left our social bowl
And rush'd into the street—there we found you
Fast in the clutches of this mountebank—
This meer anatomy—this living dead man—
We fought—and rescued you.
Ant. of E. (*looking round*) I see—
Balthazar's house!—thanks! thanks!   [*Taking his hand.*
But where's the perjur'd and confederate crew—
I will have justice!   [*Going*
Bal. (*detaining him*). Not now Antipholis—
Wait till the storm blows o'er; and in calm hour,
Appeal unto the Duke—he'll see thee righted.
Meantime, though a sad truant in the chace,
Partake our evening sports. Come, in yon bowl
Drown every care!
Antiph. of Eph. Why, yes, Balthazar—fill, fill me to the brim.

Trio and Chorus
(Antony and Cleopatra)
Come, thou monarch of the vine, etc.

The additions of the Eighteenth-Century versions are also used, especially the long amplification of the Dromio of Syracuse, about his honesty, in his very first scene.

The musical numbers are very numerous. In Act I, Luciana sings "It was a lover and his lass" (As You Like It) and the Antipholis of Ephesus "Beauty is but a vain and doubtful good" (Sonnets). The glee, "Blow, blow, thou wintry wind" (As You Like It) is rendered by the roaring crew mentioned above. In Act II the neglected Adriana warbles "Willow, willow" (Othello), and lifts up her voice in song with her sister in "Tell me, where is fancy bred?" (Merchant of Venice). A glee ends the act by further depleting As You Like It of "Under the Greenwood Tree," sung by Balthazar, Cerimon and Antipholis of Ephesus. Act III goes farther afield and gives to Angelo and the same songful Antipholis Edgar's song from King Lear, "St. Withold footed thrice the wold." Next Adriana invites her Antipholis to "Come live with me and be my love," and Luciana indulges in musical melancholy about the "Sweet rose, fair flower, untimely plucked, soon faded," from the Sonnets. This act ends with the "When icicles hang by the wall," sung as a glee by the huntsmen. In Act IV poor Adriana sings "Take oh! take those lips away" (from Measure for Measure), and later joins with Luciana in "As it fell upon a day" (from the Poems—here called Sonnets). The finale, the play having filched from many sources, now blazes up in a medley from The Tempest and A Midsummer Night's Dream. Luciana invokes "Honours, riches, marriage-blessing," and Adriana crowns all by singing

> Gentles, do not reprehend,
> If you pardon, we will mend.

Let us glance for the last time into the workshop (or factory) of Reynolds. The following gives him at his characteristic task of bringing in a song at any price; in Act I, Scene 2, Luciana speaks:

> Why does Antipholis delay so long,
> And give his wife new cause for jealousy?
> In vain I still preach patience—for she says
> That should I live to see these griefs my own,
> My boasted reasoning would be thrown aside.
> Well, I will marry one day but to try—
> Yet all things must combine to tempt me to it.
> First, the season—not when drear winter chills;
> But when, as good old calendars assert,
> Wedlock's apt season, merry springtime comes!

> Song:
> *It was a lover and his lass*, etc.

This compilation is obviously much farther from Shakespeare than was the 1816 Midsummer Night's Dream. Sampson Low published the copy of The Comedy of Errors, but after that Reynolds seems to have "lost nerve" (as well he might) and to have published no more of his adaptations. The two already discussed are therefore the last we can treat from original sources; for knowledge of the rest we are indebted to contemporary documents of another kind.

The rising tide of Genest's wrath against Reynolds begins to seethe and eddy in his comment on this production. "Reynolds in his advertisement," growls Genest, "hopes that his additional scenes will be readily pardoned as being absolutely necessary for the sake of introducing the songs —Reynolds may be assured that the only sentiments which the real friends of Shakspeare can feel towards him are— indignation at his attempt, and contempt for the bungling manner in which he has executed it." Yet Genest himself admits that the "opera" was presented twenty-seven times during the first season, and my own researches have shown me that it was frequently revived. The great success of the production was due to the scenery, the music and the cast—Liston and Farren playing the Dromios, and those lovely singing actresses, Miss Stephens and Maria Tree, Adriana and Luciana, respectively.

REYNOLDS'S TWELFTH NIGHT

Twelfth Night next fell into musical time. On November 8, 1820, it was brought out at the same theatre, with much the same puffing. It had the benefit of new scenery, machinery, dresses and decorations; besides which, the playbill states, "the Overture and whole of the Musick composed, and selected from Morley, Ford, Ravenscroft, Saville, Sir J. Stephenson, Winter, &c, and the Glees arranged by Mr. Bishop." Talk of too many cooks! Maria Tree played and sang Viola. On the playbill of November 8th, this version of Twelfth Night was announced to include musical numbers as follows: Song, "Full many a glorious morning" (Sonnets); Glee, "Who is Sylvia" (Two Gentlemen of Verona); "Even as the Sun" (Venus and Adonis); duetto, "Orpheus with his lute" (King Henry VIII)—these in the first act. In the second act King Lear and Poems (according to the programme) supplied "Come o'er the brook," and the second part of Henry IV a glee, "A cup of wine." Act III had from the "Sonnets," "Crabbed age," duetto, "Cesario, by the roses of the spring" (oddly enough, from Twelfth Night itself), and "O, by rivers, by whose falls," from the Poems. Let me pause to say that one of these numbers "from the Sonnets" never included fourteen lines of words; only six or eight lines at most would be given. The fourth act contained more sonnet-material, "O how much more doth beauty" and "Take all my loves"; its third member was "Come unto these yellow sands," from The Tempest. Act V had "In bowers of laurel" from the Poems; "Bid me discourse" from Venus and Adonis, and the original finale, "When that I was a little tiny boy" (sic). In Act IV was Shakespeare's grand masque of Juno and Ceres, from The Tempest. Failing the libretto, through the modesty or the prudence of Reynolds, I am spared the duty of telling just how or why these songs fitted in; judging from The Comedy of Errors, I should hazard the guess that they didn't. The number of songs was soon reduced to eleven.

Genest is never more amusing than when he opens fire on Reynolds. Admitting that the odious thing was acted seventeen times, Genest cries out, "In the Devil's name, why does not Reynolds turn his own plays into Operas?— does he think them so bad that even with such music as he has put into Twelfth Night, they would not prove successful?—or has he such a fatherly affection for his own offspring, that he cannot find it in his heart to mangle them?"

The critic of James and Leigh Hunt's Examiner—in this case Leigh Hunt himself—was torn with conflicting emotions; he evidently rather liked the show, though he knew, in critical justice, that he shouldn't. On November 12, 1820, he thus dubitates:

TWELFTH NIGHT.—The successful introduction of music into the *Comedy of Errors* has given rise to a similar lyrification of this delightful play. It is interspersed with songs, glees and duetts, taken from the German and English masters; and Mr. Bishop, besides adapting these to the scene with his scientific hand, has added some composition, of which though a high, it is no undeserved praise to say, that a hearer must be nicely acquainted with the varieties of musical style to distinguish it from the rest. The other modern composers are Mozart, Winter, and Sir John Stevenson, the older ones Morley, Ravenscroft, and others, who flourished during the golden age of our poetry. . . . .

Mr. Bishop has adapted the songs to the several characters "with difference discreet." *Viola's* are deep and tender; *Olivia's*, like her rank and pride, more vehement, gorgeous, and wilful; those of the others as wilful too, but light, festive, and seasonable. The whole are well executed.

. . . .

The scenery of this piece is beautiful, particularly in the Mask, which they have introduced from the *Tempest*, and which reminded us of the times of Inigo Jones and Ben Jonson. After all, we know not whether the managers and their musician have not imposed on us with the help of Shakspeare, and whether we ought not to resent these "pickings and stealings" of him on that very account. But the patchwork added to the play is at least made up from himself, and with a poet or two with whom he has been confounded. *Twelfth Night,* though calculated to be more popular than the *Comedy of Errors* and quite able to stand alone, must also be allowed to be more fitted for the introduction of songs. In short, with all our criticism and objections, we have been upon the whole much pleased; and if in candour we must mention the one, in gratitude we cannot help confessing the other.

REYNOLDS AND THE TEMPEST

Prompted by the success of this venture, Reynolds and Bishop seized upon The Tempest, "as altered and adapted by Dryden and Davenant," and therefore already sufficiently damaged, one might think. It was brought out at Covent Garden on May 15, 1821. The overture was composed by Mr. Davy, though the indefatigable Bishop "selected, adapted, and arranged" the "musick," this time by Purcell, Haydn, Mozart, Linley, Braham, Rossini and three others—obviously a mixture of schools. There was fine scenery—described on the bill, and hereafter to be referred to—many dances, much machinery, etc. The purveyors were beginning to feel the effects of having purloined so many of Shakespeare's lyrics to fill to the brim the cup of musical joy in previous "operas"; from this time on, they are forced to restore to their original setting many of the poetic gems stolen to make up the musical delights of The Comedy of Errors and its frequent successors. The process begins with The Tempest. No clue is given as to the words sung. As the version of the play was Davenant and Dryden's, we may be reasonably sure that the songs were the accumulation of a century of mistreatment of Shakespeare's fantasy. Macready was Prospero, but the other leading parts were entrusted to singers, not actors— Miranda and Dorinda to Miss Hallande and Miss Stephens, Ferdinand and Hippolyto to Abbott and Duruset, and Ariel to Miss Foote.

Evidently the novelty of this sort of entertainment was beginning to wear off, as we may judge from the review in John Bull, May 27, 1821:

> The *Tempest* has been revived at Covent Garden with equivocal success, at which we are not surprised; the system of making Tragedies Operas, and singers actresses, is an absurd one, and only serves to shew how much in the way of combination is required, in these times, to make a house; in this instance, however, the effort has failed, for the audiences have not increased in number at all since this revival, so that getting up *The Tempest*, even with additional airs, has failed "to Raise the Wind."

The Tempest in this form was played eleven times, according to Genest.

REYNOLDS AND THE TWO GENTLEMEN OF VERONA

Undeterred, however, by the law of diminishing returns, Reynolds rushed at it again, and presented at Covent Gar-

den on November 29, 1821, his musical version of The Two
Gentlemen of Verona. Of this the words and music—not
the text, thank heaven!—were published and have come
down to us naked and unashamed. These Songs, Duettos,
Glees and Choruses may be discovered by the antiquarian,
who will no doubt be pained to observe how vilely Shakespeare's plays, poems and sonnets have been forced to yield
some of their finest sweets to lend attractiveness to Shakespeare's early comedy. According to the title-page of the
printed copy of the words, "the Overture and whole of the
Musick (excepting two melodies)" were "composed by Mr.
Bishop." What liberties were taken with Shakespeare's
text may be judged by the fact that Master Longhurst
appeared as Philippo (whoever he might be) and that Miss
E. Dennett played the part of the Genius of Pleasure.
Perhaps the latter character was a friend of Proteus. Master Longhurst (or Philippo) had a good deal of singing to
do. He began the musical feast with a song from the
Poems, "When I have seen the hungry ocean gain," and
was succeeded shortly by Julia, who warbled (in the charming person of Maria Tree) eight lines of the well-known
sonnet, "That time of year thou may'st in me behold."
Julia and Philippo (a page, I guess) unite their voices in
"Say, though you strive to steal yourself away, For term
of life thou art assured mine" and six more lines.

In Act II, Sylvia sings six lines of "Oh, never say that I
was false of heart," and joins three courtiers in "Good
night, good rest, Ah neither be my share," both from the
Sonnets. Julia in Act III has a chance at the first four and
the last four lines of the noble sonnet, "When in disgrace
with fortune and men's eyes." At the end of the act,
Rodolfo, Carlos, Ubaldo and Stephano, those incorrigible
bandits of John Kemble, sing from Venus and Adonis, "To
see his face, the lion walk'd along"—but only four lines.

In Act IV Julia and all these outlaws (why?) sing "Who
is Sylvia"—already used up in Twelfth Night. A Midsummer Night's Dream supplies this same lusty chorus of
outlaws with "Now the hungry lions roar, And howling

wolves behold the moon." I can almost hear that chorus. In Act V, Julia and Sylvia unite their voices in feminine accord in sixteen lines from Love's Labour's Lost, "On a day, alack the day!" Julia alone sings one of Bishop's most popular songs, the lovely "Should he upbraid," adapted from The Taming of the Shrew. The finale is a grafting of As You Like It on a limb of the Sonnets. Sylvia sings to Valentine four lines of "How like a winter hath my absence been," and the Chorus bids the Duke receive his daughter in Hymen's words in the pastoral comedy; Julia, not to be outdone by the other lady, sings four lines of "Let those who are in favour with their stars," the chorus again, to make assurance double sure, bidding the duke receive his daughter.

Evidently more pains had been taken with the "getting up" of this show, and the management was rewarded with a run of twenty-nine performances during the first season. Genest is very Machiavellian in his comment: "This was not Shakespeare's play . . . . but degraded to an Opera by Reynolds—not printed—Dryden said of D'Urfey—'let him alone, he will do something worse presently.'"

THE MERRY WIVES OF WINDSOR

The longest-lived of Bishop and Reynolds's re-workings of Shakespeare into the operatic mould was The Merry Wives of Windsor; no doubt owing to the popularity of Madame Vestris as Mistress Page. It lasted very long, and I myself heard at Daly's Theatre in New York in the last decade of the last century, the Bishop musical rendering of the first scene between Fenton and Anne Page. As it had not been previously announced, it came to me as a distinct surprise, not to say shock. At the time of the original production, the disagreement between Henry Harris and Charles Kemble having produced disorganisation at Covent Garden, and Elliston making reckless offers at Drury Lane to discontents of note, all and sundry, Reynolds and Bishop passed over to Drury Lane and offered The

Merry Wives there. Its expected advent was heralded by John Bull, on February 8, 1824, in these uncomplimentary words:

We hear, too, that "*The Merry Wives of Windsor*" MADE INTO AN OPERA is to be produced at Drury Lane, but for the honour of human nature, we do not believe it.

We suppose this scheme—if it be truth that such a thing is in agitation—has its origin in the inglorious success of "*The Comedy of Errors,*" and the "*Two Gentlemen of Verona*" at the other house. Neither "*The Comedy of Errors*" nor the "*Two Gentlemen of Verona*" are plays of the same intrinsic power of wit and humour as "*The Merry Wives of Windsor*"; and Elliston (who takes after Covent Garden too much) ought to remember, that, although he made an Opera of "*Macbeth*" at the Circus, the same trick will not do at Drury Lane. We wonder, moreover, that Mr. Bunn . . . . does not protest against this system of travestie—it is vile and degrading. . . Only conceive Braham playing Falstaff with songs, Miss Stephens perhaps enacting Lady Macbeth, Madam Vestris (of course in breeches) delighting us in Hotspur, or Mr. Horn performing Mercutio.—It is all too absurd.

But John Bull on February 29th was obliged to recant in this notice of the performance:

"*The Merry Wives of Windsor*" has been as we anticipated it would be, produced with songs, at Drury Lane Theatre, and, as it is quite impossible not to be pleased with the singing of Braham and Miss Stephens, and with the singing and acting of Madame Vestris, the play attracts very good houses.

 . . . . . Braham sings delightfully in *Fenton*—the effect of his air without accompaniment is magical, and no proof can be stronger of the success of the new experiment of harmonising Shakespeare, than the satisfaction expressed by a succession of audiences, at once brilliant and overflowing.

Madame Vestris played the piece for her benefit, at the Haymarket, on Tuesday, October 12, 1824, and the music, as announced by the playbill of that occasion, shows how some of the now popular songs were handed on from one "opera" to another. In Act I, Fenton sings, "With thee fair summer's joys appear"; in Act II Mrs. Page sings "When it is the time of night" from A Midsummer Night's

Dream, and Mrs. Ford, the ever-useful "Crabbed age and youth," soon to serve in a third operatic comedy. Fenton and Anne sing "Love like a shadow flies." The Merchant of Venice furnishes, I know not why, to The Wives, "All that glitters is not gold" (this in Act III); in Act IV A Midsummer Night's Dream supplies to the Pages, mother and daughter, "I know a bank," and to Anne and the chorus, a finale, "Trip, trip away." The inevitable "When daisies pied" was sung by the Merry Wives in Act V. Other songs were added on the 15th; in fact, almost any popular ditty could be made to "go" in one of these confections, in their later, more inartistic days.

AS YOU LIKE IT "OPERATISED"

An interval of scarcely four months was allowed to elapse before another "opera" was born of a Shakespearian comedy. On June 30, 1824, I find the bills of Covent Garden announcing As You Like It with additional songs, &c., the words—according to the now hackneyed statement—entirely from the Sonnets and Plays of Shakespeare. Previous to the play is promised the overture to Der Freischütz, by Weber. The songs scheduled on the programme are, in order, "As it fell upon a day," "O never say," "Full many a glorious morning," "When daisies pied," "Tell me where is Fancy bred?" "Where the Bee sucks," "Under the Greenwood tree," "Blow, blow thou wintry wind," "Should he upbraid," "And is there mirth in heaven." Many of these, it will be seen, are appropriate to the play; others are introduced from previous "operatisings" of Shakespeare's comedies. I believe this to have been a mere makeshift performance, and Genest does not record it. The very first bills of the autumn, however, announce that As You Like It, " with songs and other metricals from his works, composed new for this Play by Mr. H. R. Bishop," is in rehearsal. It was brought out on December 10, 1824, and repeated several times. The music of Bishop is accessible. There is, however, an undated musical collection, the title-page reading, The Whole of the Music in As You Like It, as Performed at the Theatre-Royal, Covent Garden. Composed by Henry R. Bishop. To which are added the Three Songs Composed for the above Play by Dr. Arne. The poetry selected entirely from the Plays, Poems and Sonnets of Shakespeare. This shows that Maria Tree played Rosalind, and Miss Hammersley, Celia. The first number is a duet sung in Act I by the two girls, and is based on "Whilst inconstant fortune smil'd," from the Poems. Rosalind later has a song from the Sonnets, "Ah! me, what eyes hath love put in my head?" Arne's "Blow, blow, thou wintry wind," and "Under the green-wood tree" both are sung in their proper places; but the Sonnets are liberally filched from to make now a song for Silvius ("O thou, obdurate, flinty, hard as steel") or Celia ("Oh! Time, thou shalt not boast that I do change"). And the Sonnets, and Poems yield two glees for chorus, "Lo in the Orient, when the gracious light," or "Even as the Sun with purple-coloured face," and to Rosalind give the opportunity of singing "Crabbed age and youth cannot live together." Finally Touchstone (Fawcett) sings from the Sonnets, "Fair was my love, but not so fair as fickle." There are other songs, including Arne's "When daisies pied." Reynolds in his Life (1827) mentions no As You Like It in his list of "operatisings." His list includes only A Midsummer Night's Dream, Comedy of Errors, Twelfth Night, Two Gentlemen of Verona, Tempest and Merry Wives of Windsor. He tried the same method with certain plays of Beaumont and Fletcher, The Chances, particularly.

Before passing to the next Shakespearian "opera," I call attention to a playbill of Covent Garden for June 2, 1825. On that night, for Farley's benefit, Cymbeline was acted for the first time "these three years." In Act II, we are informed, will be sung Dr. Cooke's favourite glee of "Hark! the Lark!" But, we are further informed, that "in the course of the Evening the following Songs, &c." will be performed—thirteen in all. My first depression afterwards lifted into a mild certainty that these numbers were not part of the play, but performed, according to a very old custom, between the acts, by friends of the beneficiary. In all the other "operas" of the year the songs are stated to be sung "in the course of the comedy"; here the wording is, "in the course of the evening." Besides, with one exception, the singers, so well known as Maria Tree, Pearman, Miss Paton, etc., were not in the cast of the play. The reader is, of course, entitled to his own opinion of this unique bill. The season brought forth no repetition of Cymbeline.

THE TAMING OF THE SHREW

On May 14, 1828, The Taming of the Shrew (not acted 80 years, according to the bill) was played at Drury Lane, and repeated a very few times thereafter. The playbill announces that the overture was by Rossini, the rest of the music composed and selected by Mr. Braham and Mr. T. Cooke. The songs are "Our love was new" (Sonnets), sung by Bianca; "If Music and sweet Poetry agree" (Sonnets), sung by Hortensio; "If Love hath lent you twenty thousand Tongues" (Venus and Adonis), sung by Katharine; "Oh, do but note a wild and wanton herd" (Merchant of Venice), sung by Hortensio; "On a day" (Love's Labour's Lost), sung by Katharine; "Gamut, I am the ground of all accord" (Taming of the Shrew), a duet for Katharine and Hortensio; "If Love make me forsworn" (Sonnets), by Lucentio; "Wilt thou have Music" (Induction to the play), by Katharine; "O happy Bride" (Midsummer Night's Dream and Cymbeline), sung by Bianca and Hortensio; "Though Time drives flocks" (Poems), sung by Hortensio; "True Love is an ever fixed mark" (Sonnets), a duet for Katharine and Hortensio; "Make me a willow cabin" (Twelfth Night), by the tireless Hortensio; "If Music be the food of love" (Twelfth Night), a quartet for Katharine, Bianca, Hortensio and Pedant; and a finale, "Oh, but express Content" (All's Well that Ends Well).

Surely this is a musical feast, not to say surfeit! I shall

content myself with quoting the Times of the following day:

> Shakspeare's comedy, *Taming of the Shrew*, was revived last night at this theatre. To the present generation, this excellent comedy, in its entire state, has only been known as a literary production; although some of its dramatic incidents have been presented in an abridged state, under the title of Catherine and Petruchio. This, indeed, is the first time for we believe 70 years, that its stage qualifications have met with a proper opportunity of being duly appreciated. In the present dearth of good dramatic compositions, it is matter of surprise that theatrical managers should not oftener have recourse to these productions of our greatest bard, which, like the *Taming of the Shrew*, have long been suffered to remain in obscurity, and whose unquestionable merits ensure the success of their reproduction; when, especially, as has often been the case of late years, his plays and comedies receive the interest of musical additions, their power of attraction cannot, we should conceive, fail to be effective. A selection of sonnets from other plays of Shakspeare has been, on this occasion, added to the original ones belonging to this comedy, and they have been set to music by Braham and Cooke. Miss Ayton performed the part of *Catherine*. . . . . Besides the spirit and dramatic interest which she infused into the part, the vocal share . . . . . received that justice at her hands which reflected high credit on her musical talents. . . . . Braham undertook the part of *Hortensio*. . . . His introduction . . was . . . necessary, in consequence of the great vocal additions which had been made to it. . . . Upon the whole, however, we might have expected a better specimen of his resources in composition, as well as those of Mr. Cooke. One duet, between Miss Ayton and Braham—*Gamut, I am the ground of all accord*, certainly possesses much musical merit, and is very impressive. There was a *Rossinian* style rather prevalent in some other pieces, but we do not know to which of the composers this is to be attributed. . . .
>
> The performance met with a most favourable reception, from a very numerous and highly respectable audience.

ALL'S WELL THAT ENDS WELL

A Midsummer Night's Dream, The Comedy of Errors, The Tempest, Twelfth Night, The Two Gentlemen of Verona, The Merry Wives of Windsor, As You Like It, The Taming of the Shrew: could conquest be extended further? What comedy suitable for such treatment remained in the catalogue? At first thought one might judge the list exhausted. I confess that it was with extreme surprise that I came upon a Covent Garden playbill of October 12, 1832, announcing, with alterations and musical introductions (in three acts)—All's Well that Ends Well! It was announced with the usual pomp of phrase, promising new scenery, by the Grieves, and with Songs, Glees, Choruses, etc., selected and arranged by Rophino Lacy, entirely—of course!—from the Plays, Poems, and Sonnets of Shakespeare. For good measure was thrown in a masque (arranged from the Midsummer Night's Dream) and called Oberon and Robin Goodfellow. The characters in the masque are, besides the name-characters, the four unfortunate lovers who had been maltreated so often by the malefactors of the stage—Leveridge, Lampe, Garrick, Colman, Reynolds, and the unknown author of The Fairy Queen.

There was a great deal of music in this particular offering, and a list of it will show how far afield in Shakespeare's writings adapters desirous of novelty were forced to travel. The lyrics had long been exhausted, and fragments of the dialogue of various plays were now turned to musical account.

In Act I Miss Inverarity, the sweet singer, draws from the "Poems" an air, "Oh! Absence what a torment wouldst thou prove," and from All's Well, itself, a recitative and air, "Now, Dian from thy altar Helen flies." Mr. Wilson, according to the programme, culls from Romeo and Juliet and Othello, "Love is a smoke raised with the fume of sighs." Miss Poole, like Puck, warbles, "Oh! sometimes lurk I in a gossip's bowl." Twice the chorus lifts its lusty voice in "Trip away, make no stay," and "Pleasure reigns." I hope the reader can place these in Shakespeare's works. In Act II the same Wilson chants "Oh! never since" from A Midsummer Night's Dream, and from The Two Gentlemen of Verona and the Sonnets (according to the same veracious bill), "Except I be by Dian in the Night." With Miss Shirreff he sings a duet (Poems), "If Love make me forsworn." With Miss Horton and Mr. Henry, again, the same busy Wilson unites in a serenade, "O happy fair" (Midsummer Night's Dream). Miss Inverarity, according to the custom she established in Act I, sings from All's Well itself, "I am St. Jaques' Pilgrim." The best thing in the act, probably, was a polocca by Miss Shirreff, "If she be made of red and white" (Love's Labour's Lost). The same brilliant singer begins Act III with an air from A Midsummer Night's Dream, "Love looks not with the eyes," and from the same play culls a duet with Miss Inverarity—"Lo, gentle friends, we must be gone in haste." These two ladies, again, and Mr. Ransford make up the trio, with chorus, "If Music be the food of love" (Twelfth Night), and this trio, with the addition of the necessary Wilson, becomes a closing quartette, in "Oh! but express content" (All's Well that Ends Well).

To assign these airs properly among the *dramatis personæ*, I would say that Miss Inverarity sang Helena, Miss Shirreff, Diana (a character evidently much enlarged), Ransford sang Astringer (whoever that may be), Wilson sang Bertram, and Meadows (the quaintly named Drinkwater Meadows) played the Interpreter. Irwin was Philostrate, appearing among the characters in All's Well, not in the Masque.

The account swings full circle with another attempt on the helpless and hapless Midsummer Night's Dream, produced by Bunn at Drury Lane on November 30, 1833, compressed into two acts and serving as an afterpiece with music. It was given only a few times, though the playbills asserted that, "meeting with great favour, it will be given four times a week until further notice." After a while, the bills announced that the music was by Arne, Cooke, Stephens, Handel, Bishop, Smith, &c. These names would indicate that the musical setting was really compiled from all the Midsummer Night's Dreams that had disgraced the stage from Garrick to Reynolds. The playbills print no list of numbers sung, and the reader, possibly to his great delight, is therefore spared an enumeration, which, were it within my scholarly power, I should gladly give him.

Reynolds was not, so far as I know, concerned with the four musical perversions of Shakespearian comedy last mentioned; my indictment of him closes with what precedes As You Like It, etc. This operatic handling of the plays strikes us as remarkably curious, and the persistence of it for upwards of twenty years can only be wondered at, especially in the case of such standard stock-pieces as Twelfth Night, As You Like It and The Merry Wives of Windsor. Playgoers finally tired of the form, and the movement ceased. Taste for real opera—Weber's, Auber's and Balfe's—superseded it. Above all, the great vogue of Fanny Kemble in the late '20's, and of Ellen Tree and Helen Faucit in the early and middle '30's—these three being among the most beautiful, gifted and popular exponents of the youthful heroines of some of the comedies involved—brought back the genuine plays and banished this bastard art to the limbo of forgotten things. While the movement was in progress, it constituted a unique phenomenon; when it passed, it went into a realm of contempt along with that other operatising impulse that raged at the end of the Seventeenth Century, and gave us Shadwell's Tempest and The Fairy Queen aforesaid. When Shakespeare again became food for opera-writers, he was merely turned into libretti for Bellini, Nicolai, Goetz, Verdi, Gounod, and I know not how many besides. But that's an entirely different story.

SHAKESPEARE AND ELLISTON

It is a pleasing task to arrive at the second discussion proposed in this chapter—that of the increasing tendency which led, ultimately, to the re-establishment of Shakespeare's genuine text on the stage. Out of the low pressure of spectacle, opera, ballet and farce that dominated the management of the theatres from 1817 to 1837, we now discern the feeble flicker of a purpose to sweep away the cobwebbery of Tate and his crowd and to give—when given at all—something like Shakespeare's own plays. The teach-

FANNY KEMBLE
From a contemporary print

CHARLES KEMBLE AS MARK
ANTONY, 1340

ings of Coleridge and Lamb and Hazlitt were bearing fruit; newspaper and magazine criticism was demanding something better than the accepted stage-versions. The movement was slow, and only very tentative in the period of twenty years that we are now considering; but at least something was done; and that, too, side by side with the activities of Frederick Reynolds just described.

The first of these attempts, I am glad to say, was made by Robert W. Elliston, then acting manager of Drury Lane. I am glad to give him credit, because he has been made a sort of scapegoat by writers on the drama, from his own day to ours. Elliston was a very handsome man, an elegant light comedian, an acceptable interpreter of Macduff and similar secondary tragic characters, a boon companion, a popular man, and—a failure. His last days are best left unrecorded. But during the seven years of his directorate at Drury Lane—1819–26—he several times made a serious effort really to advance the best drama. He is often spoken of as the man who turned Macbeth into a kind of operatic pantomime, and indeed he did so; but that was during his management of the Olympic, some years before he acquired Drury Lane, and he was forced to the expedient because no theatre but the two patent houses could present the standard plays, except with musical accompaniment. To offset this vandalism, historians should speak of his services now about to be mentioned.

KEAN AND CORIOLANUS, 1820

Edmund Kean was associated with Elliston during his incumbency of Drury Lane, and in him Elliston found a willing, probably an eager coadjutor. At any rate, when an innovation was attempted, the prestige of Kean's great name was depended on to carry it through. The first of these efforts to restore Shakespeare to the stage was effected on January 24, or 25, 1820. On that evening Kean made his first appearance as Coriolanus, and the bill bore the interesting announcement that "it is the manager's inten-

tion to restore the text of Shakspeare, with omissions only."
Genest growls out something about the inconsistency, in
that case, of "inserting in the playbill 6 names, which
Kemble had given to the inferiour characters, and of which
Shakspeare never dreamt," but other critics were more
fair, and, even if they did not like the offering, vouched for
its genuineness.

The uncertainty as to the exact date of the revival is
caused by the fact that it was announced for the 24th, but,
the Duke of Kent dying, the house was probably closed
till the following evening; at any rate, the Times advertisement for the 25th announces the play for the first time,
and the same paper, on the 26th, gives the following review,
which certainly settles the matter of the date. Genest,
probably misled by advertisements for the 24th, gives that
as the date of production. Just what Elliston and Kean
attempted, may be learned from the Times criticism; also
the basis of conservative adherence to old, accepted versions
may be gathered from the attitude of the critic toward the
experiment. It certainly was not encouraging.

The tragedy of *Coriolanus* brought forward . . . . last night presented two principal features of novelty; the one, the restoration of
the text of Shakespeare to the stage, as far as was consistent with
the limit of time now usually allotted to a dramatic performance;
and the other, the first appearance of Mr. Kean in the character of
the hero. We are, of course, most reluctant to say any thing against
an endeavour, in the abstract so laudable as that of substituting the
language of our great bard for the interpolations of modern emenda-
tors; but in the present state of our stage, and especially with the
magnitude of our theatres, it does not follow that such a restoration
would be at all times judicious; and the present, in our opinion, is
one of those instances in which, as far as the audience and the actors
are concerned, it might have been better to have pursued the old
course. . . We cannot now enter into a comparison of the two:
there are many reasons why into almost every play of Shakspeare
it has been thought fit to introduce alterations, but the principal is
the absolute necessity of studying stage effect, and this object was
most successfully accomplished in the tragedy of *Coriolanus,* as it
was played when Mr. Kemble and Mrs. Siddons supported its two
leading characters. . . . .

The *Volumnia* of Mrs. Glover deserves mention: it was more than respectable; and although, as the part was originally written, much less room is afforded for the display of tragic power, she let slip no occasion when she could fitly display her talents. . . . . The scenery was very splendid, and the dresses rich and appropriate. An *Ode to Triumph*, from the pen of Mr. G. Soane, was well received. At the close the audience insisted, as usual, upon the absurdity of the re-animation of Mr. Kean to announce the repetition of the tragedy to-morrow.

A detail invites comment. The point made by the critic that "as the part [of Volumnia] was originally written, much less room is afforded for the display of tragic power," is based on the device used by Tate and Thomson, and carried on by Kemble as his addition from Thomson, of having Volumnia, as a last expedient to persuading her son, draw a dagger and threaten to kill herself unless he yield. This sickening cheapening of the character gave an actress a good chance to strike a tragic attitude of approved Eighteenth Century design, and no doubt was the "display of tragic power" in the mind of the doubting Times critic. He preferred a dagger in the hand of an actress to the dominating purpose in her mind. Kean was not a very good representative of the great Coriolanus—his small body was against him—and he did not carry on the part in his regular repertoire.

KING LEAR SLIGHTLY RESTORED

Elliston, encouraged or undeterred (I know not which), on April 24th of the same year brought out Kean as King Lear (again his first appearance in another great part in London). The success was vastly greater—Kean's Lear was a magnificent masterpiece of histrionic art. Elliston published his version of King Lear, "chiefly from Nahum Tate's Edition, with some Restorations from the Original Text." The Advertisement to the edition is interesting, and what it has to say of the scenery and costumes, I shall quote later; as to the play itself, he remarks: "The public taste long ago decided against the sublime, but terrible catastrophe of the original. . . . This edition, however, does not entirely accord with that of Nahum Tate; yet much less liberty has been taken with him than he took with Shakspeare: the main fabric has not been touched; but some of his worthless weeds have been rooted up to make room for the strength and sweetness of the immortal bard." Poor Nahum! to have applied to himself the very language that his school had applied to Shakespeare! Thus time brings in its revenges.

As a matter of fact, Elliston restores but little. Kemble, though the contour of his scenes is of Tate rather than of Shakespeare, had followed Garrick's example in making the flesh of Shakespeare's language. Elliston's version is practically identical with Kemble's. He has, however, made two important changes—and in the two greatest scenes of the play as he produced it. Shakespeare's language is restored to the opening of Lear's scene of raving on the heath, and once again the words seem big enough for the situation; the "flat rotundity" of Tate is gone forever, as it turned out. A considerable bit of Shakespeare, moreover, is put back into the exquisite scene of recognition by Lear of Cordelia (Act V, Scene 1). These two restorations, slight in themselves, raise the tone immeasurably, and make both scenes infinitely grander than they had been for many years. Besides this, there is nothing to differentiate Elliston from Kemble; but in an uphill fight involving the public conscience, moral, artistic, or literary, every little counts. The Elliston version is about like that of Oxberry.

SHAKESPEARE'S RICHARD III ACTED, 1821

Tate and Cibber were, of course, the two apparently impregnable bulwarks of Shakespearian oppression. The Lear of one, and the Richard III of the other, had been for considerably over a century in full occupation of Shakespeare's glory. Elliston by his first effort slightly undermined the position of Tate; the management of Covent Garden attempted to blow up Cibber in one fell attack.

On March 12, 1821, they produced an entirely new version of Richard III, with wholesale omission of Cibber and large restorations of Shakespeare, including the characters of Queen Margaret and Clarence. They discovered what later restorers have found in connection with this same tragedy. Inveigh as we will against the work of Cibber, it acts better than Shakespeare's. It is a pity to lose the Nemesis-figure of Margaret, and the splendid declamation of Clarence's dream; something also should be made of the tragic figure of Hastings. Cibber has made Richard a melodramatic monomaniac of crime as opposed to the subtle complexity of Shakespeare's scheming and crafty tyrant. Cibber's original verse is not good, but he had the sense to "lift" from some of Shakespeare's other plays better verse than Shakespeare put in his own Richard III. All this is true; and, whatever the cause, and with due deference to out-and-out sticklers for Shakespeare's text, first, last and always, Cibber's play—as a play—is better than Shakespeare's. It is nervous, unified, compact, where the original is sprawling, diffuse and aimless. Something of all this must have been in the mind of the critic of the Times who, on March 13, 1821, expressed his disappointment at the result of the iconoclastic experiment at Covent Garden, the night before, of restoring—in large part, at least—Shakespeare's Richard III to the stage.

COVENT GARDEN THEATRE.—At a period when Shakespeare is regarded almost with idolatry, any attempt to rescue the original text of his plays, from the omissions and interpolations which successive ages have accumulated, must at least be viewed with favour; and with that feeling we witnessed last night the representation of his *Life and Death of Richard the Third* at this theatre, which was announced to be, with a few necessary deviations, the text of the author. How far this might have been deemed by the public an improvement on Cibber's alteration, which has so long maintained possession of the stage, we are unable to state, as the condition has not been complied with, by a strict adherence either to the words of Shakespeare, or the order of his scenes. The performance last night was merely another arrangement, and certainly inferior in dramatic effect, to that of Cibber. Nothing of the character of *Margaret* is preserved, from which so much has been expected, except her first scene. The funeral of *Henry VI.* and the courtship of *Lady Anne,* are transferred to the second act, after the death of *Clarence.* Still greater liberty is taken with the speeches: those of *Buckingham* are shortened, and *Richmond* reduced to perfect insignificance. The only scene of much value was that of the council and the condemnation of *Hastings.* Macready was not so cool and indifferent as he should have been in his previous conversation with the council; but the burst of anger on baring his arm was terrific. His *Richard* is a performance of great merit, and would be still more complete if he always retained his self-command. Egerton was more powerful than usual in the recitation of *Clarence's* dream, which was one of the most applauded passages of the evening. Abbott was *Richmond;* Mrs. Faucit, *Queen Elizabeth;* Mrs. Vining, *Lady Anne;* Mrs. Bunn, *Queen Margaret.* The underlings all fell into hands that would have disgraced a country theatre.

THE LAST ACT OF KING LEAR RESTORED, 1823

This was not encouraging. All these efforts, however, must have informed the public of the actual state of affairs in the theatre—especially as criticism had become so voluminous—and the day was not far off when Macready was to reform existing conditions altogether. The last attempt I shall record in this chapter was the restoration at Drury Lane, on February 10, 1823, of the final act of King Lear— the tragic ending, as written by Shakespeare. This revolutionary, not to say epoch-making, performance was carried out by Elliston and Kean, and is simply the most significant event in Shakespearian text-building in the theatre from the time of Dryden, Tate, Shadwell and the rest to the day in which it occurred. In face of the accumulated opinion of the Eighteenth Century that the death of Lear and Cordelia on the stage "would never do," Elliston and Kean proved that it would. Much of the fight for restoration of original texts had centred in King Lear; Macready finally won the day for it with the same tragedy. But in any history of the upward struggle this Elliston-Kean version must be highly considered.

The text is unquestionably that included in the Cumberland British Theatre already referred to; its early inclusion in this series proves, as I have said, the nervous zeal with which the editors of such collections kept their fingers on the pulse of theatrical affairs. One who examines that Cumberland text will find it, up to the end of the fourth act, like Kemble's, with slight differences. Several lines are omitted in the scene (Act III, Scene 2) between Edmund and Gloster, relative to the attempts to save Lear; in Act IV, Scene 1, for the first time, the suggestive lines of Tate about Edmund's waiting for Regan in the grotto disappear from the text. Finally, Cumberland omits the part about throwing Edward's (the name still preserved from Kemble) dead body on the dung-hill.

These changes (except the second) are slight. Of course the love-affair between Cordelia and Edgar is preserved. It is in the last act that the greatest changes occur, though all is not left as Shakespeare wrote it. Strangely enough, in the first scene, Cordelia's execrable rant about saving her father still mars the close, à la Tate. But Shakespeare's scene (V, 1) between Edmund and Regan, then with Albany and Goneril, with Edgar disguised, is introduced between the first and second scenes of Act V, as they always stood in the stage versions. This, curtailed though it is, largely changes the proportion and the motivation of the act. On the other hand, Cumberland's text gives the usual amplified scene between Edgar and Gloster by the tree, not Shakespeare's very brief one. Cumberland's fourth scene is Shakespeare's third, shorn toward the close of all about Goneril's suicide, of the entrance of Kent, etc. Instead of continuing this scene to the end of the play, Cumberland's version changes to a prison, with the entrance of Lear, bearing the dead body of Cordelia.

These changes were notable as restoring to the stage, nearly intact, what must always be considered one of the most stupendous acts in tragedy. But the first part was now found not to fit; the trifling love affair injected by Tate, and the continued absence of the tragic-choric Fool, left the work monstrously out of proportion. Nevertheless, a great stride forward had been made. In view of the significance of the event, I close with the following criticism from the John Bull of February 16, 1823, cautioning the reader to remember that the writer for this paper was quite obviously hostile to Kean:

The Drury Lane management has presented to the public a novelty which was at least unexpected, we mean the restoration of *part* of Shakespeare's King Lear, which, it should appear, by the way in which they announced it in the bills, they mistook to be a restoration of the *whole* tragedy—and so, in consequence of the assertion published, we imagined it to be.

We were a good deal disappointed on visiting the theatre to find that no steps had been taken to knock away Tate's *plastering* and restore the original beautiful structure farther than concerns the *last act*, and that all the mawkish love-scenes of the bungler were still suffered to encumber the splendid work of the bard.

.   .   .   .

Nothing can be more judicious (wherever it can be done) than restoring the original of our immortal author, and we are quite sure that every man of taste will render thanks to Mr. Kean for having taken the step of bringing back the last act of King Lear nearly to its ancient purity; but with all this feeling of our own we cannot conceal the fact, that, as a public performance, it was a decided failure.

Kean's figure and general appearance is likely to excite many feelings, but certainly not that of pity . . . . . . at times the audience were almost in a titter, and more especially where he repeated, four or five times over, the word "Never—never—never—never," which exceeded, in comicality, even his own pronunciation of the word "Fool—fool—fool—fool," in Othello, and very nearly produced that most disagreeable sound to a tragedian's ear—*a horse-laugh*.

In the twenty leaderless years under review, brushing aside the frivolity of the "operatised" comedies, and the paucity of great and commanding actors, we see clearly the importance of the movement for restoration of original texts that I have just outlined.

CHAPTER XXIII

SCENERY AND COSTUMES

GAS INTRODUCED IN THE THEATRES

PERHAPS the most important single event to be noted in this chapter is the introduction of gas into both royal theatres at the very beginning of the period we are discussing. This new method of illumination probably had as much to do with revolutionising previous scenic effects as did the introduction of electric light more than a half-century later. The more light, the greater the opportunity of the scene-painter and the stage-manager. So important is the innovation in question that I may be pardoned for quoting largely. The Covent Garden bills at the opening of the season 1815–16 bear the statement that the "Exterior with the Grand Hall and Staircase will be lighted with Gas," but by the very opening date of our new period, both houses made a thorough installation of the novel medium. The Covent Garden bills at the beginning of the season of 1817–18 bear an advertisement that now seems merely quaint, but was then of vast importance.

The Proprietors respectfully inform the Publick that a new Method of

LIGHTING;

and likewise a New Principle of VENTILATING the Theatre, has been adopted. The FIRST has been effected by a MAGNIFICENT CHANDELIER, which from the Centre of the Ceiling diffuses a soft and brilliant Light around, without obstructing the View of a single Spectator. In its effect, the Body of Light is equal to 300 ARGAND LAMPS; and the Heat is directly carried off through a Tube communicating with the open Air. The SECOND is upon the Principle of a forced VENTILATION, by which the Theatre can be either Cooled or Warmed, and the Atmosphere of the different Parts of the House can be kept to one pleasant Temperature throughout the different Seasons of the Year.

157

Some objection was raised to the minor "lustres," as interfering with the view of the stage; this defect was remedied, and the playbills, within a few days, call attention to the improvement, and the generally satisfactory nature of the new methods of lighting and heating. Evidently the management prided itself on its accomplishment.

Several Additions have been made to the new *universally approved* method of LIGHTING the Theatre. The GRAND CENTRICAL CHANDELIER has been rendered still more brilliantly effective and the three Auxiliary Lustres which were complained of as impeding the Sight and destroying the Contour of the Theatre, have been removed, and GRECIAN LAMPS have been substituted, which range round the back of the Dress Circle and shed a soft medium Light, without obstructing the view of the stage. The forced VENTILATION has likewise been completed—and the CALORIFERE FUMIVORE STOVES keep the House to any degree of warmth in the most severe weather.

Drury Lane, at the same time, fell into the new system of lighting. We learn from the Examiner of September 7, 1817, that gas was installed in time for the opening of the season. The reporter greatly admires the result, "not only in front of the stage but at the various compartments on each side. Their effect, as they appear suddenly from the gloom, is like the striking of daylight. . . . It is as mild as it is splendid—white, regular, and pervading."

The lights are enclosed in glasses, and blinded from the audience by side-scenes and reflectors; but the result in every other respect is excellent, and a very great improvement; and if it is managed as well as we saw it on Friday, will enable the spectator to see every part of the stage with equal clearness. If the front-light could be thrown, as day-light is, from above instead of below (and we should like to hear the reasons why it cannot) the effect would be perfect.

Covent Garden, according to the same reporter, "has wonderful chandeliers of gas—it makes a light very bright throughout the house—only one big chandelier from the ceiling and small ones around the first row of boxes."

AN ERA OF SPECIAL PRODUCTIONS

The period we are about to consider is signalised by the carrying on of Kemble's policy of special productions for important revivals or new-workings of Shakespeare's plays; the most influential feature is the regard for greater historical accuracy in costume, starting with Charles Kemble's revival of King John, in November, 1823. This last seems to have been an epoch-making event. Aside from this, a study of contemporary playbills and criticisms will show the systematic effort to do the best for Shakespeare—to give him something like a fair show, in both senses of the expression. The policy inaugurated by John Kemble was continued by his brother at Covent Garden, and by Elliston and Bunn, successively, at Drury Lane. Names of scene-painters, mechanicians, costumers, etc., figure on the bills equally with names of actors. Altogether, lovers of suitable setting, not to say spectacle, in Shakespearian representation, had cause to rejoice; more austere critics began to deplore the attention to the material side of the performance.

THE PRODUCTION OF REYNOLDS'S "OPERAS"

To dismiss, first, the operatic Shakespeare of Frederick Reynolds, we find from the days of A Midsummer Night's Dream, in 1816, a perfect fulness of programme statement regarding the manufacturers of the performance. At Covent Garden, the scene-painters are, without important variation, through The Comedy of Errors, Twelfth Night, The Tempest, The Two Gentlemen of Verona, etc., Messrs. Pugh, Grieve, Hodgins, W. Grieve; the machinists are Saul (sometimes alone), sometimes in connection with Bradwell; the dresses by Mr. Palmer and Miss Egan. The most important of all these people are the Grieves, father, and two sons, W. and T. Grieve. They continue, these three alone, until 1832, to furnish the pictures for Shakespeare "operatised." In that year they are mentioned as the scene-painters for All's Well that Ends Well, at Covent

Garden, Bradwell still serving as provider of "decorations." Sloman now attends to the machinery, and the dresses are supplied by a pair of artists with an extraordinary combination of names—Mr. Head and Mrs. Balding.

One could wish that as much pains had been taken to outline the progress of the scenes as was taken in printing the order of the songs. Only once, to my knowledge, was this done, and then, curiously enough, the songs are not specified. I refer to the bill for The Tempest, which, on May 15, 1821, and on later renditions, provides this very interesting scene-schedule, presented, as it announces, in the following order:

Act. I. Prospero's Cave. Grieve	Interior of the Island . Grieve
The Interior of the Island. Do.	Wood . . . . Pugh
Act II. Storm and Shipwreck Do.	Volcanic Mountain and Lake
Rocky Part of the Island Do.	Grieve
Hippolyto's Cave. . . . Do	Act IV. Cave near the Shore Do.
Seashore. . . . . . Pugh	A Wood . . . . . . Pugh
Lake and Mountains by Moon-	Act V. Rocky Part of the Island
light Grieve	Grieve
Act III. Prospero's Cave, as be-	A Cave which changes . Pugh
fore Do.	to the Last Scene . . . Grieve

Twelfth Night, we learned, presented the "grand masque" of Juno and Ceres. The playbills of The Two Gentlemen of Verona (1821) stress a "Carnival in the Great Square of Milan," with a grand "Emblematical Procession of the Seasons and the Elements." In the element of Water, "Cleopatra's Galley is seen sailing down the river Cydnus," —why, no one but a deviser of spectacle could say. At Drury Lane, in 1828, there was also an attempt to beautify The Taming of the Shrew. My playbill for the second performance (May 17th) informs us that scenery is by people so notable as Stanfield, Andrews and Marinari; and it specifies some pretty sets, though what some of them had to do with Shakespeare's play I leave the reader to puzzle out for himself. In order they are set down: "Square in City of Padua, Hortensio's Villa and Gardens, Distant View of Padua by Moonlight, Petruchio's House and Italian Landscape, Part of Venice and the Adriatic,

Grand Salon and Banquet." There is a pretty eye-feast
to set before King Public.

Contemporary criticism is equally reticent. The authors
of the introductions to two of Oxberry's versions of Shakespeare are as helpful as any one I know. Of The Two
Gentlemen of Verona, the writer says (in 1823). . . "Repeated failures would probably have banished it from the
stage forever, had not the popularity attendant upon the
plan of interspersing 'The Comedy of Errors' and 'Twelfth
Night' with music, encouraged the managers to make a
similar experiment upon 'The Two Gentlemen of Verona.'
With this aid, and that of gorgeous shows and scenery, it
has lately met with some portion of favour; but, 'tis morally
certain, that were these adventitious attractions withdrawn,
it would at once relapse into its former obscurity." In
1823 Oxberry's introducer exclaims, "how satisfactorily are
our ideas of *Prospero, Caliban,* and *Ariel* embodied by a
solemn stalking gentleman in a long gown and gray beard,
a hairy man-o'-the-woods, and a robust young lady with a
pair of painted gauze wings stuck to her shoulders; and how
much the beauty as well as propriety of *Ariel's* parting
strain is increased, by its being transformed into a glee, performed by half a dozen fat chorus-singers, let down from
the ceiling in a clumsy creaking piece of machinery! The
whole affair is a futile attempt to embody beings who can
have no existence but in the imagination."

These sources failing, we can turn to the printed copy of
The Comedy of Errors (the only alteration, except A Midsummer Night's Dream, printed by Reynolds), and discover
at least a few hints. For no reason in the world, other than
operatic, the last scene of Act III is "A River surrounded
by Mountains, whose tops are covered with snow.—Across
the River is a rustic Bridge—Horns heard without—and
Balthazar, Cerimon, and others are seen crossing the Bridge
dressed as Hunters. They pause to sing 'When icicles
hang by the wall.'" Act IV ends in "An apartment in Balthazar's house—in the back is a large dining table, on which
is fruit, wine, silver goblets, &c." Both these scenes no
doubt were pleasing as spectacle; but since they have noth-

ing to do with Shakespeare and are unadulterated Reynolds, I am afraid they have but little place in an essay on the staging of Shakespeare.

Finally, I wonder if the small book of coloured costume-plates for As You Like It, published by Planché in 1825 (see page 174), represents the dresses of the operatic treatment of the pastoral comedy brought out at Covent Garden on December 10, 1824. It is possible that it does; and if it does, it brings before us something of the splendours of that by-gone day.

PLAYBILLS AT DRURY LANE THEATRE

To come to the more regular Shakespeare of Kean and the tragedians, we find our earliest documents in the playbills of Drury Lane, which begin to be more and more explicit in synopses of scenery. Elliston in the seven years of his management at Drury Lane (1819–26) made repeated efforts to mount Shakespeare beautifully. In his first season, the playbill of November 22, 1819, states that Richard III will be produced "with new scenery and splendid decorations." On January 28th, Kean was happily gratifying his ambition by appearing as Coriolanus (freed, it will be remembered, from the admixture of Thomson), and I cannot refrain from reprinting entire that part of the bill which applies to our present subject. In none of these reproductions shall I save from oblivion the names of the players who made up the cast; that part of the revival does not come within the scope of my present enterprise.

THEATRE ROYAL, DRURY–LANE

This Evening, Friday, January 28, 1820
His Majesty's Servants will perform (for the 3d time at this Theatre)
Shakspeare's
CORIOLANUS
With new Scenes, Dresses, and Decorations.

———

In Act II, An Ovation
in which will be introduced
An Ode of Triumph
Written by Mr. G. Soane, and Composed by Mr. T. Cooke

In the Course of the Tragedy, the following New Scenery:

A View in Rome, Marinari	The Capitol of Rome, Hollagan
View near the Camp of Cominius, Andrews	Another View of Rome, Marinari
The Camp of Cominius, Ditto	The Walls of Rome, Dixon

The increasingly prevalent practice of announcing the scenes and scene-painters is of great help in gathering from the past something of the secrets it has so carefully hoarded.

KING LEAR, 1820

One more bill I must produce, that of King Lear, on the third night of Kean's acting it.

THEATRE ROYAL, DRURY-LANE

This Evening, Wednesday, April 26, 1820,
His Majesty's Servants will perform (third time at this Theatre) the Tragedy of

KING LEAR

With new Scenery, Dresses, and Decorations
The Scenery by Messrs. Marinari, Andrews, Hollagan, and W. Dixon
The Dresses by Mr. Banks, and the Misses Smiths.

On April 27th, and for a short time thereafter, the bills, to the delight of future historians, contained the following illuminating schedule of scenic wonders. This and the preceding bill will show that Elliston had gathered around him an imposing group of scene-painters.

In Act III   A Land Storm

After the manner of *Loutherbourg's Eidophusicon*. Designed and executed by Marinari and Assistants; and in the course of the Tragedy, the following Scenery will be exhibited:

Antichamber in King Lear's Palace . . . . Dixon	View near Dover . . Andrews
Room of State in Palace Marinari	Chamber in King Lear's Palace Hollagan
Court before Albany's Palace Andrews	Valley near the Field of Battle Marinari
Gates of Gloster Castle . Ditto	Albany's Tent . . . . Hollagan
Forest . . . . Marinari	A Prison . . . . . . Andrews
Gallery in Gloster Castle Dixon	

Of this setting of his revival, Elliston has something interesting to say in the Advertisement to his King Lear, discussed in the preceding chapter:

In regard to the costume of the piece, it is much more easy to find fault with that which has been done, than to point out what ought to be done. . . To talk of correctness or incorrectness would be something more than absurd; all that is left is to choose the costume of any period, not too recent, and adhere to it with fidelity, or if any additions are made, to let them be the products of fancy, and not the fashion of another time.

If this reasoning be true in regard to the dresses, it must be equally so when applied to the scenic decorations. The dwellings of such a period could only have been of the rudest construction; poor Tom's hovel as it is now represented, must be on a par with the real Lear's palace . . . and how would such a style accord with the Dukes and Earls of Shakspeare?

In respect to the gold, pearls, and other ornaments adopted in this play, it may be right to observe, that the costume is borrowed from an early Saxon period, in which such decorations were profusely used. . . Most of such decorations, even to the fibula, are fac-similes of engravings from the best authorities.

If this account means anything, it means that the architecture and costumes of the play had been "conventionalised" to a period of antiquity considerably this side of the supposed time of King Lear, whose own surroundings were too rude to reproduce; but that a regard for consistency of decoration had guided the plan throughout. The setting was antique, but not oppressively or disagreeably so. In other words, it was artistic, where it couldn't afford to be too historical. Nevertheless, in whatever it did, it was conscious and aware; imagine such a thing in the day of Garrick!

The storm scene, it will be observed, was greatly stressed on the bill; it is interesting to find Loutherbourg's Eidophusikon figuring so late in the world's history. Raymond, in his life of Elliston, gives Kean considerable credit or discredit for the mechanical effects produced:

Measures were taken in the season for the revival of "King Lear" at Drury Lane. Kean had a passionate desire for playing the part, and in the scenic preparations was personally busy. Amongst other effects he had a surpassing notion for the storm. Kean had seen a mechanical exhibition in Spring Gardens (the remains of Louther-bourg's "Eidophusicon"), in which very striking porcellous effects had been produced, and which he fancied very available to his pur-pose. The proprietor was introduced at Drury Lane with this object, but he at once saw the impracticability of the scheme on such an immense area as the stage of Drury Lane. The storm, though given up on these grounds, was presently transferred to the bosom of the tragedian. To the magnitude and ruinous expense of the under-taking, Kean was positively deaf—there was either to be a storm on the stage, or no peace in the theatre. To meet his wishes, a great part of the scheme was carried into operation, and admirably executed by the artists of Drury Lane. The scenic trees were composed of distinct boughs which undulated in the wind, each leaf was a separate pendant rustling with the expressive sound of nature itself. The artists were greatly extolled.

The very success of this scene was fatal to the fame of Kean, in undertaking the part of *Lear*. The storm carried away the greater part of the applause on the few nights "Lear" was represented; and public criticism pronounced that, amidst all the leaves in the forest, not a wreath was to be found to crown the brows of the actor. *Lear* was one of Kean's failures.

Contemporary accounts tell us that by means of vari-coloured screens rotating rapidly before powerful lights, a queer combination of colours was thrown on the stage and on Kean's face, much to the detriment of the effect. All this was considerably modified after the first night. The Times of April 25, 1820, very sensibly comments on this phase of the production:

The scene of the storm was less effective than many others, because the manager, by a strange error, had caused the tempest to be exhib-ited with so much accuracy that the performer could scarcely be heard amid the confusion. He should have recollected that it is the bending of Lear's mind under his wrongs that is the object of interest, and not that of a forest beneath the hurricane. The machinery may be transferred to the next new pantomime.

If we were to behold exactly this spectacle to-day, I imagine that we should be torn with conflicting emotions. To our present experience of the wonders of staging for the century that has supervened, much of this trickery would seem inexpressibly childish and absurd; on the other hand, our feeling of immense superiority to past ages might be rudely disturbed on discovering how well—granting their limited means, in machinery and lighting—the stage-workers of 1820 really brought about the effects at which they were aiming. The advance since Garrick's day was truly amazing. Perhaps Loutherbourg is the one man mainly responsible for the improvement.

HENRY IV, PART II, 1821

To commemorate the accession of George IV, Covent Garden, in the spring of 1821, produced the second part of Henry IV, doubtless because of the opportunities afforded by the Coronation of Henry V at the end of the play. The stage, as we have seen, had, under Cibber and Garrick and Rich, successively, celebrated with Coronations the accession of George II and George III; why not now, also, that of George IV? Processions had always been the strong point of Covent Garden spectacle, and this one eclipsed all former glories. It must have been a magnificent affair. I cannot spare the reader the inclusion, in my account, of the very interesting details printed on the playbill of June 25, 1821:

Scene I. The Platform leading to the Abbey (T. Grieve)
Scene II. Westminster Abbey (Pugh)

The Galleries, Aisles, and different parts of the Abbey, filled by the various Spectators; Princes, Peers, Peeresses, Judges, Bishops, Knights, Heralds, Pursuivants, Choristers, and others who assist at the Coronation.

The Sovereign receiving the Golden Spurs, the Ring, and the Glove— the Orb and Sceptre, on the Ancient Chair of St. Edward; and the Crown being placed on his Head by the Archbishop.

The Coronation Anthem
will be sung by all the Principal Performers of the Theatre, assisted by a Numerous Choir.

Scene III. The Cloisters of the Abbey (Capon)
The Return from the Abbey to Westminster Hall.

Scene IV.   The Grand Banquet (T. Grieve).
prepared in Westminster Hall, which is decorated with the different
arms of England.

The Royal Throne,

and Table, with others for the different Nobility and Dignitaries.
. . .   Then, by sound of the Trumpets, the Entree of the Challenger
is announced, &c.

The book of the play printed at the same time gives the
order of the procession and all the "big" effects thereafter.
The reader must pardon my insistence on the right to publish the procession for his information and edification. My
only excuse is the undoubted fact that this show made a
great stir in its day, and certainly one who has journeyed
with me thus far will wish to see exactly how they managed
these things in 1821:

The Grand Coronation

Scene I

The Platform leading to the Abbey
King's Herbwoman
Six strewers of Flowers
Dean's Beadle of Westminster
High Constable of Westminster
Drums
Drum Major
Trumpets
Sergeant Trumpeter
King's Chaplains
Sheriffs of London
Aldermen of London
Masters in Chancery
King's Sergeant
King's Attorney General
King's Solicitor General
Judges
Lord Chief Justice
Choir
Groom of Victory—Organ Blower
Gentlemen of the Chapel Royal
Dean of Westminster
Prebendaries of Westminster

Herald
Barons
Baronesses
Herald
Marchionesses
Earls
Herald
Duchesses
Dukes
Norroy King at Arms
Lord Steward of His Majesty's Household
Lord Keeper of the Great Seal
Bishops
The Lord High Chancellor
The Sceptre of the Cross ⎫
The Golden Spurs ⎬
St. Edwards Staff ⎭
The Second Sword ⎫
Curtana ⎬
The Third Sword ⎭
Gentleman Usher of the Black Rod ⎫
Herald ⎬
Lord Mayor of London ⎭
Mace Bearers
Lord Great Chamberlain
Prince Humphrey
Prince John of Lancaster
Prince Thomas
Lord High Constable ⎫
The Sword of State ⎬
The Earl Marshal's Staff ⎭
The Orb ⎫
The Crown ⎬
The Chalice ⎪
The Sceptre ⎬
The Bible ⎪
The Patina ⎭

THE ROYAL CANOPY
Bishop—King—Bishop
Train Bearers
Mace Bearers   Halberdiers

___

For the *entrée* of the Challenger in Scene IV, the play-
book adds some extra details. We learn that he is "pre-

ceded by the Sergeant Trumpeter, Mace Bearer, with the Earl Marshal and Lord High Constable (on Horseback), and is himself on his War Horse, completely armed. The Herald proclaims the Challenge. The Sovereign drinks to the Champion out of a Golden Cup and Cover, which is given to the Challenger, who retires with them, always keeping his Face towards the Throne."

John Bull (July 1, 1821) reviews the performance, and at the end calls in the all-wise school-boy that I had always assumed to be the Mrs. 'Arris of Macaulay alone:

> At Covent Garden, the care and attention of the Managers has been devoted to the appropriate illustration of the Second Part of Henry IV, with the ceremony of the Coronation. A more splendid pageant never graced a Theatre; it reflects the highest credit on the proprietors for their liberality, and on those to whose particular care the arrangement of the processions has been confided.
>
> We must make one exception, which we do without any wish to be hypercritical. The introduction of the yeomen of the guard in the service of Henry IV, when it is remembered that the corps was not established till the reign of Henry VII will startle not only the venerable antiquary, but the little school-boy, who will think it a pity that some of his playfellows had not been consulted, during their holidays, upon this point. A more glaring anachronism never slipped upon the stage.

CHARLES KEMBLE'S KING JOHN, 1823

The really important event, however, in the whole period we are discussing was Charles Kemble's revival of King John, during the season of 1823–24 at Covent Garden. J. R. Planché in his Memoirs takes to himself full credit for the innovations effected. For the first time, one of Shakespeare's historical plays was staged with the utmost possible accuracy of costume, every detail being worked out with patient and loving care. I will quote at great length from Planché, who bestows upon himself an amount of praise almost beyond that of any self-recipient that I know:

> In 1823 a casual conversation with Mr. Kemble respecting the play of "King John" . . . led to a step, the consequences of which have

been of immense importance to the English stage. . . . I complained
to Mr. Kemble that a thousand pounds were frequently lavished on
a Christmas pantomime or an Easter spectacle, while the plays of
Shakespeare were put upon the stage with make-shift scenery, and,
at the best, a new dress or two for the principal characters. That
although his brother John, whose classical mind revolted from the
barbarisms which even a Garrick had tolerated, had abolished the
bag-wig of Brutus and the gold-laced suit of Macbeth, the alterations
made in the costumes of the plays founded upon English history in
particular, while they rendered them more picturesque, added but
little to their propriety; the whole series, King Lear included, being
dressed in habits of the Elizabethan era, the third reign after its termination with Henry VIII., and, strictly speaking, very inaccurately
representing the costume even of that period. . . . . . It was not
requisite to be an antiquary to see the absurdity of the soldiers before
Angiers, at the beginning of the thirteenth century, being clothed
precisely the same as those fighting at Bosworth at the end of the
fifteenth. If one style of dress was right, the other must be wrong.
Mr. Kemble admitted the fact, and perceived the pecuniary advantage that might result from the experiment. It was decided that I
should make the necessary researches, design the dresses, and super-
intend the production of "King John," *gratuitously*, I beg leave to
say. . . . . Fortunately I obtained . . . . an introduction to Doctor, afterwards Sir Samuel Meyrick, who had just published his elaborate and valuable work, "A Critical Enquiry into Ancient Arms and
Armour," and was forming that magnificent and instructive collection
now exhibiting at South Kensington. . . . He entered most warmly
and kindly into my views, pointed out to me the best authorities,
and gave me a letter of introduction to Mr. Francis Douce, the
eminent antiquary. . . .

This gentleman had assisted Mr. John Kemble when he introduced
several alterations in the costume of Shakespeare's plays, particularly
those founded on Roman history; for which latter, however, he drew
his materials from the columns and arches of the emperors, and not
from contemporaneous republican authorities. When urged to do
so, and to "reform it altogether," he exclaimed to Mr. Douce, in a
tone almost of horror, "Why, if I did, sir, they would call me an antiquary!" . . . Mr. Douce . . . most liberally placed the whole of his
invaluable collection of illuminated MSS. (now in the Bodleian
Library, to which he bequeathed them) at my disposal. He paid me
also the great compliment of lending me his fine copy of Strutt's
"Dress and Habits of the People of England," coloured expressly for
him by its author. . . . . Mr. Fawcett, the stage-manager, considered his dignity offended by the production of the play being placed
under my direction. . . . Mr. Farley—dear old Charles Farley—
also took huff. He was the recognized purveyor and director of

spectacle, and dreaded "the dimming of his shining star" . . . . .
Never shall I forget the dismay of some of the performers when they
looked upon the flat-topped *chapeaux de fer* (*fer blanc*, I confess) of
the 12th Century, which they irreverently called *stewpans!* Nothing
but the fact that the classic features of a Kemble were to be surmounted by a precisely similar abomination would, I think, have
induced one of the rebellious barons to have appeared in it. They
had no faith in me, and sulkily assumed their new and strange habiliments, in the full belief that they would be roared at by the audience.
They *were* roared at; but in a much more agreeable way than they
had contemplated. When the curtain rose, and discovered King
John dressed as his effigy appears in Worcester Cathedral, surrounded
by his barons sheathed in mail, with cylindrical helmets and correct
armorial shields, and his courtiers in the long tunics and mantles of
the thirteenth century, there was a roar of approbation, accompanied
by four distinct rounds of applause, so general and so hearty, that
the actors were astonished, and I felt amply rewarded for all the
trouble, anxiety, and annoyance I had experienced during my labours.
Receipts of from 400*l.* to 600*l.* nightly soon reimbursed the management for the expense of the production, and a complete reformation
of dramatic costume became from that moment inevitable upon the
English stage.

This gives the entire story, but the wealth of the details
thereof can be gathered only from the playbill. Let me
again reproduce the essential matter from that of January 19, 1824—some weeks after the first performance—
calling to the reader the mass of scholarship, real or imaginary, displayed therein:

COVENT GARDEN

This present Monday, January 19, 1824,
Will be revived Shakspeare's Tragedy of

KING JOHN

With an attention to Costume
Never equalled on the English Stage. Every Character will appear
in the precise

HABIT OF THE PERIOD

The whole of the Dresses and Decorations being executed from
indisputable Authorities, such as
Monumental Effigies, Seals, Illumined MSS., &c.
The Banners, Shields, and other properties by Mess. Bradwell
& Son, &c.

AUTHORITIES FOR THE COSTUME

King John's Effigy in Worcester Cathedral, and his Great Seals. Queen Elinor's Effigy in the Abbey of Fonteveraud. Effigy of the Earl of Salisbury in Salisbury Cathedral, Effigy of the Earl of Pembroke, in the Temple Church, London, King John's Silver Cup, in the Possession of the Corporation of King's Lynn, Norfolk. Illuminated MSS in the British Museum, Bodleian, and Bennet College Libraries, and the works of Camden, Montfaucon, Sandford, Strutt, Gough, Stothard, Meyrick, &c.

N. B.   The Costumes are published, and may be had of Mr. Miller, 5, Bridge-street, Blackfriars, and all other Booksellers.

John Bull, on November 30, 1823, was politely sympathetic:

The revival of *"King John,"* at Covent Garden, whether we consider the splendour with which it has been got [*sic*], the magnificence and propriety of the costumes, or the excellence of the acting, deserves the highest praise. . .   We were extremely glad to find that the favourite system of dressing up girls in men's clothes was, upon this occasion, broken in upon. . .   We cannot particularly compliment the boy who performed the part of the Prince. . .   Upon the whole, the play affords a great treat to the lovers of its illustrious author, and the drama in general . . . and . . . reflects the greatest credit upon the taste and liberality of the management.

Bell's Weekly Messenger, under the same date, is more enthusiastic:

COVENT-GARDEN.—The decided success of Shakespeare's Tragedy of *King John*, on its first representation on Monday evening, aided by the new and appropriate costume, which has seldom been equalled for splendour and effect, will, we trust, stimulate the managers to undertake the revival of other plays of the great Dramatist, with similarly correct dresses, armour, &c.   John Kemble abolished the *full-bottomed wig*, the *long waistcoats*, and *square-toed shoes* in *Richard, Hamlet, Macbeth*, and *Othello*.   It remains for Charles Kemble to complete the destruction of these *anomalies*, by the revival of all Shakespeare's *acting* Historical Dramas with the aid of costume appropriate to the period of the supposed action of the play.   Charles Kemble never more distinguished himself than by his powerful personation of the bastard *Falconbridge*.   His first and second dresses were particularly graceful and picturesque.   We never saw this distinguished actor to greater advantage.

This performance was repeated many times in the course of the year. For a while, at the foot of the bills was printed a notice to the effect that in consequence of the marked applause bestowed on the revival, "The Proprietors of this Theatre, anxious to fulfil their promise respecting Shakspeare's plays, will shortly revive the first part of King Henry IV, with the same attention to the civil, military, and legal habits of the period."

HENRY IV, PART I, 1824

This revival came on May 3rd, and again I must reproduce the essential features of the bill. This time there is an attempt to give some idea of what the scenes were—I can find no evidence that Kemble had new scenery for the famous King John revival, the bill merely stressing the costume—but with Henry IV it was different, as the reader will observe from the bill of the 6th:

THEATRE ROYAL, COVENT GARDEN

This present Thursday, May 6, 1824,
Will be acted the First Part of Shakspeare's Historical Play of

KING HENRY THE FOURTH

With the same Attention to Costume
which has been observed in the Revival of KING JOHN at this Theatre. Every character will appear in the precise HABIT of the Period; the whole of the Dresses being executed from indisputable authorities, viz. Monumental Effigies, Painted Glass, &c.

AUTHORITIES FOR THE COSTUME

Effigy of King Henry IV in Canterbury Cathedral; Portraits of Henry, Prince of Wales, the Earls of Northumberland, Westmoreland, &c. in various Illuminated MSS. in the Royal, Harleian, and other Collections.
Effigy of the Earl of Westmoreland, in Staindrop Church, Durham Sepulchral Brasses, and Monumental Effigies of various Knights of the Period in Blickling Church, Norfolk, Avel Church, Worcestershire, &c.
Painting on Glass, in St. Mary's Hall, Coventry.
Illuminated MSS. in the Public Libraries, and those of Dr. Meyrick and F. Douce, Esq.

The Sumptuary Laws passed during the Reign of Henry IV, and the works of Occleve, Camden, Dugdale, Stow, Sandford, Vincent, Strutt, Stothard, Meyrick, &c.

The Scenery

Mostly new, designed and executed by Mr. Grieve, Mr. Pugh, Messrs. T. and W. Grieve—*particularly*

The King's Chamber, in the old Palace of Westminster
The Inn Yard at Rochester, with the Castle—*Night*
Hotspur's Camp—near Shrewsbury
Road and Distant View of Coventry
Shrewsbury from the Field of Battle
The King's Tent, &c., &c.

This revival did not meet with the success of the former one, a result largely attributable to the fact that Charles Kemble played Falstaff. In his youth this versatile actor was the ideal Romeo; in his maturity he was famed as Mercutio, Benedick and Faulconbridge. How could he expect to play Falstaff—to adipose (if I may be allowed the expression) his charming personality to the physical and mental characteristics of the fat Knight? Young played Hotspur, but nothing could save the performance. Not even the papers awarded such astonished praise to the *mise en scène* as they had lavished a few months previously on King John. So soon does one become habituated to splendour, real or imaginary!

The Times of May 4, 1824, says of the revival, "the 'getting up' throughout is of the most costly and tasteful description. The Rochester scene, and the camp near Shrewsbury, are both admirably painted; and nothing can exceed the splendour of the armour and the dresses worn even by the minor characters. Two score of gentlemen, whose names one never hears, are clad in suits which 'top tragedians' would not take shame to wear."

Planché published the plates of costumes for this revival, also, in colour, and as "designed and executed on stone by G. Scharf." The next year (1825), appeared his designs (likewise coloured) for both As You Like It and Hamlet, "selected and arranged from the best Authorities"—as had been the models for King John and Henry IV—"expressly

for the Proprietors of the Theatre Royal, Covent Garden."
Concerning the plates for As You Like It, see page 162.
The reader will examine these books with great interest.
Compared with what we imagine of costume in Garrick's
time, Planché's are splendid in the extreme; judged from
present-day standards, they are stiff and uncompromising,
something like what became traditional before Irving reformed dress altogether, in light of the William Morris-
Burne Jones revelation. The student will receive no inadequate idea of Planché's work, if he examine the char-
acter-portraits of Macready, Phelps and Miss Glyn (in
Hamlet) in the present volume.

CYMBELINE, 1827

Not until 1827 did Kemble again try the same sort of
rehabilitation of ancient Kings and their garb; this time
Cymbeline engaged the attention of what one might call
his department of archæology. The Grieves painted new
scenery, and somebody (Planché says nothing of help in
any of these restorations after the above) looked up proper
authorities. The bill once more must be put in requisition.
Its display of learning will now be familiar to the reader,
and merely anticipates Charles Kean by a quarter of a century:

THEATRE ROYAL, COVENT-GARDEN

This present Friday, Oct. 19, 1827, will be acted, Shakespeare's Play of

CYMBELINE

With NEW SCENERY, DRESSES, AND DECORATIONS, executed
from the Best Authorities, and displaying as accurately as stage effect
will permit, the Habits, Weapons, and Buildings of the Gaulish and
Belgic Colonists of the Southern Counties of *Britain* before their
Subjugation by the Romans.
The New Scenery Painted by Messrs. Grieve, T. Grieve, and W. Grieve
The Dresses by Mr. Head and Miss Abbott
In Act II, Dr. Cooke's favourite Glee of Hark! the Lark by Master
Watson, Mess. Taylor, S. Tett, and Tinney
Authorities for the Dresses, Weapons, and Scenery:
Antient British Weapons, now in the Armoury of L. Meyrick, Esq.
Antient British Coins in Various Collections . . . The Welsh Triads.

The Descriptions of Julius Cæsar, Diodorus Siculus, Dionysius of Halicarnassus, Pliny, Suetonius, Dion Cassius, Pomp. Mela, and other Contemporary Writers.
The Works of Camden, Whitaker, Strutt, Meyrick, Smith, &c.

ANTONY AND CLEOPATRA, 1833

I shall close with a bill—not of the first night—of what was probably a very elaborate staging of that hopelessly impossible thing for the picture-stage, Antony and Cleopatra. This revival, effected at Drury Lane, in the autumn of 1833, employed the services of Macready and Miss Phillips in the leading characters. The reader will be interested to read the detail of the spectacle:

THEATRE ROYAL, DRURY LANE

This Evening, Monday, Dec. 2, 1833,
Their Majesties' Servants will perform Shakspeare's Historical Play of

ANTONY AND CLEOPATRA.

In Act I will be sung the
Glee: Come thou Monarch of the Vine,
by Mr. Yarnold, Mr. Duruset, and Mr. Bedford. And
An Introductory Dance,
by Mesdames Fairbrother, Foster, &c.
The following is the Succession of the Scenery:—
A Splendid Hall in Cleopatra's Palace.
A Chamber in the Palace,

GARDEN OF CLEOPATRA'S PALACE

Portico attached to the house of Octavius Cæsar, with the Capitol in the Distance.
A Hall in the House of Lepidus

NEAR THE PROMONTORY OF MISENUM

A Room in the Palace of Alexandria,
The Camp of Octavius Cæsar.
Antony's Camp, near the

PROMONTORY OF ACTIUM

With a View of the Fleets of Antony and Cæsar.
A Court in the Palace. Field of Battle, near the walls of Alexandria.
A Terrace of the Palace, the Bay, and Part of the Roman Encampment.
Cleopatra's Chamber in the Palace.

I can glean but little of critical review. This from the Times of November 22, 1833, may interest: "Shakspeare's tragedy of *Antony and Cleopatra*, adapted for representation by Mr. Macready, was last night revived with praiseworthy splendour. Every part of the drama that was necessary to the development of the story has been preserved; but some scenes and portions of scenes that did not further that object, and which rather detracted from than added to the beauties of the play, have been removed. To that extent only the alterations, by which the interest of the tragedy is concentrated, proceed. . . . The tragedy has been brought out in a truly brilliant style. The scenery is exquisitely painted, the dresses are splendid and appropriate, and the processions, which are grand, are exceedingly well arranged."

I believe the evidence cited in the foregoing pages will prove my point made in the last chapter that the leaderless age was marked by a tendency to make "productions" of Shakespeare—stock scenery and properties no longer availed. I have, I believe, selected for discussion the chief revivals of the period. The most notable feature was the Kemble-Planché effort to clothe the historical characters in array proper to the times in which they lived. There was, no doubt, a great difference in approach, attack and result, between such a production, even, as Elliston's King Lear in 1820, and the King John of Charles Kemble in 1823. The one was consistent, but to an idealised pattern of a barbaric age; the latter was as accurate as historical research could make it. The difference in weight and dignity was enormous. We shall find Macready in the short space of six years (1837–43) perfecting all that Charles Kemble attempted. From this time on, the change could be only a matter of completeness in supplying details; in intention there was little to choose between Macready and Irving.

The Dublin University Magazine (volume 61) has something interesting to say in this connection, in an article on Theatric Representation, Mechanism, and Decoration: "Purely scenic effects, about the same time [*i. e.,* in C. Kemble's *régime*] were carried to a height of perfection which the last century had never dreamed of. Dioramas by Stanfield, Roberts, the Grieves and Telbin converted the theatres in which they were exhibited into schools of painting and national galleries. Yet the elders talked of the pictorial wonders produced by Greenwood and Mariani, and of a scene by Loutherbourg painted for De Montfort, at Drury Lane, 1800, representing the chief aisle of a church or cathedral which perhaps has never been exceeded, and might still have gladdened admiring eyes, as the proprietors intended to preserve it as a heirloom, had it not perished when Holland's beautiful structure fell a victim to fire, after a short life of only fifteen years, on the night of the 24th of February, 1809."

Yet it was many years before complete reforms were effected. Two or three years after Kemble's success with King John, a writer signing himself A. M., in one of the countless theatrical publications of the time—the Olio—after speaking of his amusement at the portrait of Quin in Coriolanus, states:

But now, if you should happen to visit (and we envy not the man who is compelled to do it) the "Great Theatres" twice in one week, you may, for your edification see "Othello" performed, and witness *Iago* in an appropriate dress; but then this pleasure would be too great without alloy, too overpowering; go next night, and you may see a play of the time of Charles the Second performed in almost the same costume; there will be the same hat and feathers, the same doublet, the same boots (but these latter appear in twenty characters), and, in fact, nearly the whole dress, &c. will be the identical pieces in which the wily villain acted his part.

We went a short time since to Covent Garden, to witness the performance of "The Merry Wives of Windsor," and oh! what a medley of costume was there! *Justice Shallow, Bardolph,* and "mine Ancient," were each in dresses of different periods, and *Sir John* himself had on the jerkin, slops, hat, boots, and Scottish broadsword, which has been long since immortalized by the Staffordshire potteries as a chimney ornament; but, to crown all, *Jack Rugby* was dressed in *livery* of the time of Hogarth, and *Doctor Caius* looked like one of the portraits of *Kneller,* with a *black-wig, court-sword,* and *ruffles !* We had a female friend with us, and that compelled us to sit out the play; but as we left the house, something like a curse against the bad taste of the manager escaped our lips.

With this plague o' both your houses we may end our chapter. Apparently the time was ripe for the appearance of Macready, the complete reformer.

BOOK VI

THE AGE OF MACREADY
(1837–1843)

CHAPTER XXIV

THE THEATRES

MACREADY AT COVENT GARDEN, 1837–1839

THE six years before the act that broke the monopoly of
the patent theatres and allowed complete freedom of production to the rest, I have designated by the name of
Macready, not perhaps with complete reasonableness, but
in recognition of the fact that in four, at least, of the seasons involved, he was engaged in management and in a
decided effort to bring back to the stage something of the
dignity it had known under Garrick and Kemble. Macready failed for several reasons, the most influential of
which possibly was his character, in which egotism amounting almost to egomania struggled for the mastery over a
nervous, hesitating constitution of body that made his
whole life a succession of wailings and gnashings of teeth.
But he likewise was trying to carry on the traditions of an
earlier day, in huge theatres ostensibly devoted to tragedy,
comedy, farce and opera, with nightly change of bill; and
that, in a day of altered fashion, which favoured long unbroken runs, in smaller theatres of far less pretension.
James Anderson believes that Macready threw away most
of his chances by absolutely refusing to repeat his biggest
successes more than three times a week—the standard
repertoire being exhibited on the alternate evenings. In
this way all the momentum of a great "hit" was broken
and frittered away.

A very good account of the negotiations which led to
Macready's undertaking the management of Covent Garden in 1837 may be found in Mr. H. Saxe Wyndham's
Annals of that theatre. Macready, with his usual timidity
and prudence in money matters, stipulated to the proprietors—who had made overtures to him—that he should

incur no personal risk. On June 17th, according to his Diary, he "premised" to Mr. Robertson, "that he would not venture any part of his little property, nor make any venture beyond his own talent." On June 22nd he called on Mr. Robertson "and learned from him that the proprietors, with whom he had spoken, were very favourable to the plan . . . . of my conducting the theatre." Nevertheless Macready, on learning that the average nightly expenses of the last season were £154, was "startled"; it "made him pause." He had a financial plan of the proprietors "taking their chances" of the £7,000 rental with him "for payment of his salary," out of a reserve fund to start, as I understand it, at £1,800 and to be added to by any surplus accruing over expenses. On June 29th: "Went to Covent Garden. In my interview with Robertson and Bartley, it was mentioned that the proprietors . . . thought that I ought to incur part of the risk. To this I instantly observed, that I did not covet the office; that in risking my name, peace of mind, salary as performer, balance of loss and increased expenses, I did more than enough, and that I adhered to what I started with, viz. that I would not lay out one single shilling nor risk one farthing beyond a night's expenses."

After more parleying, a bargain was struck, evidently to Macready's advantage. On the 22nd of July, he writes in his Diary, "My mind is quite made up to enter upon the direction of Covent Garden Theatre, and I fervently and with humility invoke the blessing of Almighty God upon my efforts and labours." On the 24th he writes: "Went into the theatre to take possession of it."

MACREADY'S METHODS

The actor-manager at once started plans to produce Shakespeare with a magnificence of scene and costume till then unparalleled, probably, in English stage history. Macready gave the minutest attention to details relating to these matters, and, as his Diary shows, agonised over them as only a second-rate meticulous person can. He was greatly aided by the help of Clarkson Stanfield, who painted for him a magnificent diorama for his first Christmas pantomime and one also for his production of Henry V—to show that Shakespeare laboured under no special advantage or disadvantage. What most aided Macready, however, was the fact that Bulwer wrote for him those two extraordinarily successful romantic plays, The Lady of Lyons and Richelieu, produced in the first and second seasons respectively of his two-year tenure of Covent Garden.

Macready's company at Covent Garden would not, at first, have impressed a veteran who recalled the glories of bygone days at the patent-houses. Macready tried without avail to induce Liston to return to the stage; failing in that, he engaged Bartley, the best Falstaff of his time, but a minor one at that. In Mrs. Warner (formerly Miss Huddart) he secured the most suitable tragic actress left to the stage; she was undoubtedly the best Lady Macbeth of her day. Helen Faucit, the attractive representative of Shakespeare's younger heroines, won some of her chief renown in these two epochal years. Priscilla Horton, hard to classify, pleased in parts so different as the Fool in Lear, Ariel, and one of the singing witches in Macbeth. All three of these actresses advanced greatly in reputation during Macready's management at Covent Garden.

MACREADY'S ACTORS

Several actors, also, secured their first chance in the same company. Most notable was Samuel Phelps, whose early successes were so great that Macready reduced him to second-rate parts, with the comforting assurance that his day would come; "but I am not going to try and hasten it. I was kept back by Young and Kean, and you will have to wait for me." James Anderson, playing very delightfully young lovers, like Florizel or Ferdinand, did not conflict with Macready, and hence vaulted more quickly into a repute deserved, if not very lasting. These were the leading members of Macready's company, and, it will be seen, could not, singly or in the aggregate, have awakened thrills of anticipation in his early spectators. But all soon reached a considerable popularity, and generously abetted the manager, even to the extent of accepting reduced salaries when times were bad.

The prices of admission to Covent Garden, during the tenancy of Macready, were, boxes, 5s., second price, 2s. 6d.; pit, 2s. 6d., second price, 1s. 6d.; lower gallery, 1s. 6d., second price, 1s.; upper gallery, 1s., second price, 6d.; second price began after the third act of plays, and the second act of operas. It will be observed that these prices are considerably lower than those exacted in Kemble's day; as a matter of fact they had been considerably cheaper during some of the years immediately preceding 1837, desperate managers of Drury Lane particularly lowering or raising prices in an effort to catch the public. All had failed.

MACREADY'S FAILURE AT COVENT GARDEN

A reading of Macready's Diary must offend any except a hypochondriac. Open anywhere, and you will light upon such passages as this of April 16, 1836: "Passed a most miserably uncomfortable night, tormented and kept awake by the headache, and worried by the thoughts of this base scoundrel's [Bunn's] attempts to injure me." The reader will imagine what the diary becomes under the worries of management; indeed, it is not pleasant reading. Actors and artists and playwrights and carpenters are generally "unreasonable," and poor Macready can only fall back on his generally unbounded admiration of himself and his performances. One is relieved to learn that he ended his term of management on July 16, 1839, with a performance of Henry V. The income had apparently not equalled the outlay.

As Mr. Saxe Wyndham says, "What rendered Macready's splendid failure so particularly galling, was the knowledge that his hated rival Bunn at Drury Lane was doing huge

HELEN FAUCIT
From a lithograph in the collection of Harry MacNeill Bland

business with Charles Kean in the same Shakespearian plays Macready had to withdraw on account of their meagre drawing powers." The details of these Shakespearian revivals of the Kean-Bunn *régime* will be found in their proper place, later in our narrative.

Macready, after his failure, spent most of his time acting at the Haymarket, then starting on its brilliant career under Benjamin Webster. This theatre, originally a summer theatre and open under patent rights from May to September, had gradually been able to extend the permitted season from March to November. Hence, at both ends of the regular season it was a formidable rival to the winter houses. Finally, it remained open practically all year. Many other small theatres, now existing in London, the Lyceum, the Olympic, the Adelphi, to mention but a few, were still precluded by law from presenting any plays except burlesque, "melo-drame," operetta, etc.

THE MATHEWS-VESTRIS MANAGEMENT, 1839–1842

The now apparently doomed Covent Garden fell under the control of Charles James Mathews (Mathews the younger) and his very popular wife, Madame Vestris. They had been giving light pieces at the Olympic at a loss, and hoped, with the unquenchable hope of theatrics, to recoup in the larger theatre; verily, no amount of experience, whether one's own or another's, maketh wise in these matters. The season commenced on Monday, September 30, 1839, with a remarkable revival of Love's Labour's Lost, not produced in London since the memory of man ran not to the contrary. The manager-pair had foolishly resolved to close the shilling gallery, and were stormed on the opening night by a riot that ruined the chances of their expensive production. During their first season the ambitious couple won a great success with Sheridan Knowles's romantic play of Love, Ellen Tree very great in the leading character. The second season was notable for a revival on a scale of great splendour of A Midsummer Night's Dream, not acted in a version so close to Shakespeare's original, in all the years from Davenant to that present day; even more remunerative was Dion Boucicault's London Assurance, produced for the first time on any stage, and with attention to furniture, dresses, etc., that began an era in stage management. The third season was chiefly memorable for the début of Adelaide Kemble, who scored immense success as a singer in Norma and The Marriage of Figaro. This was the end; Mathews was frozen out of the management, and left the house with personal debts that weighed him down for many years thereafter. Covent Garden fared even worse. It dragged on for a year or two and was snuffed out as a theatre by the Act of 1843, granting the liberty of the minor theatres. In 1847 Covent Garden became an opera house, and continues such to this day.

MACREADY AT DRURY LANE, 1841–1843

One more attempt was made to save a theatre royal, this time Drury Lane. Bunn and his indeterminate successors were all eliminated and the Committee approached Macready, with the idea of having him enter upon the management. Negotiations were completed, and Macready was installed.

The term of plays began with a performance on December 27, 1841. Macready's entry under that date is characteristic: "Saw my darling babes, and, imploring the blessing of God upon my undertaking, went to Drury Lane theatre. Rehearsed the *Merchant of Venice*. Went round the various places. Gave direction on direction. My mind was over every part of the house. My room was very uncomfortable. Lay down, but got little rest. Was much disturbed by being called for as the play began; resisted for a long while, but was at last obliged to go forward. I acted Shylock very nervously—not to please myself. I saw the pantomime afterwards."

With much lamenting and groaning Macready struggled through this season and the next. His company was in great part that he had formerly engaged at Covent Garden. The number of Shakespearian revivals was about equal to that in his earlier venture. But the knell had sounded for the system of management represented by Macready. His term closed on June 14, 1843, amid circumstances best chronicled in his Diary: "Wrote out my address in anticipation of inquiry for it this evening. Went to Drury Lane theatre. Attended to business; very low in spirits; could scarcely repress the tears that rose to my eyes when Miss Horton spoke to me. Rehearsed the two or three short scenes of *Macbeth*. Gave directions to Sloman, etc., to put the scenes and properties in good order to be rendered up to the proprietors. Saw Serle on business. Dined very early. Rested and thought over my character and my address. Was in the lowest state of depression—was actually ill from my state of mind. Spoke to Mr. Willmott upon what was needful to be done. On appearing in *Macbeth*, the whole house rose with such continued shouting and waving of hats and handkerchiefs that I was quite overcome; I was never so affected by the expression of sympathy by an audience. When wearied with shouting, they changed the applause to a stamping of feet, which sounded like thunder; it was grand and awful! I never saw such a scene! I was resolved to act my best, and I think I never played Macbeth so well. I dressed as quickly as I could, and went forward to receive another reception from that densely crowded house, that seemed to emulate the first. It was unlike anything that ever occurred before. I spoke my speech, and retired with the same mad acclaim. Dickens, H. Smith, Forster and Stanfield, Serle, came into my room. They did not seem struck with my speech."

Poor, tortured soul, as Carlyle might say, well didst thou fight thy battle, but the forces of the new age were too much for thee; veritably thou didst not see until too late that the methods of Garrick would no longer avail in the early days of Victoria Regina! Therefore thou wentst to the World's dustheap, without accomplishing thy purpose. Until too late; for in that very speech which the sensitive actor fancied Dickens and the rest were not struck with, he sounded the death-note for the patent-houses. Quoted in John Bull, June 19, 1843, this address seems to us now very far-sighted and far-reaching:

Both these large theatres are now untenanted. The holders of their patents are themselves unable to present the glorious works of Shakspeare to an English audience, and yet are armed by the law with power to forbid their representation elsewhere. For were I now, after all I have given and endured to maintain the drama in these theatres—were I, excluded as I am by circumstances, from them, to attempt in a theatre lately licensed by the Lord Chamberlain for performance of the brutes and brute-tamers—were I to attempt there the acting a legitimate play, "the law, with all their might to urge it on," would be put in force to prevent or punish me! May I not ask for what public benefit such a law is framed? Or for what good purpose it is persisted in?

THE THEATRICAL MONOPOLY ABOLISHED, 1843

The Act abolishing the privileges or monopoly of the patent houses passed into a law in the same year. From that time on, any one could enact Shakespeare, wherever he pleased. Macready did not avail himself of the opportunity. Rather did his lieutenant, Samuel Phelps, aided by Mrs. Warner, rush first into the field. At the hitherto despised Sadler's Wells they began in the season of 1844–45 that series of Shakespearian revivals which continued (so far, at least, as Phelps was concerned) throughout the season of 1861–62. This, however, is a chronicle that belongs to another epoch, another way of doing things.

CHAPTER XXV

THE PLAYS

THE RESTORATION OF SHAKESPEARE

AT last we begin to arrive at the goal toward which were leading the ages already discussed, from the time of Betterton till the freedom of the theatres. The very years that witnessed the successful struggle for this freedom witnessed, also, the freedom of Shakespeare, who, like Ariel, was released from the magic of the evil spirits—in this case the adapters. From this time forth, i. e., from 1843, he was free; he could fly and he could run with his manifold charms to the audiences that chose to submit to his spell. Only three of his plays were still in bondage to Sycorax— The Taming of the Shrew, still acted as the afterpiece, Katharine and Petruchio; Richard III, not yet unshackled from the acting version of Colley Cibber; and Romeo and Juliet, ended according to Garrick. The first and third of these adaptations Macready produced during his terms of management at the royal theatres; the second he did not in that period act in any form. George Vandenhoff assures us that Madame Vestris revived Romeo and Juliet "according to the text" in her second season; if so, the tragedy was afterward sucked down in the quicksand of the popular Garrick version.

To Macready we are indebted for the impulse that brought about this revolution in public taste; yet to say this is to admit that he was the most effective agent of that taste. For several years, now, critics here and there had cried out for reformation, for a rehabilitation of Shakespeare, freed from Tate, Cibber and the rest; Elliston and Edmund Kean had already, as we know, accomplished much at Drury Lane in the decade 1820 to 1830, and probably at the very first of the following decade, Macready himself had done something to restore Shakespeare to his own plays. The revival of Antony and Cleopatra at Drury Lane, in the last weeks of 1833, was in a stage version arranged by Macready, who played the leading role. Nothing can come from nothing, of course, and Macready, in 1837, at the commencement of his two years' management of Covent Garden, could avail himself of the preparatory service of his predecessors and an awakening public conscience or taste that insisted on the brushing away from the plays of the cobwebs that had been accumulating for a century and a half.

MACREADY AT COVENT GARDEN, 1837–1839

In examining carefully Mr. William Archer's lists of the Shakespearian plays produced by Macready at Covent Garden during the seasons of 1837–38 and 1838–39, one sees that they fall into two distinct classes: (1) stock plays, performed a few times each year, with some new scenery and doubtless with care as to all details, and (2) plays made the subject of very special production, with entire revision of text, great attention to scenery, costumes, music, etc.—in other words, great revivals, new in every particular, such as many of us remember from the work of Irving and Daly. Reduced to these two divisions, we find, in the first year, that The Winter's Tale (the opening play) had four performances; Hamlet and Othello had three each; Katherine and Petruchio, Henry V, Julius Cæsar, Romeo and Juliet and Henry VIII all emerged twice, and As You Like It once. These, then, constituted the stock-plays, and, except in the case of Hamlet and Othello, later to be spoken of, I doubt if any of them were mounted with any but stock scenery or acted in any but stock versions. But in the case of three other plays—Macbeth, King Lear and Coriolanus—the account is very different; with these Macready made very elaborate attempts which were in every sense of the word "productions."

In his second season Coriolanus, Macbeth and King Lear

now naturally joined the ranks of the stock plays; they were played two, five and six times respectively. But Hamlet and Othello, which had had at least some new scenery the year before, now advanced respectively to five and eight performances. The other stock plays of the year were The Winter's Tale, Katharine and Petruchio, As You Like It, Cymbeline and Julius Cæsar. Macready concentrated all his energies on two grand revivals—The Tempest, which reached throughout the winter the astonishing aggregate of fifty-five representations, and Henry V, which attained to twenty-one. These two are all that demand consideration from us now.

The actual "productions," then, in which Macready was concerned, during his fine but financially unsuccessful reign at Covent Garden, were really only five in number—Macbeth, King Lear, Coriolanus, The Tempest and Henry V. These are all that I shall deal with in the present division of my work. Would the reader be interested to learn that none of these, except possibly Macbeth and The Tempest, brought very substantial returns to the treasury? That the first-season pantomime with a diorama by Stanfield was probably much more remunerative than the second-season Henry V with a diorama from the same able artist? That all Shakespeare combined in the first season could not equal the results attained by Bulwer's Lady of Lyons, then first brought out, and that in the second no Shakespeare, except possibly the spectacular Tempest, could rival the vogue of Bulwer's Richelieu, also then new to the stage?

MACBETH AND KING LEAR, 1837–1838

Macbeth, produced by Macready, on November 6, 1837, was the first of his Shakespearian efforts (the house opened on September 30th, with The Winter's Tale) to attract any special attention. The critics were very indifferent and superior, and condescended to only an occasional notice; Macready is shown in his Diary simply gnashing his teeth over this neglect. But Macbeth captured these elegant gentlemen, and from that time on, for the rest of the season —but no longer—the writer for John Bull is Macready's devoted slave. I cannot find that in the case of this tragedy the manager attempted any reforms in the book; he certainly retained Locke's music and all the flummery of the singing and dancing witches. Yet John Bull assures us that "the poetry of the drama is now for the first time put in motion [whatever that may mean], and its supernatural agents begin to assume their real functions." I doubt if much of Shakespeare was restored in this version; but, thanks to scenery and stage effects, Macbeth was performed during the first season on fourteen successive Mondays, and eighteen times altogether, a creditable showing.

With King Lear, produced on January 25, 1838, we come upon firm ground. The papers of the time, now awake to the importance of Macready's experiment, are exceedingly full and clear as to what was accomplished; in consequence our narrative need be but a matter of quotation. John Bull, on the 28th, begins a long review, by hitting at once upon the significant fact—that Shakespeare's play has at last been restored to the stage—for the first time, let me repeat, in over one hundred and fifty years:

Another has been added to the list of restorations of Shakespeare's plays, commenced with such taste, and so admirably carried into effect, by the manager of this theatre. Mr. Macready deserves, and will obtain, the deep respect and gratitude, not only of the playgoing but of the literary world, for his earnest and well-directed zeal to do honour to our nation's chiefest intellectual pride. . . . .

On Thursday evening—and the date will be marked in the annals of the stage—the tragedy of *King Lear* was brought out, freed from the interpolations which have disgraced it for nearly two centuries, and with the aid of scenic adjuncts, which honoured the stage and became the author. The text spoken was, to a word, that of the poet, and the conducting and machinery of the play were conceived in a noble and liberal strain, worthy a lofty art and a genuine artist.

Macready approached this occasion, one of the two or three most momentous—perhaps the most momentous—in the entire history of Shakespearian restorations, with even a little more than his customary timidity and perturbation.

On January 4th he records: "Went to the theatre, where I went on a first rehearsal of *King Lear*. My opinion of the introduction of the Fool is that, like many such terrible contrasts in poetry and painting, in acting representation it will fail of effect; it will either weary and annoy or distract the spectator. I have no hope of it, and think that at last we shall be obliged to dispense with it." Faint-hearted Lochinvar! The next day he continues: "Speaking to Willmott and Bartley about the part of the Fool in *Lear*, and mentioning my apprehensions that, with Meadows, we should be obliged to omit the part, I described the sort of fragile, hectic, beautiful-faced, half-idiot-looking boy that he should be, and stated my belief that it never could be acted. Bartley observed that a woman should play it. I caught at the idea, and instantly exclaimed: 'Miss P. Horton is the very person.' I was delighted at the thought."

Miss Horton, consequently, was chosen for the part; this choice of a woman, to us so incongruous, hardly better satisfied contemporary critics. John Bull, on February 4th, remarks that her "'poor fool and knave' is perhaps not that of Shakspeare. . . . . Still her's is a most pleasing performance, giving evidence of deep feeling; and she trills forth the snatches of song with the mingled archness and pathos of their own exquisite simplicity."

THE VERSION OF KING LEAR

The version of King Lear in Lacy's Acting Edition is, I believe, that used by Macready in his memorable revival; the cast of characters prefixed is the one engaged in his theatre in 1838, and that, I have found, is a reasonably certain test in similar cases. This arrangement of the play follows Shakespeare's with great accuracy. The first act contains Shakespeare's first four scenes in order, all, however, considerably "cut," and, moreover, throughout, some of the lines are printed with asterisks, to indicate that they were omitted in representation. These occur especially in Cordelia's farewell admonitions to her sisters, and in the scene between Edmund and Gloster. Lear's great curse, with the lines of Albany preceding it, are taken from their proper place and put at the end of the act, to effect a great exit speech for Lear.

Act II progresses in Shakespeare's order (with "cuts" and asterisks). In Scene 4, after the entrance of Lear in Gloster's castle, and before he sees Kent in the stocks, is interpolated the fifth scene of Shakespeare's Act I—the scene between the Fool and Lear, with the latter's agonised cry.

> O let me not be mad—not mad, sweet heaven!
> Keep me in temper—I would not be mad.

The act ends with Lear's rushing off into the storm—

> O fool, I shall go mad!

Up to this point the version, with its judicious "cuts," seems to me a superb acting copy. The third act restores, at the beginning, the scene between Kent and the Gentleman, bringing the ravings of Lear on the heath into the second scene. In the act there is a curious union of the two mad scenes of the King. The fourth scene begins with Shakespeare's fourth—part of the heath, with a hovel—into which is injected, much curtailed, Shakespeare's Scene 6—the farmhouse, with the entry of Gloster, Lear's imagined trial of Goneril, etc.—and then ends with the last part of the original Scene 4! This is a curious medley, but I should imagine very effective for the stage, and occasioned by the necessity for compression under the new stage conditions of scenery frequently changing—conditions which Macready was one of the first to encounter and solve.

I need not further weary the reader. Suffice it to say that in Act IV all details of the actual blinding of Gloster are omitted—not even given behind the scenes, as in Kemble. In Act IV, Scene 3 (Shakespeare's Scene 2), a few lines of Regan from Scene 5,

> It was sad ignorance, Gloster's eyes being put out, etc.

are given to Goneril. In Scene 5 of the same act (Shakespeare's Scene 6) Gloster does not "jump from the cliff";

he is prevented, as in Inchbald, Kemble and Oxberry, by the entrance of Lear. After these episodes Shakespeare's play is given with great fidelity as to situation, curtailed only within suitable time-limits. In the middle of the scene of Gloster and Edgar by the tree (Act V, Scene 2) are interpolated a few lines that I cannot identify; they are neither Shakespeare's nor Tate's.

All in all, this strikes me as an excellent stage version of the most tremendous of tragedies. Compared with even the version in use since Edmund Kean restored the catastrophe, which left the love affair of Cordelia and Edgar, and still omitted the Fool, this of Macready must have seemed very magnificent. I could not have believed that so much of Shakespeare's play could be retained and compressed within the limits of one evening's entertainment. With this production the ghost of Nahum Tate—so far as England, if not America, was concerned—was laid forever.

MACREADY'S CORIOLANUS, 1838

On March 12th of the same year Macready produced Coriolanus on a scale of unprecedented magnificence. As to the version of the play used, I must confess to having but scanty evidence. Macready, unlike Kemble, made no effort to bring out his plays in book form. His Diary informs us that publishers had approached him on the subject of an edition of Shakespeare to be edited according to his prompt-books, but apparently the actor was too nervous or too busy to undertake the task. At all events, we are forced, in considering his versions, to guess to some extent, and to take the word of reviewers and critics. Lacy's Plays will not help us in the case of Coriolanus, as it helped in that of King Lear; the edition of the former play in his series is obviously Kemble's. For some idea of the version, then, I am forced back on what the critic of John Bull gives us in his review of March 19, 1838:

The play must be looked on in the light of a new one. . . . We now have the play; we had formerly the one personage alone; to bring whom into full relief, all the rest were thrown into the shade.

The additions made by Thomson to the play [hardly a fair way of putting this, since, as we have seen, bits of Thomson's original play were injected by Kemble into Shakespeare's], as then acted, certainly fell far short of the murderous interpolations of a Tate, or a Cibber; but the retrenchments whether made by him [obviously our critic was ignorant of the true posture of affairs] or others, were numerous; and the drama, in short, was sacrificed to a strong and a noble, but a partial effect. The restorations due to Mr. Macready are large; and it must not be forgotten that if they detract from the brilliant light hitherto concentrated on the figure of *Coriolanus*, they enlarge the historical canvas to statelier proportions and severer beauties. The only portion retained of Thomson's slip-shod verse, are some half-dozen speeches that serve to connect the last scene with that in which Coriolanus yields to his mother's prayers, so as to join them [*i. e.*, the scenes] into one. This is done in order to make the termination impressive by the armed array then present on the stage. . . However, . . . he has preserved the prevention of shock at the after-change in *Aufidius'* character, by retaining, though transposed, the speech ending with, "Mine emulation hath not that honour in't, it had." A lesser fault, though still a fault, is altering the point at which *Coriolanus* foregoes his great revenge, and sees the "Gods look down at the unnatural scene." *Volumnia*, as her last effort, exclaims—

> "I am hush'd until our city be afire,
> And then I'll speak a little!"

The horrible image thus conjured up to his view, is the accumulative blow which softens his heart.

This would seem to indicate but little variation, curtailments aside, from Shakespeare's text; compared with Kemble's utter perversion of the poet's meaning in the last scenes, it must have seemed pure indeed. Macready, however, was not a great Coriolanus, and Kemble was; his success with the play on the stage was therefore almost infinitely below that of his predecessor. Alfred Bunn, certainly no friendly critic, is very sarcastic on this point. "Blessed is he that expecteth nothing, and he can never be disappointed," exclaims this rival manager. Admitting the beauty of the production, Bunn goes on: "Nothing was expected from Mr. Macready's personation of the noble Roman, and no disappointment was experienced at nothing being achieved."

SHAKESPEARE AT DRURY LANE, 1837–1838

These were the notable Shakespearian achievements of Macready during his first season at Covent Garden; his success, artistic at best, rather than financial, was embittered by the undoubted fact that Charles Kean, after some years of hard work in the provinces, was brought out at Drury Lane by the energetic Bunn, and succeeded admirably—at least in drawing crowds—in two of the very parts that Macready failed in. Bunn in his work on The Stage glories in the thought that in an engagement of forty-three nights Kean needed to play only three characters; Hamlet he appeared in twenty-one times, Richard III, seventeen, and Sir Giles Overreach, five. In the spring Kean played a return engagement, adding Othello to his repertoire. Bunn provided new setting for Richard and Hamlet. The crowds flocked after Kean, and Macready could only console himself by reflecting that sensible critics preferred the productions at Covent Garden. He may have smiled in satisfaction to read in John Bull, on February 4th, just after his own revival of King Lear "from the text of Shakespeare," a note showing the effect of his own efforts in the direction of restoring the language of the original. After stating that Kean is to play Richard III, the commentator adds, "and we trust that it will be the poet's, not Cibber's."

As a matter of fact it was Cibber's, and strongly expressed is the disappointment of the critic when he records that blighting fact a short time after; all joy went out of the performance for him. Perhaps it would be well to record here that, though Bunn took a leaf from Macready's note-book in providing expensive new scenery and costumes for this engagement of Kean, he made no effort to purify the text of the plays. In writing his work on The Stage, in 1840, he is very sarcastic again in commenting on that phrase—"from the text of Shakespeare"—now adorning Covent Garden bills, and quite obviously galling the careless Bunn himself. His chief remark is that the "casts" of Shakespeare (with any text, I suppose) were far better at his house than at Macready's. "They forgot that the Tempest, performing at the other house with the announced quotation of 'the text of Shakspeare,' owed all the attraction it possessed to the novelty of Miss P. Horton, 'My gentle Ariel,' singing while suspended in the air; because it had been infinitely better acted, and infinitely better prepared in that very theatre, 'many a time and oft.'" Much later in his very sprawling and anæmic, but occasionally interesting book, the righteously indignant Bunn cries out, somewhat inaccurately, "The hasty attempt of '*King Lear,* from the text of Shakspeare,' he made before with me, both at Drury Lane and Covent Garden—consequently there was no novelty in THAT. The restoration of 'the text of Shakspeare' in others of his plays was a mere joke, being resorted to only as it set off the hero of the piece to the best advantage." This last, as we see from the analysis of Coriolanus published in John Bull, was palpably untrue. Evidently Bunn's withers were not unwrung. He returns once more to the charge toward the end of his book, triumphantly asking if Macready's Tempest in 1838 "from the text of Shakspeare" could compare as to cast with Bunn's revival at Drury Lane in 1833, as "altered by Dryden and Davenant." Unfortunately, his contrasted casts lose much of their intended effect from the fact that Macready played Prospero in both!

MACREADY'S TEMPEST, 1838

This talk of The Tempest, however, anticipates slightly. That spirit-comedy was not produced by Macready until October 13, 1838, shortly after the beginning of his second season. He worked very hard on all details of the production, and was really nervously incapacitated by it. We know that he cut out all the words of the first scene on the ship, and gave, as Charles Kean did many years later, a magnificent moving picture to start the action and to put the audience in the mood of the spectacle to follow. John Bull, having lavishly praised his productions of King Lear

PRISCILLA HORTON AS ARIEL
From a contemporary print in the Harvard Theatre Collection

and Coriolanus, now joined the ranks of those who would be different, and severely censured the super-imposition of scenery on Shakespeare's delicate fantasy. Yet from the critic of that paper we learn of Macready's fidelity to the original text:

"That the balderdash of Dryden and Davenant, should be expunged, the Masque partially restored, and the text, necessary omissions apart, be redintegrate, were now to be expected at Mr. Macready's hands as a thing of course." At least, Macready had established a tradition for such things, and was felt to be of the winning side. No wonder Bunn read the handwriting on the wall, and tried to erase it with sarcasm.

The Tempest, like King Lear, had been one of the worst sufferers from the adapters; Macready put to his credit a literal freeing of Ariel and the other spirits and mortals of the magic isle. From 1838 Dryden and Davenant joined Nahum Tate in the shades; Dorinda and Hippolito never again raised their diminished heads on the English stage. To have restored King Lear and The Tempest—those two inveterately and incurably diseased members of the Shakespearian body—to something like their original textual purity was a feat of which any man might be proud.

MACREADY'S HENRY V, 1839

Macready decided to close his second and last season of management at Covent Garden with a very elaborate production of Henry V, with the Chorus restored. This very impersonal person is not to be found in the stage versions of Bell, Inchbald, Oxberry, Kemble or Cumberland. Genest, however, records that Garrick recited the lines of the Chorus, when Barry played Henry V at Drury Lane in 1747. As it turned out, we shall see that the Chorus became the chief feature of Macready's show, involving as it did an extraordinary progression of scenes and a diorama by Stanfield that eclipsed all glories of similar efforts in the pantomime. As nothing of foreign substance had been introduced in the rarely acted Henry V (of course I do not include the original plays on the same subject by the Earl of Orrery and Aaron Hill), Macready had no excisions to make; all he could do was to add as much of the original as he chose to an acting version depleted by John Kemble.

THE MATHEWS-VESTRIS MANAGEMENT, 1839–1842

Charles Mathews and Madame Vestris, at the same theatre, in their three years of management immediately following Macready's, moulded the policy according to their own talents, which lay entirely in the domains of comedy and farce. Tragedy they hardly attempted, but they at least began well by opening on Monday, September 30, 1839, with a revival of Love's Labour's Lost, beautifully mounted, and with a very strong cast, Mrs. Nisbett appearing as the Princess of France, Madame Vestris as Rosaline, Anderson as Biron, Harley as Don Armado and Keeley as Costard. This, so far as I can learn, was the first performance of the comedy since the closing of the theatres in 1642; the adaptation entitled The Students, published in 1762, was apparently never acted. The play was an extraordinarily choice selection for beginning Madame Vestris's season as manager, but owing to the riot on the opening night, the revival was killed in the bud, and never paid for itself.

The version she used is undoubtedly that contained in Cumberland's British Theatre, with the cast as produced by her. The only things that distinguish it from the copy of Shakespeare's play are (1) the large number of lines omitted from the text; (2) the running together of scenes to save scenery; and (3) the transposition of the first scene of Act IV in Shakespeare to the end of Act III in Vestris. These changes are such as we have become accustomed to in all Shakespearian revivals from Macready's day to ours, and, unless one insists on every word and on an Elizabethan stage, there is no reasonable objection that can be offered.

The "cuts" in the version under consideration affect chiefly the comic sections; a great deal—really a very great deal—has been taken from the scenes between Don Armado and the uncannily precocious Moth, as well as from those involving Costard and Jaquenetta. The long poetical speeches, many of them in set forms, have been rather lavishly retained, though naturally, human endurance being what it is, they have been shorn of some highly ornate lines. The comic scenes above mentioned have gained by the loss (if I may be pardoned the bull) of so much of their early Shakespearian quibbling, word-play and feeble jest. If one were to revive Love's Labour's Lost to-day (and frankly I do not see why, except as a labour of love, one should) I do not believe a better acting version could be made. Poor Madame Vestris was assailed, at about this time, by many pallid jokes on the name of the play as applicable to her own failure to make it a success.

Nevertheless, to have been the first to produce the piece since 1642 was, in 1839, something of glory and renown. The next Shakespearian effort of this management was a memorable revival of The Merry Wives of Windsor (still retaining much of Bishop's operatic music) but played in something like its original form, with Mathews as Slender, Bartley as Falstaff, and Mrs. Nisbett and Mme. Vestris as the Wives. This was played eleven times, as against nine for Love's Labour's Lost.

A MIDSUMMER NIGHT'S DREAM, 1840

In the second season Madame Vestris did another great thing for Shakespeare; she produced A Midsummer Night's Dream, practically as written by the poet, and again for the first time since 1642. The reader who has followed me thus far, will recall various attempts to turn the fairy comedy into operatic form, as in The Fairy Queen of 1692, The Fairies in 1755, or the Garrick piece in 1763; also the Reynolds adaptation of 1816. He will remember the mock-operas of Leveridge and Lampe, in 1716 and 1745 respectively; let us hope The Fairy Tale of 1763 and the after-piece of 1833 will not have escaped him. All these things literally had made ruin of Shakespeare's play, but never once in all the years from 1642 to 1840 had the Dream, as Shakespeare dreamed it, been presented on the London stage. In enumerating all the perversions of the play, one sees how it had suffered—probably more than any other single work; at any rate, we can say it had been the victim of more recurrent attacks. And now Madame Vestris revived it in almost its original form, and so gained glory equal to Macready for his restoration of King Lear and The Tempest. Indeed I may say, if I were to trace the history of Shakespearian alterations from 1660 to 1840, trace them in all their shame and futility, I could not select two greater victims of the turpitude of adapters than King Lear and A Midsummer Night's Dream, as attacked by one enemy after another.

This last true version of the fairy comedy was made by J. R. Planché, who also designed the most effective scenery. It is to be found in volume 28 of Lacy's Acting Plays, and contains (*mirabile dictu*) nothing but Shakespeare. Some of the lines usually spoken, are sung, but these and Shakespeare's lyrics are the only vocal parts included in the edition. The play is printed entire, but many lines are marked by asterisks, implying their omission by the performers. As thus presented to the reader, the play is seen to have lost nothing by additions (from other authors); probably, on the other hand, it gains as drama by the lines it has lost. Everything of importance is retained, and the play must have moved as swiftly as possible, with so much singing, to its conclusion. One's respect for Madame Vestris, the manager, is vastly increased by an examination of this prompt-book, especially when one remembers that hers was practically the first performance of A Midsummer Night's Dream on the English picture-stage—a really thought-provoking thought.

MACREADY AT DRURY LANE, 1841–1843

Madame Vestris and Charles Mathews continued in the management of Covent Garden until the spring of 1842;

but the above are their only important revivals of Shakespeare. In the last year of their term—to be explicit, on
the 27th of December, 1841—Macready again began as
manager, this time of Drury Lane. He inaugurated his
venture with a beautiful revival of The Merchant of Venice,
shorn of the silly songs and duets for Lorenzo and Jessica,
and nevertheless with both the Morocco and Arragon
scenes omitted. Two days after he met with John Kemble's success with an elaborate revival of The Two Gentlemen of Verona—that is, he met with almost no success at
all. Both of these were careful revivals, depending on
scenery and stage-setting for their chief effect. After these
opening shots from the managerial gun, Macready fell back
on the stock Shakespearian repertoire, Katharine and
Petruchio, Macbeth, Hamlet and Othello, for the rest of
the season. His great success that year was a revival of
Handel's Acis and Galatea, with startling effects and scenes
by Stanfield. This had forty-three performances, but
ought, according to Anderson, to have run on for many
more nights, if Macready could have been induced to give
up his old-fashioned notions about not allowing any piece to
play uninterruptedly until its attractiveness was exhausted.

AS YOU LIKE IT, 1842

In his last year of management (1842–43), Macready
followed the same principle of bringing out two new Shakespearian productions at the beginning and relying for the
rest of the term on stock pieces. He opened on October 1st,
with As You Like It, mounted, so far as I can judge, with
exquisite beauty, and on the twenty-fourth of the same
month, crowned his career with a magnificent revival of
King John. The remaining Shakespearian plays of the
winter were Hamlet, Othello, Macbeth, Cymbeline, Much
Ado about Nothing (this indeed in something like a new
investiture), Julius Cæsar and The Winter's Tale, surely a
very creditable showing.

His As You Like It met with great praise. His version
of the play is probably that found in Lacy's edition. It

retains a great part of the original text, and includes nothing not in Shakespeare's play, except the song, "When
daisies pied," which every Rosalind has felt herself entitled
to sing—almost to our own day. Was not Ada Rehan the
first to renounce it? Certainly Mary Anderson sang it.
John Bull, having in the past sufficiently castigated Macready for swamping Shakespeare in scenery, now once more
swings to his side with warm words of commendation. It
calls the revival of As You Like It his best effort:

And while [it says] no interpolations are admitted, the occasional
cutting is evidently a compliance with necessity, and is done to
shorten the drama, without materially injuring its wholeness as a
poetical conception. As the acts progressed, each scene tastefully
elaborated, without being overladen in any part, some around us
exclaimed, "Mr. Macready has now realised Shakspeare!" yet to
admit this opinion would deprive the artist of his fame. He has not
realised, he has done more—he has *verified* the dramatist . . . . and
on this account only could it be that scenes we have frequently witnessed and more frequently read—now truthfully presented in an
original purity, came before our minds with freshness as each was
heard or seen for the first time, and communicated a delight which,
our critical duty being fulfilled, will hereafter attract us to Drury Lane
for our personal gratification.

[Though the individual acting is, on the whole,] open to objection,
the large truth that pervades the whole drama is preserved in its
unity, and the continued and sustained delight, increasing and enlarging as the acts progressed, which we enjoyed on the night of its production, can only be placed to the amusement and the instruction the
perception of any verity is certain to impart.

We recommend our readers to see this performance. Divested of
the antiquated sentimentality of the old stage directions, almost every
scene is a new creation. It is a most masterly piece of histrionic art.

It is quite evident, then, that Macready had entirely
re-studied the play, "discarded old stage directions," as
John Bull puts it, and created an atmosphere for the pastoral comedy never known to it before. Yet some critics
thought Mrs. Nisbett's Rosalind almost a criminal offense;
I fancy from what I have read of the lady that there was
in her performance just about as much poetry as you could
take upon a knife's point, and choke a daw withal. Un-

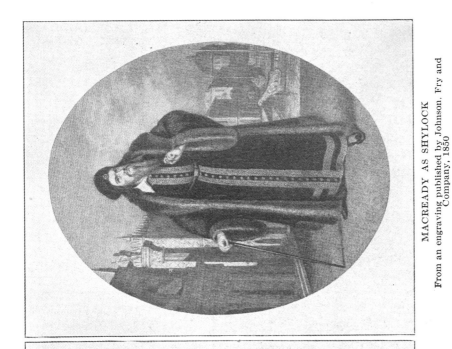

MACREADY AS HENRY IV

From an engraving published by John Tallis and
Company

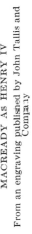

MACREADY AS SHYLOCK

From an engraving published by Johnson. Fry and
Company, 1850

doubtedly, however, her exuberant youthful charm compensated to some extent for this deficiency.

Something of this same creation of mood had been effected at Covent Garden by Macready's King Lear and Coriolanus and by Madame Vestris's Midsummer Night's Dream; it was to be the prevailing factor in Macready's last great revival—that of King John. This play had never suffered from the pirates—Kemble's King John, compared with his Coriolanus, his Tempest or his King Lear, was innocent as a hot-house rose. Macready, therefore, though he might add or take away a line or two, here and there, of the original, had nothing of importance to restore. His attention could be bestowed entirely on mounting and on the realisation of a certain unity of effect.

THE SERVICE OF MACREADY AND MADAME VESTRIS

The restoration, practically complete, of Shakespeare in King Lear, The Tempest, A Midsummer Night's Dream: this was the highly important service rendered by this last age to Shakespeare. One could wish Macready had brought back Shakespeare's Richard III, and sent Cibber's ghost to join those of Davenant, Dryden and Tate in the shades; especially in view of the entry of September 13, 1838, in his Diary: "Looked over Shakspeare's plays of *King Richard II* and *King Richard III*. Astonished at the base venality of the disgusting newspaper writers—the wretches —who dare to laud the fustian of Cibber, and tried to keep the many in ignorance by praising his trash called *Richard III.*" But it was not to be. Macready's services to the poet were finished, when he withdrew from management in 1843; from that time, till his retirement in 1851, he was merely an itinerant "star," recalling, perhaps, the tender grace of a day that is dead. Yet even in the very twilight of his career he acted for the first time in London, the part of Richard II "with singular fidelity to the text." This performance was given only twice, at the Haymarket, in the autumn of 1850, and—strange to say—in the course of the very last engagement he ever filled on the stage. I wonder what led him to it?

One leaves this period with a reiteration of the statement that the years which witnessed the last steps toward the freedom of the theatres witnessed also the liberation of Shakespeare from every adapter except Colley Cibber in Richard III and David Garrick in The Taming of the Shrew and Romeo and Juliet.

CHAPTER XXVI

SCENERY AND COSTUMES

MACREADY AT COVENT GARDEN, 1837–1839

FROM the time when the press of London began to awake to the importance of Macready's work at Covent Garden, we are at no loss to follow the scenic marvels that he unrolled before the eyes of the spectators in his theatre. Very elaborate accounts appear, especially in weekly papers, like John Bull or the Examiner; the daily Times remained cold and aloof throughout the greater part of his tenancy of Covent Garden, though it became profusely panegyrical during the later incumbency of Drury Lane. Probably the newspaper men did not, as a whole, like Macready; he was sour and unlovable, but just strong enough to demand notice in quarters unwilling to grant complete praise. Nevertheless, in his first term of management John Bull and the Examiner must have at times satisfied his craving for adulation, and in his second, the Times.

For a few months after he began at Covent Garden, his efforts, as I have said, passed unnoticed. The Examiner, to be sure, stated that "the scenes of Hamlet [October 2, 1837] were a series of glorious pictures," but Macready's Diary tells us as much: "The play was put beautifully on the stage. The audience noticed with applause several of the improvements." I am dependent on the Diary alone for statements as to the mounting of Othello (October 16th): "The Council of Forty was a scene of beautiful effect, one of the most real things I ever saw." Next day he records: "Dined at the Garrick Club; looked at the papers, not one of which noticed the *mise en scène* of *Othello !* So much for the assistance of the press!"

With the production of Macbeth on November 6th the public and the press awoke. On the evening of the production Macready writes in his Diary: "The whole play was very beautifully put upon the stage, and the audience seemed to appreciate it. I was called for, and very enthusiastically received." At last, after having been almost ridiculous in its attitude, the critic once indeed asserting that he had not had time to see the performances of The Winter's Tale and Hamlet, and was forced to attend the revival of Love in a Village or some such trifle, John Bull, November 13, 1837, highly praises the production of Macbeth: "The poetry of the drama is now for the first time put in motion, and its supernatural agents begin to assume their real functions. . . ."

Many other parts of the play were illustrated anew. We instance more particularly the scene in which the murder of *Duncan* is discovered, and the march of the army from "Birnam wood." In the latter each man was completely screened by the immense bough he carried; and the scenic illusion by which a whole host was represented stretching away into the distance, and covered as by one leafy screen, which was removed at the same time that the soldiers in the foreground threw down theirs, had all the reality of a dioramic effect.

MACREADY'S KING LEAR

This must have been an elaborate stage effect; it would hardly be tolerated in these days of electric lighting, when the line of demarcation between real and painted soldiers would be distressingly apparent to an audience. Macready, meantime, found his stride in the revival of King Lear, brought out on January 25, 1838. As to the scenic display, John Bull, to atone for previous neglect, becomes extraordinarily detailed, and puts the pictures actually before our eyes. This is almost the first thing of the kind in English dramatic criticism:

From beginning to end, the scenery of the piece, most of it new, corresponds with the period, and with the circumstances of the text. The castles are heavy, sombre, solid; their halls adorned with trophies of the chase and instruments of war; druid circles rise in spectral loneliness out of the heath; and the "dreadful pother" of the elements is kept up with a verisimilitude which beggars all that we have hitherto seen attempted.   Forked lightnings, now vividly illume the broad horizon, now faintly coruscating in small and serpent folds, play in the distance; the sheeted element sweeps over the foreground, and then leaves it in pitchy darkness; and wind and rain howl and rush in 'tyranny of the open night.'   Had such scenic imitation been introduced in some wretched melodrame, it would have been lauded to the very echo; it shall not want our eulogy at least, now that it forms the setting to a priceless diamond.

The costume is equally new, excellent, and characteristic; we would especially notice an ingenious difference of uniform, if we may use the term, by which Lear's knights are distinguished from the other retainers of the court.   It is introduced with a painter's eye to effect. . . .

Processions, marches, groups, and other accessories of the scene are managed with the same eye to apt illustration, and the same result of novel design and skilful execution.   A more admirable *coup de theatre* or one more proper to the scene and period of the drama than the sudden formation of the lists for the fight of *Edmund* and *Edgar* has never taken audience by surprise or disarmed critic.

This impresses me as the account of a nobly conceived and ably executed revival of a great tragedy; in intention nothing could surpass it even to-day.   Probably increased facilities for producing light and shade would intensify the gloom of the story, but Macready must have done remarkably well, in view of the possibilities in staging in the year 1838.

MACREADY'S CORIOLANUS

The effects of King Lear were undoubtedly surpassed in Coriolanus, brought out on March 12th.   Here again I must call in the aid of John Bull (March 19, 1838), to the end of placing a great spectacle before the eyes of my reader.   Heading its review with the inspiring caption "Shakspeare's Coriolanus," it proceeds:

And truly is this noble play so termed in the Covent Garden bills! Shakspeare is here himself; his own grand imaginings invested with reality; Patrician Rome thronged with care on the Capital; and the loud voice of the young republic threatening its citadel from the angry Forum.   The gowned nation, and the future masters of the world, whose eagles were to fly from furthest Ganges to extremest

Thule are at last shown to us as the myriad-minded poet created them; simple, stern, barbaric, cooped up in the narrow field of their early struggles and conquests. The early Rome of the English stage has hitherto been a pedantic restoration of a rude but vigorous and life-like original; a Salvator Rosa amended by a David; figures fresh from nature's mould, recast to suit the Gallic *beau-ideal ;* and the wild scenery out of which they grew, trimmed down to the beauties of Academic art. For the first time, there are now given to us the scene, and the actors on it; the hills which beetled over Tyber in precipitous strength, and the men who were as the hills that cradled them, rude, massy, and towering.

.　　.　　.　　.　　.　　.　　.　　.

The opening scene has, with admirable judgment, been selected by Mr. Macready, as a vantage ground. . . . And on this he has built up a scenic illusion that for reality, power, and masterly effect beggars all that we have ever witnessed in our own theatres, and shames even the most splendid efforts of that temple of display, the Opera at Paris; equals it, to the utmost of its magnificence, and shames it even in its strongest and least vulnerable point, historic faithfulness and antiquarian minutiæ.

And what is this first scene? A very simple one as regards the painting . . . a very vivid one as regards the tide of human existence poured upon the stage by the presence of the *dramatis personæ.* The scene represents early Rome, seen from the south-west side of the Tyber, which forms part of the foreground; beyond the river rises the steep height of the southern summit of the Capitoline hill, crowned with its *Arx* and temples; underneath, to the right, are seen the *Cloaca Maxima,* and the Temple of Vesta; whilst the remainder of the picture is occupied by the Palatine, crested with a few larger mansions, but its shelving side, up which a rude street winds its way, densely crowded with the thatch-covered huts—"*tecta pauperis Evandri,*" which, at a much later date even, contrasted with the *aurea tecta* of a more modern though still ancient Rome. . . . . When the stage becomes animated with a seemingly countless mob of barbarians, armed with staves, mattocks, hatchets, pickaxes, and their wrongs, we become sensible that it is not a mere coward crowd before us, but the onward and increasing wave . . . . . of men who have spied their way to equal franchises, and are determined to fight their way to the goal. There is no mistaking the struggle for power that has begun. It is not noble against serf, but against freeman. The illusion is still further maintained by their dress. They are no longer the mere *tunicatus popellus,* who have hitherto caricatured the Roman commonalty. In many there is an approximation to the toga; and the squalor . . . . is altogether done away with. . . .

Rome is there rough-hewn, and her sons breathe her own rude
majesty.

. . . .

But it is not with the acting of one or two parts that we now have
to do. A whole people are summoned up, and a drama instinct
with their life rolls its changes o'er the scene. The multitudes crowd
round their Tribunes; the Patricians defy or deprecate both; and all
walk, contend, harangue, stand singly, or are grouped together seemingly without reference to the spectators. Not for an instant is the
illusion suffered to be broken. We are present at the popular assem-
blies, and wild turbulence of infant Rome. The spell begun in the
first scene, is woven deftly to the last. The rude magnificence of the
Capitol is ever in contrast with the turbulent commotion of the
Forum.

We have described the opening scene. This is succeeded by the
atrium of *Coriolanus's* house, lighted through its *compluvium*, and
adorned by the tesselated floor, and shining brick-work of the period.
The square lintelled-doors; the one candelabrum; and the extreme
simplicity of the compartment are in excellent taste. The war before
Corioli is seized as an opportunity for presenting the well-known
form of the Roman camp, with its *vallum* and fosse. On the hero's
return, crowned with the oaken garland, the stage gives a marvellous
picture of a Roman holyday. It is filled with crowds of all classes,
with laurel boughs in their upraised hands; the walls and battlements
are lined with spectators; and the massy gate through which the procession moves, framed of alternate brick, and large blocks of *peperino*,
bespeaks at once the walls of Servius. To take the scenes in order,
and to do them full justice, would double the tediousness of this long
article. But we must not pass over the Senate, held in the temple
of Capitoline Jove, with its assembled fathers seated in triple rows
on their benches of stone, the lighted altar in the midst, the Consul
on his curule chair, backed by the bronze wolf to whom Rome owed
her founders, with no other ornament than its simple columns, and
the vaulted heavens seen through its open roof. Or the two views of
the busy Forum, the one displaying the Tribunal and the warning
statue of Marsyas in front, whilst high above tower the *Arx*, the
Tarpeian rock, and the fane of Jupiter Capitolinus, which rises in
Doric majesty and stretches with its hundred pillars, and massy
porticos, half across the scene; the other showing the Forum length-
wise, looking towards the Temple of Vesta, which is seen through a
centre arch, and the whole harmonised to the severe antiquity that
reigns throughout by the lowly huts and mean *tabernæ* that rest
against its pillars. The view of the port and mole of Antium, with
its *pharos*, seen by night, is in rich poetic feeling with the circum-

stance—its deadliest enemy, who "made its widows," gliding into it, like a lone spectre; and the next scene is in accordant grace, the *aula* of *Tullus's* mansion, lit by the glimmering brazier on the hearth, *Coriolanus* sitting, shrouded in his mantle on the sacred spot, which is flanked on one side by a lofty trophy, on the other by the ancestral image; the solemn beauty of the whole picture carrying us back to the most touching of all classical associations—the inviolability of the hearth. . . . . The last scene mocks description. The city frowns in the distance, begirt with the lofty and turreted walls of *Servius*, and encircled (the view is from the Appianway) by its wide moat. The Volscian army literally fills the stage with its dense files, and when the mourning Roman matrons pierce through them in long array, we breathlessly acknowledge the majesty of the historic fact, and feel that at length ROMA MORIBUS ANTIQUIS STAT.

The costume of the piece is strictly realised. Even to the *tuba palmata* of the triumpher, and the eagle-crowned sceptres of the consuls, all is correct; and the brass covered legionaries are strictly those of antique Rome. We might raise objections; wish the toga to wear its natural colour of the wool, in order to make the candidate's gown—a leading point—more conspicuous; the *fasces* to be without their axes whilst borne in the city. . . . Yet these would be captious exceptions . . . when compared with the high classical fidelity sustained throughout.

.   .   .   .

We have dwelt upon this play . . . . because it stands alone in the annals of the stage. The manner of its production is of itself a work of genius. It is the reverential yet firm filling up of a picture, whose outlines have been drawn by a master's hand; the Shakespearian spirit animates the whole. We feel it to be a subject of as much gratulation as if we had recovered another play—for it is now only that it has received a living comment and interpretation. Form and matter are equally admirable—for life is there.

It is impossible to see how praise could farther go. Yet, on April 1st, Macready is "disgusted" to see the writer in John Bull now "trimming" to Charles Kean; "he also writes ignorantly on the subject of Rome in two instances— one the site of the temples, the other the habits of the slaves." Alfred Bunn, the manager of Kean and professed foe to Macready, after ridiculing Macready's performance of the great Roman (as well he might, I should guess), proceeds: "But disclaiming all personalities, and indulging in no predilections, I cannot deny, and I will defy any one to deny, that Coriolanus was put upon the Covent Garden stage in a manner worthy of any theatre and any manager." Praise from Sir Hostis is praise indeed.

BUNN AND CHARLES KEAN AT DRURY LANE

Bunn, who brought forward Kean at Drury Lane, in order to wither the first year of Macready's glory at the rival theatre, records that he had prepared Hamlet (Kean's first play) with new scenes, dresses and paraphernalia. His playbill states that "the following, amongst other Scenes, have been painted for this Occasion, by the Messrs. Grieve: The Platform of the Castle, Another Part of the Platform, Theatre in the Court of Denmark, the Queen's Closet, Church Yard in the Vicinity of the Palace, State Apartment in the Palace." John Bull, which so slowly worked itself to a white heat of enthusiasm in the case of Macready's productions, culminating on January 28th, in its review of King Lear, now curtly dismisses the decoration of Kean's Hamlet with, "there were new scenery and dresses, but they call for no particular notice." On the contrary, the Times, which under no circumstances could be brought to praise Macready, especially commends the scenery, in its issue of January 9, 1838. "It is right that we should particularly notice the care that has been taken in getting up this tragedy. It is shameful that while thousands are thrown away on the ornaments and decorations of a paltry French melodrama, the works of Shakspeare have hardly ever been honoured with a new dress or a new scene. There has, in this instance, been a most liberal outlay on scenery, dresses and decorations. Of the scenery we would particularly speak. The opening scene, the fortress of Elsinore, the Queen's Chamber, and the ancient burying ground, where the funeral of Ophelia takes place, are most pleasing specimens of scenic painting, and infinitely creditable to the artists, the Messrs. Grieve."

Bunn, having for many times presented Hamlet, with the

attraction of Kean and the new scenes, was moved to perform a similar service for Richard III. The playbill is now far more ambitious in its statements, and announces boldly, in opposition to Macready's boasting about the actual text of Shakespeare (Bunn had at least a sense of humour), that the play will be produced "as altered by Cibber." Then follows a grand flourish in Bunn's best manner:

With New Scenery, Dresses, and Decorations.
The Scenery Painted by
Mr. Grieve, Mr. T. Grieve, and Mr. W. Grieve.
The Costumes, from eminent Authorities, by Mr. Palmer, and Mrs. Benton.
The Properties, Armorial Bearings, and General Decorations, by Mr. Blamire.

The following new Scenery has been prepared for the occasion:—
The White Tower.
By-Ward Tower
Vaulted Chamber in the White Tower
Interior of Old St. Paul's
in which is seen
The Body of King Henry lying in State
State Chamber in the Tower
Gallery in the Tower.
The Palace!
A Street in London
A Landscape near Tamworth.
Bosworth Field!
Richmond's Camp
Richard's Tent!
Another Part of Bosworth Field
The Battle Field.

The Times of February 6, 1838, again praises the show. "Much care has been taken in getting up the play. The scenery, by the Messrs. Grieve, is beautifully painted. The view of the interior of Old St. Paul's, with the lying in state of Henry VI., forms a very brilliant and imposing scene. It is an immense improvement on the old practice, when a lumbering gingerbread coffin was dragged across the stage.

The dresses are new, and in strict accordance with the costume of the age."

Twenty years afterwards, when Charles Kean was producing his elaborate Shakespearian revivals at the Princess Theatre, the Grieves were his chief scene-painters; they thus bridge times distinctly old with those distinctly modern. Their last service during Kean's first season with Bunn was a complete new setting for Othello, revived on May 16th, with Kean in the title-role. The scenic programme will bear repeating, and sounds very attractive to-day. Unfortunately, I could find no newspaper account of the scenery.

Theatre Royal, Drury Lane
This Evening, Wednesday, May 16th, 1838
Her Majesty's Servants will revive Shakespeare's Tragedy of
Othello
The following is the order of the New, and extensive Scenery,
Painted by
Mr. Grieve, Mr. T. Grieve, and Mr. W. Grieve
The Grand Canal
A Street in Venice
Council Chamber
Sea Port of Cyprus!
Exterior of Guard House
Chamber in the Palace of Cyprus
Apartment in the Palace
The Bed Chamber!

It will be observed that it was in two of the plays with which Macready had had no success—Othello and Hamlet—that Kean had captured the town; in all probability the setting, even, surpassed Macready's. Can one be surprised, then, at Macready's soreness, his disgust at the "conceit [this from Macready!] of this insolent young man"?

MACREADY'S TEMPEST, 1838

It will be remembered that Macready's first great effort during his second season at Covent Garden was The Tempest, first shown on October 13, 1838. This was a great

success, and was given fifty-five times. The Diary of the
day following the production reads: "Could not recover
myself from the excitement of last night. The scenes of
the storm, the flights of Ariel, and the enthusiasm of the
house were constantly recurring to me." Unfortunately,
the King of France having marched his army up the hill,
began now to march them down again. In other words,
John Bull's enthusiasm began materially to abate; began
that now very familiar cry as to whether the poetry of
Shakespeare was not swamped in scenery, and Macready
was made to appear as one reducing poetry to palpable
prose. The sensitive man must have been galled by what
John Bull had to say on October 21, 1838:

> The manner in which the play of *The Tempest* has been produced
> here seems to have commanded universal eulogy from the press. . . .
> Crowded houses, too, and the genuine verdict of heart-sprung applause
> swell the full chorus of Mr. Macready's triumph. Yet we, who till
> now have been foremost with our cheers, are, however reluctantly
> compelled . . . . to express our dissent from the general verdict.
>
> .   .   .   .
>
> The first scene of the play, as now presented, gives the clue to the
> grand mistake which has misled its producer. He has supposed
> that the *material* horrors of the tempest were uppermost in the
> author's thoughts as a means of producing an impression on the
> spectator; and, accordingly, a mimic vessel is outrageously bumped
> and tossed about on waves that we can liken to nothing save tiny
> cocks of hay, painted green, and afflicted with a spasm. . . .
> . . . . In the very next scene, *Prospero* enters by a flight of rocky
> steps, with *Miranda* at his heels, for the sake of a good stage effect.
> . . . . In a similar spirit is the formation of what is termed a pic-
> ture when the two seat themselves, *Prospero* on a high stone couch,
> and *Miranda* on a lesser one at his feet, like a child on a stool. This
> is "affectations." In the same aim at trifling effects, when *Ferdinand*
> is disarmed, . . . the sword is made to fly over his head. . . And we
> may observe that the red fire, Salamander spirits, and trumpery phan-
> tasmagoria . . . are, in our opinion, altogether unwarrantable. . . .
> For into an Easter-piece, and a very indifferent one, has *The Tem-
> pest* been transformed. *Ariel* is whisked about by wires and a cog-
> wheel, like the fairies in Cinderella. . .
>
> .   .   .   .
>
> We repaired to the first representation of the play with high hopes.
> But on witnessing it . . . . . we left with a misgiving that we had

been in the wrong when we advocated the use of scenic resources to their utmost extent, as accessories to the mental triumphs of the stage. Still, remembrances of *Coriolanus*, *Lear*, &c., intervened to prove that provided they are made subservient to the higher purposes of the scene, they do indeed aid the dramatic "illusion."

At any rate, one receives from this account the impression of much material splendour in the production. Probably Priscilla Horton as Ariel, flying about on wires, overtopped the impression created by Helen Faucit as the gentle Miranda. Dryden's Dorinda and Hippolito were gone, but how much worse are these characters than flying wires raised to a stellar magnitude? This is a question too delicate for a mere historian to answer.

MACREADY'S HENRY V, 1839

Macready, finding that Shakespeare (and others), with or without scenery, could not be made to pay, decided to withdraw from the management of Covent Garden. He signalised his retreat by a very elaborate revival of Henry V, restoring the Chorus, now portrayed in the character of Time, and with a panoramic background painted by Clarkson Stanfield. This was the crowning triumph of Macready's career as manager, and was produced on June 10, 1839. He changed his tactics to the extent of the following programme-announcement: "It may be advisable, if not necessary, to depart so far from the custom of the management, as to offer a few words of explanation.

"The play . . is a dramatic history . . and the poet . . . has adopted from the Greek Drama, the expedient of a Chorus to narrate and describe intervening incidents and events.

"To impress more strongly on the audience, and to render more palpable these portions of the story . . . . the narrative and the descriptive poetry spoken by the Chorus, is accompanied with Pictorial Illustrations from the pencil of Mr. Stanfield." Bunn, whose own programme quackery and puffery was proverbial, unjustly seizes upon this instance to show the hypocrisy of his enemy in his former announcement of intention as to such matters.

By the time of this production critics in general were becoming nervous about so much magnificence for Shakespeare; would it kill him, as effectively as in the past he had been killed by lack of suitable adornment? Yet one must admit, said Master Critic, that the show was very fine. Let us read the Times of June 11th, vocal at last, and when its support came too late to save the venture:

COVENT-GARDEN THEATRE

Last night Shakspeare's *Henry V.* was produced with that elaborate magnificence and that minute attention to proprieties of scenery and costume which have characterized the "Shakspearian revivals" as they are called, of this theatre. While, however, we praise the magnificence of the pageant, it must be remembered that it is as a pageant we praise it, and we still retain an opinion formed long ago, that excessive pageantry is no sign of a revival of the drama. . . However great the attempt to represent closely an army on a battle field, still the obviousness of the attempt can only render its fruitlessness more apparent. . . The discrepancy between the stage and reality still remains.

Thus much by way of general reservation. As a scenic spectacle the play of *Henry V.*, as produced last night, merits unqualified praise, and we scarcely know whether most to admire the care, taste, and research displayed in the design, or the beauty of the execution. The most novel and ingenious idea is the accompanying the Chorus (spoken by Vandenhoff in the character of Time) by a succession of painted illustrations by Stanfield. At first the curtain is removed, and discovers another curtain appropriate to the piece, adorned with the arms of England and France, and with a border formed of the escocheons of the principal characters of the piece. When this is withdrawn, Time is discovered upon a circular orifice occupied by clouds, which dissolve away, and present an allegorical scene representing "the warlike Harry," with "famine, sword, and fire at his heels, leashed in like hounds." This scene vanishing, the play begins. The picture that . . . . preceded the second act exhibited Cambridge, Scroop, and Maskam [*sic*] receiving bribes from France. The third act was ushered in by a moving diorama, by far the most splendid piece of scenery presented on the occasion. The English fleet is seen leaving Southampton, its course is traced across the sea, and the audience are gradually brought to the siege of Harfleur. By an ingenious arrangement the business of the act begins before the

TWO SCENES FROM MACREADY'S REVIVAL OF HENRY V

From Scharf's Recollections of the Scenic Effects of Covent Garden Theatre during
the season of 1838–39

diorama has quite passed, and the picture, as it were, melts away into the actual siege by the characters. The grouping, confusion, and truth of this scene is excellently managed. Another moving diorama, representing the French and English camps prior to the battle of Agincourt, introduced the fourth act, and another of the King's triumphal entry into London, brought in the fifth. Here, and indeed the whole of the scenery, was beautifully painted; but the siege of Harfleur was the grand point. The battle of Agincourt produced no effect; a little smoke was made to obscure the stage, and by a pantomime-trick process, the troops painted, as if in the distance, were converted into the same troops engaging. The fault was that the transformation took place immediately before the audience.

An even better description of Stanfield's great effects may be gleaned from a review in the Oddfellow of June 15, 1839:

The second act is introduced by . . . .; the third by a moving diorama (the most splendid piece of machinery we ever saw in a theatre), depicting the voyage of the English fleet to Harfleur, views between which town and that of the place of embarkation (Southampton) form the different subjects. On the ship's arrival at Harfleur, the siege is commenced, and while it is thus being represented, the curtain is raised, and the action of the opening scene describes the same thing. If, out of the many excellencies which were so obvious, any particular one can be extracted for more commendation . . . it is assuredly this portion of the piece. The melting away of the pictorial into the real siege was truly wonderful; and the transition was managed with such consummate skill, that it was utterly impossible for any one to detect the precise moment at which either the one ended, or the other commenced.

John Bull, now converted to its theory that too much scenery was worse than no feast, felt called on to praise with a very exalted sense of its own superiority. I confess that this kind of criticism has always wearied me; it is so very easy to produce, and is generally founded on the intense personal conceit of the writer. *He* could do so much better himself; *he* knows exactly what the public wants, etc. At any rate, John Bull declares on June 17, 1839:

The battle of Agincourt, which there is no reason for bringing on the stage, is represented by a pantomimic trick; the scene changing, as by the wave of Harlequin's wand, from a champaign to a field of battle strewed with the dead and dying; and to make the matter worse, the painting is so indifferent, or so indistinct, that it is only by a stretch of fancy one can make out the artist's intent. So far has this rage for over-embellishing his author led Mr. Macready that at the conclusion of the fourth act, which ends with these words, spoken by *King Henry*—

> Do we all holy rites;
> Let there be sung *Non nobis* and *Te Deum*, etc.

the actor literally kneels down with his soldiery, and the curtain falls to the solemn strains of an organ, brought from England we suppose for the purpose. . . .

Too much praise cannot be given to the appointments of the play; to the general fidelity of the costume; or to the general beauty of the scenery, which, however, is very unequally painted. The artist's *chef-d'œuvre*, to our eye, is the field of Agincourt, with the camp fires by moonlight. Such a sky we never saw on canvass [*sic*] before— 'tis the firmament indeed. The interiors are given in strict accordance with the authorities for the period, and take the imagination back at once to the time. Mr. Macready has cared for neither expense nor labour to do homage to his author, and we honour him for it. We are only sorry that his zeal has outstripped his discretion, and that he who has shown so much taste and discrimination in other things should have erred so grossly in this. In fact, he has gilded the refin'd gold.

LOVE'S LABOUR'S LOST, 1839

Perhaps, in view of such tempered critical mercy to his efforts, Macready might have felt justified in handing over to other hands the obligation of producing Shakespeare on a scale of elegance in accordance with his deserts. His successors at Covent Garden were the younger Mathews and his brilliant wife, Madame Vestris. Of their opening attraction, Love's Labour's Lost, John Bull gives a good account on October 7, 1839. Drury Lane being a chaos, at present, the Grieves transferred their services to the rival house. Says John Bull:

The performances were Shakspeare's comedy of *Love's Labours Lost*, and a new farce called *Alive and Merry*. The scenery in the first was excellent; being from the practised pencil of the Grieves. Its gem was a little rustic background with a pool in front, which

might have been painted by Stanfield or Roberts. The opening
scene, however, which displays the whole stage, and gives a reach
of country far as the eyes can carry, will be the favourite of the mil-
lion; and, put to the general vote, would carry the day against the
finest scenic efforts which we remember to have seen of those eminent
artists. The costume is equally correct and gorgeous; the stage
arrangements neatly devised; the acting, we speak collectively, miserable.

A MIDSUMMER NIGHT'S DREAM, 1840

"The acting miserable"; and the critic was speaking of
the efforts of Anderson, Cooper, Harley, Keeley, Madame
Vestris and Mrs. Nisbett, people we have been taught to
reverence as among the finest of their age! Verily no critic
can project himself far into the future! Passing this phase
of the subject, we arrive at the great production of the
second season of the Mathews-Vestris *régime*—the epoch-
making restoration to the stage of something very like
Shakespeare's own Midsummer Night's Dream. Of the
preparations for this J. R. Planché, who adapted the play
and designed the last great scene, furnishes the best account. He says:

A third important revival was Shakespere's "Midsummer Night's
Dream" on a scale of great splendour, and for the first time with
the overture, wedding march, and other music by Mendelssohn.
When this revival was first suggested, Bartley said, "If Planché can
devise a striking effect for the last scene, the play will run for sixty
nights." I pointed out that Shakspere had suggested it himself,
in the words of Oberon to his attendant fairies—

"Through the house give glimmering light,

.   .   .   .

Every elf and fairy sprite
Hop as light as bird from brier,
And this ditty after me
Sing, and dance it trippingly."

It was accordingly arranged with Grieve, the scenic artist . . . .
that the back of the stage should be so constructed that at the command of Oberon it should be filled with fairies, bearing twinkling
coloured lights, "flitting through the house," and forming groups and
dancing, as indicated in the text, carrying out implicitly the direc-

tions of the author, and not sacrilegiously attempting to gild his refined gold. The result was most successful, and verified Bartley's prediction.

It will furnish food for conjecture to examine the scenic version of Mme. Vestris's Dream, as printed in Volume 28 of Lacy's Acting Plays:

Act I, Sc. 1.	Hall in the Palace of Theseus—with view of Athens.
Sc. 2.	Room in Quince's Cottage.
Act II, Sc. 1.	Moonlight landscape—High sloping bank, 3 E. R.— Small made-out bank against it. do. R. C. up stage. do. 4 E. L.—flowery bank, 4 E. L., fireflies, etc.
Sc. 2.	The previous scene works off gradually and discovery [sic] another part of the wood.
Act III, Sc. 1.	Moonlight—transparent wood—platform colored and rising ground, crossing from the back, R. Water piece joining it and running off L.—[In the course of this scene occurs the stage direction: The moon sinks very gradually; the rays disappear from tops of the trees; daylight continues to increase until the lights are full on].
Act IV, Sc. 1.	The Wood.—Titania's bower—sloping bank, 3 E. R., with Slote and concealed bower.
Sc. 2.	Room in Quince's house.
Sc. 3.	The transparent Wood, as in Act III, Sc. 1, which changes to sunlight.
Act V.	Hall of statues, with raised stage in the centre hung R. the back with curtains. Couch R. and two Grecian stools—two do. chairs, L. . . . Change to another part of the Palace—staircases, R. and L. —raised stage to form a staircase and platform centre—smaller staircases lead from the platform to side stairs—gallery running along the back from R. to L.—Parisian lanterns of various colored paper for all the fairies.

At the same time that this revival killed the tendency to alter and re-write Shakespeare's fairy play, it also brought into being the now generally accepted practice of mounting it with historical accuracy as to costume (supposedly Athenian) with corresponding architecture, furniture, etc.

This one learns from the ever-helpful John Bull of November 23, 1840:

This reclamation apart, and a little grumbling at the prudery which has changed the Indian boy . . from a slim youth . . into a little child with an uncommonly dirty head of hair . . . . these petty and invidious murmurs apart, and apart, too, unqualified condemnation of a ballet most injudiciously and unnecessarily introduced, *A Midsummer Night's Dream* has at length been put on the stage in a style which must satisfy the most fastidious voluptuary in scenic art.

The locality of the play is well marked by a magnificent view of Athens in the first scene; the fairy haunts follow, green, fresh, and sylvan; and the concluding scene of this rainbow-coloured vision is perfectly magical. Yet we are inclined to think, with reference to the production of the entire play, that an occasional preference of the suggestive to the actual would be more in keeping with the fairy texture of the drama, and would take greater hold of the fancy. Were, for instance, the change to this brilliant last scene preceded by a complete darkening of the theatre, the fairies but to show themselves torch in hand in all points as suddenly to vanish, and to leave each pilaster, frieze, architrave, and cornice distinctly outlined in glow-worm light, the conclusion, with the exception of the epilogue to be sung off the stage, and *Puck*, to speak the epilogue but half advancing from some leafy capital . . . . the obtruding sense of the similarity of this scene, gorgeous as it is, to the finale of a ballet at the Opera, would at least be avoided. . . .

The costume for the most part rests upon authority, and is as correct as the scenery of the Grieves is beautiful; yet authority might be found for dresses falling in more graceful lines than those worn by *Demetrius* and *Lysander*, and the Amazonian garb put on *Hippolyta*, whatever Etruscan vase may say to the contrary, might advantageously, and at least with equal correctness, be exchanged for a more becoming as well as a more modest costume. The fairies are clad . . . in virgin white, and immaculate silk stockings. For the benefit of our lady readers, we may explain that the porringers or straw baskets which hang at the back of *Demetrius* and others, are *petasi* or hats.

Mme. Vestris's labours for Shakespeare ended, practically, with this production; both the time and she were out of joint for such efforts. I believe she will go down in theatrical history as the woman who produced London Assurance with a profusion of modern drawing-room appurtenances—

furniture, draperies, carpets, ottomans, etc. She has also been said to be the first—and in this very comedy—to introduce a "box-scene" on the London stage.

MACREADY AT DRURY LANE, 1841–1843

The last consistent effort in this period to make special "productions" of Shakespearian plays was Macready's in his two years of management at Drury Lane, terminating in the spring of 1843. In his first year, The Merchant of Venice, which began the belated season on December 27, 1841, and the seldom-acted Two Gentlemen of Verona, on December 29th, were splendidly mounted. Of the first of these, Mr. William Archer in his life of Macready states that "for the first time (so far as I know) in the case of a Shakspearian revival, a synopsis of the scenery was issued —an honour hitherto reserved for pantomime and spectacular drama. Even now the list of scenes found no place on the play-bill, but was relegated to a small fly-leaf." The reader will remember that many synopses of scenes for Shakespearian revivals had been printed on playbills of the last twenty years or more, though they were not so printed during Macready's occupation of Covent Garden. But, as we learn from the review in the Times, these synopses were now distributed on little bills to the audience.

THE MERCHANT OF VENICE

The critics were unanimous in praise of Macready's settings for his first two Shakespearian productions; apparently he had taken a lesson, and was careful not to overdo. His scenery, though excellent, was not allowed to take precedence of the drama and the poetry. John Bull, regarding The Merchant of Venice, assumes a very lordly and patronising tone; the article was meant to be corrective of vulgar public taste, and the critic could not deign to describe scenes. On January 3, 1842, therefore, he merely states that "all the accessories of *The Merchant of Venice* were in good taste—properly subdued, yet sufficiently prominent, brilliant and elegant as the dialogue they illustrated— aiding the general effect without in any part interfering with or overlaying the poetic purpose of the drama; and having notified thus much, we will now pass from these minor matters to consider the play itself together with the present stage version of it."

The Times, having ignored, as we have seen, a great part of Macready's initial effort of four years previously, now thunders forth approval. On December 28, 1841, it gives us as much material as we could possibly desire, which I reproduce with the remark that I am amazed such effects could be accomplished in that day and generation:

The scenery is in the best possible taste, very beautiful, and yet nicely discriminated, so as not to overbalance the drama. The effect of the tribunal, with the forty, was most imposing, reminding us of that produced by the Roman Senate in Mr. Macready's revival of *Coriolanus*. The moonlit garden in the fifth act is particularly beautiful, sparkling with soft light, and melting away into a poetic indistinctness at the back. To give every completeness to the plays at this house, little bills are gratuitously distributed, containing descriptions of the scenery, with a short notice of the usages of the time in which the dramatic action is supposed to occur. We give as a specimen, the one distributed for the *Merchant of Venice*.

The costume of the play, in its present revival, is that of the 16th Century.

Act I. Scene 1,—Venice. The Church and Place of St. Mark.— Marshall.

Scene 2. Interior of Portia's House on the mainland.— Tomkins.

Act II, Scene 1.—Venice. Shylock's house on the canal, with distant view of the Campanile.—Marshall.

Scene 2. The interior of Shylock's House, looking out upon the Canal and the Dogana.—Marshall.

Scene 3. Venice. The Church and Place of St. John and St. Paul.—Marshall.

Act III. Scene 3.—Venice. The Gates of the Arsenal.—Tomkins.

Scene 4. Vestibule of Portia's House on the Mainland.— Marshall.

[*Scenes 1 and 2 of this act are not specified in the Times.*]

Act IV. Scene 1.—Venice. A Court of Justice. The arms on the tribunal of Venice and her tributary states Istria, Candia, Cyprus, Dalmatia, &c.—Marshall.

In Venice, the tribunal for criminal cases and two others were composed of forty judges, ordinarily presided over by one of three selected from the council of the Doge, and draughted for the most part, if not wholly, from the members of the Senate.

The Doge, on all public occasions, was attended by his particular officers, knight, esquires, captains, heralds, &c. The right of sitting in the councils and on the tribunals was among his privileges.

Act V. The Garden of Portia's Palace on the mainland. —Tomkins.

THE TWO GENTLEMEN OF VERONA

In regard to The Two Gentlemen of Verona, we are left considerably more in the dark. Our wise guides have lost (in two days) their youthful enthusiasm, and return to their earlier note of immense superiority to such gewgaws. Besides, as they both say, Macready was toning down very considerably. More praise at less expense was not a bad idea for him. Of the revival in question, the Times on December 30th says: "Some beautiful scenery was introduced, but not so as to overlay the drama. A new and splendid curtain made its first appearance last night. It is of crimson velvet, with a broad gold fringe, and ornamented with large gold wreaths of laurel." John Bull, on January 10th, agrees: "As to scenery, it was admirably put upon the stage—quite enough was done and yet not too much. All was excellent taste, controlled by sound judgment in this respect. The dresses, also, though in some particulars almost grotesque, and as a whole apparently hardly in unison, were nevertheless smart, cleanly, and not unpleasant in effect. The characters were, in truth, rather underdressed (for the comedy in its spirit seems to demand a gay costume) particularly so in the case of Lucetta."

By the time the second season began, both of these papers were in a far more "coming-on" disposition, if not quite in holiday mood. On Saturday, October 1, 1842, Macready brought out what seems to have been a really beautiful revival of As You Like It, perhaps the first carefully considered "production" the play ever had. He established throughout a certain effect, which, for lack of a better name, we may designate by the much-abused word "atmosphere." The Times of October 3rd is very explicit:

Mr. Macready commenced his second season here on Saturday, to all appearances resolved to carry it on in the same spirit . . . . . as in the former one. Revivals of both plays and music invested with all the charms of Stanfield's scenery, and every other accessory to stage effect which can be devised, and entrusted to a most complete company . . . . form the staple motive of attraction. . . .

. . . . The songs interspersed in the piece, of which not one was omitted, were all most effectively executed. . . .

. . . And now let us say a word about one of the greatest features of the performance—namely the scenery and "getting up," than which nothing could be more admirable, and, in the minutest particular, more complete. Every scene was a complete picturesque study, and above all the wrestling scene deserves mention, in which the new effect was introduced of including the space where the wrestlers encounter with ropes and staves, round which the courtiers and spectators stand, pressing eagerly forward, watching every movement of the combatants. The effect of this was most vivid, and the natural manner of the two wrestlers through every vicissitude of the struggle elicited shouts of applause.

What is probably a reproduction of this really exquisite scene, I offer for the delectation of the reader.

KING JOHN, 1842

King John followed on October 24, 1842, and was Macready's last attempt at a complete staging of a Shakespearian play. This was a very elaborate spectacle, probably the most expensive and exhaustive during his tenure of Drury Lane. It would seem to have carried to the extreme of perfection the correctness of detail established by Charles Kemble in Planché's re-mounting of the same play in 1823. The Times of the 25th gives us assurance of the beauty of the show:

The revival of *King John* last night is, taken as a whole, a great work. Mr. Macready has brought before the eyes of his audience an animated picture of those Gothic times which are so splendidly illustrated by the drama. The stage is thronged with the stalwart forms of the middle ages. The clang of battle sounds behind the scenes, massive fortresses bound the horizon. The grouping is admirably managed. The mailed figures now sink into tranquillity; now, when the martial fire touches them, they rouse from their lethargy, and thirst for action. The sudden interruption in the third act to the temporary peace between John and Philip Augustus was a fine instance of the power of making the stage a living picture. The Englishmen and Frenchmen who had mingled together parted with the rapidity of lightning, the hurried movements, the flashing swords, bespoke the turbulent spirit of the old barons. A quiet mass of glittering accoutrements had suddenly burst into new combinations of animation and energy. To the smallest *minutiæ* was this attention to what may be called the decorative characters of the piece directed. The citizens of Angiers, who watched the conflict from their walls, and whose countenances eagerly followed the various movements in the distance may be mentioned as a minor instance of excellent training for a complete effect. There was much beautiful scenery in the piece. The fortified town of Angiers, the castle from which Arthur leaps, solidly constructed edifices, the various scenes of battle-fields, were all bold and strongly characteristic.

.   .   .   .

King John is a "hit." Macready announced it for repetition twice a week amid vociferous applause, and the principal actors were called for.

The cast, I may break my not unbreakable rule by saying, was exceptionally strong, Macready appearing as the King, Phelps as Hubert, Anderson as Faulconbridge, and Helen Faucit as Constance.

It may be well to quote from John Bull of October 31st, if only to learn the name of the scenic artist, Telbin, later of great fame in Charles Kean's heyday:

The play has been put upon the stage with the utmost liberality. Every scene, and apparently every dress is new. Good taste directs

SCENE FROM AS YOU LIKE IT, AT DRURY LANE THEATRE
From an engraving by T. H. Ellis after a drawing by T. H. Shepherd

profuseness, and while more is done than was absolutely necessary
for effect, in no instance does a mistaken zeal overlay what it pre-
tends to embellish. . .

The new scenery is painted by Mr. Telbin—the first appearance,
we think, of this artist's talent on the stage of a National Theatre.
He has fancy in design . . . breadth of style . . . and a force . .
in which he has no equal.

The dresses were tasteful and characteristic. The exuberances of
the period were judiciously softened down, while the prevalent features were retained.

The very best description of the effects accomplished is
to be found in the remarks on the production prefixed to
the Lacy edition of the play—probably Macready's stage-
version. I quote this entire:

We have had nothing so great as the revival of this play. In the
first scene, King John appears enthroned and surrounded by his
barons, hurling defiance at the French King; the Gothic hall being
hung with tapestry, but above showing the bare stone walls, adorned
with only a canopy over the chair of state, and the carved timbers of
the roof, exhibiting the rude pomp of elder days. In the next scene,
the chivalry of France and England, arrayed in the glittering panoply
of war, meet before the gates of Angiers; the lofty ramparts and bas-
tions of the town, stretching out in dim perspective along the river's
bank, frown defiance on the rival forces; and while the two monarchs
hold parley with the citizens on the walls, we have full opportunity
to note the details of this sumptuous and striking scene. The quaint
heraldic devices on the shields and surcoats of the Knights, enliven
with their gaudy hues the glitter of their coats of mail; the regal
habiliments of the Kings, the flowing robes of the ladies, the parti-
coloured habits of the ladies, and the flaunting banners adding a
brighter glow to this warlike pomp; the host of warriors are in frequent action, and the shifting of the throng, as each party advance
and retire, produces new combinations of colour that prevent the
eye from being fatigued. In the succeeding scenes the Pope's Legate
swells the pageant with the pomp of the Romish church, and brings
new elements of discord into play: the grief of Constance now casts
a shade of gloom over the dazzling scene; and the subsequent entrance
of King Philip, defeated and cast down, attended by a few dejected
followers, prepare the way for the catastrophe of Arthur's death.
The contrast of this and the following scenes with those that have
gone before, is striking to the most careless observer: John is seen
again enthroned, but shorn alike of pomp and power; his abasement

before the Pope's Legate is followed by a second defeat in his own kingdom, his death by poison concluding the tragedy.

In this revival, the accoutrements are complete, from the helmet to the spur of each mailed warrior. Not a distinction is missed in the appointments. From citizen to baron, gentleman to knight, soldier to servant, priest to King, gradations are marked with picturesque exactness. The scenery has had the same attention. The council-room, the field before and after battle, the fortifications of Angiers, the moated and embattled fortress of Northampton, the glitter of the royal tent, the gloom of Swinstead Abbey—they have all the character of truth, the character of simple and strong fidelity.

May I be permitted to end with a brief account of the very last dying gasp of Covent Garden at the beginning of Macready's last season at Drury Lane? John Bull of November 14, 1842, speaks of a revival of The Tempest, during the brief, inglorious management that had just succeeded the Mathews-Vestris failure. This management lasted but a few months and with it the noble history of Covent Garden as a theatre for plays practically ceased. According to John Bull, the spectacular Tempest in Covent Garden dead surpassed that of Covent Garden, dying, under Macready:

The first scene discovered a huge vessel, fully rigged and manned, tossed about on a tempestuous ocean. The size of the ship, and the ingenuity with which it was managed, now rising so as to discover the keel, and then dipping to the level of the stage, seeming to sink into the mimic waters, rendered the effect particularly real, to which the ease with which the apparently weighty machine was worked, and the facility with which it tacked about, helped to contribute. . . . . Simply regarded as a piece of mechanism, the invention, for the fidelity with which it realised its intent, was wonderful, and the tumult of applause its exhibition elicited fully deserved. . . . Mr. Macready omitted [in his performance of two years before] the dialogue, and presented only the ship—which was managed in a very inferior manner—indeed there is no comparison to be made in that respect. On the present occasion the dialogue is spoken, yet— is more than the ship presented?

.   .   .   .

The scenery is all new, and in its character altogether higher than that employed to illustrate the same piece formerly. The luxuriance of the foliage, and the boldness of the eminences suggest a tropical climate, but care has been judiciously taken not to define any particular locality. The mechanical changes were also improved upon —and the last scene of the fourth act made more impressive by adherence to the author's design.

This is the end of my scenical song, up to the freedom of the theatres. I have traced, so far as I could from the material at my disposal, the development from the stock scenery of earlier previous generations to the complete "production" of Macready's time, in which every detail was scrutinised with an eye to unity of effect. So far as I can see, Macready's King Lear, Coriolanus, Tempest and King John were as carefully planned and executed as one of Irving's later revivals. The difference in effect in the latter's performance was largely due to greater facilities of lighting, archæological research and higher development of public taste. But granting all this, Macready was trying to do just what Irving tried to do—to present Shakespeare with the greatest possible beauty and appropriateness of decoration.

One improvement remains to be noted—the introduction, during the last years of this period, of the lime-light. This highly important innovation has been ascribed to the year 1855, the occasion of Charles Kean's Henry VIII, but J. R. Anderson told Mr. W. J. Lawrence (Notes and Queries, Seventh Series, vol. VIII) that he distinctly remembered the use of this revolutionising adjunct during Macready's incumbency of Covent Garden in 1837–38. Macready, to be sure, soon gave up the luxury, because of its expense (30s. a night!), but the essential thing is that the lime-light was utilised somewhere toward the close of the Macready régime.

BOOK VII

THE AGE OF PHELPS AND CHARLES KEAN
(1843–1879)

CHAPTER XXVII

THE FREEDOM OF THE THEATRES

THE ACT OF 1843

THE passing of Macready from the management of Drury Lane synchronised with the passing of the glories of the two great patent theatres. The conviction had long been strengthening that these theatres were too large for thorough understanding, not to say enjoyment, of the spoken word, and this, together with increasing speculation by inartistic managers and increasing public zest for spectacle, song and dance, drove the bark of monopoly at last on the rocks. Earnest reformers, also, agitated the principle of a free theatre, unhampered by legal convention, and preached the educative value of drama to be given wherever an audience could be induced to gather within the walls of a theatre. London had become too large to draw through the heart of Covent Garden and Drury Lane all the life-blood that flowed in constantly extending suburbs undreamt of by the inhabitants of Mayfair and the City. Macready, as we have seen, advocated in his farewell address at Drury Lane the revoking of the exclusive monopoly of the patent theatres. A few months later his advice was carried out by Parliament, and, from 1843, any theatre was free to produce Shakespearian and other "legitimate" plays, under only such jurisdiction as was demanded by a respect for public safety.

No longer, thereafter, was it necessary, as at Garrick's début in 1741, to "sandwich" a play between the two parts of a concert, or, as in Elliston's day at the Surrey (in 1809), to convert Macbeth into a *ballet d'action*, in order to give the manager an opportunity of performing the character of

237

the witch-driven Thane. Nor was any outlying theatre again compelled, as was the Royal Coburg on February 14th, of a year unspecified in the bill to which I have access, to attract an audience by the announcement of "a Grand and Terrific Historical Caledonian Drama, founded on Shakespeare's sublime Tragedy of Macbeth, interspersed with Characteristic National Marches, Chorusses, Combats, and Processions, entitled, The Fatal Prophecy! or, the Scottish Regicide." Not that the humble south-suburban Coburg was attempting anything different in kind from what one nightly saw at the more exclusive Theatres Royal. It merely wore its rue with a difference more crude; a cruel law and a melodrama-loving audience pounded its art into something a little coarse for human nature's daily food in the West End. Hamlet, I find by the bill of February 4, 1828, was converted by the Coburg into a "New Grand Serious Drama, in Three Acts," and, in order to quiet official nerves, the management gravely announced that "this Piece is not an alteration or adaptation of Shakespeare's admirable Tragedy of the same name, the Language, Incidents, and in many respects, the Plot, being wholly different. It is partly founded on the celebrated French Tragedy by Ducis, and partly on a French Serio Pantomime from the same story. . . . It is confidently hoped, that from these materials has been produced a Melo-Drama, possessed of as powerful an Interest, and as abundant of striking Incident, impressive Situation, and terrific Effect, as any that has hitherto appeared." No doubt the Coburg would have preferred to produce Shakespeare pure and undiluted, but what could one do in sight of the authorities?

Even before the act of 1843 there had been more or less open defiance of the law. Alfred Bunn, to whom we are so largely indebted for information concerning this period, informs us that "one Mr. Rayner, who had opened a theatre in the Strand, defied the Duke of Devonshire, and had refused to obey the King's own commands to close it, now received a formal license. The Haymarket Theatre, whose license of four months had grown into one of eight, now obtained an extension of two more, and by virtue thereof completed a season of ten months." The annual licenses of the English Opera House were extended; also those of the Adelphi and Olympic Theatres. Obviously, with managers refusing to obey the law, even when the officers of the law preluded their commands with a "Please!" and with the officers of the law themselves extending theatrical privileges at a rate ruinous to the monopoly, there was nothing to do but throw the legal fiction into the dust-heap, and let the drama sweep on unhindered through channels never conceived of in the days of Kemble and Edmund Kean.

THE PASSING OF COVENT GARDEN AND DRURY LANE

With the withdrawal of their government props the two royal houses at once collapsed, thereby proving what their opponents had so long maintained. Covent Garden had a few months longer as a home of the drama; in 1847 it became permanently an opera house, and Melpomene and Thalia became merged into Calliope and Terpsichore. Drury Lane, immediately after the withdrawal of Macready, fell into the hands of his inveterate enemy Alfred Bunn. For some years he, too, turned the great national theatre to what stage-historians regard as the base uses of opera; here the undying Bohemian Girl with Balfe's music and Bunn's own words was produced, as well as Wallace's Maritana. Only in 1844 did Bunn revert to the glories of the past; in that year Charles Kean played here the usual Shakespearian and classic repertoire, and with a success as gratifying as it was unexpected. But four years later Bunn brought in (at Garrick's Drury Lane!) the Cirque National, from the Champs Elysées, and exterminated thereby both himself and the theatre of England's fondest hope. The best two seasons for a decade or two were those of the management of James Anderson (1850–51). They were very unsuccessful financially, nearly bringing Anderson to ruin, but at least they brought no blush of shame to his cheek. Anderson, distinguished product of the Macready school, opened in January, 1850, and produced As You Like It, Othello, Julius Cæsar, and other Shakespearian pieces, with the usual accompaniment of Sheridan Knowles and others of his school. Finding the fare apparently innutritious to the treasury, in his second year he made an elaborate production of Azael, the Prodigal, founded on Scribe and Auber's L'enfant Prodigue. The spectacular glory of this, and the dramatic success of Ingomar, first produced at this time, made up a large part of this latter season. Anderson kept the theatre open for 232 nights, and lost £9,161. He was followed by an American circus, that made thousands of pounds. Verily, the dark days of Drury Lane seemed unilluminable.

The theatre passed through many managements, three in succession lasting a week each. Finally, E. T. Smith, a publican, an ex-policeman and an artistic sinner, acquired the lease for £3,500, and, in 1852, opened with Uncle Tom's Cabin. He was in possession for about ten years, furnishing any pabulum the kitchens supplied. It would be unfair to say that none of the feast was palatable to sensitive appetites. Occasionally Shakespeare emerged in due course, but not with the air of one on his native heath. The most interesting items I find in a none too exhaustive study of programmes of the period show Gustavus Vaughan Brooke appearing here in the autumn of 1853 in his usual parts— Othello, Shylock, Richard III, etc., supported by the American actor, E. L. Davenport, who for several seasons had been a strong feature of the London theatres. Helen Faucit, the perennial, had been at Drury Lane the year preceding, in her usual repertoire of Shakespeare and Bulwer, but, for years thereafter, the famous old theatre could hardly hold up its head, artistically, among the rapidly increasing London playhouses. Not until the *régime* of F. B. Chatterton (1864–79) did anything like the former splendour hover above the stage of Old Drury. We leave it, now, to pass to the real leaders among the theatres of the first days of freedom for all.

RISE OF NEW THEATRES

For the years from 1843, until Samuel Phelps deserted Sadler's Wells in 1862, the last-named theatre and the Princess's in Oxford Street were unquestionably the scenes of the greatest glory of Shakespeare. At Sadler's Wells for eighteen years Phelps established a Shakespearian record that still endures, and at the Princess's from 1850 to 1859 Charles Kean raised his banner above the walls of the Philistines, and made the finest productions, scenically, of Shakespeare witnessed up to that time; he very clearly handed on the torch to Henry Irving of blessed memory. These two houses were pre-eminently the home of Shakespeare in London, so long as they lasted under the managements I have mentioned, and to their achievements the present part of my chronicle must be largely devoted; but other theatres bore their part in early and mid-Victorian history and will receive treatment in the pages that follow.

As might have been foreseen, the liberty of the theatres brought at first a kind of license (not in the censor's meaning of the word). Too many of the former "minor" theatres boldly stepped into the ranks of the major, and surfeited the public with excess of the "legitimate." Of these, within reasonable hearing distance of Bow Bells, were the Olympic, in Wych Street, and the Princess's aforesaid (before the days of Charles Kean). Farther away, to the north, was the Theatre Royal, Marylebone, and to the south, the Surrey, a very unfashionable but well-meaning place which proved through many years that even Cinderella could wear Shakespearian slippers. It was really a sort of combination-house for itinerant stars, whom it supported with its more or less competent stock-company. All these things now seem very far away, and their glory withers before the steady fame of Sadler's Wells, the Princess's under Charles Kean, and the Haymarket under Benjamin Webster. But they must receive due notice.

I may close preliminaries by stating that the multiplying of the theatres was both the cause and the effect of a cir-

cumstance inherent in the withdrawal of patent rights from
the big theatres. Many actors attached to those patent-
houses, from Macready, Phelps, Mrs. Warner and Helen
Faucit to minor "great" ones, found themselves without
permanent employment, and naturally drifted from one
theatre to another, filling star engagements, whether in town
or country. Hence the need of many theatres; hence,
equally, the need of many stars. Hence lamentations as
well, by the oldest inhabitant of pit or gallery, as to the
vast superiority of former days over these purposeless,
meaningless times, in which we most do congregate and
grumble.

THE HAYMARKET

For ten years after 1843 the Haymarket was the most
fashionable theatre in London. Opened in 1821 on a site
next door to that occupied by the Little Theatre in the
Haymarket, which we have known for just one hundred
years, the Haymarket now to be discussed had grown vastly
in popularity and had, as we have just learned, been allowed,
a year or two before 1843, to extend its season to ten
months, in direct opposition to the original rights of Drury
Lane and Covent Garden. In 1837 it came under the
management of that excellent actor and gentleman, Benjamin Webster, by whom, till his retirement in 1853, it was
raised to its topmost fame. The history of this delightful
theatre for the first ten years of the freedom of the theatres
is—except for that of Sadler's Wells—the most pleasing to
be chronicled in the present chapter. Certainly it is the
most charming, though the history of the Princess's for the
years immediately following 1853 is more splendid.

The bill for the opening of the season on April 17, 1843,
seems to indicate that Webster was already anticipating
the new day to be inaugurated shortly after by the passage
of the act granting freedom of production to all theatres.
The advertisement is a perfect forest of capital letters, exclamation points, and promises of good things to come.
"During the recess," we are informed, "the theatre has

undergone Extensive Alterations, the Proscenium has been entirely remodelled, and the whole of the Interior decorated in the most Costly and Elegant Style! By a curtailment of the useless portion of the Stage in front of the Curtain [goodbye, apron!], and advancing Orchestra and Lights near the Actors and Scenic Effects, the Lessee has been enabled to appropriate the portion so obtained, to form a certain number of Orchestra Stalls, which can be retained for the parties taking them the whole of the Evening."

This curtailment of the "apron" and consequent sequestration of part of the pit for orchestra stalls that could be "reserved," strikes me as the most modern note found in my journey through hundreds, possibly thousands of playbills of the London theatres. I wonder how the "pittites" felt about the invasion of their democratic domain by those aristocratic stalls? Were they consoled by the announcement immediately following that, "for the comfort of those visiting the Pit, backs have been placed to all the Seats"? Was this really a sop to surly Cerberus?

At any rate, all, "stalled" and "backed" equally, could rejoice in the subsequent notice that "among the most important Improvements, is the introduction (for the first time) of Gas as the Medium of Light! A Brilliant Centre Chandelier has been erected [why not *suspended*, O Benjamin?]," etc. There is more glorious rhetoric on the bill, giving the names of the artisans and artists who installed these wonders, but I hasten to what, after all, is far more important, the roster of the amazingly brilliant company engaged for the season, far more brilliant, though not less virtuous, than Sadler's Wells could ever afford, or Charles Kean's Princess's, either, for that matter. Madame Vestris, Madame Celeste, Mrs. Glover, Julia Bennett (afterwards the well-liked Julia Bennett Barrow of the Boston theatres), William Farren, Charles Mathews, Buckstone and Webster were the leaders; Charles Kean was engaged for a limited starring engagement, and in the autumn Mrs. Nisbett appeared.

This company (excepting Kean) it will be observed was

best fitted for comedy, and it may be said at once that the Haymarket through a large part of the ten years of its glory under Webster was most noted for its productions of Sheridan, Goldsmith, Colman the elder and Colman the younger, Holcroft, Morton, etc. Modern comedy of refined quality was also produced, but throughout the period of Webster's management, Shakespeare and the "legitimate" tragic writers were frequently acted only by great stars on protracted visits. Kean was the first of these visitors, and on June 12, 1843, appeared as Hamlet, with Mrs. Warner (specially engaged) as the Queen, Julia Bennett as Ophelia, and Howe, who came to America in 1883 with Henry Irving, as Claudius. During his engagement Kean went through his regular classic repertoire. But, without "stars," Webster early began to "do" Shakespeare occasionally. The Merry Wives enjoyed a long run from January 10th to February 19th, 1844, with Madame Vestris and Mrs. Nisbett as the merry ones, Mathews as Slender, Webster as Evans, etc. On March 16th of the same year came an amazing revival of The Taming of the Shrew, "from the original text," Induction and all, and "as acted divers times at the Globe and Blackfriars Playhouses," that is, without scenery, in the modern sense of the word, and with something approximating the stage conventions of the Elizabethan time. "Amazing" is the only adjective suitable to express my surprise at the discovery of this incident, so far in advance of our present efforts toward such a method of presenting Shakespeare on the stage.

These successful experiments with Shakespeare may have been the cause of the considerable enlargement of the stage noted on the playbill for the opening of the second season, September 30, 1844; if so, at the beginning, old comedies beautifully played made this house, nevertheless, more like the famous Wallack's of the third quarter of the Nineteenth Century in New York, rather than like the Shakespearian theatre the last season might have led one to expect it would be. In the autumn of 1845, however, Shakespeare came into his own again. Helen Faucit and James Anderson joined Webster's forces on October 20th, and, though the original Pauline naturally opened in The Lady of Lyons, she was playing Rosalind on November 5th. This was as nothing, however, to the sensation of December 29th, when Charlotte and Susan Cushman appeared as Romeo and Juliet, "from the text of Shakespeare," and inaugurated a run that was to carry them, three nights a week, nearly throughout the season. On June 25th they appeared as Viola and Olivia in a special production of Twelfth Night, Buckstone and Webster appearing as Sir Andrew and the Clown, respectively. Romeo and Juliet was played for the last time on July 11th.

I must hurry to the end. The season of 1846–47 contains no Shakespeare, but 1847–48 and 1848–49 were banner years for the bard. Helen Faucit, Mr. and Mrs. Charles Kean, Mrs. Nisbett and other notabilities joined the company. The Taming of the Shrew was repeated; Mrs. Kean made a great hit as Viola on November 11, 1848, and on December 14th, she and her husband appeared in a beautiful revival of The Two Gentlemen of Verona. Later in the season, elaborate productions introduced the same distinguished stars in Hamlet, The Merchant of Venice, Othello, etc. The supporting company included J. W. Wallack, founder of Wallack's Theatre in New York, and Laura Addison, who had just left Sadler's Wells.

For the opening of the season of 1850–51, Webster announced a veritable galaxy: Macready, Mrs. Warner, the Keans, Mrs. Nisbett, Wallack, Webster, Buckstone, Keeley, Priscilla Horton, etc. They all appeared (Macready and the Keans not together, but in successive brief seasons) in many memorable performances of Shakespeare. The last notable Shakespearian season of Webster was that of Macready's farewells to the stage in the autumn of 1850, during which he appeared for the first time in his career as Richard II and played all his great parts many, many times. He was supported by E. L. Davenport and the inevitable, useful Mrs. Warner. In the spring and summer of 1851 J. H. Hackett met success as Falstaff in The Merry Wives of Windsor. With Charlotte and Susan Cushman, Mrs. Mowatt, Hackett and Davenport gloriously succeeding on the London stage in these years, the American invasion might be described as "on" in full force. One of the latest of the new arrivals on the stage of Webster's Haymarket was Barry Sullivan, whose Hamlet (February 7, 1852) set London a-quiver with its eccentricity of reading.

Webster retired from the management in 1853. At his benefit, on March 14th, he said, somewhat pathetically, before the curtain, "Those who remember this theatre when I first took it sixteen years ago, . . . must perceive the extensive alterations, . . . and improvements, that I have accomplished during my tenancy; abrupt angles have given way to curves, and my circles, especially from their present occupancy, appear graceful in the extreme. I have backed the pit, and could, in another sense, for respectability against any pit in London. I have stalled off what was originally the orchestra. . . The proscenium I have widened 11 feet, and entirely remodelled it, and introduced gas for the fee of £500 a year, and the presentation of the centre chandelier to the proprietors; and, behind the curtain, money has not been spared to render the stage as perfect for dramatic representation as its limited means will furnish. In fact, I have expended, with no ultimate advantage to myself, on this property over £12,000, besides paying more than £60,000 in rent; yet I have met with anything but a generous consideration in return by the party most interested in the result."

Webster passed to the management of the Adelphi, and was succeeded in the management of the Haymarket by Buckstone, who carried on its fortunes for upwards of twenty-five years. With his *régime* Shakespeare was relegated to the background. In the early '60's Sothern startled the body dandiacal by his performances of Lord Dundreary, and in the early '70's Madge Robertson (Mrs. Kendal) acquired renown in the fairy or poetic comedies of W. S. Gilbert. In the early '60's Ellen Terry was a member of the company. Yet under Buckstone Shakespeare was not wholly neglected. In 1854 and 1855 Charlotte Cushman filled engagements here, playing Queen Katharine and Romeo, though Meg Merrilies was then, as always, her most popular character. On June 4, 1855, Helen Faucit appeared as Juliet to the Romeo of Barry Sullivan. On September 30, 1861, Edwin Booth made his début in London, enacting Shylock. In this and other Shakespearian parts he was liked, but not enthusiastically. By 1861 the Haymarket was universally recognised as the home of comedy, and Booth's efforts in tragedy suffered on this account. By an irony of fate he was followed by Sothern, who made his great hit in Our American Cousin, drawing from the well of English undefiled many a bucketful of money and applause. After the retirement of Webster, the Haymarket ceased to be a factor in the Shakespearian field; nevertheless, the beautiful and lamented Adelaide Neilson played there her later London engagements during which she captivated again as Rosalind and Juliet. At this house, also, she first essayed (April, 1876) the character of Isabella in Measure for Measure—a superb portrayal. Her exquisite Viola in Twelfth Night first delighted the London public in February, 1878, as it had captivated New York, the previous spring, at Daly's Fifth Avenue Theatre. The curtain fell in 1879—and at the Haymarket— on the last London performance of this gifted woman. The next season she played in America. Her death occurred in Paris in August, 1880.

SADLER'S WELLS

If the Haymarket was the most fashionable theatre in London during the greater part of our period, Sadler's Wells was the most democratic. This remarkable house, under the leadership of Samuel Phelps, probably did more to popularise Shakespeare in the course of eighteen years (1844–62) than did any other theatre in the whole domain of English theatrical history.

There was something daring in Phelps's plan. The theatre at Sadler's Wells stood far from the theatrical and fashionable centre of London, in the distant region of Islington, known to many Londoners of to-day merely as a name painted on a 'bus. In 1765 the brick house immortalised by Phelps succeeded a wooden structure in the same region, and for many years thereafter was noted as a cheap and often disreputable resort, in which variety performances, tight-rope walking, tumbling, etc., alternated with performing dogs, etc. Grimaldi, the famous clown, appeared at Sadler's Wells annually, to the delight of a loyal audience, retiring in 1828. In 1804 the theatre fell under the management of Charles Dibdin, and "began," to quote H. Barton Baker, "that series of nautical dramas with sensational effects and real water, that obtained for it the name of the 'Aquatic Theatre,' and formed its principal attraction during the next forty years. For these effects a gigantic tank, fed from the New River, was constructed beneath the stage, and a drama entitled *The Siege of Gibraltar* was produced; in this piece real vessels floated on real water for the bombardment of the fortress; the heroine fell from the rocks into the sea, and her lover plunged after her; there was a naval battle and a ship afire, from which the sailors sprang into the waves to escape the flames, and in another scene a child was cast into the water and rescued by a Newfoundland dog. The tank was ninety feet long, five feet deep, and in some places twenty-four feet wide; there was a second over the stage, fifteen feet square and five feet deep, for waterfall effects. In a play called *The Island* . . . . . the stage was raised bodily to the roof for one act which was performed upon the tank."

Year after year, again to quote Mr. Baker, "the bills are very monotonous." Terrific melodramas, ballets and pantomimes succeed each other, with Grimaldi a regular annual feature. Dramatic versions of Walter Scott were at last given here in the decade 1830–40, and slightly raised the quality of the entertainment offered. But the audience at this place was throughout of rough, turbulent and frequently disreputable character.   The "Wells" was far, far away from the Haymarket.

And it was in this unpromising building with its disorderly clientele that Samuel Phelps was to carry out his great life-work.   The way in which he reduced his audiences to politeness and earnest loyalty and attracted to his house the best brains and characters from a better-bred neighbourhood has been recounted from many points of view.   The long series of splendid performances that appealed to a vast democratic throng from Pentonville and Islington and Mayfair is more legitimately the subject of our present discourse.

Just why Phelps should have selected this remote scene of endeavour I have not discovered; it seems to have appealed to him, possibly because of its remoteness and difficulty.   Associated with him for two years were the distinguished tragic actress, Mrs. Warner, her husband (as treasurer), and T. L. Greenwood (as acting manager).   An Address issued to the public said that "Mrs. Warner and Mr . Phelps have embarked in the management and performance of Sadler's Wells Theatre in the hope of eventually rendering it what a theatre ought to be—a place for justly representing the works of our great dramatic poets. . . . .   Each separate division of our immense metropolis, with its 2,000,000 of inhabitants, may have its own well-conducted theatre within a reasonable distance of the homes of its patrons.

"For the North of London, they offer an entertainment selected from the first stock drama in the world, re-inforced by such novelties as can be procured by diligence and liberality."   The address concludes modestly with a plea for indulgence for shortcomings and a promise of steady endeavour for improvement.   From the first, we may add, Phelps's partner Greenwood was a strong adjutant; according to John Coleman, "he not only attended to the financial department, and took the weight of the production of the pantomime off his [Phelps's] hands, but he also watched the waves of public opinion, and steered the ship in accordance therewith"; a kind of Lacy to Phelps's Garrick, I take it.

In this unfashionable neighbourhood, in a house far from elegant or luxurious, for eighteen years Phelps toiled on, amid universal acclaim, establishing a repertoire of classic plays almost unparalleled. Not only did he produce with utter adequacy all of the plays of Shakespeare except Richard II, the three parts of Henry VI, Troilus and Cressida, and Titus Andronicus, but he revived such forgotten Elizabethan worthies as Beaumont and Fletcher's King and no King, and The Maid's Tragedy (under the title of The Bridal), Massinger's City Madam and Fatal Dowry, Webster's Duchess of Malfi, Rowley's A Woman never Vext, as well as the more familiar Rule a Wife and Have a Wife, A New Way to Pay Old Debts and Venice Preserved.

The company at Sadler's Wells could not afford to be very superior; Phelps, like Irving and Augustin Daly, preferred, indeed, to train novices into professional competence. This is, perhaps, the test of a great manager and producer. At any rate, Phelps had the discomfort of seeing his best people constantly deserting. George Bennett and Henry Marston remained throughout the greater part of the eighteen years, as did the serviceable Miss Cooper; but one "leading lady" succeeded another in such quick order that they were like the woe that doth tread on another's heels, so fast they follow. Mrs. Warner departed at the end of the second season, her place being taken by Laura Addison, a new actress, who won immediate favour in some of Helen Faucit's best parts. Miss Addison also remained but two seasons, and was in turn followed by Isabel Glyn, who likewise was instantly successful. In the course of years she proved to be that undesirable thing, a one-part player, though in her case the part was the exceedingly difficult one of Cleopatra, the more's the mystery. Miss Glyn left in the autumn of 1851, and Miss Atkinson, a distinctly inferior actress, took her place. From this time on, leading actresses, in the Warner-Glyn sense, were almost non-existent at Sadler's Wells; the repertoire had to be

SAMUEL PHELPS AS
MACBETH

SAMUEL PHELPS AND MISS
GLYN IN HAMLET

From engravings after daguerreotypes by Paine of Islington

MRS. WARNER AS HERMIONE

From an engraving published by
John Tallis and Company

LAURA ADDISON AS IMOGEN

From an engraving after a daguerreotype
by Paine of Islington

adjusted accordingly. Some of the more notable of Phelps's
latest revivals—Timon of Athens, Henry IV, Part II,
Henry V, Pericles, The Tempest and A Midsummer Night's
Dream—need no pronounced female personality, and
Phelps dispensed with the Warners and Glyns and reaped
unto himself a richer harvest of praise and possibly of money.
At any rate, the history of his constantly vanishing leading
ladies might, if truly told, make interesting reading.   One
can only end by admitting that a slight loss in artistic credit
is involved; Kemble and Siddons, Charles Kean and Ellen
Tree, Irving and Ellen Terry fill the imagination more
richly than does the single personality of Samuel Phelps.
The glories of Sadler's Wells will occupy us in the succeeding
chapter.

THE PRINCESS'S THEATRE

The Princess's is chiefly remembered for the splendid
Shakespearian reign of Charles Kean (1850–59); but for
five years previously it had housed some notable productions of the bard.   The always interesting Charlotte Cushman and Macready are involved in that earlier history.
The Princess's, opened, after alteration from the Queen's
Bazaar, as a theatre in 1840, had passed in 1843 into the
hands of Maddox, a principal mortgagee.   At first he continued an earlier style of offering, operas and to some extent
what we should now call "vaudeville."   In 1844 he had a
great success with J. W. Wallack in Don Cæsar de Bazan,
and passed, thereby, with a sort of natural transition, from
romantic drama to tragedy.   On February 14, 1845, Charlotte Cushman made her first appearance in London, as
Bianca, in Fazio.   She next appeared as Lady Macbeth
to the Macbeth of Edwin Forrest.   Though Forrest failed
lamentably, possibly, as he alleged, through the efforts of
Macready's partisans, Miss Cushman was at once acknowledged as the greatest English-speaking tragedienne of her
time—an estimate the English never altered.   She remained
for eighty-four nights—not consecutive—at the Princess's,
playing Juliana and Julia, and, from the Shakespearian list,

Rosalind and Beatrice. She was indubitably the sensation of the year; in December following she was, as we have seen, engaged at the Haymarket in the memorable revival of Romeo and Juliet.

From October 13th to November 21st, Macready was at the Princess's in a round of his best-known Shakespearian parts; he returned for another month's stay, January 26–February 27, 1846, and once more, from April 13th to well in the summer of the same year. Hence at a bound the Princess's leaped very high into popularity and prosperity in the Shakespearian field. Not in vain had come to it the cry of the freedom of the theatres. Macready played here again in two engagements in the spring and fall of 1847. In the first, he was supported by Creswick and Mrs. Warner. In the latter, he played Macbeth, Wolsey and Othello to the Lady Macbeth, Katharine and Emilia of Charlotte Cushman.

Interesting to students of the American stage was the début at the Princess's on January 5, 1848, of the Americans, Mrs. Mowatt and E. L. Davenport. They opened in The Hunchback, but soon showed their mettle in a charming performance of Much Ado about Nothing. These American artists, like Miss Cushman, though of course not to the same degree, succeeded emphatically. They, however, remained but a short time at the Princess's, and won their best laurels on the stages of the Theatre Royal, Marylebone, and the Olympic, in Wych Street. Davenport was later at the Haymarket and Drury Lane. As a matter of fact, if I were to offer a guiding string through the intricate Shakespearian activities of these years, I could not think of a better than that furnished by the history of E. L. Davenport in his flittings from theatre to theatre. With him invariably went performances of the plays of Shakespeare.

Macready, it will be observed, filled all his important London engagements—except the last, at the Haymarket—at the Princess's. His final engagement with Maddox extended from February 21st to April 14, 1848. In the first four weeks he played Macbeth, Wolsey, Othello, Hamlet, Lear, to the opposite leads of no less a personage than Mrs. Butler (Fanny Kemble), who made a not startlingly successful return to the stage.   After her departure he added other stock parts to his repertoire.

Cushman, Macready, Davenport, Mrs. Mowatt, Mrs. Warner: verily the Princess's had had its giant race before Charles Kean, in partnership at first with Robert Keeley, assumed control of the house on September 28, 1850.   The lavish and scholarly productions of this conscientious man will form a main staple of news in subsequent chapters; suffice it here to state that, in addition to other good plays, old and new, he carefully produced, from newly studied texts and with unstinted outlay, scholarly and financial, twelve of Shakespeare's greatest works.   He expended thousands of pounds where Phelps spent possibly but hundreds; he gave to Irving and Tree a formula followed in all their later revivals.   He retired on August 29, 1859, richer in fame and experience than in financial profit.   But he is with Kemble, Macready and Irving in the distinguished company of scholarly actors and producers, if not with his father and Garrick and Betterton as one of the immortal interpreters of Shakespeare.

At the Princess's, under his successor, Augustus Harris (father of Sir Augustus of recent Drury Lane renown), Henry Irving played, among other parts, Osric in Hamlet; in the next year, on October 27, 1860, Harris first introduced Charles Fechter to a London audience.   It was not until March, 1861, that this distinguished actor, with Gallic art and Gallic intonations, appeared as Hamlet, upsetting all tradition as to stage business, reading of lines, etc., and by his unusualness securing a "run" unprecedented for this particular tragedy.   London took sides and argued vociferously, pro and con, while the box office overflowed.   When on October 23, 1861, Fechter, at the same theatre, attempted the part of Othello, even his most ardent Hamlet-worshipper was forced to admit that his portrayal was a mistake. Fechter shortly assumed the management of the Lyceum, and went from rather bad to very much worse in finance and popular favour. He introduced on the Lyceum stage many improvements, almost revolutionary, in stage machinery, and had renewed success with a production of Hamlet.

The last notable Shakespearian event at the Princess's, within the period we are covering, was a revival of Antony and Cleopatra, in May, 1867. In this, Miss Glyn, bridging gracefully the eighteen years since she had first played the part at Sadler's Wells, was again a perfectly satisfactory representative of the serpent of old Nile. On this reincarnation we drop the curtain at the Princess's.

THE MARYLEBONE, THE OLYMPIC, THE SURREY

The Haymarket, Sadler's Wells, the Princess's: quite indisputably these were the fortresses—the first-named if only occasionally—of Shakespeare during the initial twenty years of the freedom of the theatres. But others now crowd into notice. Of these the Theatre Royal, Marylebone, exacts but a passing notice. Hither, after leaving Sadler's Wells, Mrs. Warner betook herself as manager, and brought out many of Shakespeare's plays, not lavishly, I suspect, but very well. Her own acting in a special production of The Winter's Tale resulted in a not despicable success to her early experience. In 1848, from April 24th to May 8th, Macready condescended to play an engagement with her company. In the autumn of 1848 came Mrs. Mowatt and Davenport, and stayed, by renewal of engagements, for half a year. They began the season with As You Like It. In the autumn of 1849 they came again, and out-Cushmaned the great Charlotte by appearing in an epicene version of Romeo and Juliet, Fanny Vining (Mrs. Davenport) as Romeo, Mrs. Mowatt as Juliet, and Davenport as Mercutio. This same combination appeared also in Cymbeline and Twelfth Night. The Theatre Royal, Marylebone, was a pretty house, and it obviously gave pretty performances of Shakespeare. Beginning on April 8, 1850, the fiery Gustavus Brooke appeared here for a brief season in his inevitable Othello and in Hamlet.

This is all there is to record of the theatre in Marylebone. I bring it in here, not because it bears in any pertinent way on my subject, but to show the reader how all the managers were up and doing in the field of Shakespeare. Mrs. Warner's management was a brief, if not inglorious thing. William (J. W.) Wallack, the younger, was manager here in 1855, keeping alive the sacred flame of Shakespeare.

The Olympic invites more detailed and more loving comment. The early days of this house are associated with the management of Vestris and Mathews and with farce and operetta. But after the opening of Shakespeare to the "minor" theatres, the Olympic management proudly stalked into the arena. 1848 was the banner year in this not very strange and not very eventful history. On January 3, 1848, Gustavus Vaughan Brooke at this house made his first appearance in London in his favourite part of Othello. Some agnised that a new Edmund Kean had arisen; but very shortly this glow-worm gan to pale his ineffectual fires, chiefly (sad to relate) in strong drink, and those who had most ardently supported Brooke began to cool in the light of evident facts. But for some years he had a following of no mean dimensions. He was succeeded here by Mrs. Mowatt and Davenport, who seemed to be trying every London theatre to see which they liked best.

The old Olympic burned to the ground on March 29, 1849, but a new Olympic was immediately built, and in it, on February 4, 1850, Othello was performed by an admirable cast: Brooke as Othello, Davenport as Iago, Fanny Vining as Emilia, and Mrs. Mowatt as Desdemona. In November and December, 1850, Brooke and Helen Faucit were playing here in a round of the "legitimate." At the same time Macready was vigorously "farewelling" at the Haymarket, with the late Olympic Davenport as his chief support, Phelps was pursuing his successful career at Sadler's Wells, and Charles Kean was just starting his at the Princess's. Verily, in the autumn of 1850, the London playgoer had much choice in Shakespeare on the stage.

An interesting appearance at the Olympic—interesting to Americans at least—was that of Laura Keene in 1851.

The younger J. W. Wallack and Helen Faucit (where was *not* Helen Faucit in these years?) were playing here in July, 1851, and on November 3rd of the same year Laura Keene played Rosalind. On November 24th she appeared as Juliet. The name of this charming lady is indelibly written in the history of the American theatre.

The Olympic, then, at the mid-century was vigorously glorifying Shakespeare. Its later history, under the successive brief reigns of Farren, Alfred Wigan and F. Robson, leads it far from Shakespeare to melodrama, of the variety of The Ticket of Leave Man, Henry Dunbar, etc. It, like the Theatre Royal, Marylebone, is included here, not because it contributed anything of novelty or note in the Shakespearian chronicle, but because for a few years it rushed in where bigger theatres feared—if I may so put it —to tread, and kept Shakespeare very much alive.

And as to the Surrey, that popular house, across the river, over by Lambeth way? The great Macready accepted a two weeks' engagement here in 1846, and, throughout the greater part of our period, Creswick was part manager and sole heavy tragedian of the theatre. Of this bald, bold actor the story goes that he once confessed he should like to triple the parts of the Ghost, Polonius and First Gravedigger in Hamlet; but in that event there would be no one to play Hamlet! Let us hope he referred only to Lambeth. Well, I did not bring in the Surrey merely to record these meagre happenings. On the contrary, I eternise the place solely because there on the 23d of April, 1864 —the three-hundredth anniversary of the birth of Shakespeare—was produced, probably for the first time since it was originally acted, the Second Part of Henry VI. The reader will please remember, nevertheless, that the Surrey played much Shakespeare in the period we are discussing.

DRURY LANE REBORN

Lest the reader, wearying of this Banquo-line of theatres, should cry out in horror against my damnable iteration, I

CHARLES KEAN AS HAMLET   MRS. MOWATT AS BEATRICE

From engravings after daguerreotypes by Paine of Islington

MACREADY AS HAMLET AT THE SURREY THEATRE

From the *Illustrated London News*

hasten to assure him that but little remains to be treated.
Drury Lane, having suffered severe eclipse under the successive tyrannies of Bunn and E. T. Smith, emerges at last
into something like the light of day under the kindly min-
istrations of Edmund Falconer and F. B. Chatterton.

It is a great pleasure to find old Drury once more taking
its place in the van of Shakespearian production.   Phelps
retired from Sadler's Wells in 1862; Kean, as we remember,
gave up control of the Princess's in 1859.   The field of
Shakespearian endeavour, as exemplified in the service of
Kemble, Macready and the two actor-managers just mentioned, was therefore left vacant.   But before believers in
such a system had had time to ask nervously and apprehen-
sively, "Who next?" help came from a most unexpected
quarter—Edmund Falconer, writer of popular melodramas,
like Peep o' Day, which in 1861 saved his earlier management at the Lyceum.   He was a prolific writer and not a
bad actor—a second-rate Dion Boucicault.   In 1863, with
F. B. Chatterton, he assumed the management of Drury
Lane.

The new impresarios at once effected a bold and successful stroke.   They engaged the ever popular Phelps,
who, since giving up Sadler's Wells, had had a rather distressing experience under the management of the difficult
Fechter; and for many years thereafter, as the historical
imagination likes to recall, the leading London theatre and
the leading English actor—Charles Kean died in January,
1868—conjointly made the best Shakespeare history on the
London stage.   The story has been often told, and is easily
accessible in the life of Phelps by John Coleman, in that by
W. May Phelps and John Forbes Robertson, and in the
history of Drury Lane Theatre by Edward Stirling.

The first appearance of Phelps with the Falconer-Chatter-
ton management was in Byron's Manfred, mounted with
superb spectacular display.   This play was followed by a
magnificent revival of Henry IV, Part I, got up to celebrate
the tercentenary of Shakespeare's birth (1864).   In the
next season came a revival of the second part of the same

history, and wonderful productions of Othello, Cymbeline and Macbeth, in the last two of which Helen Faucit returned to the stage, to the great delight of her still devoted public. Helen Faucit was one of the few lucky ones who never grew old, or not, at least, until she was very old. Falconer was forced by financial stress to retire in 1866, and thereafter for thirteen years Chatterton was in sole charge of the national theatre.

His record is on the whole one to be proud of. Throughout the greater part of his term Phelps's name is on the bills. King John, the Brothers Webb in The Comedy of Errors, a spectacular Faust, Byron's Marino Faliero, these are some of the mainstays of the '60's. But experience, I regret to say, forced Chatterton to enunciate the famous epigram, "Shakespeare spells ruin, and Byron bankruptcy." In light of this conviction, he turned to Walter Scott, and produced, first, Halliday's adaptation of The Fortunes of Nigel, called King o' Scots, in which Phelps appeared, and, second, the same adapter's Amy Robsart, founded on Kenilworth. In the latter, in 1870–71, the beautiful Adelaide Neilson stepped into the front rank of living actresses. Phelps and Miss Neilson appeared together, on September 23, 1871, as Isaac of York and Rebecca in Halliday's dramatisation of Ivanhoe.

But thanks to the lovely Neilson, whose early death has left her ever young and ever fair in memory, Shakespeare once more demonstrated his unfailing charm at Drury Lane on December 19, 1870. On that evening Miss Neilson entered on her embodiment of Juliet, which to this day lingers in tradition, in history and in the hearts of old playgoers as the perfect representation of the character of the hapless daughter of Capulet. No one since has effaced this impression, and no one seems likely to do so. If Garrick was the great Lear, and Kemble the great Coriolanus; if Mrs. Siddons was the great Lady Macbeth, and Edwin Booth—to Americans at least—the great Hamlet; Adelaide Neilson is to Americans and English alike the great Juliet. Forever must we love and she be fair. It is pleasing to think that this assumption—after a timid début in the character years before—was first seen on the historic stage of Drury Lane. On December 18, 1871, Miss Neilson played Rosalind at the same theatre, and shortly afterwards appeared in New York, there to captivate every lover of Shakespeare.

Little else, Shakespearian, need detain us in the history of Drury Lane. In September, 1873, a curtailed Antony and Cleopatra was gorgeously mounted with spectacle, dance and song; and, in 1878, The Winter's Tale brought back to the stage something like the wreck of Charles Dillon. On February 4, 1879, Chatterton, whose finances had been growing worse and worse, left Drury Lane forever. In the autumn of that year it was reopened by Augustus Harris with a successful production of Henry V, in which George Rignold, who had succeeded magnificently in the play in New York in 1875, first enacted the hero-King in London. Charles Calvert had brought out a sumptuous revival of the piece in Manchester in the early '70's, and sold the production outright to Jarrett and Palmer of Booth's Theatre in New York. The success of the venture in New York, with the handsome Rignold, is a matter of American theatrical history. In 1879 Rignold brought the play to the notice of Londoners, who, in this case, it is amusing to note, received their Henry V from Manchester, *via* New York.

A CONCLUDING MISCELLANY

It must not be assumed that in the thirty years or more of our present chronicle Shakespeare was marked off definitely by productions at certain specified theatres, and that other houses refrained from poaching. On the contrary, hardly a house of repute failed at one time or another to hang the banner from its walls. Throughout the period the theatres I have just briefly characterised were the prominent producers of the dramatist, but they stood out against a background of Shakespearian endeavour, vague yet definite, shifting yet permanent. Shakespeare was too good to be left unacted. At the St. James's, for instance, in 1860, Barry Sullivan again appeared as Hamlet, a Hamlet somewhat more temperate than that he had exhibited at the Haymarket in 1852. Nevertheless, as I have stated, the Haymarket, Sadler's Wells, the Princess's, and, latterly, Drury Lane, were head and front of the endeavour.

In the decade of the '70's, however, while Shakespeare might be found unexpectedly anywhere, and consistently nowhere, certain performances won recognition. Ada Cavendish, a painstaking actress, was successful as Rosalind, at the St. James's in 1878; for Juliet she was totally unfitted by temperament and appearance, handsome as she undoubtedly was. Just as in the late '40's, Shakespearian activities might be traced to some extent in the constant change of *milieu* on the part of E. L. Davenport, so in the '70's we are equally assisted by following the journeys of Samuel Phelps from theatre to theatre. John Coleman has scheduled these for us, but from the itinerary I shall select only a few interesting details. At the Queen's Theatre in Longacre, in 1870, he renewed an earlier triumph as Bottom in a notable revival of A Midsummer Night's Dream. Under Hollingshead at the Gaiety, he played, at Christmas, 1874, Falstaff in a superb production, hereafter to be described, of The Merry Wives of Windsor. Acting from time to time in various London theatres, Phelps "assisted" as his last great effort in John Coleman's revival of Henry V at the Queen's Theatre, September 16, 1876. Coleman himself, as manager, generously pre-empted the part of Henry V, but in a prologue made up of parts of Henry IV, Phelps played the King.

It will be seen, then, that some of the more important of the later Phelpsiana are associated with the Queen's Theatre. But this house hands down the record of other endeavours. Here, in November, 1871, was revived The Tempest, with much spectacle, song (Arne's and Purcell's) and dance, including the masque, "with the descent of Juno in a car drawn by peacocks," to quote Dutton Cook (Nights at the Play), and a grand ballet terminating the third act. Ariel, according to the same lively chronicler, was "afflicted with certain attributes of the ordinary ballet girl," but otherwise not unsatisfactory. I am chiefly interested to learn that the pulchritudinous George Rignold played Caliban, "with tusks and pasteboard jaws," but "in the right spirit." This unimaginative production I decline to discuss further, and dismiss it, paired with a Cymbeline of April, 1872, at the same theatre. In this latter, Dutton Cook asserts that "some attempt has been made to invest Cymbeline's palace with the characteristics of Anglo-Saxon architecture; and Posthumus assumes a kind of Viking guise." But who could have cared when the Imogen was hardly more than an amateur, the same lady, in fact, who capered about as Ariel in the recent Tempest?

Pass we to pleasanter things at the Queen's. At this theatre came, on September 14, 1872, to continue till September 28th, a production of Romeo and Juliet by George Rignold and Adelaide Neilson. Matinee girls of the '70's in New York can shake their gray locks in speechless wonder at a promise so alluring, as they read of it now, perhaps, for the first time; just how their more sedate English cousins regarded the treat I am unable to say. But a combination of the handsome George Rignold and the beautiful Adelaide Neilson strikes me as the best that could possibly be offered impressionable theatre-goers of the year 1872. They appeared together once or twice at benefits in New York in the balcony scene, but never, I believe, in the whole play.

THE BANCROFTS' MERCHANT OF VENICE, 1875

A Shakespearian production demanding report is the colossal failure of the Bancrofts at their famous Prince of Wales Theatre in Tottenham Court Road. This tiny house, the birthplace of the Robertson cup and saucer comedy, was diverted from its placid career in April, 1875, for a splendid revival of The Merchant of Venice. In this Ellen Terry played Portia for the first time in her life; but alas! the acting of Shylock by Charles Coghlan—superb actor when properly cast—killed the production. I shall speak of this performance in its place.

As a kind of exotic posy, I gather together, at the close, the record of certain distinguished foreigners who, in all the years we are discussing, brought to the attention of Londoners continental methods of interpreting Shakespeare. Fechter I have already mentioned. Before his day, however—in June, 1852, to be exact—a German company appeared at the St. James's Theatre, playing on alternate evenings with a French company headed by the great Rachel. In the course of the season Emil Devrient enacted Hamlet, with German conscientiousness and lack of magnetism, avoiding "points," and especially emphasising Hamlet's love for his mother. This performance was, of course, in the German tongue. In broken English, on the other hand, was Stella Colas's Juliet, exhibited, with great success, at the Princess's in 1863–64. George Henry Lewes did not like this performance; but therein he differed from most critics, amateur and professional. Two far greater artists warbled the native wood-notes wild in their own Italian. In July, 1857, Madame Ristori played Lady Macbeth at the Lyceum, and thereby "Lady Macbeth," according to Henry Morley, became "the entire play." But who cares, when it is a matter of subordinating Duncano, Re di Scozia, and Macbetto? Signior Vitaliani, as Macbeth, says Morley, allowed Madame Ristori to dominate him throughout the tragedy; and, after the sleep-walking scene, and the announcement of the death of Lady Macbeth, "short work is made by the adapter of the following part of the play, which is condensed into a single page of the libretto." Madame Ristori enacted Lady Macbeth in later London seasons. Finally, Tommaso Salvini, perhaps the greatest actor of modern times, took London by storm at Drury Lane, in the spring of 1875, with performances of Othello, which, by their fiery rage and Oriental animalism, surpassed

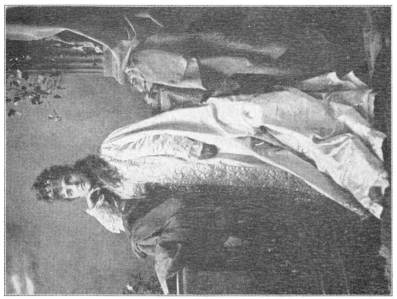

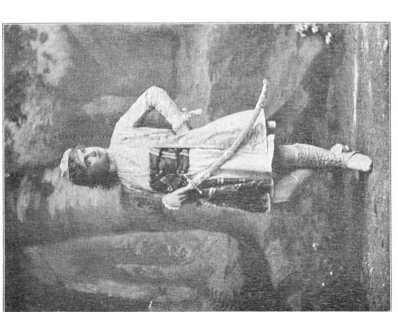

ADELAIDE NEILSON AS VIOLA   ADELAIDE NEILSON AS JULIET

From photographs by Sarony of New York

any rendering of the Moor hitherto seen. Public opinion at once divided on the question of whether Shakespeare's Othello was this great primitive, elemental character, or the chivalrous, gentlemanly soul previously exhibited on the stage. Whatever the view on this problem, there could be no doubt as to the cyclonic force of Salvini's impersonation, or the consummate art with which it was carried out. His Hamlet, his Macbeth and his King Lear, though finished and in many respects great performances, never captured the public heart as did his Othello. Ernesto Rossi played Lear at Her Majesty's in June, 1882. His supporting company used the English tongue, he, the Italian. On one evening during the engagement he played the last two acts in very broken English; he attempted no other part during the engagement, which was a failure. Quoth the Athenæum of June 24th: "Signor Rossi quits our stage with a promise to return when he is able to act in English. For the performance of that promise we shall wait with resignation."

All these foreign efforts I dismiss with the statement here made. Their effect, in every case, was a matter of acting, and therein some were potent and influential. But for our history the stage versions employed were a matter of no importance whatever; as a matter of fact Stella Colas—the only one of the five to use an English text—reverted to Garrick's Romeo and Juliet, eighteen years after Charlotte Cushman had discarded it. And as for the Macbetto of Madame Ristori! Finally, in regard to scenery, throughout their careers Madame Ristori and Salvini were sublimely indifferent to it, as their genius entitled them to be; Devrient, of course, used stock setting in his very brief season at the St. James's, in 1852, and Vining's rehabilitation of Romeo and Juliet for Stella Colas, in 1863-64, is not worth considering beside Kean's great revivals of the previous decade or Chatterton's in the years immediately following. These foreign invasions I therefore dismiss from further mention in the history.

THE LYCEUM AND IRVING

With the foregoing chronicle of English actors and managers finishing their careers, one might assume that the end had come for Shakespeare. The facts fortunately proved to be entirely contrary. For the better part of the decade 1870–80 the Lyceum Theatre gradually came to the front— to the chief place—thanks largely to the acting of Henry Irving. The theatre was leased in 1871 by the American, H. L. Bateman, primarily for the exploitation of his daughter Isabel, whom he hoped to induce London to accept as it had accepted her sister Kate a few years before. London, in this case, disappointed expectation, but it greeted with increasing enthusiasm the work of the leading actor, Irving, who had, indeed, been noted heretofore as an interpreter of character parts in comedy or melodrama. From Irving's first appearance as Mathias in The Bells, on November 25, 1871, he became a marked man. He passed from success to success, until on October 31, 1874, he appeared as Hamlet —his first great Shakespearian assumption. His performance was "different," and attracted London for the unprecedented run of two hundred nights. Macbeth followed on September 18, 1875, but this—though it lasted eighty nights—was a comparative failure, as were the remaining Shakespearian efforts of Irving during the Bateman management—Othello, on February 14, 1876, and Richard III, on January 29, 1877, though to Richard, at least, the critics were kind. These were the only Shakespearian pieces produced during the Bateman management; on December 30, 1878, Irving opened the theatre under his own sole direction, and from that date begins his history as a great Shakespearian producer. I may be pardoned, therefore, for passing lightly over these early performances, in view of the overwhelming importance of his own later generalship. It seems wise, however, to bring them in the account in this place. After all, Irving was—by reason of his Hamlet at least—a famous impersonator of Shakespeare when Samuel Phelps died in 1878. His career with Bateman must there-

fore conclude the Phelps period rather than form the preliminary chapters of the Irving period—the period from his
occupancy of the Lyceum in 1878 until he made his last
appearance on its stage in 1902.

CHAPTER XXVIII

THE PLAYS

FINAL RESTORATION OF SHAKESPEARE'S TEXT

IN the multiplicity of Shakespearian activity just indicated for the thirty-five years following the Act of 1843, the reader will neither expect nor desire detailed treatment of the stage versions employed. Rather will he be grateful, I suspect, for some thread to guide him through the tangled maze. That thread he will find, as I have found it, in the determined effort of the stage-leaders to carry on the work of their best predecessors from Elliston to Macready in restoring the text of Shakespeare to the theatre. This effort, it will be remembered, had succeeded in banishing all perversions, or at best, innocent emendations of Shakespeare, except Cibber's Richard III and Garrick's Romeo and Juliet and Catharine and Petruchio. Aside from these, the Shakespeare plays presented, however cut and however transposed in scene-order, were presented in the words of Shakespeare. Even Shakespeare's own Romeo and Juliet, according to George Vandenhoff (Leaves from an Actor's Note-Book), had been presented by Mme. Vestris during her second season at Covent Garden, but so inadequately that it had perished almost at birth; thereafter the Garrick adaptation had held undisputed possession of the boards.

The opening years of the new order were to see even these last strongholds of Seventeenth and Eighteenth-Century oppression stormed and at least temporarily razed. The leaders of the attack were Benjamin Webster and Samuel Phelps, and to them we owe, from 1843 to 1850, the most interesting final episodes in the battle that had waged continuously for nearly two centuries, a battle for the staging of Shakespeare as written by the poet himself, and not as "improved" by every petty artisan of the theatre who might assume himself to be greater than the greatest.

The first restoration was, from many points of view, the most remarkable: the Haymarket production of The Taming of the Shrew, "from the original text," as the playbill proudly announces, and "as acted divers times at the Globe and Blackfriars Playhouses, 1606." This performance was undoubtedly the first complete acting of the farcical comedy since the days before the closing of the theatres in 1642. The reader who has followed the history from Lacy's Sauny the Scot in 1667, through the two fragments known as The Cobler of Preston in 1716, thence onward to the "ballad-opera," A Cure for a Scold, in 1735, and Garrick's Catharine and Petruchio in 1756, down to the other "opera," with Shakespeare's own title in 1828, will observe that the original play has never, until the present moment, crept into our history. On March 16, 1844, Webster, then in flood-tide at the Haymarket, was moved to revive Shakespeare's piece, Induction and all, and—most remarkable!—with screens and curtains, in lieu of scenery, thereby anticipating by more than half a century the most pretentious and self-righteous scene-devisers of to-day. One of the few remaining Shakespearian comedies had thrown off its shackles, and made its way to success as it was originally planned. Webster and Mrs. Nisbett played the tamer (spelled as Daly many years later spelled it—Petrucio) and the tamed, and made great "hits." The play was given many times during the season, and was reproduced with equal success two years later. Webster, in summing up the achievements of his management of the Haymarket, counted this, as Pascoe tells us, among his highest and most glorious. And well he might! I may anticipate by stating that Phelps on November 15, 1856, revived the play, also "from the text of Shakespeare," at Sadler's Wells. Phelps elected to play the part of Christopher Sly, and seems to have made a great impression, probably from the mere exhibition of versatility. According to the review of Phelps's performance in the Morning Advertiser, "the entire five acts were rigidly played"—rigidly in that nothing was omitted—"and it must be confessed that to hackneyed play-goers of the modern school, the earlier scenes occasionally dragged; but the audience"—and this was typical of Phelps's earnest, eager hearers—"the audience, we firmly believe would not have lost a word. They come with the antique feeling to this theatre, throw themselves into the story, and having, by close attention and an intelligent sympathy, made personal acquaintance with the characters, they desire to know the history and the end of every one of them." Obviously, they dined earlier in Islington, and took their play-going more seriously than did the denizens of Mayfair.

So much for Catharine and Petruchio and its defeat by Shakespeare's own version. Yet Katharine and Petruchio (the usual spelling since Kemble's day) was too good an afterpiece to be permanently dislodged, and even Phelps went back to it at need. But the deed had been done; two great managers had shown the attractiveness of The Taming of the Shrew, and their achievements lingered in memory till Augustin Daly in the Irving period introduced to London the matchless Katharine of Ada Rehan.

PHELPS RESTORES RICHARD III

Phelps, enthroned among loving subjects, dealt the second blow at the Shakespeare-who-was-not-Shakespeare; this time Colley Cibber's Richard III went down at least to temporary defeat. On February 20, 1845, the original play was brought out at Sadler's Wells. The playbills announce Richard III "with the restoration of the text of Shakespeare," and go on modestly as follows: "In order to meet the spirit of the present age, so distinguished for illustrating and honouring the works of Shakespeare, and with at least an honest desire of testing truthful excellence over all attempted improvements, this restoration is essayed, in lieu of the alteration, interpolation, and compilement of

Colley Cibber, which has so long held possession of the stage." Later bills report that the play, "having been received with complete approbation, will be repeated three times a week until further notice." A comparison of the cast of Phelps's production with the *dramatis personæ* of the Cambridge text will show that the version at Sadler's Wells must have employed a great deal of the original tragedy; only the son and the daughter of Clarence, the Archbishop of Canterbury (obviously joined by Phelps with his brother of York), Vaughan, Urswick and the other priest, and Tressel and Berkeley are lacking. This shows close adherence to Shakespeare.

Of such adherence there can be no doubt after reading the Times review of February 24th. Says the "Thunderer":

Mr. Phelps and Mrs. Warner have well asserted their independence by the production of Shakspeare's *Richard III*, in the place of the ordinary compilation by Colley Cibber. We do not mean to say that every line, or even every scene, of the original play is preserved. There are several liberal omissions, and some parts are transposed, but the construction and march of the play are Shakspeare's.

And a very different play it is from the common version. . . The whole of the scenes belonging to Henry VI, and, of course, that monarch himself are omitted, and the play begins, as it ought to do, with Richard's soliloquy. . . . The murder of Clarence, with the dream . . . . is restored to its proper place. The wailings of the three bereft mothers, the Duchess of York, Queen Margaret, and Queen Elizabeth, return to the boards, as also does the Council, with the accusation of Hastings. . . . .

Whether actors who have to play Richard will like Shakspeare so well as Cibber we very much doubt. . . . Many of his "points" fall away . . . including some of the most effective. The famous "Off with his head, so much for Buckingham," the imprecation after he is mortally wounded, the second scene with Lady Anne . . . are all demolished at one fell swoop. Mr. Phelps, who played Richard on Thursday night, did not attempt to make it a character of points. . .

What is lost on the side of Richard is more than compensated to the play by the restoration of Queen Margaret. . . For it is this character that gives unity to the play. She is the incarnate Nemesis,—the revelation of Fate,—almost the Chorus of the play. Mrs. Warner played her admirably. She entered with the aspect less of a human enemy than of some supernatural being. The intensity and violence of her hate were terrific. . . It was decidedly the most effective character of the piece. . . . . With a young gentleman, named Ward, who made his *début* as Edward IV (omitted in Cibber's version), we were much pleased. The King only appears on the point of death, and the languor and breaking strength were given with a degree of delicacy and judgment that promises exceedingly well.

Our guess as to the elimination of some of the royal children is verified by the review in the News of the World, quoted—as usual without date—in the biography of Phelps by May Phelps and Forbes Robertson. This summary of the proceedings is interesting in itself, but particularly in view of the fact that some of the material of scenes eliminated was worked over in scenes actually presented. This was not very different from the practice of Cibber himself, and we rather regret finding Phelps indulging, if ever so slightly, in the same old discreditable game. The News of the World informs us that auditors "have the original text, with such alterations only as were necessary either to reduce the play within acting length, or obviate some otherwise insurmountable difficulty. We refer to the second act. In lieu of two scenes with the Duchess of York and the children of Clarence in one place, and with the child of Edward in another, and a third scene with some citizens, the subject of their discourse is worked into a conference between Gloster, Buckingham, and Hastings, &c. after King Edward is carried out dying; when Gloster sounds his doubtful friends as to the probability of their assisting him in his attempt to obtain the crown. A scene after the retirement of Edward, and the re-appearance of the Queen lamenting his death, was necessary; and it is a matter of discussion whether the scene thus arranged has been conceived in a becoming spirit, and executed with due reverence for the great author. The whole of the language employed being adapted from other parts of the play, may be urged in its favour. This is the only alteration of great importance; in other places compression only is observed, with occasionally the introduction of a few lines (Shakspeare's) to conclude an act or make a graceful exit." This long-felt necessity of concluding an act on a big speech was part of the change that came in with the drop-curtain; the concluding tableau at once fixed itself in the minds of stage-managers as the ultimate of endeavour.   Nothing could be more foreign to the spirit of Shakespeare as written.

Richard III, then, was the first great effort of Phelps at restoring an original to the stage.   There were liberal omissions and some parts were transposed, as we have seen; but what the audience witnessed and heard was mostly Shakespeare, not Cibber.   What was the result?   Obviously, it was that of the revival of Shakespeare's text at Covent Garden in 1821; actors still continued to perform the Cibber adaptation.   And why?   Because it is, say what we purists will, a better acting medium—it is more compact, more thrilling, more "pointed" for a star actor.   The sad part remains to tell: Phelps acted Richard but seldom during his tenancy of Sadler's Wells, and then, in his very last season (1861–62), revived, after many years, Richard III—in the Cibber version!   W. May Phelps in his biography of the actor says that for this he holds himself responsible. "Having seen Mrs. Warner's magnificent performance of Queen Margaret, I told him I was quite certain Miss Atkinson could not act it."   Possibly Phelps himself was not reluctant to return to the more showy Gloster of Cibber— an actor-made, almost "actor-proof" part.   Charles Kean in the next decade played the Cibber version at the Princess's, and Shakespeare's Gloster did not re-emerge till Henry Irving enacted him at the Lyceum, in January, 1877. The Cibber play, as I have said before, still tyrannises, in the theatre, over Shakespeare's.   No star-actor of a Gloster likes to see the Nemesis-figure of Margaret walk away with all the honours; possibly that is why Cibber altogether eliminated the character of the grief-crazed queen.

CHARLOTTE CUSHMAN AS ROMEO, 1845

The next restoration was under Webster's management at the Haymarket, on December 29, 1845, when Charlotte and Susan Cushman appeared as Romeo and Juliet, entirely from the Shakespeare text. The restoration is accredited to Charlotte Cushman, who insisted on discarding the Garrick flummery. The version of the play in Lacy's edition is undoubtedly that in use at the time; the printed cast of Webster's revival is a criterion. A glance at this will show how little is gone; hardly worth collating for, if I may so put it. The part of Lady Montague is restored, the business of the first act, with references to Rosaline, is given fully, Mercutio's Queen Mab speech is in proper place, by night, not in a grove by daylight, as in Garrick, Juliet gives her "banished" scene, which Adelaide Neilson and Mary Anderson, later, omitted, and a great deal of the fuss with the Capulets and the Nurse, prior to the attempted awakening of Juliet, is wearily gone through with. Even the reconciliation of the Capulets and the Montagues follows on the death of the lovers. This is to give almost too much of Shakespeare; but it is hard to be a reformer and to be moderate at the same time.

This revival placed Miss Cushman on the highest pinnacle of fame in London, and was the great feature of the season, 1845–46. It was repeated, according to Mr. William Archer, eighty-four times. Phelps followed Miss Cushman's lead in his revival of the play on September 16, 1846, "with the original text," he himself playing Mercutio to the lovers of Creswick and Laura Addison, and the Nurse of Mrs. H. Marston; a good cast, utterly lacking what Charlotte Cushman so richly supplied—the flash of genius.

PHELPS'S KING LEAR AND WINTER'S TALE, 1845

The preceding narrative has shown the restoration to the stage of three Shakespearian plays hitherto acted but in mutilated or garbled form. Even before the last of these restorations, however—Charlotte Cushman's Romeo and Juliet—Phelps had gone much farther than had Macready in staging, almost complete, two other works that had long suffered at the hands of the enemy. These were brought out at Sadler's Wells, in November, 1845, just one month before the Haymarket Romeo and Juliet. The first was King Lear, on the 5th, with the Fool first played by a man, be it noted, and with, apparently, very great fidelity to the author. The Athenæum hymns its praise in terms that leave no doubt. "We have contended," it says, "for the purity of Shakespeare's text, and have welcomed every approach to it on the stage. We therefore commended Mr. Macready's revived version of King Lear; but, nevertheless, regretted the dislocation of some of the scenes, and the injurious falling of the curtain at the end of the first act on Lear's curse. We have lived to see all this effectually reformed. King Lear as now performed at this theatre follows the text and order of Shakespeare's scenes, with some few inevitable omissions, but with no alterations. The scene, hitherto omitted, between the King and the Fool, which closes the first act, excels in pathos. . . It was capitally acted. . . . The tragedy is, of course, in its restored state, long; but there is a felt progression in it which interests the spectator." Bell's Weekly Messenger further states that "Mr. Phelps, with a more lively faith [than Macready, who had made "certain sacrifices" to the "supposed taste of his audience"] in the power of Shakespeare, on Wednesday last produced the entire play as it came from the mind of its immortal author." Bravo, Phelps!

The second of the revivals I have mentioned was that of The Winter's Tale, brought out two weeks later, on the 19th. The speed with which these productions followed each other shows that Phelps relied far more on poetry than on scenery. In the next decade both he and Charles Kean could "produce" hardly more than one revival yearly, so exacting were the demands of the mechanical agencies involved. But in the '40's The Winter's Tale could follow another revival, in two weeks. The Athenæum informs us that, though particular "attention has been paid to the general *mise-en-scène*," . . . nearly every word of the original text is repeated, and that the second scene of the fifth act, so long wont to be mutilated [the scene involving Autolycus, first with the Gentlemen, then with the Shepherd and the Clown] is restored—a merit this, deserving unqualified commendation."

PHELPS RESTORES MACBETH, 1847

Another service Phelps was to perform. The last vestige of alteration now survived in the witch-scenes of Macbeth, with the verbal accretions by Davenant and their musical decoration by Locke. Lady Macduff also had long been banished from the scene. Phelps resolutely set to work to remove these blemishes, and on September 27, 1847, brought out Macbeth, with the now familiar slogan, "from the text of Shakespeare." The Times, on the following day, succinctly sums up the difference:

It is highly characteristic of the present disposition to revere the memory of Shakspeare, that his text has been followed with that severe conscientiousness which marked the performance of last night. The music, with the interpolated words to which it is set, has been dropped, Lady Macduff and her son are restored, the old man talks of Duncan's horses eating each other, and last, but not least, Macbeth is killed *off* the stage in the orthodox manner, and his head is brought on the pole. There is no half-measure in this. Mr. Phelps having raised the Shakspearian banner, waves it gallantly indeed.

Again a comparison of playbill and of *dramatis personæ* in the Cambridge text will show how closely Phelps followed his master. Only the character of the English doctor is omitted from the bill, showing that the unnecessary scene involving this person (in Act V, Scene 3) was erased from the exhibition. Phelps was apparently more conscientious in such matters than was his brilliant rival of the next decade at the Princess's; but his audiences were probably more earnest and more exacting.

F. G. Tomlins, in Douglas Jerrold's Weekly Newspaper (quoted by W. May Phelps), is a bit more philosophic than the "Thunderer" in his review of Phelps's accomplishment: "Of all the attempts to restore Shakspeare's plays we consider this the boldest. Precisely because it had been so little altered, in comparison to others, was it difficult to restore it. Connected also with noble music . . . many persons still think it was an allowable innovation. All such thinkers we refer to the reproduction at this theatre. . . . For the first time for nearly two hundred years could a correct view be obtained by an audience of the play in its entirety; and never did its proportions come out more perfectly. By inserting only the portion of the Witches designed by the author, their agency and their potency became obvious. . . . Four short scenes, in curt dialogue, divided between three and sometimes four individuals, make up the whole of this terrible machinery. But never was the supernatural more effectively introduced."

As in the case of one or two of the restorations previously discussed, Phelps's efforts, I am sorry to say, did not produce lasting results. Charles Kean, in his spectacular revival at the Princess's, on February 14, 1853, restored all the business of the singing witches, and once more deleted Lady Macduff and her child from the *dramatis personæ*. Probably he gauged West End taste in so doing; farther to the north, at Islington, they liked their Shakespeare pure.

PHELPS'S ANTONY AND CLEOPATRA, 1849

One of the most notable of Phelps's productions at Sadler's Wells was Antony and Cleopatra on the 22nd of October, 1849. This, according to W. May Phelps, was from the original text, and therein came nearest, since Garrick's of 1759, to realising Shakespeare's conception. The 1813 revival at Covent Garden was, as we know, a silly admixture of Shakespeare and Dryden; Dutton Cook tells us that Macready's effort in 1833 was not without Dryden alloy. But Phelps, in the revival of 1849, gave Shakespeare undiluted, though, from the exigency of the case, Shakespeare's forty-two scenes were, by running together and by transposition, reduced considerably in number. Forty changes of scenery would demand something more than human in the way of scene shifters and stage directors, especially on a small, not remarkably well-equipped stage like that of Sadler's Wells. The loyalty of Phelps to his cause, however, may be judged from the fact that only three characters, and those less than minor, are missing from the list on his playbill; excepting Taurus and Seleucus and Silius— who were they, O my reader?—no one is missing from the play as cast by Phelps. With so great an opportunity for doubling or even trebling, I consider such loyalty little short of heroic. If Phelps had followed the custom, invariable with Charles Kean in the next decade at the Princess's, of printing synopses of scenery, we should have a clearer idea of what he did with Antony and Cleopatra; as it is, he condescended only in the case of Pericles in 1854 to give us of later days so palpable a help toward an understanding of his plan. Finally, lest the reader be misled by wandering fires, I may warn him that the Complete Works of Shakespeare, "edited by Samuel Phelps" and published in 1854 by Willoughby & Company, stand merely as a *nominis umbra*. They are not, alas! acting versions, nor are they even good versions of the originals; Coleman tells us the editorial task was performed by Phelps's right-hand man, E. L. Blanchard. We may assume, therefore, that Phelps merely lent his name to the publication as many actors have done, since his time, down to the days of the Henry Irving Shakespeare. Phelps's own stage versions are not accessible. In the case of Antony and Cleopatra, we fall back on our general confidence in Phelps's conscientiousness in such matters, and support our faith by a statement in John Bull (October 27, 1849) to the effect that the tragedy "has been played exactly [note the word] according to Shakespeare's text, without any of the liberties usually taken by modern adapters."

PLAYS INFREQUENTLY ACTED

I would stress the fact that this production was the last definite restoration of the original text in any Shakespearian play, during the years of the period we are now discussing. It is also a restoration in another sense, that of bringing back to the stage a play so infrequently acted, previously, that its revival came with the effect of complete novelty to a generation that had not known it before.   Antony and Cleopatra was thus, it will be seen, a restoration in both senses.   For the rest of the discussion I shall consider restorations of Shakespeare only in the second sense.   Cibber and Garrick might again supersede Shakespeare in Richard III and Romeo and Juliet, but no one would henceforth be so absurd as to think he could actually re-write any play of Shakespeare.   The race of Tate was extinct. Therefore, I shall hereafter be called upon merely to chronicle revivals of the dramatist's plays not often seen on the stage.   The great masterpieces of the poet were constantly acted, in form approximating the original; but these I leave, to pass to matter more unusual, in recording attempts, almost always futile, to make the hitherto neglected plays of the poet acceptable to a public that in general liked them not.

One of the earlier of these trials, within the years we are searching, was Benjamin Webster's with The Two Gentlemen of Verona, at the Haymarket, on December 14, 1848. In spite of the fact that Mr. and Mrs. Charles Kean appeared as Valentine and Julia, with Creswick as Proteus, and Webster and Keeley as Speed and Launce, and in spite of new scenery and considerable music, the revival was not a great success.   This particular play will be but love's labour lost for any manager; and, except for laudation from critics and scholars, he is not likely to reap a rich harvest for his pains.   Phelps was to discover this in the next decade at Sadler's Wells.   The public undoubtedly feels that the play is a weak forerunner of Twelfth Night, and that one may as well wait for performances of the stronger work.

In the same year, March 3rd, the student will be pleased to learn that the Olympic Theatre brought out an interesting item in the Shakespeare Apocrypha—the play of Sir

John Oldcastle. This deserves mention here for its novelty merely; it is not related directly to our subject. The only critique with which I am familiar is in the Illustrated London News of March 4, 1848, and shows weakness everywhere in the production. "The performance of this work . . . was far from satisfactory. It was not played according to the original text, and, although the chief characters were well filled . . . . it failed to awaken the mildest enthusiasm. There is something singular in the fascination which makes 'legitimate' managers persist in routing up these musty mediocrities, when every experiment turns out a greater failure than the preceding one." So much for Sir John Oldcastle, and the honest effort of the Olympic management; I am not sure that the play was repeated. The next night G. V. Brooke played Hamlet.

PHELPS'S ACTIVITIES, 1850–1862

The more notable of the Shakespearian revivals at Sadler's Wells, up to the mid-year of the century, have been detailed. The baker's dozen of years remaining to Phelps's management saw the completion of his scheme to bring on the stage the greater number of Shakespeare's plays. Six only he failed to produce, and five of these are probably unactable. The most memorable of his restorations—in our second meaning of the word—were so important that their fame still abides among the few who really care for the theatre. These were, in order, Timon of Athens, September 15, 1851; Henry V, October 25, 1852; A Midsummer Night's Dream, October 8, 1853; Pericles, October 14, 1854; The Comedy of Errors, November 8, 1855; The Taming of the Shrew, November 15, 1856; Love's Labour's Lost, September 30, 1857; Coriolanus, September 15, 1860.

These revivals, it is observed, occur at the rate of about one annually; the explanation, unquestionably, lies in the increased exigency of the situation scenical. Of course, during the years discussed Phelps had a very large repertoire, classical and modern, with the varied delights of

which he regaled his loyal public. I have cited only the
more remarkable of his revivals; but it must be remembered that, along with his constant repetition of the more
familiar Shakespearian plays, he, from time to time, revealed
whatever dramatic values inhere in less frequently acted
comedies like Measure for Measure, All's Well that Ends
Well and The Two Gentlemen of Verona. The bill changed
frequently, sometimes nightly, and a great revival, even in
its early days, was enacted generally but three times a
week. Friday and Saturday were "off" nights, and on
them Phelps seldom appeared, as John Coleman's humorous
account attests. The amount of work involved in keeping
up to the high level of all these performances must have
been enormous; in some respects Phelps's might be rated
as the last great repertoire theatre in English annals.

I shall, in the pages that follow, take up only the finest of
the revivals in the list cited above. One at least, The
Taming of the Shrew, has already been instanced; several
of the others, remembering Phelps's zeal in restoring the
original text, we may safely pass by. Three on which a
considerable part of his glory rests, I will now examine in
order.

TIMON OF ATHENS, 1851

So far as I know, Phelps's was the only near approach
to a performance of Timon of Athens in the history of the
English stage; Shadwell's alteration, originally produced in
1678, had held the stage, with intervals of silence, up to
1745. Cumberland, after much bickering, had induced
Garrick to bring out his version in 1771, and Thomas Hull
had perpetrated another in 1786. Until 1816, when George
Lamb restored something like order to the play, Shakespeare's creation or anything approximating thereto, had
been conspicuous by absence from the boards. Phelps's
revival, therefore, was a complete novelty, and it was a
brave thing to attempt. Before an Anglo-Saxon audience,
at least, the lack of feminine interest is an insuperable disadvantage; the only women characters, as we know, could

hardly be admitted to polite society. Furthermore, Timon is, for all practical purposes, an unsympathetic person; there is something peculiarly unpleasing in the serious stage illustration of the adage about a fool and his money. And except for the faithful Flavius and the snarling Apemantus, Shakespeare has provided few distinctly individualised characters. All the more honour, therefore, to Phelps, who saw possibilities in the original play, and mounted it very splendidly, in September, 1851.

By this time the opportunity for scenic display was appealing to him more and more, and this aspect of his production is stressed by the reviewers. But that the play was not permitted to be submerged in scenery, we learn from positive statements; the notice of Henry Morley, in the Examiner, on the second revival of the play in 1856 is so good that I have no hesitation in reproducing it here at considerable length. The entire review may be found in Morley's Journal of a London Playgoer, under date of October 18, 1856:

A main cause of the success of Mr. Phelps in his Shakespearean revivals is, that he shows in his author above all things the poet. Shakespeare's plays are always poems, as performed at Sadler's Wells. The scenery is always beautiful, but it is not allowed to draw attention from the poet, with whose whole conception it is made to blend in the most perfect harmony. The actors are content also to be subordinated to the play, learn doubtless at rehearsals how to subdue excesses of expression that by giving undue force to one part would destroy the balance of the whole, and blend their work in such a way as to produce everywhere the right emphasis. . . . .

This is the case especially with "Timon." . . . . . Every member of the company is taught to regard the poetry he speaks according to its nature rather than its quantity. The personators of the poet and the painter in the first scene of the "Timon" as now acted, manifestly say what Shakespeare has assigned to them to say with as much care, and as much certainty that it will be listened to with due respect, as if they were themselves Timons, Hamlets or Macbeths. Nobody rants . . . . . nothing is slurred, a servant who has anything to say says it in earnest, making his words heard and their meaning felt; and so it is that, although only in one or two cases we may have observed at Sadler's Wells originality of genius in the actor, we have nevertheless perceived something like the entire sense of one of Shakespeare's plays, and have been raised above ourselves by the perception.

This great service then Phelps performed; he put on Shakespeare as a whole, with every detail realised.   As to Timon of Athens, we may be sure that justice was done the text, and that most of the scenes were given, "cut" only as the exigencies of the stage demanded.   Of this we may convince ourselves by comparing the playbill with the *dramatis personæ* of the Cambridge edition.   Every member of the long list of characters is found on the bill, excepting only the Fool, and he, I suspect, appears in another guise.   This is being very fair to Shakespeare; and no one else, so far as I can learn, was ever so faithful to his trust, from Betterton to Irving and Tree.   Phelps gave more of Shakespeare in a play than did any other of the actor-managers for two hundred and fifty years.

A MIDSUMMER NIGHT'S DREAM, 1853

We have traced the history of Shakespeare's fairy comedy from the entry in Pepys's Diary, through nearly two centuries of dreadful vicissitude, to Madame Vestris's revival in 1840.   It was, however, to Samuel Phelps that this beautiful creation owed its first adequate production. There was, we know, something garish about Madame Vestris's, but precisely the opposite effect—the soft enchantment of a moonlit vision—was realised at Sadler's Wells in October, 1853.   The scenery was, of course, a prevailing characteristic of the revival, but every criticism I have read—and what theatre-lover has not read many?—emphasises the poetic verisimilitude of the accomplishment. This is one of the few instances in which the almost impossibly difficult was effected—Shakespeare's fairies and his mortals mingled for once in a misty, moonlit charm so enthralling that the auditor lost all sense of things as they are and allowed himself to be transported to a poetic realm hitherto unknown and undreamt of.   It was the first wholly satisfactory presentation of Shakespeare's fairy play of which dramatic annals make record. It gave most of Shakespeare's text, well spoken by trained actors. Phelps as Bottom—a very great performance—was the only "star" in the cast.

PERICLES, 1854

The wonder is, not that Pericles should have been unperformed in the course of two centuries (Lillo's Marina, of 1738, hardly causing a ripple of excitement, and an edition of the play printed in 1796, "as intended to be performed at the Theatre Royal, Covent Garden," never having reached its goal—the stage), but that even the hardy Phelps should have ventured on the production of it. Yet this he did in 1854. Better even than we in our studies he realised the disjointed and fragmentary character of the play; only too keenly he must have foreseen its limited acting-possibilities. In all probability he wished to make headway against the vogue of Charles Kean's magnificent revivals at the Princess's, and at one blow re-establish his own prestige as the most intellectual manager of the time. Pericles at least offered opportunities for unlimited scenic display; traversing a large part of the ancient world, its action carries one from scene to scene of splendour almost unparalleled in the painter's experience.

For reasons unknown to me, Phelps's bill of this play— "copyright and entered at Stationers' Hall," it warns imitators and pirates—carries unusual information as to the production. Every scene is printed, distinctly localised, and with the names of such of the characters as appear for the first time therein. In other words, cast of characters and scene-synopsis are given together in very interesting fashion. By carefully comparing these scenes and characters with Shakespeare's text, we have an infallible clue to the order of events in Phelps's version.

But first, what of Gower, the chorus-like figure, who appears very frequently throughout the original play, naïvely informing the reader of intervening acts and episodes in the passage from one disjointed scene to the next? Evidently this was a problem for Phelps; at last he decided to omit this important, but (I should expect) boring figure, and to make up the deficiency in a way that his steady panegyrist, Henry Morley, can approve of but with one auspicious and one drooping eye. To our surprise, almost our dismay, we discover that Phelps supplies some of the necessary links to the story by "writing into" the action certain passages from the monologues of the deleted Gower. I am sorry to report this of the virtuous Phelps; but the truth must be told, though idols fall. Morley, under date of October 21st, in his Journal, tells the sad tale:

In the revival of the play Mr. Phelps was left to choose between two difficulties. The omission of Gower would be a loss to the play, in an artistic sense, yet the introduction of Gower before every act would very probably endanger its effect in a theatrical sense, unless the part were spoken by an actor of unusual power. The former plan was taken; and in adding to certain scenes in the drama [would Morley had been more explicit here!] passages of his own writing, strictly confined to the explanation of those parts of the story which Shakespeare represents Gower as narrating between the acts, Mr. Phelps may have used his best judgment as a manager. . . .

The change did, inevitably, to a certain extent, disturb the poetical effect of the story; but assuming its necessity, it was effected modestly and well. The other changes also were in no case superfluous, and were made with considerable judgment. The two scenes at Mytilene, which present *Marina* pure as an ermine which no filth can touch, were compressed into one; and although the plot of the drama was not compromised by a false delicacy, there remained not a syllable at which true delicacy could have conceived offence.

Let us return to the bill of the play, and the light it throws on Phelps's version of Pericles. All of Shakespeare's characters appear in the cast, except the Pandar, whom one gladly misses. The first act is given in three, not four scenes, merely by running together the second and third. I suspect that this already overladen scene is filled with parts of Shakespeare's Act II, Scene 4, since the list of characters in the bill calls for Escanes, easily omitted up to now, and three Lords, who have almost nothing to do before this bit in the second act, where indeed they have much. Both scenes take place, as labelled in the one scene on the bill, in Tyre. Phelps's second act otherwise follows Shakespeare, except that scenes 3 and 5 are run together, an any sensible stage manager would run them together on a stage richly laden with scenery. The third act contains Shakespeare's first two scenes, but the playbill incomprehensibly (to me) omits Shakespeare's next scene, at Tarsus; that in which Pericles leaves his infant Marina in charge of Cleon and Dionyza. Perhaps, as this was a repeated scene, or bit of staging, it was not re-announced on the bill. I am led to believe the scene was given, because Morley's synopsis of (evidently) the acted play, expressly states that, "being at this time near Tharsus, and remembering that Tharsus owes to him a debt of gratitude, *Pericles* makes for Tharsus, in order that he may place his infant with the least possible delay upon sure ground and under tender nursing." I cannot say whether or not Shakespeare's fourth scene of this act—that between Cerimon and Thaisa—was run on the second scene of the same act, involving the same characters. Knowing the stage as I do, I think it quite likely.

The remaining parts of the play are all Marina's and her father's. Phelps's version (according to the playbill) opens with the scene of the abduction (whether or not the "bit" of recrimination between Cleon and Dionyza is transferred from Scene 3 to conclude the episode, I cannot say), but the act otherwise contains only the scenes of Marina in the house of the woman of Mitylene, here given as one unbroken series of events (and enough at that). The last act comprises the great scene of recognition on board Pericles's ship and that in the Temple of Diana at Ephesus. They were connected by a moving panorama of the passage from Mitylene to Ephesus—one of those stage effects so popular at the time.

This was the last of Phelps's really great new productions at Sadler's Wells. The final eight years of his tenancy saw noble performances of all the repertoire, but the newer revivals were of plays not so rarely acted, or, as in the case of Pericles, never acted in the times of recorded history. With Pericles, therefore, we take leave for the present of the worthy Samuel Phelps.

CHARLES KEAN AT THE PRINCESS'S

Enter Charles Kean. During his first season at the Princess's (1850–51) he was associated in management with the popular comedian, Robert Keeley, and possibly for this reason, possibly because the novelty had not yet shaped itself to a settled policy, the Shakespearian performances, though good, attained but little of the distinction so marked in the productions of the subsequent years. The season lasted thirteen months, from September 20, 1850, to October 17, 1851, and the profits were £7,000, largely owing to the Great Exposition of 1851. During the thirteen months involved, Twelfth Night (the opening bill) was repeated forty times; Hamlet, fourteen; As You Like It, four; The Merchant of Venice, twelve; and Henry IV, Part II, twenty-two times. This, though a good showing for Shakespeare, was a slight record compared with that of seasons soon to follow.

The versions of the plays used need not detain us here; I doubt if they received any supervision from Kean. In the second season, however, when Kean was sole manager, he did two notable things. He opened, on November 22, 1851, with The Merry Wives of Windsor, "divested," as J. W. Cole, his eulogist, informs us, "of the operatic and textual interpolations by which it had been too long disfigured," in fact ever since 1824, when the Reynolds-Bishop medley was produced at Drury Lane. So long as Madame Vestris played Mrs. Page, the Shakespearian text was doomed to wear the golden chain of Bishop's music. Now Kean discarded all that, and, as Cole glowingly relates, "the fine, racy dialogue was no longer impeded by the introduction of bravuras, interminable duets, and flourishes." To give the reader an idea of the excellence of

Kean's company, composed of far better individual talent than Phelps's, I may say that Mr. and Mrs. Kean played the Fords, J. Vining and Mrs. Keeley the Pages, Bartley, Falstaff (and he was the very best of his time), Keeley, Sir Hugh Evans, Ryder, Pistol, Alfred Wigan, Doctor Caius, Harley (the best living comedian), Slender, and Drinkwater Meadows, Shallow. This was about the best cast possible in a London theatre of that day. The comedy ran twenty-five nights, and established the reputation of the house.

The second important Shakespearian event was the revival, on February 9, 1852, of King John. This was the first of that series of Shakespearian productions for which the Princess's, under Kean, was to become famous, even to our own day. From the date of this production, Kean was noted as the first really great producer of Shakespeare in anything like our modern sense, involving absolute historical accuracy as to scenery, costumes, and accessories; every production was the result of minute search for sources, study of originals, examination of historical documents, consultation with experts, archæological and artistic, and an unwearied striving for unified and beautiful effects. Kean's programmes became wonderful in their citation of authorities for styles in dresses, armour, architecture, etc. His published acting versions bristle with notes of fearsome, not to say appalling, scholarship. The poor man probably was too much of a scholar to be a great actor, but at least he had the fun of revelling in his scholarship, and of challenging all comers to prove him guilty of a single anachronism or a single point misplaced. Contemporaries, of course, ridiculed and burlesqued him for his scholarly programmes, but the public snatched a fearful joy in swimming in the mighty sea of questions raised on every programme handed out to the patrons of the theatre.

Kean honestly thought that this was doing the very great thing for Shakespeare; the plays were not properly presented unless every detail of decoration was in accord with a unified plan. This idea persisted throughout the career of Henry Irving and most of the career of Beerbohm Tree. It is only within a few years that many people have decided the best thing to do for Shakespeare is to give his plays undecorated by anything except what he himself supplied—the verse, with a minimum of scenery.   But neither Kean nor Irving could have conceived of such a state of mind.   This is a contribution of the Twentieth Century.

And what of the plays, as staged by Kean?   Naturally, with such weighty masses of scenery, requiring time for manipulation, the plays could be given only in part; cutting must be very liberal, to allow time for intermissions, and to send the audience home at a proper hour.   Furthermore, scenes must be run together to use, with least expenditure of time in shifting, the very heavy, elaborate "sets" built up to astonish the playgoers with their novelty and solidity. Cutting and transposition of scenes, also the placing of scenes in settings to which, in reason, they could not possibly belong; these are the invariable accompaniments of Shakespearian productions arranged according to the Kean-Irving formula.   They must be accepted as inevitable, and are indeed gladly so accepted by the majority of playgoers, who have become spectators in the theatre, rather than auditors —auditors of the finest poetry in the language.   When this is said, most has been said concerning Kean's versions. He prated much of the integrity of the text as spoken on his stage, and certainly nearly everything there spoken— except in Richard III—was Shakespeare, without alloy of inferior craftsmen; but so much of the original was not spoken that Kean was like a man who swore to speak the truth and nothing but the truth, blandly ignoring the fact that the *whole* truth was also required.   What Kean gave was nothing but Shakespeare; but alas! the great deal that he did not give was also Shakespeare.   This, however, was expected in his day.

KEAN'S KING JOHN AND MACBETH, 1852–1853

An examination of all but one of the twelve plays he chose to publish—those of his first season not specially "got up" he did not publish—will reveal the justice of my remarks. The first in point of time, King John, omits only one brief scene, and gives all the rest in Shakespeare's order; but there is hardly one scene which is not severely "cut"—sometimes almost to the bone. Somehow, one manages to forgive this, in view of the gorgeous stage spectacle provided; the very next production of Kean, however, supplies a grievance hard to be condoned—the restoration of all the Locke-Davenant ballet-operatic stuff in Macbeth, magnificently staged at the Princess's, on February 14, 1853, and played sixty times in the course of twenty weeks. This, and Richard III, and, to a slight extent, Much Ado about Nothing, were the only plays of which one cannot say that it was all Shakespeare that was presented. Since Phelps had in 1847 abolished all these detestable additions, Kean had no defense for their restoration except the purely sensuous attraction to eye and ear. To make room for this desirability, he omits the scene of Lady Macduff and her son, which Phelps had restored; also that of the drunken porter. A Kemble survival makes poor Seyton perform all the menial services required by the bloody-minded Macbeths. Every time a servant is required, the ubiquitous Seyton answers the summons; he even opens the gate —*vice* the porter deleted—for the inopportune entrance of Macduff, just after the murder of Duncan. The part about the fatal storm—the colloquy between the Old Man and Rosse—is missing. Lady Macbeth does not appear in the scene following the discovery of the murder, nor does Donalbain. The English Doctor is not brought into the scene between Malcolm and Macduff in Act V. Finally Macbeth is slain on the stage. This version, therefore, is not different in theory from that of Kemble; Phelps's good service in restoring the original seemed, for the moment, to have been in vain. Kean brought back some fine poetry that Kemble had omitted, chiefly in the first two acts; but, in spite of that, his production of Macbeth distinctly set the clock back, as far as the west end of London was concerned. Worse even than this was his resurrection of Cib-

ber's Richard III, on February 20, 1854, nine years after
Phelps had restored the original.   This he had the grace
not to include in the twelve "Shakespearian" plays he edited
for publication, and I am, therefore, relieved of devoting to
it more than very brief notice.   In this case the whirligig
of time brought in very quick revenges: the play ran only
nineteen nights, and the extravagant mounting was a complete loss.

KEAN'S HENRY VIII, 1855

During this season, 1853–54, Mrs. Kean had suffered
from a serious and protracted illness; her services had,
therefore, not been available.   Possibly, if she could have
played Queen Margaret, the original Richard III might
have been given.   On her return, toward the close of the
next season (on May 16, 1855, to be exact), Henry VIII
was presented with a wealth of scenery, costumes and
effects, and enjoyed a hitherto unprecedented run of one
hundred consecutive nights.   This was the first of a rapid
succession of Shakespearian revivals that brought to the
theatre uninterrupted acclaim and prosperity, and led to a
fifty-year habit of spectacular display in all "big" Shakespearian productions.   Though Kean had begun two or
three years before with King John and Macbeth, Mrs.
Kean's illness had sadly disarranged his plans; now, with
her restoration to the stage, he was able to accomplish all
that he desired, and for four years startled London with
one magnificent spectacle after another, until thoughtful
critics began to fear that Shakespeare was doomed to be
merely an excuse for scenery, rather than the scenery an
aid to Shakespeare.   From this time to the end of his
career as manager, he atoned for the Locke-Davenant
absurdities in Macbeth and the Cibber Richard III by
giving Shakespeare only, if not Shakespeare entire.   Henceforth, no dross was allowed to mingle with the gold, though
the gold was always—alas!—clipped.

Shakespeare's historical plays, as well as most of those
of his contemporaries, sadly lack unity; the Elizabethans

felt that they must honestly pack in every episode of importance in the life of the King who gave the title to the play. Henry VIII suffers particularly under this weakness, and he would be a rash purist who would insist on the preservation on the stage of all the material of the last two acts. Undoubtedly the dramatic interest ceases with the death of Queen Katharine. As regards the acting version of Kean, then, we must admit that he has given the skeleton (or more) of all that is dramatically feasible; that he presents all the scenes—and in Shakespeare's order—that bear on the tragedy of the King, the Queen and Wolsey. They are diminished greatly in substance, but the spirit remains. Furthermore, he gives more of the last episodes than did his successors, Irving and Tree.

In making his version he even restored, as his preface proudly asserts: "The scene in which the two Cardinals, Wolsey and Campeius, visit Queen Katharine in the Palace of Bridewell, after the trial . . . . is now restored, for the first time. The '*Vision*' in the chamber of the dying Katharine, at Kimbolton Castle, replaces the introduced song of Patience. . . . The fifth act has of late years been entirely omitted. The portion relating to the christening of the royal infant, the Princess Elizabeth, is now restored. Any further addition would extend the representation beyond reasonable limits."

It may be observed that the first two are, indeed, the changes that differentiate Kean's version from Kemble's; the latter, however, retained even more of the Gardiner-Cranmer material preceding the christening of Elizabeth. Kean also restored to Griffith the lines in the scene of Katharine's death which Kemble—following Bell—gave to Cromwell—because he originally played Cromwell, I suppose. In the course of the action Kean introduced his favorite device of a moving panorama, this time of London, as it appeared in the reign of Henry VIII. All in all, his acting version is good, granting the necessity—imposed by scenery—of the heroic excision he made from the body of the text, even in the episodes actually presented. Without being too reactionary, we may congratulate the Londoners of 1855, who saw and heard this beautiful revival of a great tragedy.

THE WINTER'S TALE, 1856

Kean's next attempt was a superb Winter's Tale, revived on April 28, 1856, and played thereafter consecutively for 102 nights. The most radical change was the substitution of the name of Bithynia for Bohemia, that same old sea-coast troubling Kean's scholarly mind, while his producer's eye, as his preface informs us, saw a chance to utilise Asiatic costumes in Bithynia for contrast to the Greek dress of the earlier scenes in Syracuse. As to his cuttings from the body of the text, the reader will be pleased to learn that they are chiefly in the scenes of humour at the close. Autolycus, the Clown and the Shepherd are far less garrulous in Kean than in Shakespeare. This is particularly true of Autolycus; his part in Act V, Scene 2, is given to Dion, who thus relates the great discovery of Perdita by her father. Autolycus gone, the Clown and the Shepherd automatically disappear; lament them who will! For myself, I consider it a rather good acting version of The Winter's Tale, for the year 1856.

A MIDSUMMER NIGHT'S DREAM, 1856

To give an idea of what Kean meant by presenting Shakespeare according to the text, we may carry mathematics to that unmathematical thing, The Midsummer Night's Dream, which he produced on October 15, 1856, and with which for the 150 nights of its performing he achieved probably his prettiest success as a manager. While it is true that, with one notable exception, Kean gave the play according to the text of Shakespeare, it is so shrunken a body he offered that one could only exclaim, "What a falling off was there!" For instance, the first scene of the first act is reduced from 251 to 161 lines, and among those missing are most of the finest passages of poetry in the play. A change in the text itself occurs at the beginning of Act II. Puck's opening speeches are given to a Fairy; and why? In order that the audience, fresh from late and fashionable dining, might have the thrill of beholding Puck rise on a mushroom, the while music sweetly played! The ensuing speeches between Oberon and Titania are frightfully mangled, Titania's 'These are the forgeries of jealousy,' yielding most of its life-blood in being reduced from 38 to 9½ lines. This indubitably is buying scenery at a high cost. Act III, Scene 2 (really Shakespeare's Scene 1) is cut from 463 to 226 lines. The play toward the close is allowed to retain more of the original material; but, as a serious attempt to present one of the most poetical of plays, I know of no acting version—"with the original text"—less satisfactory than this. We must fall back on our faith in scenery to atone for what the poem has lost.

RICHARD II AND THE TEMPEST, 1857

The season in which the Midsummer Night's Dream was produced was almost a year in length—from September 1, 1856, to August 21, 1857. In the course of these twelve months Shakespeare was presented 290 nights at the Princess's—a very remarkable record. This was undoubtedly Kean's banner year, not only in number of Shakespearian performances but in number of splendid Shakespearian revivals. In addition to A Midsummer Night's Dream, he brought out on March 12, 1857, the seldom-acted Richard II, and kept it going for 85 nights; and on July 1st he surpassed all previous attempts with a truly gorgeous Tempest, somewhat in the style of a pantomime, to be sure, but still The Tempest. This assuredly surpasses all records within my ken.

Kean's version of Richard II is what one might expect from an actor-manager who played the principal part. Everything is sacrificed to the character of the hapless monarch. For instance, Aumerle, one of the most interesting personages in Shakespeare's tragedy, is reduced to practically the vanishing point. Not only is his first important scene—that between himself and the King, following the banishment of Bolingbroke—omitted, but all the matter pertaining to his treason is eliminated from the last act. This of course abolishes Shakespeare's Scene 3 of Act V, the plea of the Duchess of York for her son—her part thereby suffering dramatic annihilation—and the imposing business of Bolingbroke's pardon. Why not thus reduce Aumerle and even Bolingbroke, when the star must be "featured" as Richard, and also much scenery provided and—shifted? Other scenes less reprehensibly but entirely "cut" are that between the Captain and Salisbury in Wales (Shakespeare's Act II, Scene 4, which indeed one might expect to go) and that before Bristol Castle, with Bolingbroke and York, and including the death of Bushey and Green (Shakespeare's Act III, Scene 1), a bit that might well have been spared.

These and other "cuts," however, were probably made to provide for a very elaborate wordless spectacle of the entry into London of the wretched Richard in the train of the conquering Bolingbroke. For this much vaunted show, Kean, I am convinced, would have broken many jars of the finest poetic honey. Yet, in the second scene of Act V, he permits York to tell his duchess all the events of the pitiful exhibition thus pictorially represented at the end of Act III. Verily the ways of managers are past finding out. Perhaps audiences in 1857 pardoned, for the sake of this spectacle, the loss of such passages as I have mentioned; if so, they would gladly give up the first 105 lines—as Kean compelled them to do—in the scene of the abdication of Richard in Westminster Hall, the acted scene beginning with the entrance of York, and wholly discarding the long episode of the Bishop of Carlisle. In conclusion, I may do Kean the justice to say that he did not spare his own part either; for instance, in Richard's last scene, his pathetic speech beginning, "I have been studying how I may compare This prison where I live unto the world," is cut from 66 to 16½ lines, a veritable self-abnegation on the part of the man who might have spoken the entire 66! The reader sees that the version I have attempted to describe has gained much in unity of action and vastly in sharpening of the main character. It is much better than others of the century, and perhaps for Kean's purposes was as good as one could expect.

The Tempest is "cut" in a rather different way. No scene is omitted, but every scene is shorn of some of its chief poetic beauties. The text bristles with descriptions of scenery, dancing, and mechanical effects, but one will look in vain for many of the noblest lines Shakespeare ever wrote. Perhaps for the wonderful stage representation of the ship storm-tossed at sea, spectators willingly dispensed with every word Shakespeare had provided for the situation, and frankly accepted the inevitable as a mid-Victorian moving picture; but what of the glorious scene that follows —that with Prospero, Miranda and Ariel, reduced from 501 to 339 lines? Since all the scene is great poetry, one can judge how much great poetry was sacrificed. After this, one learns without protest that from Act II, Scene 1, the episode of Alonzo, Sebastian, Antonio and the rest of that storm-driven crew, 140 lines have been expunged before the entrance of Ariel. This one might forgive, but never the injury to the lovely scene of log-bearing and love-music in Act III, veritably shrunk to the skeleton of its once rounded and youthful beauty. In lieu of this, who would choose all the wondrous spectacle of the banquet scene, the anti-masque of animals, etc., or the ship on a calm sea, that closes the play? Even in 1857 the Shakespearian enthusiast must have left the theatre with a feeling of disappointment, not to say resentment and disgust, resolving hereafter to seek his poetry at Sadler's Wells, where scenery was less in evidence.

KING LEAR AND THE MERCHANT OF VENICE, 1858

1857 was, as I have said, Kean's banner year for novelty of play and splendour of staging. The following year saw him reverting to those good old "stand-bys," King Lear and The Merchant of Venice. These, also, he brought out with great attention to scenery and costume, but, after all, Londoners of that day could not be expected to become excited over plays so frequently acted everywhere.

Kean's version of King Lear, played April 17, 1858, is very like that in Lacy's Acting Plays, which I have assumed to be Macready's. The order of the scenes is very similar, though the parts of speeches retained or omitted in some cases differ considerably. The first act ends, as did Kemble's and Macready's, with the curse upon Goneril, omitting the subsequent scene between Goneril, Albany and Oswald, the last of whom, by the way, is called merely *Steward* throughout the tragedy. Shakespeare's Scene 5, between Lear and the Fool, is not given here, though part of it—as in Macready's (?) version—begins the third scene of Act II, the entry of Lear into Gloster's castle—an absurd place to find it. But this is the price we pay for the drop-curtain, which must be made to fall on a striking tableau or a striking speech; and what could be more striking than Lear's curse on Goneril? Likewise, the second act ends with Lear's exit—"O fool, I shall go mad!" necessitating the omission of all that follows, between Regan, Goneril, Gloster and the rest.

The most striking resemblance to the Lacy (Macready?) text is in Kean's Scene 4, of Act III—the Heath, with a Hovel. In this, Kean gives almost all of Shakespeare's text, up to the entrance of Gloster; omitting Gloster, for the moment, he brings in the trial of Goneril from Scene 6. Then Gloster enters, as in Shakespeare's Scene 4, gives some of his speeches as in Scene 4, and ends with his speeches from Scene 6 of the original. This, the reader sees, is very much after the Lacy (Macready?) pattern. Kean omits all of Shakespeare's Scenes 5 and 7—the blinding of Gloster. Furthermore, he omits Gloster's fall from the cliff, which is, as in Kemble, interrupted by the entrance of Lear. The rest of the play runs on briskly to Shakespeare's conclusion, cutting liberally what the employment of much scenery will not permit it to use. Perhaps, for its time and place, it did no great injustice to Shakespeare.

The Merchant of Venice, brought out magnificently on

June 12, 1858, with transferring and transfusing of scenes, and with considerable curtailing of speeches, manages to give something not very prejudicial to the purpose and meaning of Shakespeare's play. Both of Portia's suitors, Morocco and Arragon, are restored; they had not figured in Kemble's version, nor do they appear on the playbill of Phelps's Sadler's Wells. Kean in his preface justly claims the credit for bringing back these parts, "for the purpose of more strictly adhering to the author's text, and of heightening the interest attached to the episode of the caskets." In doing so, however, he does not hesitate to reduce Morocco's "choosing" speech from 48 to 16 lines, or Arragon's from 34 to 25; but, after all, the audience could at least see that Bassanio was not Portia's only suitor. The scene, by the way, in which Bassanio chooses the leaden casket is "cut" with almost a desperate hand. Portia's first speech is reduced from 24 to 6½ lines, her big speech, "Away, then, I am lock'd in one of them," from 23 also to 6½. Bassanio's choice-speech is cut from 35 to 19 lines, his second speech, from 35 to 15. One would have to ponder to determine just how far such a performance came to justifying Kean's boast about playing "from the text of Shakespeare." All the lovely poetry of Jessica and Lorenzo in the moonlight at Belmont is also sent to the limbo of unused, if not forgotten things. Perhaps one might sum up as to Kean's Merchant of Venice by admitting that it is a good acting play without undue favour to lines that happened to be poetical.

HENRY V, 1859

The last two revivals of the Kean *régime* were Much Ado about Nothing (November 20, 1858) and Henry V (March 28, 1859). Of Much Ado I shall say but little in this place; if the play is given at all, it must be given about as Shakespeare wrote it. It is seldom "cut" to a noticeable degree. The only variants I shall note are some interpolated lines at the end of Act IV, Scene 1, the scene in which Benedick promises to kill Claudio. A foot-note tells us that "the lines in italics are an introduction, which custom has grafted on the play." The silly lines aforesaid, to the effect of "You'll be sure to challenge him?" "By those bright eyes, I will," etc., are found in Oxberry, and not in Inchbald; they therefore must have grown up after the day of Kemble. A few unidentified lines, in addition, close the play with a sort of "tag." Kean ought to have been ashamed to leave in these lines at the end of a career of management priding itself on purity of text. In conclusion I may say that he omitted the scene of Beatrice's visit to her cousin on her wedding morn, and Claudio's penance at the supposed tomb of Hero.

His edition of Henry V sins—if it is sin—merely by omissions. The first scene in Act I—that between Ely and Canterbury—is entirely gone, and Canterbury's long speeches in the second are mercifully cut and "telescoped" into something approximating limits humanly possible for actor and audience. The first scene involving Dame Quickly, Pistol and the crew from Eastcheap is likewise expunged, and the second brought in, apparently, merely to apprise us of the death of Falstaff. As usual in Kemble and his successors, the Boy's long speech beginning, "As young as I am, I have observed these three swashers," is introduced to end this scene, from its proper place in the second scene of Act III. I shall not pursue my way through the rest of Kean's version; suffice it to say that, except for liberal curtailment of speeches, he follows Shakespeare's plan with a consistency not unworthy of praise. As do all preceding versions, his omits the lesson in English between Alice and the Princess. With this play we take leave of Kean as a re-arranger of Shakespeare.

CHARLES KEAN'S POSITION

In light of the evidence, then, it is clear that Kean, in an age notable for restoring Shakespeare to the stage, must be regarded as something of a reactionary. The man who, in the decade after Phelps had re-staged Shakespeare's Macbeth and Richard III as originally written, brought back Locke and Davenant and Colley Cibber; the man who cut away great portions of the poetry to make room for spectacle—this man must be reckoned considerably less great than Phelps or even Benjamin Webster. When it comes to all the adjuncts of scenic display, however, the record is changed; then Kean takes his place as the legitimate forerunner of Henry Irving—as Irving was forerunner of Tree —perhaps ranking with both for excellence in that domain in which each in his own day was supreme. These three are incontestably the great exemplars of a system now possibly obsolete—a system which brought about a setting almost veritably real in effect, that transplanted to the stage of a theatre almost perfect reproductions of the locale of a Shakespearian scene, whether it was a canal in Venice, the forum of ancient Rome, a room in an English palace or a council-chamber in a French chateau. The scene passed from resemblance into reality, and the actors seemed literally to live in the environment constructed for them by scene-painter, carpenter and mechanician. The result was frequently of surpassing beauty, but it crowded out great parts of the play, and consumed the time gained thereby in necessary manipulation of scenery. We thought it very grand in its day; now a newer generation regards it as very mid-Victorian—a dreadful thing.

BACK TO DRURY LANE IN THE '60's

Kean's vaulting ambition probably o'erleapt itself in expenditure and in trouble; he retired in 1859 and passed from the history of the English theatre. The record returns, by poetic justice, to the great national theatre, to Drury Lane, now managed by that F. B. Chatterton who finally formulated the epigram about Shakespeare spelling ruin. Before the birth of that memorable word it will be remembered that he enlisted in his service Samuel Phelps, who had just abdicated at Sadler's Wells. In the labours of these two at the national theatre, the decade of the '60's finds its best results in the production of Shakespeare, Byron and other poetic dramatists.

HENRY IV, PARTS I AND II, 1864

Their first Shakespearian offering on the elaborate scale now customary was presented during the tercentenary of Shakespeare's birth, in 1864. The first part of Henry IV was presented on Easter Monday with Phelps as Falstaff, Walter Montgomery as Hotspur, Walter Lacy as the Prince, John Ryder (a first lieutenant of Kean at the Princess's) as the King, and Mrs. Edmund Falconer as the Hostess—a very excellent cast. What interests us now is the inclusion, in the cast, of the name of Lady Glendwyr, as it is affectedly spelled. This is the first time, to my knowledge, that the song of the Welsh lady had annoyed the ear of any Harry Percy on the stage from the days of Betterton and before. The Illustrated London News of April 2nd is happy over the restoration. "The revival," it says, "was distinguished by one commendable feature. The great Glendower scene, hitherto omitted, was supplied. . . . The whole scene is thrown in most artistically by the poet as a point of repose, and should never have been omitted. We are happy to say that, though timidly acted, it proved eminently successful and effective." In other respects the drama was faithfully put on the stage; only one scene—the last of Shakespeare's Act IV, that of the rebels in the Palace of the Archbishop of York, always omitted in acting—was missing, as a glance at the version printed in Lacy's Acting Plays will show. Aside from this, every scene is presented in Shakespeare's order, and with so slight a curtailment that one might call it a model of Shakespearian adaptation to the stage. The revival was a great success, and enjoyed a run of several months, during the season of the Shakespeare tercentenary jubilee.

In view of this success, it is perplexing to find the second part of the same play revived in the autumn of the same year by the same people at the same theatre with a slovenly text hardly differing from that in use from 1773 onwards. The version presented, also to be found in Lacy, omits as usual the Induction by Rumour, the first scene at Wark-

worth Castle, in which the sick Northumberland is informed
of the death of his son, and Act II, Scene 3, at the same
place, the episode of Northumberland, his wife and Lady
Percy. All this is according to hoary tradition. Another
convention followed by the text is the transference of the
King's soliloquy on sleep from its proper place in Act III
to the beginning of the fourth act, where it serves as a
preliminary to the beautiful scene between Henry and his
son, just prior to Henry's death. This constitutes all the
matter of Act IV, and brings it about that the King appears
only in this act. Perhaps there are advantages in concen-
tration of dramatic interest in such an arrangement. The
more serious scenes throughout the play are considerably
cut, but nevertheless the not very interesting third scene
of the first act is retained—the scene in the Archbishop of
York's palace—much reduced in lines, and even in personnel, Lord Bardolph being excised and Mowbray dowered
with what is left of his rather lengthy speeches. Perhaps
the adapter feared an audience might be confused between this Bardolph and that other in Falstaff's rabble
rout.

As a matter of fact, this version was made largely with
an eye to the single purpose of displaying the remarkable
versatility of Phelps. Whereas, in the first part of the
play, he had enacted Falstaff, in this he "doubled" the
parts of the King and Justice Shallow—a remarkable feat.
Hence, all of the King was thrown in high light in Act IV,
and the Shallow scenes were strongly accentuated at the
close. The earlier parts of the play merely hurried on to
this consummation devoutly to be wished—the exhibition
of the popular actor in parts so widely different as to exhaust
terms of wonder in the vocabulary of the spectator. Phelps
had played both parts at Sadler's Wells, also.

THE COMEDY OF ERRORS AT THE PRINCESS'S, 1864

Meanwhile, let us return to other interesting events in
the history of the tercentenary in the spring of 1864. At

the Princess's, a house which could never forget its past glories, was effected a revival of The Comedy of Errors, played continuously without the fall of the curtain, and yet with as many scenes—eleven—as Shakespeare's five acts require; in fact with one more, since the version breaks a scene in two, playing the first half within the house of the Antipholus of Ephesus, the second half in the street outside.   An examination of the text, as printed in Lacy's Acting Plays, will show that rather unusual respect has been paid to Shakespeare; all his scenes are given in his order, and the only change is found in the usual cutting out of lines and speeches.   As given, without intermissions and as a straightforward narrative, it was a unique experiment, deserving attention equal to that excited by Webster's revival in 1844 of The Taming of the Shrew with little, if any, scenery.   In its day it triumphed by the beauty of its stage pictures and the extraordinary performance of the Dromios by the Brothers Webb, who were so exactly alike that the audience was in bewilderment throughout the evening.

HENRY VI, PART II, 1864

Even more interesting was the revival in this memorial season, and on the very day of the birth so portentous— April 23rd—of the never-before-acted second part of Henry VI. Of course I remember, as does the reader, the various attempts of Crowne, Ambrose Philips, Theophilus Cibber, and another unnamed one (in 1817) to place on the stage something resembling various fragments of Shakespeare's tragedy; but, while remembering, I must admonish that these were a long way from the original. And now, after many years, the Surrey Theatre, unfashionable and unpretentious, astonishingly in the tercentenary celebration revived the best of the three plays on Henry VI, and gave to the well-liked James Anderson the task of "doubling" the Duke of York and Jack Cade. This looks like a dwarfing of the leading figures of Humphrey, Duke of Gloucester and his haughty duchess. All that I know of the perform-

ance—which ran for only a week—I quote from the London
Illustrated News of April 30th:

> The noblest effort at properly celebrating Shakspeare was made
> at this house on Saturday last [*i. e.*, April 23rd]. A revival of the
> greatest importance was worthily accomplished, and with the greatest
> success. Mr. Anderson placed on the boards "The Second Part of
> Henry VI."—a drama which has not been played for 270 years—and
> so placed it as to make it noticeable as a revival, or rather restoration
> to the stage, of an utterly neglected work. . . . The multitude of
> characters needful for the action tried, of course, the resources of the
> management; but the difficulties were overcome by doubling and
> even trebling some of the characters. Mr. Anderson himself took
> two characters—the Duke of York and Jack Cade—both of which
> he performed with remarkable effect. The first he strengthened with
> speeches taken from the part of Warwick, and thus has an oppor-
> tunity of denouncing Suffolk for the murder of Duke Humphrey. . .
> He throws a certain amount of eccentricity into the part of Jack
> Cade, which is at least amusing. Mr. Fernandez assumed the parts
> of Suffolk and Alexander Iden, and in his conflict with Jack Cade
> manifested much picturesque power. The fight, indeed, was ex-
> traordinarily good, and of itself worth seeing. . . . The accessories
> of the piece were sufficient, and the scenery abundant.

I can only repeat that the figures of the Gloucester-pair
seemed to have been dwarfed in this revival; in spite of
that, the affair is very interesting and well worth greater
attention than the more aristocratic journals—the Times,
for instance—were inclined to bestow on it. Search through
the pages of this paper was unrewarded by even a line of
comment on an effort so well deserving a column.

ANTONY AND CLEOPATRA, 1867 AND 1873

Performances of Shakespeare were given very frequently
in London during the years with which I am dealing; the
patience of my reader will endure reference only to those
that were in some way revivals or restorations of unusual
proportions. Secure in this belief, I pass by all but the
essential, and come to two performances of Antony and
Cleopatra, revived by Phelps in 1849, and not importantly

since.   In 1867, at the Princess's, still struggling valiantly to keep up its prestige, the tragedy was played, once more with Miss Glyn, not indubitably eighteen years older than in her glory at Sadler's Wells.   The version of the play is to be found in Lacy, and a poor thing it is.   Charles Calvert had used it previously in Manchester.   Shakespeare's forty-two scenes are reduced to nineteen, by running together or by omission.   I do not see how a careless auditor could have known what it was all about.   The first act, by no reprehensible economy, runs Shakespeare's five scenes together as two, but at the beginning of Act II the hand of the assassin begins to be visible.   The first scene, Messina, at Pompey's house, is the first to go; soon after, the third, Cæsar's house, with Antony, Cæsar and Octavia, follows suit.   Scene 4 also is discarded.   This gives plenty of time and space for the two elaborate sets of Misenum, with ships at anchor, and the great tableau on board Pompey's galley.   In the first act, I may say, by favouritism almost all of Alexas's speeches are given to Mardian, and in the second act Mardian becomes the messenger who bears to Cleopatra the ill news of Antony's marriage.   Evidently Miss Glyn's Cleopatra was too ladylike to give him the beating that Shakespeare's Cleopatra thought he so richly deserved.

The third act comprises nine scenes, selected from Shakespeare's third and fourth acts.   It may be easiest to describe it by telling what has been omitted.   The first scene of Shakespeare's Act III—the plain in Syria, with Ventidius and Sicilius—is missing, also the second, the anteroom in Cæsar's house; Scene 4, with Antony and Octavia, is not used, nor is Scene 5, with Enobarbus and Eros.   The character of Octavia, in fact, appears only briefly in the sixth scene.   Shakespeare's tiny eighth and ninth scenes are also deleted, as is the twelfth, in Cæsar's tent.   The reader can see for himself how little, except Antony and Cleopatra and their doings, remains of Shakespeare's third act; so little, in fact, that several scenes from Act IV can be run on, without inconvenience, to fill out the demands of the new act. From Act IV, then, the adapter helps himself to as much as he needs of Shakespeare's first scene, Cæsar's camp at Alexandria; his fourth, the arming of Antony; his sixth, Cæsar's camp again, and his eighth. The intervening scenes are rejected. As a warning, let me again state that I am here, as usual, calling into use the scene-divisions in the Cambridge edition of Shakespeare's tragedy.

Calvert's fourth act has three scenes—Shakespeare's ninth, Cæsar's camp, with the death of Enobarbus; his twelfth, the palace, with Scarus, Antony, Charmian, Cleopatra, Alexas and Mardian, and his fifteenth, a Monument, with the death of Antony. All the rest is eliminated ruthlessly. The fifth act omits Shakespeare's first scene, and closes the history with the long episode of Cleopatra's death. Frankly, I admit that I do not know what can be done with Shakespeare's great tragedy on the stage; it is so episodic, so devouring in its demands on the stage-manager and on the attention of an audience, that I hardly see how it can be presented at all. At all events, such a mangled version as this of Calvert's is hardly Shakespeare's play; a world tragedy is reduced to a love-episode in Alexandria and its environment.

The revival in 1867 was not a success. Nor was that of September 20, 1873, at Drury Lane, when the tragedy, reduced by Andrew Halliday to four acts and twelve scenes, was brought out with unwonted splendour of song, dance, procession and spectacle. Even more than the version at the Princess's this reduces all to a mere exposition of the loves of the two chief characters. The Times, of September 22nd, shows the damage that had been done to what many regard as Shakespeare's greatest poem, if, obviously, not his greatest play:

Mr. Halliday has, as he says, addressed himself to the task of clearly representing the passion of the "single pair," and has therefore struck out all that is connected with Pompey. He has also done much in the way of omission and redistribution, thus reducing to 12 scenes the 33 of the original. By his modifications he has avoided those leaps from Egypt to Rome, and back again, which passed unheeded by our ancestors, but which harmonize ill with our present respect for unity of place. Thus the play, which is in four acts, has become widely different from that which years ago Mr. Phelps produced at Sadler's Wells.

In Mr. Halliday's piece the principal scenes in which the lovers appear are preserved, though frequently fused together at the pleasure of the author. All that occurs at Rome is brought within the limits of the second act; the scene of all the rest is Egypt. . . . The omission of the scene in which Enobarbus kills himself on the stage lessens the effect intended to be produced by the bluff old soldier.

Dutton Cook, in his Nights at the Play, adds a few details of the proceedings, which justify a reproduction of his paragraph:

The work has been reduced to about one-half of its original length, and is now performed in four acts. Pantomimic scenes have been introduced, realising the famous description of Cleopatra's progress in her burnished barge upon the Cydnus—the river being transferred, for the convenience of the adapter, from Cilicia to Egypt—and introducing a Roman festival with processions of Amazons, ballets, and songs of boys in honour of the nuptials of *Antony* and *Cleopatra*. Further the battle of Actium, with the defeat of Cæsar by the combined fleets of *Antony* and *Cleopatra*, is depicted with surprising animation and completeness. Indeed, nothing could be better in their way than these exhibitions of scenic art and stage management. Mr. Beverley's paintings are in his best manner, the costumes and accessories are most splendid, while crowds of supernumeraries fill the scene and enhance the effect of the picture. A more magnificent spectacle can hardly have been produced in a theatre than is contained in this revival. . . . Upon the other hand, it must be said that the integrity of the work has suffered. No line is spoken that is not Shakspeare's, but then the lines of Shakspeare that are not spoken are very many indeed. The transposition of the scenes, so as to preserve "unity of place" as much as possible, has been skilfully managed, and is without doubt a reasonable alteration. . . But Mr. Halliday's excisions are certainly inordinate. *Pompey*, with his friends *Menas, Menecrates,* and *Varrius*, has altogether disappeared; the rival camps of *Cæsar* and *Antony* are not presented; the treachery of *Enobarbus* is but briefly treated, and his death is omitted; while the scene between *Cæsar* and *Cleopatra* finds no place in the new version of the play. These are among the most important of the omissions; but generally there has been much paring away of poetry to make room for pageantry. . . . The spectators readily accepted Mr. Chatterton's conditions, and "Antony and Cleopatra," ruthlessly docked but gorgeously adorned, was welcomed with extraordinary applause.

THE BANCROFTS' MERCHANT OF VENICE, 1875

I pick up pearls where I find them, and, passing by much that is hardly startling, I come to the unique production in April, 1875, of The Merchant of Venice by Mr. and Mrs. Bancroft on the tiny stage of their famous theatre in Tottenham Court Road—the Prince of Wales. Just why these masters of modern "cup and saucer" comedy should hit upon the idea of thus producing a very familiar play of Shakespeare's, it is very hard to say. But the histrionic mind knows no discouragement and always looks for new worlds. The preceding season they had had a great success with a revival of The School for Scandal, re-arranged in five solid acts, and, as if that were sufficient reason, now seized upon The Merchant of Venice. The result was a pitiable failure, owing chiefly, as I have said, to a very bad Shylock by Charles Coghlan and in spite of a perfectly exquisite Portia of Ellen Terry—a characterisation then first revealed. Somehow this production has got itself entangled in the imagination with something of the charm that belongs to lost causes. Mr. (now Sir Squire) Bancroft, in The Bancrofts: Recollections of Sixty Years, is very interesting on the subject of this failure, "of which we shall continue to be proud." His account of the version used and of the scenery is so inextricably bound together that I shall not be so cruel as to separate one element from the other. The scenery was selected from views actually studied in Venice with their scene-painter, and the result could be unusually elaborate, because, as Sir Squire Bancroft says, the tiny stage permitted of only one set to the act. Hence the scenes were re-arranged and transposed in a rather high-handed way. Let his story show how this was accomplished:

I took upon myself the great responsibility of rearranging the text of the play, so as to avoid change of scene in sight of the audience, and to adapt the work, so far as possible, to its miniature frame; being greatly fortified in my researches by the discovery of the following passage by . . . Dr. Johnson [in which he shows that the quarto editions have no distribution of acts, and that "it lies open to a new regulation, if any more commodious distribution can be proposed."]

. . . Perhaps there will be no better opportunity to describe the sequence of scenes I eventually decided on, for I often have regretted that I did not print the play as we produced it. The first tableau, "Under the Arches of the Doge's Palace," with a lovely view of Santa Maria della Salute, contained the text of the opening scene and the third scene of Act I, the dialogue being welded together by carefully arranged processions and appropriate pantomimic action from the crowd of merchants, sailors, beggars, Jews, who were throughout passing and repassing. The second tableau was in Portia's house at Belmont, and opened with a stately entrance of Portia, and her court, to the strains of barbaric music, which announced the arrival and choice of the golden casket by the Prince of Morocco. After his disconsolate departure, came the dialogues between Portia and Nerissa from Act I, Scene ii, followed by the announcement of the Prince of Arragon, and his choice of the silver casket. In the third tableau we returned to Venice, a most quaint spot of the old city being chosen for the outside of Shylock's house, which, without exception, was the most extraordinary scenic achievement in so small a theatre, the close of the scene being the elopement by moonlight of his daughter. This tableau was then repeated by daylight for the scene of the "Jew's rage" with Salanio and Salarino, and his subsequent frenzied interview with Tubal. The fourth view was a repetition, with some changed effects, of the hall in Portia's palace, where Bassanio chose wisely from the three caskets, and heard afterwards of Antonio's arrest. The next tableau was the "Trial Scene," and the last, "Portia's Garden at Belmont."

The words of the songs from some of Shakespeare's other comedies were introduced, and sung by boys as Portia's pages, but no syllable of the text was altered, transpositions of the dialogue alone being necessary for my arrangement of the play.

THE LAST OF PHELPS, 1876

The reader sees how the career of Phelps furnishes a leading string throughout this period. That name recurs for the last time in our chronicle, in connection with what would seem to have been an absurd performance of Henry V, played at the Queen's Theatre, on September 16, 1876. This was a unique performance which rendered poetic justice for an earlier second part of Henry IV (1719). In that, the first part of Henry V was used as an epilogue; in this, scenes from Henry IV, Part II, served as a prologue. The parts used were first, the episode of the King (with his soliloquy on sleep) and his son—the episode of the crown and the dying King, and, second, the reconciliation of Henry V and the Chief Justice. Why this should serve as a prologue to the stirring drama of Henry V—unless for the imposing curtain-tableau of the Coronation of Henry V— it would be hard to say; but it enabled John Coleman, a poor actor and at that time manager of the Queen's Theatre, to kill two birds in one play. Possessed of the services of the eminent Phelps he could put him forward as the father and, before the audience assembled to see this famous actor, he himself could gratify a cherished ambition to play the son. The only flaw in the scheme was that it did not work very well; one act of Phelps hardly made up for four of Coleman. But in an age ostensibly devoted to bringing back Shakespeare as he was written, we must animadvert on this eccentric offering. It rather hurts to see Phelps crowning a noble career in this unworthy way. He acted again, but this was the last "production" with which he was associated.

DRURY LANE AGAIN, 1878–1879

One of the last productions of Chatterton at Drury Lane was The Winter's Tale, in October, 1878; Charles Dillon played Leontes, not as he would have played the part in his prime. There were, of course, spectacle and show and music, but, as the arrangement was Charles Kean's of years before at the Princess's, it need not detain us here. My authority as to the version used is Dutton Cook's Nights at the Play. After the accession of Augustus Harris to the Drury Lane management he won most fame and fortune with melodrama of an unashamed front, but he began his career at this house with a production of Henry V, by George Rignold, who had for several years previously set maiden hearts a-flutter from New York to San Francisco and back again, with his virile, handsome personality and his dashing style. This version, as we have seen, originated with Charles Calvert in Manchester, whence it came to London, belated, *via* all America, as it were. No one else has ever equalled the fame of George Rignold in the part of Henry V.

The version used in this world-conquering production (Rignold afterward carried it to Australia) is found in the Acting Plays of Samuel French. It gives practically all of Shakespeare's scenes, except the very first, that between Ely and Canterbury, also deleted by Kean; the rest, some of them greatly "cut," are present in regular order and with a fair degree of poetic language. The two Quickly-Pistol scenes are run together, the boy as usual ending with the customary monologue that no manager seems tempted to reject, though most insist on transferring it to this place from its Shakespearian place on the stricken field in France. The entire fourth act of Rignold's version is given over to a spectacular entry of the victorious Henry into London, the basis of the show being the same old chronicle unearthed by the indefatigable Charles Kean. Alice's instructing the Princess in English is moved from its proper place, to the beginning of the fifth act, where it just precedes all the grand business of the marriage arranged in the Troyes Cathedral. This transfer no doubt conduces to unity of interest, the poor princess being in danger otherwise of being "lost in the shuffle," incident to the changing of so many battle scenes.

HENRY IRVING (1874–1878)

The events described above all fell definitely within the Phelps-Kean period—its rise, its glory, its decline and fall. They were, for us, backward-looking things; but the reader will keep his eye on the Lyceum Theatre, where, from 1871 to 1878, Irving was building up a substantial reputation, and making the Lyceum a forward-looking thing. His appearance there, under the Bateman management, I have recorded. Here, of the four Shakespearian revivals of that management, I shall discuss but one—Richard III. Hamlet must be reserved for the opening of the Irving management in 1878; Macbeth for the mid-period of that management in 1888. Othello is eliminated because it is a negligibility in Irving's career, both in 1876 and in 1881. Besides, Shakespeare's Othello is so closely knit that no adventurer has ever trifled with it.

Of Irving's Richard III of 1877 it is not too much to say that it is nearly the worst very modern version of a Shakespearian play with which I am familiar. It is egregiously "cut." For instance, the vengeful Margaret is reduced to one scene, her first, and frightfully "cut" at that. The dream and the murder of Clarence are given, but reduced to very short limits. The arraignment and arrest of Hastings also are retained, considerably curtailed. The scene of the women before the Tower is inexplicably omitted, but, later on, the Duchess of York and Queen Elizabeth (without Margaret) revile Richard as he passes by. Why the great figure of Margaret should be revived to so little purpose, it is hard to see. I should say that, though little except Shakespeare is found in the Irving version, so much Shakespeare has been removed that the story becomes almost unintelligible. The thing goes to oblivion by its own unworthiness.

SUMMARY

I have endeavoured to carry the reader from 1844, when Phelps and Webster began seriously to do something for Shakespeare, to 1879, when most of the managers, except the newly started Irving, were about ready to agree with Chatterton of Drury Lane that Shakespeare spelled ruin. I have covered, as well as I could, the activities of Phelps and Kean and their lesser contemporaries. In the thirty-five years involved every play of Shakespeare, except Titus Andronicus, Troilus and Cressida and the first and third Henry VI had been presented in adequate and usually in splendid manner. Garrick's mauling of Romeo and Juliet was no longer visible in a London theatre, and only in questionable outlying districts was his Katharine and Petruchio to be seen. Colley Cibber was toppling on his Richard III throne. Managers still fitted Shakespeare to scenery, rather than scenery to Shakespeare. But one thing was clear: every one realised that everything spoken must now be Shakespeare. The day of rewriting was past forever.

CHAPTER XXIX

SCENERY AND STAGING

WEBSTER'S TAMING OF THE SHREW, 1844

THE youthful reader will be surprised, possibly disgusted, to find, at the beginning of this discussion, account of a performance of Shakespeare without scenery and with screens and curtains arranged to produce the effects necessary to a complete enjoyment of the dramatic picture. It is ever the privilege of the very youthful to make for themselves the interesting and highly novel discovery that the grass is green, and to find out, with utter disgust, later on, that their grannies knew it all the time. We thought that screens and curtains were so uniquely Twentieth-Century! At any rate, we must all be somewhat startled to learn that Benjamin Webster, at the Haymarket, in March, 1844, was induced by the resourceful Planché to bring out The Taming of the Shrew with what was then considered to be an approximation to the Elizabethan manner, *sans* scenery, *sans* spectacle, *sans* everything hitherto thought essential to the proper representation of Shakespeare. Is not this an interesting experiment to follow so close on the freedom of the theatres?

Furthermore, the result was highly satisfactory, in 1844 and in 1846, when the comedy was again revived. The wonder is that no other attempts were made in the same direction. I quote from the Times of March 18, 1844, to show the reader exactly what Webster and Planché accomplished. The prevailing features, it will be observed, are the scene of the usual kind for the Induction, the curtains, screens and placards for the play itself, and the "make-up" and dressing of the characters. This bit of reviewing is respectfully submitted to those who believe the last decade to have originated the idea of such staging. Says the Times:

The greatest credit is due to Mr. Webster for reviving the play in the shape in which we find it in Shakspeare's work, and for producing it in a style so unique that this revival is really one of the most remarkable instances of the modern theatre. It was a suggestion of Tieck's that the plays of Shakspeare should be acted on the sort of stage which existed in the time of Elizabeth and James I, and although the revival at the Haymarket does not exactly follow this suggestion, still it is in the same spirit, and allows the audience to judge of the effect of a play unaided by scenery. The "Induction" in which Christopher Sly is discovered drunk by the sporting lord, is played in the ordinary manner before a scene representing an inn; but when he is removed into the hall, there is no further change, but the play of the *Taming of the Shrew* is acted in the hall, two screens and a pair of curtains being the whole dramatic apparatus. By the mere substitution of one curtain for another, change of scene was indicated, and all the exits and entrances are through the centre of the curtain, or round the screens, the place represented being denoted by a printed placard fastened to the curtain. This arrangement, far from being flat and ineffective, tended to give closeness to the action, and by constantly allowing a great deal of stage room, afforded a sort of freedom to all the parties engaged. The audience did not in the least seem to feel the absence of scenery, and though the play lasted three hours and a half, the attention of the house never failed, and a play could hardly go off with more spirit. . . .

 . . . . The players who appear in the "Induction" were so made up as to give a sort of resemblance to Shakspeare, Ben Jonson, and Richard Tarleton. The costumes were very handsome and appropriate, and the whole does great credit to Mr. Planché, under whose superintendence the play was produced. A drop-scene has been painted for the occasion, representing a view of London, with the Globe Theatre as one of the principal objects.

GENERAL PRINCIPLES OF STAGING

For the first two decades of our period we shall undoubtedly make best headway if we confine our researches to the work of Phelps and Charles Kean. Playbills throughout these twenty years lay stress on the fact that plays are presented "with new scenes, costumes and accessories"; I suspect that, frequently, in the announcement lurks far more of promise than of performance. I have no doubt that theatres like the Haymarket, the Olympic and the Princess's (even before it passed into the hands of Charles Kean) were provided with a large stock of good scenery; I am equally sure that Othello and The Merchant of Venice had out-door scenes in common, that Venice even lent a neighbourly hand to Verona in the mounting of Romeo and Juliet or The Two Gentlemen of Verona. And who cared? Flats or drops shut or fell before more elaborate sets in third, fourth and fifth grooves; chairs and couches were shoved on, and disappearing legs of scene-shifters left the stage empty for Desdemona or Juliet or Portia. And again who cared? Convinced of this, I offer the student reproductions of cuts in the Illustrated London News which I take to be pretty exact representations of what could be seen on the stage of the most fashionable theatre in London—the Haymarket—when Macready was deemed the best tragic actor and Charlotte Cushman the best tragic actress. The first shows Macready as Iago and J. W. Wallack as Othello in what I consider a perfectly adequate setting at the Haymarket; it is reproduced from the Illustrated London News of December 1, 1849. The second represents Miss Cushman as Romeo and Miss Swanborough as Juliet, at the same theatre, and is taken from the same paper under date of February 10, 1855. Both these studies merit deep attention; the general "get-up" of each scene is as good as anything we should expect to-day in any but a specially prepared revival. The more one looks at such things, the less he pities his ancestors and the less he plumes himself on the superior advantages of his own generation.

SAMUEL PHELPS AT SADLER'S WELLS

The pictures I have presented seem to me to be worth pages of hazarded description. I, therefore, offering them as typical "stock" stage-sets of the '40's and '50's, pass on to the special productions at the two widely contrasted

CHARLOTTE CUSHMAN AND MISS SWANBOROUGH IN ROMEO AND
JULIET, HAYMARKET THEATRE, 1855
From the *Illustrated London News*

J. W. WALLACK AS OTHELLO AND MACREADY AS IAGO, HAYMARKET
THEATRE, 1849
From the *Illustrated London News*

houses of Phelps and Kean.   The contrast in method in the
productions of these men merits a word.   In their own day
partisans ranged on one side or the other; the adherents of
Sadler's Wells spoke much of purity of text, poetic effect,
scenic delights guided by perfect taste and accomplished
at a minimum of expense; by inference, they threw in a
suggestion against the Princess's as a gaudy temple of spectacular display, with something too little of Shakespeare
and altogether too much of smothering scenery.   Doubtless
there was something in all this, as there was also something
in the answer of the Princess's that the West End is not so
serious as Pentonville, and that, if people will not go to
hear Shakespeare alone, it is better to induce them to hear
him through their eyes, with all the allurement of beautiful
pictures.   This was the argument in the '50's, and the
basis for the argument it will now be my pleasant duty to
elucidate.

I may add, however, a word of John Coleman, from the
Memoirs of Samuel Phelps.   "The productions at both
theatres," he maintains, "were equally distinguished by
artistic taste and excellence, although it must be admitted
that in the majority of instances those at the Princess's
were infinitely more splendid."   Of Phelps he says: "His
limited resources, and the small area in which he moved,
restricted him from the sumptuous embellishments and gorgeous splendour of previous, and, indeed, of later revivals.
His staff of auxiliaries, even in his greatest works, rarely
exceeded two-score, but he contrived to multiply his resources by a process as ingenious as it was amusing."

This process Coleman illustrates by reference to Phelps's
revival of Henry V, and his account is too good to be curtailed.   Let Coleman speak: "In Henry V, in the march-
past before Agincourt, the troops defiled behind a 'set
piece' which rose breast high.   Madame Tussaud modelled
eighty wax heads—these were fitted on 'dummy' figures of
wicker work, clad in the costume and armour of the period.
Every man of the gallant forty carried two of these figures,
one on either side, attached to a sort of frame-work, which

was lashed to his waist; hence it seemed as if they were marching three abreast.

"As they tramped past, banners streaming, drums beating, trumpets braying, the stage seemed crowded with soldiers, and the illusion was so perfect that the audience never once discovered the deception."

When it is recalled that Kean, according to his last speech at the Princess's, in 1859, employed, for his greatest spectacles, 550 persons, something of the difference in method and effect may be derived. Coleman, again, informs us that Phelps "had a capable and industrious assistant stage manager in Mr. 'Pepper' Williams," while his partner, Greenwood, also attended to the financial department and freed Phelps of unnecessary business burdens. His scene-painter, Frederick Fenton, was a main tower of strength, and constantly consulted as to plays to be produced, adaptation of texts "to the exigencies of scenic arrangements," etc. In other words, Phelps's was a compact little army under competent and loyal officers; for eighteen years it kept the banner flying over Sadler's Wells, to the inspiring music of Shakespeare's verse within. From every point of view, this is a notable epoch.

SOME OF PHELPS'S EARLY SUCCESSES

Of the thirty-one plays of Shakespeare produced at Sadler's Wells, all, I am sure, were presented with entirely adequate scenery, costumes and effects. It would be worse than confusing to enter upon the details of these, one after the other. The reader will, I am sure, prefer to stress the more important and take for granted the adequacy of the others.

The first I shall consider will be the highly important restoration of Shakespeare's own Richard III, on February 20, 1845. The account of the News of the World almost sets the production before us, and greatly increases our respect for Phelps as producer: "The play has been placed on the stage with remarkable care and attention; the records of antiquity appear to have been searched for authorities in costume, scenery, and manners." Thus would it seem that Phelps handed on the torch from Charles Kemble to Charles Kean; but "while the stage arrangements are wisely kept subordinate to the play itself"—and this is Phelps— "they yet constitute an admirable representation of the habits and customs in Court life and City life of the time. Cheapside, with a view of which the play opens, the ancient palace architecture, the Tower, and Baynard's Castle, with approach of the Mayor by water, are extremely picturesque scenes; and the last act presents a succession of effects. . . . . Instead of the continual changing of scene and running about of parties, first to one tune and then another . . . . . . the action takes place as it has been described by Shakespeare. Richmond is observed marching onward with his army; and then we are carried to Bosworth Field, where the tent is literally set up in the presence of the audience. On the other side of the brook that divided the contending armies Richmond's [query: Richard's?] tent is then raised, and the constant movement of leaders of the two forces, the variety of costume and banners, and the earnestness of every actor employed [this is again Phelps] constitute a picture of remarkable perfection. Night having closed in with a kind of dioramic effect [spirit of Macready!], two cressets are planted at the entrance of Richard's tent, which throw a faint light over the forepart of the scene; whilst in the background the ghosts of Clarence, Lady Anne, the Princes, and Buckingham are advanced between the two tents, by some ingenious process, but so far only as to be dimly visible to the audience; this partial obscurity, and the deep stillness that is preserved on the stage, just allow the imagination to play without over-exciting it; and the effect is extremely good. The dawn of morning is accompanied with the distant hum of preparation, then the faint roll of drums is heard mingling with the bugle call, and increasing with the impatience of the troops. The fight and final struggle of Richard and Richmond were represented so vividly and impressively, that at the fall of

Richard the conclusion of the piece was delayed by the continued shouts of the audience.''

Surely we may express thanks to the by-gone critic who thus palpably sets before us the life of that production; it is the next best thing to witnessing the show.

The Times of November 28, 1845, gives a brief but sufficient account of The Winter's Tale just revived at Sadler's Wells. This was not, in truth, one of the more famous of Phelps's recensions of Shakespeare, but I reproduce the criticism of the Times, as strengthening the impression of the great care of Phelps in all the departments of production and as showing the beauty of the staging at his theatre:

> One does not often see a play got up in such a creditable style. . .
> There is a certain life infused . . . which displays itself in the exertions of the actors employed, which asserts itself in the costumes, which speaks through the very appropriate scenery, and which altogether leaves a most exhilarating impression on the spectator.
>
> .   .   .   .
>
> The scenery is entirely new, for the most part consisting of felicitous representations of classic interiors, decorated in the polychromatic style. The famous scene of the statue is so managed as to produce a most beautiful stage effect. The light is so thrown, and the drapery is so arranged, that the illusion is all but perfect, the stately figure of Mrs. Warner, who looked the statue admirably, contributing in no small degree to the beauty of the picture. The moment the curtain was removed, the applause of the audience broke out with immense force. The storm in the third, and the rural scene in the fourth act, are also specimens of clever stage-management.

PHELPS'S MACBETH, 1847

In Macbeth, produced on September 27, 1847, Phelps began to exhibit some of the peculiarly individual traits of mounting since associated with his fame. We have seen the unearthly effect of the Ghosts in his Richard III; in Macbeth the Witches and their appearances and disappearances were managed with almost uncanny supernaturalism. From many accounts available, I select that of the London Times of September 28th. "Mr. Phelps," it says, "has

gone to work at the production in a style of his own, ...
and placed an impress of genius on the whole affair. To
the banquet scene he has given an air of primitive rudeness,
and has so arranged the tables that Banquo's ghost appears
with better effect. The battle scenes and the groupings on
a large scale are all so managed as to produce a massive
appearance, and the costumes, being by no means after the
ordinary fashion, occasion a novelty of combination. Most
admirable is the manner in which the witches are treated,
the preternatural aspect which is given to them evincing a
spirit which is really poetical. The common intervention
of a gauze half removes them from reality, but the ingenious
expedient of thickening the gauze in the lower part, so that
they are suddenly concealed when it rises, effects as near an
approach to a 'vanishing' as possible. When the witches
address Macbeth and Banquo, they are not, as usual,
placed in the front of the stage, but crouch upon an obscure
rock at the back, and when they have vanished thence by
means of the gauze, they are seen in profile floating across
the sky. As a spectacle, this representation of *Macbeth* is
one of the most original ever seen."

Lloyd's Weekly Journal gives an admirable idea of the
entire production, again accentuating that green gauze with
which readers of Phelps's memorials grow so familiar.
Really, with Phelps, green gauze assumed almost epic proportions. "The first scene was very very skilfully managed. . . . The stage was darkened to a much greater
degree than usual, so much so that but the imperfect outlines of the weird sisters were visible. In front only a dim,
lurid light played, and as the hags stepped backwards, the
darkness, aided by a combination of gauze screens, procured
one of the most perfect effects of vanishing we ever saw.
The gradual clearing of the air too, after Macbeth's interview with the sisters, disclosing the lines of the victorious
army in the distance, was well conceived and cleverly executed. It seemed the natural brightening up of nature
relieved of the presence of the foul sorcerers."

Altogether, I feel justified in remembering most, with

Phelps, his wonderful effects of darkness visible. But other scenes won the approval of Lloyd's. "Macbeth's castle at Inverness was another effective scene, but we mention it principally as being the first attempt we have seen to reproduce some of the local features of the pleasant site —the steep wall-crowned hill, and the river rushing beneath. The alarm scene of the murder was admirable. Nobles, knights, squires, pages and vassals, armed with every species of ancient weapons picked up on the spur of the moment—here a halberd, there a battle-axe, now a pike, anon a blazing pine torch, rushed tumultuously upon the stage. . . . The final scenes were spirited in the extreme. The old conventional business of a general action—a flourish of trumpets every two or three minutes, with a single combat between, was very properly dispensed with. If ever a *mêlée* was well imitated upon the stage, it was in this representation of the tragedy. Looking through heavy Gothic balustrades, you saw the crowd of combatants. A sally of the defenders of the castle now driving out their besiegers; anon a fierce rally of the English soldiers beating back the troops of Macbeth; while forth from the *mêlée* with difficulty disentangling themselves from the fighting, rushing crowd—now Macbeth, now Macduff, now Siward, would struggle forward for a conspicuous place. Macbeth's head is also introduced on a pole, as directed by Shakespeare."

Does not this impress the reader as a wonderfully interesting performance? And does he not dimly gather the notion that it was more a matter of fine stage management than of elaborate scenery? But what of costumes? As to this Lloyd's informs us that the tartan used since Macklin introduced it in 1773 was abandoned, as too late a wear for the early times of Macbeth. Instead, there were "primitive mantles, with their heavy bars and ponderous folds," harmonising well "with our notions of the early, almost traditional period of the play." Bravo, Phelps, Greenwood and Fenton! Bravo, people of Islington who supported these efforts, at the price—mind!—of sixpence in the gallery, and a shilling in the pit, while more fashionable

Londoners stayed charily away from Shakespearian revivals nearer their own habitations.

The four most notable productions of Phelps at Sadler's Wells, seem to me, from aught that I could learn from history, to have been Antony and Cleopatra (1849), Timon of Athens (1851), A Midsummer Night's Dream (1853) and Pericles (1854). With three of these I shall close my discussion of his scenic activities at his famous theatre. Timon I shall leave unsung, because, so far as I see, its chief interest lay in the fact of its being a revival of a long-neglected classic.

Oddly enough, in spite of the great opportunities for spectacle in Antony and Cleopatra, and though Phelps did not neglect them, it is Miss Glyn's performance of the Queen that is chiefly stressed in contemporary accounts. On the whole, I suppose we should be pleased at this. The scene of revelry on Pompey's galley was most admired in its day, and that, with some other stray hints, stands out in the account in the London Times of October 24, 1849, which follows:

. . . To produce a visible picture consistent with the poetical one drawn by the dramatist has been the great object of Mr. Phelps. His Egyptian views, decorated with all those formal phantasies with which we have been familiarized through modern research, give a strange reality to the scenes in which Cleopatra exercises her fascinations. . . . The scene on board the galley of Sextus Pompeius . . . the spirit with which the revelling of the triumvirs and their host is represented, the classical fitting up of the banquet, and the jollity of those who share it, render this one of the most striking scenes of the play.

Something, but not much, is added in the review from the Illustrated London News of October 27th:

The Egyptian scenes are exceedingly *vraisemblable* ; that on board of Pompey's galley, with the banqueting sovereigns of the world as drunk as cobblers, is exceedingly life-like. As it is managed, too, on the boards, it is rendered one of the most picturesque and exciting incidents in the representation. Mr. Phelps, in particular, aided the pictorial, by his well-studied bacchanalian attitudes, some of which were exceedingly fine. The illusion was almost perfect; the actor could scarcely be recognized through the disguise. . . .

A similar effect was produced on Miss Glyn. . . She combined grace and dignity—all the fascination of a Vestris with the majesty of a Pasta. . . . Gorgeous in person, in costume, and in action. . . . Withal she was classical, and her poses severely statuesque. Her death was sublime. . . Altogether, Miss Glyn's performance of Cleopatra is the most superb thing ever witnessed on the modern stage.

From the same issue of the Illustrated London News I reproduce a drawing of one of the scenes. The background, faintly sketched, is unquestionably Egyptian in mass and outline; even the mural figure is decked out with Egyptian head-dress. But what of Miss Glyn's Cleopatra? Is it not dressed for a party in the West End of London rather than for a happening in the palace of the Ptolemys? To me it indubitably is, and distressingly so. Miss Glyn garbed thus, with how large a grain of salt am I compelled to take contemporaries' eulogies of the archæological correctness of the entire production? Alas!

A MIDSUMMER NIGHT'S DREAM, 1853

The production of Shakespeare's fairy comedy is generally conceded to be the greatest triumph of Phelps's career. This was due to his performance of Bottom, to the excellence of the ensemble, but chiefly to the remarkable degree to which the dream itself was realised. Perhaps Henry Morley's account is the best, as reproduced from the Examiner under date of October 15, 1853:

Mr. Phelps has never for a minute lost sight of the main idea. . . . He knew that he was to present mere shadows; that spectators, as *Puck* reminds them in the epilogue, are to think they have slumbered in their seats, and that what appeared before them have been visions. Everything has been subdued at Sadler's Wells to this ruling idea. The scenery is very beautiful, but wholly free from the meretricious glitter now in favour; it is not so remarkable for costliness as

SCENE FROM ANTONY AND CLEOPATRA, SADLER'S WELLS THEATRE,
1849

From the *Illustrated London News*

SCENE FROM ANTONY AND CLEOPATRA, PRINCESS'S THEATRE, 1867

From the *Illustrated London News*

for the pure taste in which it and all the stage arrangements have been planned [the usual note for Phelps's critics]. There is no ordinary scene shifting [observe this!]; but, as in dreams, one scene is made to glide insensibly into another. We follow the lovers and the fairies through the wood from glade to glade, now among trees, now with a broad view of the sea and Athens in the distance.

The observant reader here perceives the presence of a diorama or moving-scene, so beloved of managers, the second half of the Nineteenth Century, especially in connection with this very play, now perhaps enjoying its first really worthy performance. "And not only," proceeds Morley, "do the scenes melt dream-like one into another, but over all the fairy portion of the play there is a haze thrown by a curtain of green gauze [Phelps again!] placed between the actors and the audience, and maintained there during the whole of the second, third and fourth acts. This gauze curtain is so well spread that there are very few parts of the house from which its presence can be detected, but its influence is everywhere felt; it subdues the flesh and blood of the actors into something more nearly resembling dream-figures . . . throwing the same green fairy tinge, and the same mist, over all. A like idea has also dictated certain contrivances of dress, especially in the case of the fairies. . . .

"The main feature—the Midsummer Night—was marked by one feature so elaborated as to impress it upon all as the central picture of the group. The moon was just so much exaggerated as to give it the required prominence. The change, again, of this Midsummer Night into morning, when Theseus and Hippolyta come to the wood with horn and hound, was exquisitely presented. And in the last scene, when the fairies, coming at night into the hall of Theseus, 'each several chamber bless,' the Midsummer moon is again seen shining on the palace, as the curtains are drawn that admit the fairy throng." This part of Morley's pæan ends with the usual note concerning a Phelps production: "Ten times as much money might have been spent on a very much worse setting of the Midsummer Night's Dream."

Very much the same note is struck by Douglas Jerrold

in Lloyd's. "It is dreamland," he cries. "There is a misty transparency about the figures that gives them the appearance of flitting shadows. . . . You fancy you can see the moon shining through them. There they dance and whirl, and are puffed about first from one side and then to another, like a cloud of silver dust. . . The best way to enjoy it is, to half-close your eyes, and to resign yourself completely to the influence of the scene."

Jerrold tells us that "the scenery was quiet and subdued, as sylvan scenery at night should be. . . . . . There are not more than three or four scenes in the whole play, and yet so artistically are the different changes of moonlight, fog, and sunrise produced, that you imagine you have been wandering through an entire forest, with a fresh prospect meeting you unexpectedly at every turn."

And the costumes, and the fairies? Again we are told that they "harmonize with the scenery. . . . The fairies, as they glide in and out of the trees and foliage, give you an idea that they have actually stepped out of them . . . . and by long residence . . . had become imbued with the colour of them. They were none of your winged, white-muslin fairies [thank Heaven!] with spangles and butterfly wands, but were real, intangible shadowy beings that . . . . would infallibly at the first cockcrow melt into thin air." And Jerrold tells us that all was done noiselessly, as though "the smallest sound would have broken the spirit of the dream."

I am convinced that this was the best performance of the Midsummer Night's Dream ever given in London; of no other can I read such glowing, such convincing eulogies. Surely Jerrold and Morley knew whereof they wrote, and I accept their judgment implicitly. I have always loved to read of this production; I have faith in it.

PERICLES AT SADLER'S WELLS, 1854

The year following, Phelps made a revival with more gorgeous effects, with his nearest approach to the splendour of the Princess's, then launched under the profuse management of Charles Kean.   Pericles was brought out on October 14, 1854, why I cannot imagine.   So disjointed a vessel seemed bound to wreck on the rocks or in the gale.   Yet by the magnificence of the setting Phelps pulled a victory from predicted defeat.   He seems to have been attracted by the possibility of presenting strange antique architecture, costume, dance, and manner, not in one country, but in many.   Ancient Greece and the Orient were to be transported bodily to the purlieus of Islington and Pentonville. On no other production, apparently, did Phelps ever lavish so much costly scenery; had Charles Kean's gorgeous production of Sardanapalus moved him to this act of extravagance?

Whatever the cause, the result was splendid in the extreme.   Again I quote from Henry Morley, under date of October 21, 1854: "Of the scenery, indeed," he states, "it is to be said that so much splendour of decoration is rarely governed by so pure a taste.   The play, of which the text is instability of fortune, has its characteristic place of action on the sea.   *Pericles* is perpetually shown (literally as well as metaphorically) tempest-tost, or in the immediate vicinity of the treacherous waters; and this idea is most happily enforced at Sadler's Wells by scene-painter and machinist.   They reproduce the rolling of the billows and the whistling of the winds. . . .   When he [Pericles] is shown on board ship . . . the ship tosses vigorously. When he sails at last to the temple of Diana of the Ephesians, rowers take their places . . the vessel seems to glide along the coast, an admirably painted panorama slides before the eye; and the whole theatre seems to be in the course of actual transportation to the temple of Ephesus, which is the crowning scenic glory of the play. . . .   Now the spectator has a scene presented to him occupied by characters who appear to have stepped out of a Greek vase; and presently he looks into an Assyrian palace, and sees figures that have come to life and colour from the stones of Nineveh.   There are noble banquets and glittering processions, and in the banquet hall of King Simonides, there is a dance which is a marvel of glitter, combinations of colour, and quaint picturesque effect. There are splendid trains of courtiers, there are shining rows of vestal virgins, and there is Diana herself in the sky."

This must have been a wondrous spectacle; how could Phelps afford it, far out in Clerkenwell at popular prices? The Times, of October 16th, adds some details as to the panoramic voyage of Pericles to Ephesus: "An admirably equipped Diana, with her car in the clouds, orders his course to her sacred city, to which he is conducted by a moving diorama of excellently painted scenery. The interior of the temple, where the colossal figure of the many-breasted goddess stands in all its glory amid gorgeously attired votaries, is the last 'bang' of the general magnificence."

With this superb spectacle, I leave the Phelps *régime* at Sadler's Wells. Before closing, I beg to repeat that, during its eighteen memorable years, all the plays presented were presented with care, with adequate setting, with entirely satisfactory results. But it would be misleading to consider many of them as mounted with the extreme expense and beauty of Macbeth, Antony and Cleopatra, A Midsummer Night's Dream and Pericles. These were among the glories of the house, and stand far above other productions.

THE SURREY THEATRE, 1853

Another precaution may be necessary, lest the reader assume that elaborate efforts to decorate Shakespeare were manifested only in the more famous theatres. Sadler's Wells, itself, had begun under Phelps only as a modest venture in an outlying district, and probably, in the regions farther to the south of fashionable London, the popular Surrey rather plumed itself on occasional pretentious revivals. Perhaps, after all, this humble handmaid of the drama deserves more attention than it has ever received from historians of the stage. At any rate, I cannot refrain

from calling to notice my playbill for "the first night of the
Dramatic Season" there, on October 3, 1853.   The offering
is, for the first time at this theatre, "the Grand and Poetical
Play of The Tempest, from the Text of Shakespeare"
[note this last touch, to see how movements spread].   The
bill stresses the facts that the play is "produced under the
Direction of Mr. Creswick; the Dioramic Illusions by the
Scientific Inventor, Mr. Childe; the Masque & Dances produced by Mr. Frampton; the Gorgeous Scenery by Mr.
Dalby and Assistants; the Mechanical Effects by Mr. Rough
[under the circumstances, a name of ill omen?]; the Dresses
by Mrs. Maria Browne; the Decorations and Appointments
by Mr. T. Eallett."   And the cast was certainly good: Creswick as Prospero, George Bennett as Caliban, and Fanny
Wallack (dear to American memory) as Miranda.   The
scenery is announced with a flourish worthy of Alfred Bunn:
"View of the Neapolitan Fleet at Anchor [why?], with a
Dioramic and Pictorial Illusion of a Storm and Wreck;
Enchanted Island and Cell of Prospero; Extensive Indian
Landscape; a Wild and Barren Landscape; a Desolate
Mountain Region; a Grand Masque, [with] Harvest Fields
and Arcadian Landscape, Rustic Characteristic Dance by
the Nymphs and Reapers; Cave and Seashore; the Sun-
Illumined Ocean; Flight of Ariel."   Veritably, in reading
this bill of promised delights, the playgoer might have rubbed
his eyes, to assure himself that he was really in the democratic Surrey, and not in Charles Kean's Princess's, far
across the river; at least, in Sadler's Wells, even farther
to the north.   Doubtless files of programmes would yield
more such special efforts of a past now very remote.   I do
not suppose the Surrey was frequently taken up with spectacles so splendid,—for Shakespeare, at any rate.

CHARLES KEAN AT THE PRINCESS'S

Lavishness, not occasional, but practically universal,
was reserved as a crowning feature for the productions of
Charles Kean at the Princess's during the decade of the

'50's. But even here certain of his revivals stand above the generality for splendid effect. His collected stage versions of Shakespeare are twelve in number, but of these two at least, Hamlet and Much Ado about Nothing, may be dismissed at once from our discussion. Mrs. Kean's niece, Mrs. F. M. Paget, presented to the South Kensington Museum nearly four hundred water colours, about 7 by 9½ inches in size, representing sets for Kean's plays, and with the names of the artists written in in Kean's hand. An article by Mr. Edward F. Strange on these pictures will be found in the Magazine of Art (vol. XXVI, 1892). An earlier impression of mine as to the comparative inconspicuousness of the mounting of the two plays mentioned above is confirmed by Mr. Strange's statement that for Hamlet on January 12, 1858, Kean—I do not know why— "was content to rely on the stock scenery and properties," and that for Much Ado about Nothing, on November 20, 1858, "the scenes were good in average, but not of special distinction."

Of the remaining ten plays, except Macbeth, Mr. Strange has much to say of both scenes and scene-painters; he also writes of the setting for Cibber's Richard III, which Kean had the grace not to include in his collected Shakespeare, published in 1860. Mr. Strange I shall quote occasionally, but meantime pass on to the acting versions, as supplying scenic details very germane. One caution is necessary: the editions of the plays published singly during the run of the work involved are more elaborate in scene direction than are those found in the collected plays, and from these earlier versions I shall draw my present help. The acting versions of Kean, I may say, are scholarly in the extreme; authorities in costume and architecture are cited with an accuracy that must have awed the playgoers into whose hands they fell. Furthermore, each act is followed by notes that remind one only of text-books prepared for hapless schoolchildren; capital letters printed after words in the text direct to these fearfully academic disquisitions. My reader should look up some of these texts to observe at first hand what Dutton Cook calls a passion for archæology that was "almost crazy." Kean was no doubt greatly aided in these matters by J. R. Planché, whose name frequently graces our chronicle.

Beginning with Macbeth, the second of his imposing revivals, Kean issued with his bill of the play the material used as an introduction to the printed text; therein every playgoer was informed of the scholarly reasons why the spectacle was clothed and built in exactly the manner visible on the stage. The whole disquisition fairly bristled with names of long-forgotten worthies, classical, mediæval and renaissance. It was as good as going to school, or, better, attending a present-day popular lecture. An example from the introduction in the collected works, supplied for the first of the great revivals—King John, February 9, 1852— will show the mettle of Kean's (or Planché's?) scholarship:

There is little difficulty in collecting safe authority for the costume of King John's reign. Tapestry, illuminated manuscripts, and tombs supply abundant evidence. The habits of many of the principal characters are copied from monumental effigies, care having been taken that those who outlived King John, and were buried under the sovereignty of Henry the Third, are not clothed in emblazoned surcoats, such as appear on their respective tombs, since no instance of such ornament occurs before the year 1250.

Coeval ruins still in existence bear correct testimony of Norman architecture. The Room of State in the first act is copied from the Hall in Rochester Castle. Each succeeding scene is arranged from specific remains of the twelfth and thirteenth centuries.

Kean concludes by stating that he brought out this play partly as an educational service; with a sincere desire "to convey information to the general public through the medium of refined amusement." I believe this was true, and that this desire was the actuating cause of the large number of historical plays revived by him at the Princess's. If, however, the reader was impressed by the introduction to King John, what will he think of that to Macbeth, produced on February 14, 1853? Here we have archæology rampant—at least for a theatre programme, with which now it was issued. I cannot spare the reader, any more than Kean spared his patrons; but my reader, like the patron, is not forced to peruse and ponder:

The very uncertain information which we possess respecting the dress worn by the inhabitants of Scotland in the eleventh century, renders any attempt to render this tragedy attired in the costume of the period a task of very great difficulty. . . .

In the absence of any positive information handed down . . . . I have borrowed material from those nations to whom Scotland was constantly opposed in war. The continual inroads of the Norsemen, and the invasion of Canute, in 1031, who, combining in his own person the sovereignty of England, Norway, and Denmark, was the most powerful monarch of his time, may have taught, at least, the higher classes, the necessity of adopting the superior weapons and better defensive armour of their enemies; for these reasons I have introduced the tunic, mantle, cross-gartering, and ringed byrne of the Danes and Anglo-Saxons, between whom it does not appear that any very material difference existed; retaining, however, the peculiarity of "the striped and chequered garb," which seems to be generally admitted as belonging to the Scotch long anterior to the history of this play; together with the eagle feather in the helmet, which, according to Gaelic tradition, was the distinguishing mark of a chieftain. Party-coloured woollens and cloths appear to have been commonly worn among the Celtic tribes from a very early period.

Diodorus Siculus and Pliny allude to this peculiarity in their account of the dress of the Belgic Gauls; Strabo, Pliny, and Xiphilin, record the dress of Boadicea, Queen of the Iceni, as being woven chequer-wise, of many colours, comprising purple, light and dark red, violet and blue.

There is every reason to believe, that the armour and weapons of the date of *Macbeth* were of rich workmanship.

Harold Hardrada, King of Norway, is described by Snorre as wearing in the battle with Harold II, King of England, A. D., 1066, a blue tunic and a splendid helmet. The Norwegians, not having expected a battle that day, are said to have been without their coats of mail.

This mail appears to have been composed of iron rings or bosses, sewn upon cloth or leather, like that of the Anglo-Saxons. Thorlef, a young Icelandic, or Norwegian warrior of the tenth century, is mentioned in the Eyrbiggia Saga, as wearing a most beautiful dress, and it is also said that his arms and equipments were extremely splendid.

On second thought I *will* spare my reader further details, stating merely that this fearsome introduction of Kean's proves by seals and monuments, and by Meyrick in his work on ancient armour, that knights and barons bold of the Eleventh Century must have dressed about as they appeared on the stage of the Princess's Theatre. The scholarship wends its way securely through Alexander I of Scotland, David I, etc., until we land on Kean's statement that he has equipped Siward and his son in the leathern suits called Corium or Corietum, which were introduced among the Saxons in the Ninth Century. I hope my reader is as relieved as I to learn of this archæological detail, and can enjoy, so much the more, in historic imagination, the lines of Shakespeare as delivered by characters so correctly garbed.

Kean ends by informing us that "the Scotch had probably improved greatly in their architecture and habits of living during the age just anterior to the Norman Conquest of England, and under these considerations, the architecture, previous to the Norman Conquest, has been adopted throughout the play. During the five centuries which preceded that event, the Anglo-Saxons made great advances, and erected many castles and churches of considerable importance; they excelled in iron work, and ornamented their buildings frequently with colour. On this subject I have availed myself of the valuable knowledge of George Godwin, Esq., F. R. S., of the Royal Institute of Architects, to whose suggestions I take this opportunity of acknowledging my obligation."

After such a preliminary *credo*, no one could rationally doubt the good intention of Kean. I cite this elaborate *ante-mortem* as illustrating Kean's methods of production; for later revivals, I shall quote less liberally. I may end this preliminary view by stating that Kean, in his farewell speech at the Princess's in 1859, animadverted bitterly on those who had not liked his efforts, scholarly as they were. He said, "I have been blamed for depriving Macbeth of a dress never worn at any period, or in any place, and for providing him instead with one resembling those used by surrounding nations. Fault was also found in my removal of the gorgeous banquet of gold and silver vessels, together with the massive candelabra (such as no Highlander of the

Eleventh Century ever gazed upon), and with the substitution of the more appropriate feast of coarse fare, served upon rude tables, and lighted by simple pine torches."

Of King John and Macbeth I here take leave, with the statement that the Witch scenes of the latter were very well managed, with storm and mist and supernatural disappearances. It will be remembered that Kean restored the Davenant-Locke material. One effect of a peculiarly Kean-like organisation occurs at the end of Act III, after Davenant has done his worst, with singing and dancing witches. At the very close, Hecate ascends into the air, the witches disappear, and then, in all the majesty of complete capitals, THE MIST DISPERSES, AND DISCOVERS A BIRD'S-EYE VIEW OF THE ISLAND OF IONA. Why? Heaven knows, unless it were to bring down the curtain on a fine transformation, to rival the Christmas pantomime, and to send the glad eye of the spectator with more cheer to the solemn perusal between acts of the notes about costume and other archæological matter so learnedly supplied with the bill of the play.

KEAN'S HENRY VIII, 1855

The first of Kean's revivals that catches the fancy is Henry VIII, on May 16, 1855. This I shall dwell on at greater length. Kean, in his now customary introduction, asserts that "to give full effect to this noble play, information has been sought from every source which could contribute to the realisation of what may be almost termed the domestic habits of the English Court, three hundred years ago. Shakespeare has so closely followed Cavendish . . . . the grand festival at York Place is so clearly described by the early historian . . . that there is no difficulty in conveying an exact picture of the entertainment. . . ." He continues:

In the disposition of the stage at the trial of Queen Katharine, I have again followed Cavendish, as well as the corresponding account in D'Aubigné's "History of the Reformation."

The christening of the future Protestant Queen Elizabeth was sol-
emnized with all the rites of the Church of Rome, at the Grey Friars,
Greenwich (not a vestige of which now remains); and I have taken
advantage of the historical fact of the Lord Mayor and City Council
proceeding to the royal ceremonial in their state barges, to give a
panoramic view of London, as it then appeared, concluding with the
old Palace of Greenwich, where Queen Anne Boleyn resided at the
time.   These views have been copied from a drawing by Antony Van
Den Wynyerde, A. D., 1543.

.   .   .   .

Strutt observes . . . that the whole of the life of Henry VIII
(especially during the time when . . . Wolsey was in favour),
abounded with processions and princely shows of grandeur and magnificence.   This pageantry Shakespere [and, one may interpolate,
Charles Kean] has vivified, ... and has thus produced, as Coleridge says, "a sort of historical masque or show play."
Where it has been possible to find music sufficiently ancient to
coincide with the period of the play, it has been introduced.   The
remaining portions, together with the overture, entr'actes, and duet
of "Orpheus with his Lute," have been composed by Mr. J. L. Hatton. [Kean then specifies the old tunes, including "Lightie Love
Ladies," said to have been Shakespeare's favourite air, which is
introduced before and after the vision of Queen Katharine.]

Kean rightly says that this play abounds in opportunity
for show, pageant and procession; of this he availed himself more than had any of his predecessors, restoring a
scene or two merely for the pageantry involved.   Few
before his day or since gave both the coronation of Anne
Boleyn and the christening of her daughter.   I can best
show the production by quoting liberally from the book of
the play as prepared by Kean.
The first scene is in Old Palace Yard, Westminster, copied
from a drawing made by Van Den Wynyerde in 1543, and
no doubt very solid and substantial.   The train of Wolsey
is preceded by a trumpet march, and comes in this order:

4 Trumpeters
6 Guards
Pursuivant, with the great silver-gilt mace of the Chancellor
2 Gentlemen, with silver-headed staves
Gentleman, carrying the Great Seal of England

2 Gentlemen Ushers, with wands
Priest carrying Cardinal's hat
2 Gentlemen Ushers with wands
2 Laymen, carrying silver pillars
2 Priests, carrying silver crosses
8 Henchmen, supporting the canopy over Cardinal Wolsey, and followed by
2 Pages
2 Secretaries
2 Chaplains
8 Footmen
6 Guards

The second scene is the "Council Chamber, a restoration of the painted Chamber at Westminster, from Capon's drawing in *Vetusta Monumenta*. It opens with a flourish of trumpets, Bishops, Judges, and Lords of the Privy Council discovered. Enter, L. H., four Mace Bearers, Lord Chamberlain, the Lords; the King enters, leaning on the Cardinal's shoulder.

"The King takes his state. The Lords of the Council take their several places. The Cardinal places himself under the King's feet, on his right side. A noise within, crying, Room for the Queen, who enters, ushered by Norfolk and Guildford; she kneels. The King rises, places her by him."

The fourth scene is the "Presence-Chamber in York Palace. Music. A small table under a state for the Cardinal; R. H. a longer table for the guests, C." The guests enter, and shortly, preceded by a flourish of trumpets, pursuivant with mace, two silver pillar-bearers, two gentlemen ushers, the lord cardinal, himself, enters and takes his state. Two pages attend to him. Of course there is the usual entry, later, of the King and twelve others, as maskers, habited like shepherds, preceded by sixteen drummers and fifers, and sixteen torch-bearers. This must have filled the stage with bustle and animation.

As usual for the execution of Buckingham, the scene is the King's Stairs, Westminster, taken from the same drawing as Act I, Scene 1. There is great confusion of a crowd,

at first, then "enter Buckingham, R. U. E.   Two tip staves
before him; the axe, with the edge towards him, and Guard;
with him Lovell, Vaux, Sands.   The Duke's barge discovered with four rowers, at the foot of the steps leading to
the water.   Buckingham's exit is by this barge, which
slowly moves off, L. H."   This no doubt was impressive
stage machinery in 1855.

The next highly picturesque tableau is that of the Queen's
trial (Act II, Scene 4).   Kean's staging was different from
Kemble's; he minutely describes it:

> The scene is a Hall in Blackfriars.   The Court assembled to try
> the divorce of Henry and Katharine.   The two Cardinals sit in the
> centre, on a raised platform, as Judges, with their respective suites
> on each side of them.   Below them, the Secretaries.   To the right
> of the Cardinals a throne for the King, and to the left a raised chair
> for the Queen.   The bishops, Doctors of Law and Divinity, and Peers
> are seated between the Legates and the throne.—Trumpets sound.
> Enter four Trumpeters, two Mace Bearers, Garter King-at-arms,
> two Mace Bearers, Sword Bearer, Lord Chamberlain, Six Henchmen
> surrounding the King; Norfolk and Suffolk; they pass across to R. H.,
> the King takes his seat.
> Enter Queen Katharine, eight Ladies in Waiting, four Bishops, and
> Griffith, her Gentleman Usher.   The Queen sits L. H., the Women
> surround her.

This must have been an imposing tableau, hardly surpassed by Irving and Tree of later days.   The third act
begins with a scene in the Queen's Palace at Bridewell, in
which is introduced "a chimney-piece, designed by Holbein
for that palace, from a drawing in the British Museum."

Acts IV and V are very short, but in them Kean managed to crowd a great deal of spectacular splendour.   The
first scene of Act IV is a platform erected for the procession
to Queen Anne Boleyn's coronation, and leading to the
west door of Westminster Abbey.   The order of the procession runs thus:

> A lively flourish of trumpets; then, enter
> 4 Trumpeters
> 2 Judges

Gentleman with the Purse containing the Broad Seal
Gentleman with the Mace
Lord Chancellor
Choristers singing
Mayor of London bearing the Mace
4 Aldermen
Garter King-at-Arms in his coat of arms, and on his head a
  gilt copper crown
4 Pursuivants
Marquis Dorset, bearing a sceptre of gold, with him the Earl
  of Surrey, bearing the Rod of Silver with the Dove
Duke of Suffolk, bearing a long white wand as High Steward,
  with him the Duke of Norfolk, with the Rod of Marshal-
  ship
4 Barons of the Cinque Ports bearing the Canopy over the
  Queen, on each side of her the Bishops of London and
  Winchester
The Duchess Dowager of Norfolk, bearing the Queen's train,
  followed by Ladies
The Procession passes across the stage from L. H. to R. H.

The second scene of the act contained that which was, unquestionably, the finest tableau of the spectacle—the Vision of Queen Katharine, hitherto unrepresented for a century or more. The sketch of this—reproduced from the Illustrated London News of June 2, 1855—gives, I am sure, but a faint impression of this scene, in which it has been asserted unwarrantably that the limelight was first used on the London stage, and in which Ellen Terry, then a very little girl, posed as the top angel—though this was in 1858, at a later revival, not at the original, in 1855; so much at least I gather from Ellen Terry's Story of My Life.

Of the scenery and effects in general, J. W. Cole, Kean's eulogist, has this to say: "The order of *Wolsey's* march as he is passing to the council chamber, the dazzling splendour of the banquet at York Place, the solemnity of the execution of *Buckingham*, the distribution of the court for the trial of the divorce question between the King and *Katharine of Arragon*, the etherial beauty of the vision in the scene of

SCENE FROM HENRY VIII AT THE PRINCESS'S THEATRE, 1855
From the *Illustrated London News*

SCENE FROM THE WINTER'S TALE AT THE PRINCESS'S THEATRE, 1856
From the *Illustrated London News*

her dream and death . . . . .; these bold and truthful innovations are exclusively the result of Mr. Kean's close
examination of his subject, and are as entirely new as they
are superior in value and reality to the old conventional
arrangements they have so happily superseded." Miss
Terry gives even more valuable testimony. She refers to
the splendours of Charles Kean's stage, a stage on which
she made her début at the age of six. "It has been said
lately," she states, "that I began my career on an unfurnished stage, when the play was the thing, and spectacle
was considered of small importance. I take this opportunity of contradicting that statement most emphatically.
Neither when I began nor yet later in my career have I
ever played under a management where infinite pains were
not given to every detail." Miss Terry asserts her faith
in "a beautiful and congruous background," and proceeds
to say that "child as I was, the beauty of the productions
at the Princess's Theatre made a great impression on me,
and my memory of them is quite clear enough . . . for me
to assert that in some respects they were even more elaborate than those of the present day." This is high praise
from the coadjutor of the incomparable Henry Irving, and
lends special emphasis to her remark that "the production
of Henry VIII at the Princess's was one of Charles Kean's
best efforts. I always refrain from belittling the present
at the expense of the past, but there were efforts here which
I have never seen surpassed, and about this my memory is
not at all dim."

This is conclusive from one who lived through the finest
period of Irving's work and Tree's, and it justifies the
extravagance of the Times of May 17, 1855, which cries
out, "We will run the risk of being charged with exaggera-
tion by declaring in most unequivocal terms that the play
of 'Henry VIII,' as produced last night at the Princess's
Theatre, is the most wonderful spectacle that has ever
been seen on the London stage." In the Vision, the Times,
of May 21st asserts further, of Mrs. Kean as Katharine,
"The attitude in which, half-rising from her couch, she fol-

lows with her eyes the departing forms, might serve as a study for some picture of a saint's 'ecstasy.'"

As if the foregoing glories were not enough, Kean began, as we have seen, the fifth act by a moving panorama of the journey of the Lord Mayor from the City to Greenwich, to the christening of the infant daughter of Henry VIII and Anne Boleyn.

This work of supererogation in a spectacle already replete with processions and gorgeous scenes must have greatly impressed Kean's audiences. The book of the play informs us that these views have been copied from a drawing by Van Den Wynyerde (1543), and proceeds to say that the panorama "represents London, as it appeared in the reign of Henry VIII, commencing at the Palace of Bridewell, and passing the Fleet Ditch—Blackfriars—St. Paul's—London Bridge—The Tower—Limehouse—the Celebrated Man of War, the Great Harry (copied from the Model in the Room of the Admiralty, Somerset House)—Barges of the Lord Mayor and City Council on their way to Greenwich, to attend the Christening—Greenwich Palace, Park, &c., &c." The panorama finally ends and merges into a scene of the Interior of the Church of the Grey Friars, Greenwich, "restored from contemporaneous buildings, in the absence of absolute vestiges." In this church occurs a gorgeous christening ceremony in which figure the King, Norfolk, Suffolk, the Lord Chamberlain, Lords with gifts of great standing bowls, lords and ladies, Duchess of Norfolk, godmother, bearing the child richly habited in a mantle, the Marchioness of Dorset, the other godmother, Lord Chancellor, Lord Mayor, Sheriffs, Aldermen, Archbishop of Canterbury, Bishop of London, etc. I suspect, however, that the reader has had enough of pageantry, and I conclude by echoing Miss Terry's faith in this as one of the bravest of stage spectacles. It must have cost three or four times what Phelps expended on his usual productions at Sadler's Wells. One last word: according to the Illustrated London News of June 2, 1855, "the number of set scenes has rendered one of the contrivances of the French stage necessary. Fold-ing curtains of magnificent velvet are occasionally let down, while the requisite scenic arrangements are being made."

Beginning with The Winter's Tale, on April 28, 1856, Kean entered on a series of performances of possibly even greater magnificence. In his now expected preface he shows clearly that the contrast between Greek civilisation at its most beautiful (pictorially) and Asiatic life of a more barbaric pomp chiefly led him to the decoration of this play. The conviction that Syracuse at its highest rivalled Athens in splendour of architecture induced him, he tells us, to place "before the eyes of the spectator, *tableaux vivants* of the private and public life of the ancient Greeks, at a time when the arts flourished to . . perfection." Accepting Sir Thomas Hanmer's substitution of Bithynia for the still vexed Bohemia, he was enabled "to represent the costume of the inhabitants of Asia Minor at a corresponding period." To crown the shepherd scene in Bithynia, he ventured "to introduce one of those festivals in honour of Bacchus, known under the title of '*Dionysia.*'"

A reading of the directions for scenery in the text, as issued, and of all the directions for dance and spectacle, will convince the reader of the efforts employed in the production. Kean tells us that he called in, for advice on the architecture, and other archæological details, George Godwin, F.R.S., and George Scharf, Jr., F.S.A. For the music, of which, as usual, Kean made much, James A. Davies, Lecturer on Music, supplied supervisory control. The scene-painters, under the direction of Grieve, were the best in London, and included Telbin, W. Gordon, F. Lloyds, Cuthbert and Dayes—a glittering galaxy. Rather, however, than reproduce the scene-directions of the acting version, I shall quote the glowing description of J. W. Cole, in his Life and Theatrical Times of Charles Kean:

As the curtain rose, we saw before us Syracuse at the epoch of her greatest prosperity, about 300 B. C., and gazed on the fountains of

Arethusa and the Temple of Minerva. After the short introductory scene . . . . we passed to the banqueting-hall in the Royal palace, where *Leontes, Polixenes, Hermione* and guests were discovered reclining on couches, after the manner of the ancient Greeks. Musicians were playing the hymn to *Apollo*, and slaves supplied wine and garlands. Thirty-six resplendently handsome young girls representing youths in complete warlike panoply, entered, and performed the evolutions of the Pyrrhic dance. The effect was electrical.

Charles Kean is nothing if not archæological, and we must all be consoled to learn from his text of the play, that "the cornice on which the roof rests is supported by Canephoræ." A similar thrill is imparted by the information that the first scene of Act II is the Court of the Gynæconitis, or Women's Apartments, "a beautiful interior," according to Cole; in the next scene, according to the same enthusiastic chronicler, "a representation of one of the dreary 'Latomiæ,' or excavated dungeons, known as the 'Ear of Dionysius,' conveyed a corresponding idea of the severity with which the guiltless *Hermione* is treated." In view of all this archæology, does any reader wonder at the statement of Ellen Terry about the care for detail on Kean's stage— Ellen Terry, who made her first appearance in a speaking part—that of the child Mamilius—in this very production?

Let us return to Cole, who tells us that "the third act comprised the trial of *Queen Hermione* in the public theatre at Syracuse, the usual hall of judgment on great public occasions. The arrangement of the stage here presented an astonishing instance of scenic illusion. The area is extremely limited; yet, by pictorial and mechanical combination, it appeared to expand to colossal proportions. . A wonderful realization was presented by the dense assembly of auditory and officials; by the imposing appearance of the King on his throne, with sages and councillors ranged beside and on each side of him; by the arraigned Queen, borne in on her litter, with attendant females; and by the solemn procession of the Oracle. . . These were grouped together, and the varying emotions of the whole assembly reflected in animated gesticulation and expression. . . ."

The two parts of the play were joined together in the original by a Chorus, who speaks of the events of intervening years. Kean accompanied this speech by a gorgeous pageant or allegorical representation, which would have delighted the court of Charles I, or the patrons of Dorset Garden, as completely as the naïve denizens of Mayfair in the time of Kean. The entire scheme of the "machinery" and its manipulation can best be gleaned from the unwearied Cole: "Clouds now descended and filled the stage, leading to a classical allegory, representing the course of *Time*. As these clouds dispersed, *Selene*, or *Luna*, was discovered in her car, accompanied by the *Stars* (personified by living figures), and gradually sunk into the ocean. *Time* then appeared, surmounting the globe, no longer represented by the traditionary bald-headed elder, with his scythe and hour-glass, but as a classical figure, more in accordance with the character of the play, as now represented. He spoke the lines. . . As *Time* descended, *Phœbus* rose with surpassing brilliancy in the chariot of the Sun, encircled by a blaze of light which filled every portion of the theatre. The group appeared to be derived from that in the centre of Flaxman's Shield of Achilles. The horses were modelled with a life and fire that would have done honour to Baron Marochetti himself. The statue-like grace and immobility of *Apollo*, as he stood in the car, reining in his impetuous steeds, impressed a universal conviction that this figure also was artificial; but the living reality was conveyed in the most startling manner, when, at the full height of his ascent, he suddenly raised his right arm to lash a restive courser. The effect baffles description. The entire allegory may be pronounced the greatest triumph of art ever exhibited on the stage."

This must have been a wonderful show. It "dissolved," Cole tells us, into the palace of Polixenes. There were two other great scenes, employing full stage. The first, the scene of the Shepherd's festival, in Act IV, was—again to quote Cole—"rich in the luxuriance of Eastern foliage, with a distant view of Nicæa, the capital of Bithynia, on the lake Ascania. Nothing could be more delightful than this complete change from the palatial magnificence of the earlier portion of the play. . . . . A dance of shepherds and shepherdesses comes in so naturally, and was performed with such exquisite grace, and a musical accompaniment so completely in harmony with the scene, that we almost fancied ourselves in Arcadia during the golden age. . . From this delicious dream we were roused by the boisterous merriment of the *Dionysia*, or grand festival of the vintage, in honour of Bacchus, executed by an overpowering mass of satyrs, men, women, and children, in wild disguises, and with frantic energy. There must have been at least three hundred persons engaged in this revel of organized confusion."

The last scene of importance was that of the statue, reproduced—opposite page 336—from a print in the Illustrated London News of May 10, 1856. I must say I like it, and can well accept Cole's account as authentic: "The procession by torch-light, the passing round the peristyle within which the statue is placed, the grouping when Hermione was discovered," are all commended. Yet even with all this, Mrs. Kean, we know, from pictures, and from Ellen Terry's evidence, wore her hair " drawn flat over her forehead and twisted tight round her ears in a kind of circular sweep"; and amazed by "the amount of petticoats she wore," starched, "in defiance of the fact that classical parts should not be dressed in a superfluity of raiment."

The above record of Charles Kean's production of The Winter's Tale will show how little truth, as Miss Terry says, there was in the persistent statements that she made her first appearance on an "unfurnished" stage. The child-débutante of 1856, in Charles Kean's theatre, was the immortal leading actress in his successor's (Henry Irving's) Lyceum; and both managers had exactly the same ideal of Shakespearian production.

Charles Kean's path, like that of other producers in our history, was beset by the petty animosities so galling to a sensitive nature. Chief among the attacks was the now very common cry about smothering Shakespeare in scenery. In the case of The Winter's Tale the Times, which had so highly extolled Kean's Henry VIII, neatly phrases the doubt. "The Winter's Tale," it animadverts, "produced at the Princess's Theatre with extraordinary magnificence of decoration, has revived the question of the artistic legitimateness of those gorgeous accessories with which Mr. Kean has more than once decked out the Shakespearian dramas. The point is by no means settled, as some critics seem to think, by the consideration that Shakespeare himself could never have, in fact, contemplated such a representation of his play. If any test at all can be applied, it must be furnished by the dramatist's own conception of the scene in which his personages moved—by the manner in which they were ideally presented to his mind; and if we can convince ourselves that Shakespeare—with whatever vagueness—conceived his Leontes, his Hermione and his Perdita, as surrounded by the very life and scenery of actual Greece, we must be grateful to Mr. Kean for supplying an element which the poet himself was only forced to exclude by the imperfect mechanism of the Elizabethan stage."

Thus does the Times neatly pose a question that perplexed Macready's more unsympathetic critics, that perplexed Kean's, Irving's and Tree's; I cite it here to show that there is literally nothing new under the critical sun. Kean, at any rate, was grieved and harassed by the reiterated statement that he sacrificed Shakespeare to setting. In reality, he believed his elaborate mounting distinctly added to the poetic effect of the plays produced.

KEAN'S MIDSUMMER NIGHT'S DREAM, 1856

After The Winter's Tale had run its 102 nights, Kean reverted to a play offering similar effects; though why, since neither he nor Mrs. Kean could appear in it, he should have selected A Midsummer Night's Dream, it is somewhat difficult to discover. Probably the opportunity for spectacle again invited. He put it on with all the allurements of song, musical enchantment (Mendelssohn's), moonlight (though of a stage variety), scenery and costume. He ignored, as his Preface learnedly boasts, the probable architecture of the era of buildings in the time of Theseus, 1200 B. C., "which were rude in construction, and of the simplest material," and selected a later period. Hence, "the Acropolis on its rocky eminence, surrounded by marble temples, has been restored, together with the theatre of Bacchus." Cole must again be called into court; he asserts that before the eyes of the spectators was placed, on the rising of the curtain, a "restored view" of Athens; " we saw, on the hill of the Acropolis, the far-famed Parthenon, the Erechtheum, and the statue of the tutelary goddess Minerva, or Athena; by its side the theatre of Bacchus in advance, the temple of Jupiter Olympus, partially hiding the hall of the Museum; and on the right, the temple of Theseus." This not uncrowded scene also included the summit of Mars Hill. It was apparently but a back-drop, since the front scene was a Terrace adjoining the Palace of Theseus, overlooking the City of Athens.

If Cole liked this setting, Morley did not. Under date of October 25th, he urges that such a setting, beautiful as it is, is in too hard and fast contrast to the fairy scenes. The poetry was missing—the now familiar cry. But what of those fairy scenes? Cole is jubilant about them:

The introduction to the haunt of the supernatural beings; the first appearance of Oberon and Titania, with their attendant trains; the noiseless footsteps of the "shadow dance" on the moonlit greensward, with the undulating reflections . . .; the wood, peopled with its innumerable fairy legions . . . the melodious music composed by Mendelssohn . . . the perpetual change of scene and incident; the shifting diorama; the golden beams of the rising sun glittering on the leaves; the gradual dispersion of the mist, discovering the fairy guardians, light and brilliant as gossamer, grouped around the unconscious sleeping mortals; the dazzling magnificence of the palace of Theseus. . . .

But again Morley disagrees. He likes the diorama of the second act—invariable concomitant of this play at the time; it is "a dream-like moving of the wood, beautifully managed," but it is "spoilt in effect" because Oberon stands before it "waving his wand, as if he were exhibitor of the diorama, or a fairy conjuror causing the rocks and trees to move." Furthermore, "the fairy ring" revealed, calls down scathing scorn, because in it is Titania's shadow dance. "Of all things in the world a shadow dance of fairies! If," says Morley severely, "if anything in the way of an effect of light was especially desirable, it would have been such an arrangement as would have made the fairies appear to be dancing in a light so managed as to cast no shadow, and give them the true spiritual attribute. Elaborately to produce and present, as an especial attraction, fairies of large size, casting shadows made as black and distinct as possible, and offering in dance to pick them up, as if even they also were solid, is as great a sacrifice of Shakespeare to the purposes of the ballet-master, as the view of Athens in its glory was a sacrifice of poetry to the scene-painter."

In this revival Kean indulged in the familiar transformations with which subsequent performances of the same play have familiarised us. Puck's first appearance shows him rising on a mushroom. Ellen Terry, the Puck of the production, reveals one of the secrets of the prison-house. "When Puck was told to put a girdle round the earth in forty minutes, I had to fly off the stage as swiftly as I could, and a dummy Puck was whirled through the air from the point where I disappeared." One night, Miss Terry informs us, she caused great laughter. The dummy fell and the real Puck ran out and picked it up, receiving therefor a "sound cuff" from some one in authority. Morley is particularly acrid in comment on such flummery. "We get at the end, a ballet of fairies round a maypole that shoots up out of an aloe, after the way of a transformation in a pantomime, and rains down garlands. Fairies, not airy beings of the colour of the greenwood, or the sky, or robed in misty white, but glittering in the most brilliant dresses, with a crust of bullion about their legs, cause the curtain to fall on a splendid ballet; and it is evidence enough of the depraved taste of the audience to say that the ballet is encored." Morley asserts that he makes these comments in no censorious mood; but I do not believe him.

Let us end with a description of the concluding scene by the ever-happy Cole, who sings of "the dazzling magnificence of the palace of Theseus at the close, thronged on every staircase, balustrade and corridor, with myriads of aerial beings," who "join in an unseen and unheard epithalamium on the mortal inmates." This final tableau is like that of Madame Vestris's in 1840; why not, since Planché had a hand in both? Laura Keene's production of the play in New York in 1859 was evidently modelled on Charles Kean's. It had, I suspect, as his had, more of the pantomime elements than had Phelps's, and to that extent offended judicious critical taste. What has Puck to do, rising on mushrooms—especially dressed as was Ellen Terry —with belts and garlands of flowers! Anyhow, the people liked Kean's revival of the Dream sufficiently to keep it on view for 150 nights.

KEAN'S RICHARD II, 1857

Perhaps wearied with all the mythical and fairy-like adjuncts of these last two great revivals, Kean turned again to the historical plays, and brought out, as a companion picture to his King John and Henry VIII, a gorgeous and archæologically accurate presentation of a play that even Phelps never attempted—Richard II. Did Kean's magnificent production anticipate one by Phelps and render it therefore useless, not to say hazardous?

My scenical report has already grown so long that I will content myself by reproducing the account of the performance of Richard II published in the Illustrated London News of March 21, 1857, supplementing by the scene of Richard's humiliating entry into London, from the same issue. This was the main feature of the show, but the architectural aspects of the scenery were so splendid that

SCENE FROM RICHARD II AT THE PRINCESS'S THEATRE, 1857

From the *Illustrated London News*

SCENE FROM THE TEMPEST AT THE PRINCESS'S THEATRE, 1857

From the *Illustrated London News*

one gains, in reading, an idea of one magnificent set after another of solid sombre masonry "cased in the unfeeling armour of old time." This is stressed in the account in the London News that follows:

Mr. Kean has wisely gone beyond the drama to the Chronicles, and between the third and fourth acts has presented to sight the humiliating entry into London of Richard II in the custody of Bolingbroke. This is one of the most gorgeous and effective scenes that we ever witnessed on the stage. Commencing with the Dance of Itinerant Fools as described in "Strutt's Sports and Pastimes of the English," we are presented with the multitudes that crowd the streets, the balconies, and the housetops, and witness numerous little episodes, skilfully acted out by competent performers, preparatory to the main event of the scene. Nothing can be more impressive than the entrance of Bolingbroke on his white charger, followed by Richard on his humble steed, all sad and woe-begone, utterly subdued by the execrations of the mob. The words recorded by the chroniclers are spoken on the stage by the usurper and the crowd, but Richard passes over in melancholy and heart-broken silence. Such an interlude as this Shakespeare would himself have doubtless approved of, as a fitting illustration of historic fact. Its tendency is to realize the whole of the action. . . . .

The other scenes, rich and various as they are in their appointments, are strictly confined to their bearing on the actual text. The Privy Council Chamber in the Palace of Westminster presents its walls and roof decorated with the badges and cognizances of *Richard II* ; and the lists of combat at Gosford-Green are graced with the Royal pavilion, containing the King enthroned, attended by his nobles, the effect of the scene being enhanced by its apparent interminability. The bed-room in Ely House surrounds the dying hours of old *Gaunt* with appropriate grandeur; while the advance of *Bolingbroke's* army through the wilds of Gloucestershire is actualized to the senses by picturesque artifices and numerous stage expedients. Added to these, we have the excellent restorations of the entrance to St. Stephen's Chapel, Pembroke Castle, and Flint Castle; with representations of Milford Harbor, Welsh scenery, and certain famous localities of London, such as Westminster Hall and the Traitors' Gate of the Tower. The Dungeon in Pomfret Castle, and St. George's Hall at Windsor, complete the splendid diorama composed by the scenes of this revival.

The costume of the piece is varied and exceedingly accurate. It is principally taken from the illuminations to the French metrical history . . . . in the British museum; but other works have been consulted with effect. The music also merits attention. It has been composed and adapted by Mr. J. L. Hatton.

The skill with which all this scenic magnificence has been introduced, without impairing the dramatic interest or interfering with the histrionic excellence, deserves more than ordinary praise.

That the reader may have, at first hand, an idea of Kean's great pageant of the entry of Bolingbroke and Richard into London, I quote it entire from his acting version:

HISTORICAL EPISODE

LONDON.—*The fronts of the houses adorned with tapestry and hangings, as on occasions of public rejoicing. A vast concourse of people occupying the streets, in expectation of the arrival of Bolingbroke, Duke of Lancaster, and the deposed and captive King Richard the Second. The incidental amusements of the crowd are taken from* "*Strutt's Sports and Pastimes of the English,*" *including the*

DANCE OF ITINERANT FOOLS

The Dance Tune is supposed to be as old as the Reign of Edward the Second.

TRUMPET MARCH.   ENTER PROCESSION

City Trumpeters

City Banner.   Banner of St. Paul

Guards

City Mace Bearer. Lord Mayor's Banner. City Sword Bearer

Sheriff of London. Lord Mayor. Sheriff of London

Aldermen

Banner of the Mercer's Company

Captain and Company of the Mercers (Armed)

Banner of the Grocer's Company

Captain and Company of the Grocers (Armed)

Banner of the Fishmonger's Company

Captain and Company of the Fishmongers (Armed)

Banner of the Goldsmith's Company

Captain and Company of the Goldsmiths (Armed)

Banner of the Linen Armourers (Armed)

Captain and Company of the Linen Armourers (Armed)

Banner of the Saddler's Company

Captain and Company of the Saddlers (Armed)

Banner of the Baker's Company

Captain and Company of the Bakers (Armed)

Royal Banners

Noblemen in Civil Costume

Minstrels
Duke of Lancaster's Banner
Girls with Flowers

Knight in Armour	BOLINGBROKE	Knight in Armour
Knight in Armour	on	Knight in Armour
Knight in Armour	HORSEBACK	Knight in Armour

Guards
Captain, and Band of City Archers
The Duke of Lancaster is received with shouts of enthusiasm

Bolingbroke. Thanks, my countrymen and loving friends, I thank you, countrymen.

Voice from the Crowd. Long live Henry, the noble Duke of Lancaster!
Shouts

Another voice. Welcome, long wished for Duke of Lancaster, may all joy and prosperity attend you.
Shouts

Another voice. Such a lord deserves to be king!
Shouts repeated

Bolingbroke. My lords, and friends, here is King Richard, I deliver him into your custody, and beg you to do with him as you wish.

Different voices. God save thee, Bolingbroke! Heaven preserve thee! Welcome, Bolingbroke!

General shouting of Long live the Duke of Lancaster!
[*Flourish of Trumpets and other instruments, the ringing of bells, &c., &c.*

KING RICHARD IS RECEIVED IN SILENCE

An open space is kept round him that all may see him, and a boy comes forward, pointing with his finger, and saying, Behold King Richard, who has done so much to the Kingdom of England!

Murmurs from the Mob

Voice from the Mob. Now are we well avenged on him who has governed us so ill!

Exclamations. To the Tower with him! to the Tower with him!

An old soldier, who has fought under the banner of Edward the Black Prince at Cressy and Poictiers, accompanied by his grandson, endeavours to pay homage to the son of his former commander, but is prevented by the mob, and treated with contempt. The procession passes on, and the

DROP FALLS

This is about the most elaborate synopsis of a stage procession with which I am familiar; the picture seems to have been, also, more elaborate than any I have seen in a Shake-spearian play. It was the glory of this particular production, and with its success I close the discussion of the much-vaunted revival. Cole ejaculates, "the music, the joy-bells, the dances, the crowded balconies and windows, the throngs in the street [Ellen Terry informs us she was the boy that climbed to the top of a pole], the civic processions, the mailed warriors, the haughty *Bolingbroke*, the heart-broken *Richard*, the maddening shouts of gratulation which attend the one, while the other is received with silence, gradually deepening into murmurs, groans, and insults, the scrupulous accuracy with which every dress and move-ment is pourtrayed"; all this, emphasises Cole, bewildered with astonishment and admiration. Furthermore, this was Kean's masterpiece. "The scene," says Cole, "altogether surpassed the glories of *Wolsey's* banquet and ball in Henry the Eighth, or the maddening reality of the Dionysian pas-time in the Winter's Tale."

KEAN'S TEMPEST, 1857

Once more Kean returned to the realm of imagination, completing what I have called his banner year with a superb production of The Tempest, on July 1, 1857. He himself played Prospero, and Kate Terry, Ariel. This elder of the remarkable Terry children had already played Titania, when Carlotta Leclercq gave up the part, and was, the next year, at the age of sixteen, to be the youngest Cordelia known to the stage.

Kean's version of The Tempest began with a remarkably vivid representation of the ship in the storm, "the arrange-ments of which," according to the Illustrated London News of July 4th, were "entirely new and appalling in the ex-treme. The flaming deck of the vessel, as it tosses and turns, with its helpless crew," was "a direful spectacle." Says Cole, it struggles "against the combined fury of winds and waves," and ultimately seems "to founder with all on board. As the mist of the storm disperses, the sun slowly

rises on the magic island, the sea subsides, the waters recede
from 'the yellow sands,' and *Prospero* is discovered with
Miranda, standing on the point of a rock, superintending
the effect of his art."

This storm was one of Kean's triumphs, but The Tempest had other wonders. As Cole informs us, "a great
triumph of scenic exhibition is reserved for the third act.
A long perspective of desolation gradually changes from
barrenness to tropical luxuriance; trees rise from the earth,
fountains and waterfalls gush from the rocks; while naiads,
wood nymphs, and satyrs enter, bearing fruits and flowers."
The masque of Juno, Iris and Ceres chiefly occupied the
fourth act, which concludes with the hunting of Caliban
and the sailors by a legion of goblins "copied from furies
depicted on Etruscan vases."

Another great scenic effect was that of "some allegorical
illustrations," as the Illustrated London News puts it,
"representative of Prospero releasing the spirits who had
served him so well." For this, Night, according to Cole,
"enshrouds the scene. The released spirits take their
flight from the island, through the air; morning breaks, and
shows the royal vessel floating gently, and in perfect trim,
on the unruffled waters. *Prospero*, standing on the deck,
delivers the epilogue. The ship gradually sails off, the
island recedes from sight, *Ariel* alone occupies the scene,
suspended in the air . . . . while a distant chorus of spirits
dies softly away as the curtain falls."

Kean, throughout, brought on many mechanical tricks
suggestive of the court of Charles I and of Dorset Garden
Theatre. Cole must again supply the details: "*Ariel* formerly walked on and off the stage . . . moving with the
substantial attributes of mortality. . . . Now, we were
really presented with a 'delicate spirit,' at one moment
descending in a ball of fire; at another rising gently from a
tuft of flowers; again, sailing on the smooth waters on the
back of a dolphin; then, gliding noiselessly over the sands,
as a water-nymph; and, ever and anon, perched on the
summit of a rock, riding on a bat, or cleaving mid-air with

the velocity of lightning. The powers of modern stage mechanism are almost as marvellous as the gift ascribed to the magic wand and book of *Prospero*."

This, then, was Kean's performance of The Tempest, probably the most beautiful and astonishing ever put on the stage, unless Shadwell's in 1673-74 was equally brilliant scenically. Purists then, like purists now, lamented their lost fragments of Shakespeare; but the average theatregoer simply revelled in the show for a long succession of performances.

KEAN'S LAST PRODUCTIONS

The three following revivals of Kean at the Princess's I shall pass over more rapidly; fine as they were, the echoes of them have rung more faintly through the intervening years.

The first was King Lear, played on April 17, 1858. Kean, with his passion for archæology, tells us in his preface that he had deemed it advisable "to fix upon some definite epoch as the supposed time of action," and "the Anglo-Saxon era of the eighth century has been selected for the regulation of the scenery and dresses"—with him a very essential feature. The scenery, as usual by those best of scene-painters, Grieve, Telbin, Gordon, Lloyds, Cuthbert, Dayes, &c., presented some decidedly rude and primitive effects. Of King Lear, Cole contents himself by saying that Kean "has so skilfully employed the resources which unwearied research enabled him to collect, that . . in the pictorial accompaniments, whether sylvan or architectural,—in the dresses, arms, and implements,—he presented us with an original picture of early Saxon England." Mr. Edward F. Strange, in the Magazine of Art (1892) informs us that "the best scenes were the Room of State in Lear's palace (Lloyds), with its adornments of hunting trophies and weapons, Cuthbert's Exterior of the Duke of Gloster's Castle, and Gordon and Grieve's two views near Dover, in which a strong suggestion from Turner was marked."

This production passed on the tradition—as to Saxon setting—derived from Macready and Phelps, to Irving.

In the next revival at the Princess's,—The Merchant of
Venice, on June 12, 1858,—I suspect Kean was a great
innovator in stage management. He was the first, I believe, to bring on the stage the bridges, the canals, the gondolas, the crowds, the carnival-mummers of Venice—at
least the first to do it in the sense that Bancroft and Irving
and Tree did it. He tried to give, not only Shakespeare's
play, but a huge bustling picture of Venetian life. I fancy
it was a very splendid exhibition he built up around the
story of the pound of flesh. Let us hope Shakespeare's
reasons did not become, like Gratiano's, but as two grains
of wheat in a metaphorical bushel of scenery.

At any rate, in this revival, Kean, according to Mr.
Strange, took "his costume from Veccellio and Jost Amman,
and all his architecture from actual buildings." Cole again
brings the living verity before us. "The curtain draws
up," says he, and what a theatre-feeling we get at the
words, "the curtain draws up and we discover ourselves in
Venice. . . Not represented as of old, by the traditionary
pair of flats of Gothic aspect, . . but we see the actual
square of St. Mark with the Campanile and clock-tower,
the cathedral, and the three standards, painted from drawings taken on the spot. . . . . Throngs of picturesquely-
contrasted occupants gradually fill the area, passing and
repassing. . . . Nobles, citizens, inquisitors, foreigners,
traders, water-carriers, and flower-girls are there"; also a
little girl carrying a basket of doves, one Ellen Terry, as
her memoirs show; "a flourish of trumpets announces the
approach of the Doge, who issues in state procession, on
his way to some public ceremony."

Another scene extolled by Cole is in the second act—"a
general view of Venice, taken from one of its most picturesque points, containing the canals, bridges, and gondolas.
. . . Here the abduction of Jessica takes place. . . .
There have been many beautiful exhibitions of dancing
and merriment in the Princess's Theatre, . . . but none
that in general estimation . . . equalled this. A Venetian
carnival is a thing of itself. . . . The great wonder is how,

in so small a space, such an appearance of vast extent could be conveyed, and how so many groups, and such complicated movements, could be so gracefully organized." A reading of the stage-directions in Kean's acting-text will strengthen this impression. First, old Gobbo enters over the bridge—a new and delightful effect in 1858, though we Irvingites cannot be moved by it. Next enter Bassanio, with Leonardo and Stephano in a gondola (from L. H.). Later on Gratiano enters in a gondola (R. H.). As a supreme test of mechanism, two gondolas come on together when Gratiano and Lorenzo in one, enter L. H. and Salarino and Salanio in another, L. H. S. E. They all land. Launcelot brings his letter on, over the bridge. The bridge and gondolas on the canal are utilised constantly for exits and entrances, and after the flight of Jessica there is general merriment by maskers, revellers, etc., bringing down the curtain on a scene of bustle and confusion then realised for the first time in this play.

Cole is very enthusiastic about the setting of the trial scene, which takes place in the Sala dei Pregadi, or Hall of the Senators. . . . The architecture and ornaments are "from punctiliously indisputable authority." Kean's management of stage-crowds had now become proverbial, and the "dumb magnificoes, the subordinate officers, the clerks, heralds, and secretaries, the spectators crowded in the galleries and doorways, all demonstrate the same interest . . . and produce a succession of pictures in which nothing is out of keeping, but which satisfy the eye and critical judgment."

Of Much Ado about Nothing played on November 20, 1858, I can find nothing that warrants special mention. Cole tells us that the effects were lavish and lost nothing in comparison with those of The Merchant of Venice. But he cites only two. "The opening view, the harbour of Messina, was quite a pictorial gem. The gradual illumination of the light-house and various mansions, in almost every window, the moon slowly rising and throwing her silver light upon the deep blue waters of the Mediterranean, were managed with imposing reality.   Then followed the masquerade, with its variegated lamps, bridge, gardens, and lake, seen through the arches of the palace." Brief as is this account of Cole, it strengthens, I am sure, a feeling that has been growing on the reader that there was a pettiness of detail in some of Kean's effects—the stage was "cluttered." To say this is, of course, to judge him by present-day standards, but the impression remains. Irving never crowded his stage like this; one remembers Shylock, not the carnival, Portia, not the magnificoes and secretaries. Yet Irving had the adjuncts, but reduced to their proper place.

KEAN'S HENRY V

With the production of Henry V, beginning March 28, 1859, Charles Kean relinquished the management of the Princess's, and passed from London theatrical history. He subsequently played engagements in Australia and in the United States; his death occurred in January, 1868. Mrs. Kean—the delightful Ellen Tree—survived him by many years. The two great scenes of the revival of Henry V were the storming of the bridge at Harfleur, and an interpolated mass-picture, like that of Richard II, this time representing the triumphant entry of Henry into London after the battle of Harfleur. These, as Mr. Strange says, must have been splendid and effective.

A novel and clever effect was introduced in the fourth chorus—recited by Mrs. Kean in the character of Clio (in itself a novelty, since the Chorus when played at all had always been chanted by a man). In the fourth chorus, Mrs. Kean paused after the words,

> And chide the cripple tardy-gaited night,
> Who, like a foul and ugly witch, doth limp
> So tediously away,

the while the scene opened and discovered the interior of a French tent, with the Dauphin, the Constable, Orleans, and others, playing at dice. Twenty or more lines of the familiar scene are actually spoken by these characters, and then, the scene closing in, Clio proceeds with the words of the Chorus until she has delivered

> unto the gazing moon
> So many horrid ghosts,

when the scene re-opens, discovering the English camp, with a group of soldiery praying. After a pause the scene shuts. Clio is then allowed to proceed to the close with her speech in what I am sure was the matchless elocution of Mrs. Kean—last survivor of the giant race before the flood.

For information as to the great entry of Henry V into London I am indebted to a note in the Lacy acting edition of the play. At the end of the fifth Chorus, that edition interjects the words of the old chronicler on which Kean based his stupendous show. The reader who has followed my account of Kean and his activities, will have no difficulty in reconstructing the spectacle as it dazzled and delighted playgoers in 1859. Says the Lacy text:

> Mr. C. Kean has thought it advisable to introduce here . . . . . an
> Historical Episode
> Old London Bridge, from the Surrey side of the River
> Reception of King Henry the Fifth
> On entering London
> After the Battle of Agincourt.

In foot-notes follow

Extracts of King Henry's reception into London from the anonymous Chronicler, who was an eye-witness of the events he describes:—
" And when the wished for Sunday dawned, the citizens went forth to meet the King . . . *viz.* the Mayor and Aldermen in scarlet, and the rest of the inferior citizens in red suits, with parti-coloured hoods, red and white. . . When they had come to the Tower at the approach to the bridge. . . Banners of the Royal arms adorned the Tower, . . . and trumpets, clarions and horns sounded . . . . and in front there was this . . . inscription upon the wall, ' Civitas regis justicie.' . . . And behind the Tower were innumerable boys representing angels, arrayed in white, and with countenances shining with

gold, and glittering wings, and virgin locks set with precious twigs of laurel, who at the King's approach sang. . .

"A company of Prophets, of venerable hoariness, dressed in golden coats and mantles, with their heads covered and wrapped in gold and crimson sang with sweet harmony, bowing to the ground, a song of thanksgiving.

.   .   .   .

" Beneath the covering were the twelve kings, martyrs and confessors of the succession in England, their loins girded with golden girdles, sceptres in their hands, and crowns on their heads, who chaunted with one accord at the King's approach.

.   .   .   .

"And they sent forth upon him round leaves of silver mixed with wafers, equally thin and round.   And there proceeded out to meet the King a chorus of most beautiful virgin girls, elegantly attired in white, singing with timbrel and dance; and then innumerable boys, as it were an angelic multitude, decked with . . . white apparel, shining feathers, virgin locks, studded with gems, and other resplendant and most elegant array, who sent forth upon the head of the King passing beneath, minæ of gold, with bows of laurel; round about angels shone with celestial gracefulness, chaunting sweetly. . .

" And besides the pressure in the standing places, and of men crowding through the streets, and the multitude of both sexes along the way from the bridge . . . . scarcely the horsemen could ride through them.   A greater assembly, or a nobler spectacle, was not recollected to have been ever before in London."

I must not close without quoting from Kean's farewell speech, on the last night of his management, August 29, 1859.   He said, "in this little theatre, where £200 is considered a large receipt, and £250 an extraordinary one, I expended in one season alone, the sum of £50,000.   During the run of some of the great revivals, as they are called, I have given employment . . . . to nearly 550 persons.   In improvements and enlargements to this building . . . . I have expended about £3,000.   This amount may, I think, be reckoned at about £10,000 when I include the additions to the general stock, all of which, by the terms of my lease, I am bound (with the exception of our own personal wardrobe) unconditionally to leave behind me."

Miss Terry writes the unbreakable word on this management and on all others of similar ideals. "I believe," she says in summing up her memories of the Princess's, "I believe that although the receipts were wonderful, Charles Kean spent much more than he made during his ten years of management. Indeed, he confessed as much in a public announcement. The Princess's Theatre was not very big, and the seats were low-priced. It is my opinion, however, that no manager with high artistic aims, resolute to carry them out in his own way, can ever make a fortune." Perhaps Miss Terry would not object to the amendment—"can ever *keep* a fortune."

THE INTERREGNUM, 1859–1879

For the twenty years between the retirement of Kean and the first definitive appearance of Irving, as sole manager of the Lyceum, "resolute" and able "to carry out his high artistic ideals in his own way," the record traverses, as we have seen, a series of scattered performances at various theatres, Drury Lane being the most conspicuous.

FECHTER'S HAMLET, 1861 AND 1864

The first production that engages us is Fechter's notable Hamlet at the Princess's in March, 1861. This was more notable as an entirely new reading, with novel stage-management, business, etc., than as a distinctly brilliant scenic representation. Nevertheless, it must not be forgotten that Fechter did for Hamlet what Phelps and Kean had done for Macbeth; he removed all velvet and lace from the dressing and garbed the Danes of Hamlet's supposed era in rude habits that breathed a Viking air through the play. Furthermore, the architecture and the furniture were made to fit in with this primitive apparel. The Times of March 22, 1861, gives the best idea of the innovations. "After the fashion of the German stage," it tells us, "he indicates Hamlet's Scandinavian nationality by a profusion of flaxen hair, and carries to perfection an assumption of that dreaming, unpractical look which is scarcely to be

associated with a dark complexion." Fechter's Hamlet
was seen at its best after the actor undertook the management of the Lyceum Theatre. From Mr. Austin Brereton's
history of the Lyceum I learn that Fechter shortly after
assuming control altered the stage of the house very considerably for the mechanical effects then in vogue.

Of Hamlet as revived May 21, 1864, at the Lyceum, the
Times of May 23rd gives adequate account. "That all the
modern means that have been devised for the purpose of
scenic effect would be employed on this occasion had been
confidently expected, nor were expectations disappointed.
. . . Mr. Fechter, in his revival, has two objects in view.
One of them is to give an antique Danish colouring to the
whole piece; the second is to present certain effective situa-
tions under a new aspect. The first of these objects can
be only approximately attained. . . Mr. Fechter has presented his audience with massive architecture of the Norman style, and the dresses of the mediæval period. Rosencrantz and Guildenstern are no longer attired in that conventional costume which is vaguely associated with the
courtiers of Spain or Italy, but are dressed like Northern
warriors—bluff fellows, with thick beards, coarse leggings,
and cross garters, and the other personages are after the
same model, Mr. Fechter of course retaining that peculiar
black dress and blonde hair which became so famous at
the Princess's." In this production Kate Terry was very
admirable as Ophelia, antedating her famous sister Ellen's
success in the same part by fifteen years.

More specific details may be gathered from Professor
Brander Matthews's Stage Traditions:

A large part of the action of "Hamlet" was made to take place
in the main hall of the castle at Elsinore. . . This hall filled the
stage; it had broad doors at the back, and above this portal was a
gallery with smaller doors at both ends leading off to upper rooms and
with curving stairways descending on either side. Most of the exits
and entrances were made by means of one or another of these stairways; and Fechter utilized them artfully when the time came for the
killing of the King. The throne upon which Claudius sat to behold

the fencing was on one side. Kate Field's record of the business, in her biography of Fechter, conforms to my recollection of it:—
"The moment Hamlet exclaimed

> 'Ho! let the door be locked.
> Treachery! Seek it out!'

The King exhibited signs of fear; and while Laertes made his terrible confession, the regicide stole to the opposite stairs, shielding himself from Hamlet's observation behind a group of courtiers, who, paralysed with horror, failed to mark the action. Laertes no sooner uttered the words

> 'The King's to blame!'

than Hamlet turned suddenly to the throne in search of his victim. Discovering the ruse, he rushed up the left hand stairs, to meet the King in the centre of the gallery and stabbed him. . . As he descended the stairs the potent poison stole upon Hamlet, who, murmuring

> 'The rest is silence!'

fell dead upon the corpse of Laertes, thus showing his forgiveness of treachery and remembrance of Ophelia."

To Mr. J. Ranken Towse I am indebted (New York Evening Post Magazine, December 20, 1919) for interesting details of Fechter's management of the always troublesome Ghost:

When Charles Fechter first played "Hamlet" at the London Lyceum an astonishing effect was secured by an exceedingly simple device. The ghost delivered his long speech, standing in an archway, apparently in the full light of the moon. As he began to scent the early morning air he began to fade—without any motion on his part or any darkening of the stage—and grew dimmer, by degrees, until he vanished altogether. This was about as spectral a bit of business as could be imagined. It was brought about as follows: The ghost stood behind a large concealed wheel which, when started, caught up, at each revolution, a fresh piece of some almost transparent stuff, artfully tinted to match the background, until the requisite thickness was obtained. The ghost apparently melted into thin air.

THE SHAKESPEARE TERCENTENARY, 1864

It will be observed that Fechter's revival of Hamlet at the Lyceum fell in the period of the tercentenary of Shakespeare's birth. The great Shakespearian success of this celebration, however, was the fine revival of the first part of Henry IV at Drury Lane, in which Phelps played Falstaff. The scenery by Beverley was highly extolled, and consisted of the following sets, as set forth in the playbill:

King's Ante-Chamber
Apartment in the Palace
Throne Room
Old Inn Yard
Road to Gadshill
Apartment in Warkworth Castle
Room in the Boar's Head, Eastcheap
Bishop's Palace, Bangor
Rebel's Camp, Shrewsbury
Road to Coventry
King's Camp
Rebel's Camp
Field of Battle near Shrewsbury
(Sunset)

The great feature of the production, scenically, was the representation of the battle of Shrewsbury. Fortunately I am able to supply from the Illustrated London News of April 2, 1864, a pictorial replica, and the reader will agree that it justifies the encomium of the letterpress: "The fifth act of the drama was placed on the stage with accessories which will command for it a long possession of the boards. The Shrewsbury battle-field was divided by a long ridge, and the numerous combatants, arrayed in bright armour, were concealed under its shelter, until, rising from their ambush, they filled the stage with their glittering figures, all in vivid action and stirring conflict. The brilliant effect . . . roused the audience to repeated plaudits. The new scenery . . . has been painted by Mr. Beverley, and the whole constitutes the most worthy dramatic effort of the time."

The reader remembers that during the celebration of 1864 the Webbs were appearing at the Princess's in a version of The Comedy of Errors, played continuously throughout twelve scenes. The scenery and setting in general were greatly admired, and formed a main part of the very successful revival. But I feel it unnecessary to detain the reader further. After all, the stage waits for Henry Irving, and we must not keep it waiting too long.

ANTONY AND CLEOPATRA, 1867 AND 1873

Of Miss Glyn's appearance as Cleopatra at the Princess's in May, 1867, I will pause hardly longer than necessary to exhibit a picture from the useful Illustrated London News of May 25th, which shows the great advance in *vraisemblance* of Egyptian effect over the production of Phelps, in 1849, as illustrated by the same journal. At least, this advance is incontrovertible in the matter of costume. The Illustrated London News, in the same issue, assures us that "some capital scenery, by Mr. T. Grieve, has been transferred from the Manchester Theatre; and the costumes employed are brilliant and beautiful. Mr. F. Lloyds, also, has built up for us Pompey's galley, and placed it in the moonlight and on the rippling water in a manner to enchant all beholders."

The synopsis of scenery for this revival, as printed in Lacy's acting version of the play, sounds particularly attractive. It calls in succession for a room in Cleopatra's Palace at Alexandria; Cæsar's House in Rome (both these by T. Grieve); Lepidus's House in Rome, with Rome in the Background; Cleopatra's Palace, near Misenum; Pompey's Galley; Cleopatra's Palace again; a plain near Actium; Cæsar's Camp; Antony's Camp; Alexandria; Banks of the Nile (by T. Grieve); and the Monument (another picture by Grieve). This all promises well, but of the production as a whole a sort of postscript to the Lacy acting edition has some severe things to say. "In the revival at the Princess's, excepting Antony's, there was not one Roman suit beyond the requirements of ancient Bartholomew. The armor of the Triumvir was passable in shape, but in quality was equal to that which should be worn by a cen-

SCENE FROM HENRY IV, PART I, AT DRURY LANE THEATRE, 1864

From the *Illustrated London News*

turion. The Egyptian dresses were utterly beneath contempt. . . . . The scenery (with the Colosseum, 60 years before a stone of it was laid) was well painted, but it reproduces the faded hues of 1855, not the brilliancy of 2000 years ago."

So much for the short-lived revival of 1867. That of 1873 at Drury Lane received far higher praise for its scenery. A just estimate of this exhibition, and that is what it was— an exhibition in which Shakespeare was butchered to make a scenic holiday for London playgoers—a just estimate of it may be gathered from notices in the Times of September 22nd, and the Illustrated London News of September 27th. Says the first of these authorities:

As a spectacle *Antony and Cleopatra* is most gorgeous; perhaps exceeding anything which has yet been brought out by Mr. Chatterton at Drury Lane Theatre. If the "purists" object that Mr. Halliday has travelled from the text to find opportunities for the introduction of scenic effects, it cannot be denied that he has travelled to good purpose. That he may show the barge in which Cleopatra first met Antony on the Cydnus, he supposes that when Antony leaves Egypt for Rome, she accompanies him to court in the self-same barge, and thus enables Mr. William Beverley to produce a pictorial illustration of the words of Enobarbus which could scarcely be surpassed. The marriage of Antony and Octavia gives occasion for a Roman festival, liberally furnished by Mr. John Cormack with dances and processions, and from which a chorus of boys may judiciously be removed. But the crowning picture is the naval battle between the Romans and the Egyptians which is introduced at the end of the third act. The appearance of two contending galleys and the heartiness with which their respective crews showered arrows on each other raised the audience . . to a state of excitement which would not be calmed till Mr. Chatterton came before the curtain.

And says the second:

The play now opens with the entrance of Cleopatra, the scene being a chamber of that great queen's palace in Alexandria, where, too, an Egyptian dance is introduced with characteristic effect. The scene is of so striking a nature that Mr. Beverley was enthusiastically called for, an honour also repeated . . . at the conclusion of the act, which closed with the exhibition of her Majesty's state barge afterwards described by Enobarbus, in which Antony and Cleopatra depart together for the coast. . . .

The second [act] concludes with another [spectacle] scarcely so legitimate. The scene is in Rome, and a festival is supposed to take place in honour of the wedding of Antony and Octavia, in which we are treated with four processions, and a new song . . . sung by Miss Banks and a choir of thirty boys . . . followed by a ballet, called the Path of Flowers. . . . The third act concluded with the naval battle between the Romans and the Egyptians. . . . Altogether, the stage and its appointments were worthy of the stage of the national theatre.

THE BANCROFTS' MERCHANT OF VENICE, 1875

The haphazard and occasional character of Shakespearian production at this time can be appreciated only by a study of old books. If ever the theatre was without a leader it was from 1862, when Phelps gave up Sadler's Wells, till 1879, when Irving undertook the sole management of the Lyceum. In this time no theatre could be depended on to supply poetical drama at even irregular intervals; it was supplied or not, just as things happened. Meantime, we come to the still famed production of The Merchant of Venice by the Bancrofts on the tiny stage of their Prince of Wales Theatre.

Part of the scenic details of the revival have been included in my account of the acting version prepared. Mr. Bancroft tells us that he and his wife spent a portion of the summer of 1874 in Venice, selecting views, and adds so many facts concerning the production that we almost revisualise its unforgotten glories. Announcing that the formation of the plan preceded its execution by full twelve months, he continues:

There [at Venice], as arranged beforehand, we met George Gordon, our chief scene-painter. . . . Every hour seemed occupied in settling to what purpose we could best put it, and very carefully we chose picturesque corners and places from the lovely city to make good pictures for our narrow frame. In the Palace of the Doges we saw at once that the Sala della Bussola, with its grim letter box, the *Bocca de Leone*, was the only one capable of realisation within our limited space; and this room we resolved should be accurately reproduced for the trial of Antonio. . . . We also arranged to show different views of Venice in the form of curtains between the acts of the play. We bought many books, we made many drawings, we were satiated with Titian and Veronese, we bought many photographs.

. . . Much charming music was specially composed by Meredith Ball, which should not be allowed to perish. The views of Venice shown between the acts—comprising the Campanile and column of St. Mark, the Rialto, and a view of the Grand Canal—were beautiful pictures by George Gordon, who, with his friend and fellow-worker, William Harford, devoted months of labour to the scenery. The utmost realism was attained. Elaborate capitals of enormous weight, absolute reproductions of those which crown the pillars of the colonnade of the Doge's Palace, were cast in plaster, and part of the wall of the theatre had to be cut away to find room for them to be moved, by means of trucks, on and off the small stage, which although narrow, fortunately had a depth of thirty-eight feet. The scenic artists also consulted a great authority, E. W. Godwin, who kindly gave them valuable archæological help.

The play throughout was well received, but never with enthusiasm. . . . It all looked so unlike a theatre, and so much more like old Italian pictures than anything that had previously been shown upon any stage in all the world. . . . Some of the dresses seemed to puzzle many . . . notably those worn by Bassanio and by the Venetian nobles . . . in their beautiful velvet robes of state reaching to the ground, the striking and correct costume of the Prince of Morocco and his gorgeous attendants, and that of the equally picturesque Spanish nobles who accompanied the Prince of Arragon. I need not add that the painters were loud in praise of all this.

It may be that it all came a little before the proper time, and that we saw things too far in advance.

Ancient consolation of those that fail!

THE CLOSE OF THE STORY

A production of The Merry Wives of Windsor shall be told of in the words of its perpetrator, John Hollingshead, in whose Gaiety Chronicles the account is found. For strength of cast, and promise of scenic equipment, this strikes me as too good to be passed by. Let Mr. Hollingshead speak for himself, and introduce the Gaiety Theatre to our history:

Having Mr. Phelps as my principal actor at Christmas 1874 . . . I decided to put burlesque on the shelf for a short time and to produce the *Merry Wives of Windsor* . . . .
I cast [it] as follows: . . . . Sir John Falstaff, Mr. Samuel Phelps; Mr. Ford, Mr. Hermann Vezin; Sir Hugh Evans, Mr. Righton; Mr. Page, Mr. Belford; Fenton, Mr. Forbes Robertson; Dr. Caius, Mr. Arthur Cecil; Slender, Mr. J. G. Taylor; Justice Shallow, Mr. J. Mac-Lean; Host, Mr. Gresham; Pistol, Mr. Soutar; Robin, Miss Maude Branscombe; Mrs. Page, Mrs. John Wood; Mrs. Ford, Miss Rose Leclercq; Anne, Miss Furtardo; Dame Quickly, Mrs. Leigh.

.   .   .   .

Alfred Thompson designed the dresses, and Messrs. Grieve, Gordon, and Harford painted the scenery. The Windsor Forest scene was the work of Mr. Grieve, Senior. I got my friend Arthur Sullivan . . . to compose special music for the play, and I induced Mr. Algernon Swinburne to write the following song, which I took the liberty of inserting in the text of Shakespeare.
This song was set to music by Arthur Sullivan, and sung by Miss Furtado.
The revels round Herne's Oak were performed by a trained band of singing boys, who did justice to Arthur Sullivan's music, which is now a concert classic.

This piece was played at the Gaiety, December 19, 1874; A Midsummer Night's Dream followed on February 15, 1875; The Tempest, April 10, 1875, and Much Ado, April 26th. Ada Cavendish played in the last piece. This was a brave Shakespearian effort for a house foredoomed to become the home of burlesque of a peculiarly British type.

I close this chronicle in the words of Dutton Cook, from whose Nights at the Play I glean all that seems necessary to tell the last fading glories of Drury Lane, before it developed into the great temple of melodrama under Augustus Harris. The reader will remember a revival in the very last days of Chatterton at that theatre of The Winter's Tale, produced on September 28, 1878. The account in

Dutton Cook brings the performance visibly before us, and may be quoted entire:

Mr. Charles Kean's arrangement of the text has been followed, and some attempt has been made to imitate the scenic splendours and illusions of the grand revival of the play at the Princess's in 1856. The allegorical exhibition of the Flight of Time, with *Luna* in her car and *Phœbus* in his chariot, has not been attempted; but a grand Pyrrhic dance is introduced in the first act, and an uproarious Dionysiac festival occurs in the fourth. The trial of *Hermione* takes place in the theatre at Syracuse, and Bithynia is throughout substituted for Bohemia, pursuant to the suggestion of Sir Thomas Hanmer in 1744, and the example set by Garrick in 1756. The bear that should eat Antigonus does not appear at Drury Lane, however; at the Princess's, it may be remembered, this animal figured conspicuously, chasing the *Antigonus* . . . with peculiar zest. . . . But certainly the representation at Drury Lane, if it may not altogether compare with Mr. Kean's revival—the result of profuse expenditure, exceeding painstaking, and an almost crazy fondness for archæological accuracy —is as complete in regard to stage decoration and musical embellishments as a general audience could possibly desire. Several new scenes have been painted, the costumes are very brilliant, and the dancers and supernumeraries crowd the stage.

What could be added? What, for that matter, could be added to the same critic's review of George Rignold's Henry V, that opened Augustus Harris's management of Drury Lane, in November, 1879?

He is most heroically pugnacious of aspect; he looks a born leader of fighting men; he exhibits indefatigable vigour alike as swordsman and orator; he overwhelms his foes both by force of arms and strength of lungs. As, falchion in hand, clothed in complete steel, with a richly emblazoned tabard, he stands in that spot so prized by the histrionic mind, the exact centre of the stage, the limelight pouring upon him from the flies its most dazzling rays, and declaims speech after speech to his devoted followers, he presents as striking a stage figure as I think I ever saw. . . . . In support of the actor the play-bill asserts that 400 supernumeraries are employed; I cannot believe that there are quite so many. Drury Lane is rich in scenery suitable to the legitimate drama, and in costumes, armour, and weapons of a mediæval pattern; the play is presented, therefore, quite in the manner of a "grand revival," if not absolutely with fresh appliances.

One touch in the above compels us to pause. The implication that the scenery was old and stock material of Drury Lane may be erroneous; why may it not have been the Manchester-New York setting, a bit the worse for wear, as it might well be, after so long a service? The production at any rate had seemed very splendid to New York four years earlier.

And what of Irving? Oddly enough, nothing. Irving had to become his own manager, before his productions merited inclusion in any chapter on scenery. Bateman was a niggard, I fear.

CONCLUSION

The reader has seen the stage prepared for Irving. In the period between 1843 and 1879 the most interesting events were the *régime* of Phelps at Sadler's Wells and that of Charles Kean at the Princess's. For some years (1850–59) these two represented the dynamically opposed theories of management involving faithfulness to text with adequacy of setting, and gorgeousness of setting with curtailment of text. Kean, scenically, offered the high lights of the period. Chatterton's efforts at Drury Lane (1864-78) were less whole-hearted and therefore less successful. The general tendency of the period throughout was, however, to mount Shakespeare's plays with great pomp and ceremony, whenever any but the most perfunctory performances were attempted. Irving, though Bateman had given but little, inherited this tradition when, in December, 1878, he assumed sole charge at the Lyceum. He carried the tradition to its highest perfection of taste, if not of gorgeousness —perhaps to the highest it can or will ever go—and him we may regard as the supreme representative of a school now somewhat in disfavour, especially with the young and revolutionary.

BOOK VIII

THE AGE OF IRVING

(1879–1902)

CHAPTER XXX

THEATRES AND PRODUCTIONS

SUPREMACY OF THE LYCEUM

THE Lyceum, at the accession of Henry Irving to sole management on December 30, 1878, became at once the leading theatre of London, perhaps of the English-speaking world. The glory that had been Drury Lane passed without delay to this house and abided there till it was snuffed out by the departure of Irving in 1902. For the period of more than twenty years of his management, however, even when success began to be harder of attainment, there was no question of the fixed status of the Lyceum in the affections of London playgoers. By happy chance, moreover,—and it was hardly more than chance,—the theatre held its supremacy, as the home of important Shakespearian production, even when Irving was absent on provincial tours or on his increasingly frequent visits to America.

Here, for instance, during the first three of Irving's engagements in the United States and Canada (seasons of 1883–84, 1884–85 and 1887–88) Mary Anderson played winter-long engagements in repertoire, with two elaborate Shakespearian revivals; and here, in the autumn months of 1895, 1897 and 1898, respectively, Forbes Robertson started on his career as an independent actor-manager, in Shakespearian productions soon to be noted; here, again, in 1890, Augustin Daly's company appeared in the performance of As You Like It, the particular beauty of which—Ada Rehan's Rosalind—had charmed New York during a large part of the season preceding. Here, finally, in the winter of 1900, Mr. F. R. Benson made his first incursion into London with that Shakespearian repertoire company that it was once hoped would revolutionise Shakespearian production and, with something of Elizabethan simplicity of presentation, bring back something of the Elizabethan zest for Shakespeare in the theatre. This history covers a wide range and to a great extent tells the fortunes of Shakespeare in the age of Irving. Of course there were many productions at other houses, but the Lyceum was the recognised upholder of Shakespearian tradition during all those years. In public sentiment and in prestige it was the National Theatre.

Before proceeding in the direct line, I cannot refrain from calling attention to the international aspect of the foregoing statements. Throughout the last quarter of the Nineteenth Century the voyage across the Atlantic became a pleasure, and was indulged in freely by actors of both Great Britain and the United States, with greater or less artistic and financial reward. At any rate, a history of either the English or the American stage for those twenty-five years includes many names and productions well known in both countries. Henry Irving and Ellen Terry were figures as familiar in New York as in London; Ada Rehan and John Drew and Mary Anderson were acclaimed in the British capital even more enthusiastically than in the purlieus of Broadway or Tremont Street or the Loop in Chicago. Forbes Robertson in later years has become even more an international figure. This of course was true of more than the Shakespearian players, but it is with them only that I am concerned at present. To a great extent, however, it will be seen that a history of Shakespeare on the London stage during the period of Irving is almost equally a history of Shakespeare on the American stage.

Miss Terry, in recalling her experiences there, says "my mental division of the years at the Lyceum is *before* Macbeth, and *after*." For the moment she asserts that her reason for this division lies in the fact that this was "the most important of all our productions," because of the preparation involved, and the amount of discussion evoked. I suspect that the latter is the impelling reason. Much later in the story of her life, Miss Terry affirms that "perhaps Henry Irving and I might have gone on with Shakespeare to the end of the chapter if he had not been in such a hurry to produce Macbeth. We ought," she thinks, "to have done As You Like It in 1888, or The Tempest." She gives a list of Shakespeare's plays that Irving should have brought out before Macbeth. Some of these are questionable, but there can be no doubt that Miss Terry is more than hinting at what most of Irving's admirers fully realised —his utter inability—physical and temperamental—to give a satisfactory rendering of the Thane. The tide of success for his management at the Lyceum began to turn after this gigantic, if noble or at least nobly conceived, failure. Therefore, in saying that her recollections of the Lyceum divide into the periods before and after Macbeth, Miss Terry is merely saying that they divide into the two periods, respectively, of glittering success and of long-extended but inevitable progression toward heart-breaking failure.

This time-division of the great actress seems admirable for my purposes. I shall therefore begin by giving an account of the leading Shakespearian performances in London from December 30, 1878, when Irving inaugurated his management of the Lyceum, until December 29, 1888, when he made his ill-advised production of Macbeth. The reader will not desire for all those years a complete list of Shakespearian presentations by itinerant players at outlying theatres; he will be satisfied, I am sure, with the record of the chief presentations, with some slight comment on their significance for our history. The leading revivals I feel reasonably certain may be found in the pages immediately following.

IRVING AS MANAGER

The account, then, begins with Hamlet at the Lyceum, in the very last days of 1878. For this Ellen Terry was engaged to play Ophelia, and thus entered on the memorable association with Irving that lasted throughout the years of his tenancy of the Lyceum and brought about the most satisfactory artistic results of the entire period.

It is a great pleasure to bear witness, once more, to the

superlative excellence of the Irving productions. Of the setting I shall speak later; but as to the acting of the Shakespearian plays I state positively that nothing so generally impressive has been seen in my time. This is true despite the fact that Irving was really not a great Shakespearian actor; he produced very elaborately something like twelve of the poet's plays in the years of his incumbency at the Lyceum, and in only two of them, I honestly believe, was he extraordinarily fine. English critics liked his Hamlet, but Americans, nurtured on the art of Edwin Booth, did not. In fact, few Americans, critics or laymen, cared for any of his Shakespearian impersonations except Shylock and Cardinal Wolsey. Irving's limitations fitted him for eccentric character-parts of a melodramatic turn like Mathias or Louis XI or Dubosq; they also permitted him, curiously enough, to shine in Charles I or Dr. Primrose or Becket. But for the grand tragic characters—Hamlet, Macbeth, Lear—he was utterly unsuited; his dreadful voice and his ungraceful figure prevented a realisation of his ideals.

Irving was, however, a great manager; he knew how to get the very best results from his actors, individually and collectively. Of Ellen Terry—the unique Beatrice, Ophelia, Portia—it is unnecessary to speak. The leading men in successive seasons were Forbes Robertson, William Terriss and George Alexander, handsome, romantic actors, all capable of reading verse and interpreting poetry; the leading women were Jessie Millward and Winifred Emery. Genevieve Ward was frequently engaged for "heavies," especially in the extra-Shakespearian field. But what of the others—Martin Harvey, Tyars, Mead, Howe, Johnson, Wenman, Mrs. Pauncefote, Maud Milton? These make an aggregation of excellence not equalled or even approached in recent days. To see them together in Shakespeare—above all, to hear them in Shakespeare—was a blessing. If Nature denied to Irving the vocal equipment necessary for a beautiful reading of poetry, it amply endowed him with the teacher's faculty for making others read beautifully.

ELLEN TERRY AS BEATRICE

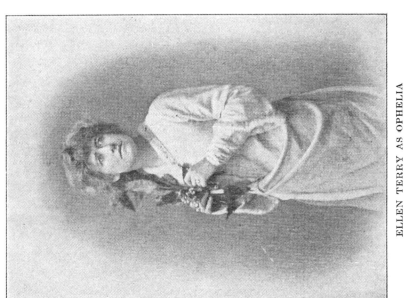

ELLEN TERRY AS OPHELIA

From copyrighted photographs by Window and Grove of London

With these actors, then, Irving held sway at the Lyceum for more than twenty years. Some of them left to become managers or stars on their own account; but the majority remained till the end, and the company never appreciably deteriorated. It was repertoire rather than actors that brought about the ultimate failure. Irving had exhausted the list of parts—Shakespearian and otherwise—for which his limitations rendered him available. Besides, from 1896 his health began to fail.

IRVING'S HAMLET (1878–1879) AND SHYLOCK, 1879

There was no sign of this, however, in 1878, when the more than twenty-year campaign began. Hamlet, although Irving had played it for two hundred nights in 1874–75, now ran for one hundred and eight performances, thanks probably to the additional delight of Ellen Terry's Ophelia. Other pieces (of the non-Shakespearian list) followed, until on November 1, 1879, Irving brought out the Shakespearian play with which his fame is chiefly associated—The Merchant of Venice. This in all ways was recognised as a notable event, and stamped the Lyceum as the theatre of theatres for two decades to come. In this revival Ellen Terry reappeared as Portia, a part in which stage history affords her no rival. The play achieved the astounding record of two hundred and fifty consecutive performances.

EDWIN BOOTH AT THE PRINCESS'S, 1880–1881

Staying on this permanent success of the Lyceum management, we may digress to other notable matters in the season of 1880–81. On November 6, 1880, Edwin Booth began a long engagement at the Princess's Theatre, newly rebuilt, but rather remote from the theatrical centre. He was perhaps ill-advised in selecting Hamlet for his début; he was no longer of youthful appearance, and Irving's performance of the Dane was now accepted in London as undisplaceable by a new aspirant. Booth, as a matter of fact, appeared old-fashioned to critics willing to accept the new methods of Irving. The beauty of his voice and elocution was acknowledged, but, according to some critics, he strove too hard for "points," he rolled his eyes too much and he gesticulated too much. The naturalistic method, inaugurated by Fechter and perpetuated by Irving, was beginning to make its impress felt. America was grieved at the failure of its favourite actor to capture London playgoers, but Booth, despite opposition, and with the tragedy of his wife's mortal illness facing him daily, pluckily carried on his engagement for one hundred and nineteen nights, ending on March 26th with performances, in double bill, of Shylock and Petruchio. He came to receive high critical approval as Bertuccio and Richelieu, and, in the Shakespearian field, as Iago (but not as Othello) and King Lear. The last-named play was produced on February 14, 1881, and enjoyed a fair degree of popularity. Some critics even hailed it as a great performance. But, in general, the engagement was a failure, and caused some rankling in American hearts. The episode closed by an engagement at the Lyceum generously arranged by Irving, in which for four weeks the two actors alternated the parts of Othello and Iago, with Miss Terry as Desdemona and William Terriss as Cassio. The engagement began on May 2, 1881, and constituted the last attempt of Irving to mount Othello on this stage. It allowed Booth to return to America with a little factitious glory, but it convinced Irving—and to his great disappointment, according to Miss Terry—that he himself could not act the Moor. The revival, according to the best opinion, revealed two masterly Iagos and two unsatisfactory Othellos; but, even within these limits, the London critics stood loyally by their own Irving in assigning the palm for superiority in performance of the Moor's Ancient.

MADAME MODJESKA'S JULIET, 1881

Another event was the attempt of Madame Modjeska to convert London playgoers to her way of acting Juliet. This

was made at the Court Theatre on March 26, 1881. The
lady had been winning great success in the modern emo-
tional French drama, and, in spite of her maturity and her
marked accent, had the temerity to attempt the great love
tragedy before an audience the least ready in the world
to accept Shakespearian verse from the lips of a foreigner.
In this revival Forbes Robertson first appeared as Romeo,
and Wilson Barrett played Mercutio. Critical London
received this offering with mixed delight; the meeting of
Romeo and Juliet and the balcony scene were sweetly and
sympathetically played by the Polish actress, but in the
tragic dénouement she lacked force. And there was always
the accent to forget or to try to forget. I must say I sym-
pathise here; I saw Modjeska in many Shakespearian parts
and I admired her perfect skill and her charming personality
in all, but forever and forever there was Shakespeare spoken
with an accent that I could not for one moment put out of
my consciousness. One simply had to accept Modjeska's
Shakespearian impersonations despite this severe draw-
back. Juliet was, so far as I know, the only Shakespearian
part she played in London.

THE SAXE-MEININGEN COMPANY, 1881

Perhaps it is better for foreigners, if they wish to act
Shakespeare before English-speaking audiences, to do so
in their own language, as Ristori and Salvini and Rossi did.
This, at any rate, was the plan of the next notable foreign
effort to portray Shakespeare in London. I refer, of course,
to the far-famed troupe from the Royal Theatre of Saxe-
Meiningen, which appeared at Drury Lane Theatre, beginning on May 30, 1881, and continuing for several weeks
during the height of the season. This organisation prided
itself on perfection of ensemble, which often, as in this case,
means mediocrity of individual performance, and on extraordinary accuracy and picturesqueness of stage-management, especially in the handling of mobs or other great
masses of humanity. In this latter respect, the visit of

these foreigners had a lasting effect on the English stage, particularly in the work of Irving, then beginning his career as manager. They opened in Julius Cæsar, and followed with other plays, the only Shakespearian being easily discernible under their German titles of Was Ihr Wollt and Ein Wintermärchen. All were given in the translations of Tieck and Schlegel. But of course Londoners—unless German Londoners—cared nothing for a Teutonic translation of the poet; what interested all was the lesson in staging offered by the visitors from a small German theatre. At the same theatre on May 14th, two weeks before the arrival of the Germans, the American John McCullough had appeared as Othello—less than two weeks after the Irving-Booth performance at the Lyceum and during the run of that unique production. Who could have expected success under these circumstances? Hardly even McCullough, I should think.

IRVING'S ROMEO AND JULIET, 1882

After all these foreign incursions, Londoners no doubt went back with delight to the next important Shakespearian revival at the Lyceum, standing like a great sea-mark among the multitude of theatres. Here on March 8, 1882, Irving made what Ellen Terry calls his first elaborate, pictorial production of a Shakespearian play—Romeo and Juliet, brought out almost exactly a year after Modjeska's careful staging of the same tragedy at the Court. In the management of stage crowds it was at once seen that Irving had profited by the visit of the Meininger the preceding season. As to the acting, it may be admitted unreservedly that the weak feature was the Romeo of Irving. Terriss played Mercutio, and I fully agree with that luckless wight who suggested that the assignments might have been exchanged to the great advantage of the performance. Luckless I call this man, because his remark brought down upon him the vials of Ellen Terry's wrath. With Miss Terry I also agree in protesting that Irving was far more intellectual than

Terriss; but Romeo was also romantic and amorous and brave and handsome and manly, and all these things Terriss seemed to be preëminently, to the end of his days. And there is no denying that Irving's Romeo suggested few, if any of such attributes. For Miss Terry's Juliet one must also predicate comparative failure. The deepest tragic notes were not included in her scale, delightful as that scale was in timbre; this she was to prove through the rest of her career. Lady Macbeth was not for her, nor Volumnia; neither, presumably, would Constance have been. Even the gentler sorrows of Juliet were beyond her; Ophelia's pathetic madness represented her farthest reach on the tragic side. But Miss Terry was always lovely to see and hear, and people liked her Juliet, even if they could not forget Adelaide Neilson's. For the rest, Mrs. Stirling played the Nurse, Fernandez the Friar, and George Alexander, then hardly more than a beginner, Paris. All the minor parts were excellently performed, and this fact, together with the beauty of the setting, carried the play to a series of one hundred and sixty-one performances.

IRVING'S MUCH ADO ABOUT NOTHING, 1882

Of what Shakespearian production of Irving does the reader instinctively think when his mind turns to those blessed days now past forever? If his experience is like mine, I am convinced that the answer will be Much Ado about Nothing. This, I believe, was the bright star in the crown. If anything more exquisite was ever put on the stage, I envy those who saw it. In this production all factors were united to the end of a perfect joy. The setting and all the accessories reached the highest point of excellence, but first to fond memory's lure recurs the Beatrice of Ellen Terry—one of the famous impersonations in theatrical history. No word can be added to the volume dedicated to its witchery. In the enjoyment of this lovely performance one even forgot the angularity of Irving's Benedick, and realised that the entire rendering of the play was as near to perfection as human art can go. And, to make up any possible deficiency on the male side, how generous was Irving the manager in providing the Claudio of Forbes Robertson, and the Don Pedro of William Terriss, with an incomparable pair of older men in Fernandez and H. Howe for Leonato and Antonio! To prove that generosity could even further go, Jessie Millward was cast for Hero—the best Hero I have ever seen. This unmatchable aggregation appeared first in the comedy on October 11, 1882, and continued to appear in it two hundred and twelve nights successively. Then came Irving's first American tour, at the end of which he re-appeared at the Lyceum on May 31, 1884, resuming the run of this adorable revival until it reached its two hundred and forty-third performance on July 5th.

IRVING'S TWELFTH NIGHT, 1884

It was followed immediately, on July 8th, by a revival of Twelfth Night—the last new Shakespearian production of Irving till the fateful Macbeth of 1888. The reader will see for himself how few of Shakespeare's plays were brought out by Irving; Tennyson's Becket hardly atoned for the meretricious glitter of the colossally successful Faust or other melodramatic showy attractions of the years to come. Twelfth Night introduced Irving as Malvolio and Miss Terry as Viola, but it never ranked as a success of the Irving *régime*. It soon went to the storehouse.

WILSON BARRETT AND MARY ANDERSON, 1884

Though this is the end of Irving for the present, it is not the cessation of important Shakespearian activities. On October 16, 1884, Wilson Barrett, who was in those days regarded as a possible future rival of Irving, opened the Princess's Theatre with a much-discussed revival of Hamlet, which restored and re-interpreted many lines of Shakespeare and became a pretty subject of conversation where

men most do congregate. For a season it seemed as if a
new tragic actor had arisen and a new force had been
brought into the dying places of the drama. It proved to
be a flash in the pan, but nevertheless this revival will demand our consideration later.

The Lyceum, however, was not to be eclipsed. During
Irving's first absence in America, in the season of 1883–84,
his stage had been occupied by the beautiful Mary Ander-
son, who had appeared in a round of "legitimate" plays,
Ingomar, The Hunchback, The Lady of Lyons, and in
Gilbert's Pygmalion and Galatea. Irving was again tour-
ing the United States and Canada in the following season,
and once more Mary Anderson, become immensely popular, was at the Lyceum. This season she inaugurated—on
November 1st—with a magnificent revival of Romeo and
Juliet, playing the heroine to the Romeo of Terriss and the
Nurse of Mrs. Stirling. It ran throughout the winter.
Probably no more beautiful picture was ever revealed than
was the Juliet of this accomplished woman; what it lacked
in passion it made up in declamatory power and in physical
charm. Certainly it made all succeeding Juliets seem pale
in contrast.

THE KENDALS' AS YOU LIKE IT, 1885

We are dealing with the decade of the actor-manager, of
Wyndham at the Criterion, of the Bancrofts and, later, of
Beerbohm Tree at the Haymarket, of John Hare and the
Kendals at the St. James's, of Wilson Barrett at the Princess's. This was a time, generally, of small theatres and
modern plays. But occasionally, as with the Bancrofts
and their revival of The Merchant of Venice in 1875, the
lure of Shakespeare proved too strong to be resisted. In
January, 1885, the Hare and Kendal management brought
out As You Like It on the unaccustomed stage of the very
attractive and fashionable St. James's Theatre. This was
as great a performance of a poetical comedy as could be
made entirely out of prose. The scenery was unusually

beautiful, but Kendal as Orlando, Mrs. Kendal as Rosalind, Linda Dietz as Celia and John Hare as Touchstone were entirely out of their element. I yield to none in my admiration for the art of Mrs. Kendal, who had a command of technique surpassing that of any contemporary actress; but poetry was sadly lacking in her composition. Hence Ellen Terry—the living personification of poetry—with less art, perhaps, went so infinitely beyond her in appeal. I bring in this revival of As You Like It more as a curiosity than as an artistic force; for similar reasons one might include a pictorial revival of The Comedy of Errors at J. S. Clarke's Strand Theatre on January 18, 1883, Mr. Clarke—brother-in-law of Edwin Booth and a very accomplished comedian—playing the Dromio of Syracuse. But why dwell on trifles?

MARY ANDERSON'S WINTER'S TALE, 1887

After Irving's second tour of America and the passage to America of Mary Anderson's Romeo and Juliet, the Lyceum stage fell heir to its greatest financial success—W. G. Wills's dramatic spectacle, Faust, in which Irving played Mephistopheles, George Alexander Faust, Miss Terry Margaret and Mrs. Stirling Martha. This poor thing ran uninterruptedly for three hundred and ninety-six nights, and consequently and perforce was carried to America in the season of 1887–88. During Irving's absence Miss Anderson again occupied the Lyceum with a beautiful revival of The Winter's Tale, in which, for the first time in the history of the play, she "doubled" the parts of Hermione and Perdita, and in which Forbes Robertson played Leontes. Produced on September 10, 1887, it ran throughout the greater part of the season. As a spectacle it was very beautiful. Needless to say, Miss Anderson in the classic robes of Hermione—especially in the statue scene—and in the pink dress and leafy coronal of Perdita was a vision of surpassing loveliness. In the latter part, especially, she proved that she also could act, and act very well. The rustic dance in which Perdita figured is one of the imperishable memories of all who saw it.

DALY'S TAMING OF THE SHREW, 1888

With the account of the success of another American production I close my story of the first part of the Irving period. On May 29, 1888, at the Gaiety Theatre, Augustin Daly first showed his London public what he could do for Shakespeare. In two previous visits, during the summers of 1884 and 1886, respectively, he had exhibited his fine American company in modern farce and comedy. He now presented them in the superb revival of The Taming of the Shrew, which had enjoyed a run of one hundred and twenty nights in New York in the season of 1886–87. This was the first time London had seen the play in its entirety since the days of Samuel Phelps at Sadler's Wells. The tasteful production of Daly was an immediate success, thanks largely to the glorious Katharine of Ada Rehan. Her performance was at once hailed as among the very few greatest Shakespearian representations, not only of that age but of all time. Such it remains in theatrical history, and on its triumph I ring down the curtain on Ellen Terry's first division of the Irving *régime*—the period before Macbeth.

IRVING'S MACBETH

Irving revived Macbeth on December 29, 1888, almost ten years to a day since he had inaugurated his management at the Lyceum. During that decade he had produced but six Shakespearian plays, surely not an imposing number from the standards of Kemble and Phelps. The explanation lies in his success with melodrama and Faust, and in his three season-long visits to America. These causes were to operate as an even greater deterrent in the remaining years of his tenancy. As a matter of fact, his Shakespearian revivals were, as I have said, very few during his whole career, and in that respect contrast rather unpleasingly with those of Beerbohm Tree. Only six more were to follow, up to and including the unfortunate Coriolanus of 1901, the swan-song of Irving's management.

But there was no melancholy note in the production of Macbeth. Irving's prosperity and repute were at their height; his Macbeth was prepared with all the confidence born of years of success, and anticipated with delight by countless admirers. Irving had failed as the Thane in 1875, and there was no reason to expect that he would be acceptable now. For better or worse, certain traditions have grown up about the character, and most of these Irving was bound to violate. For instance, he was not able to look big and warlike, his voice was rasping and nasal, quite incapable of coping with the "big" speeches, and in every way he suggested the ascetic, intellectual visionary, rather than the bluff warrior. Hence he was forced to portray Macbeth as a neurasthenic, madly driven by ambition to a murder planned in his mind even before the encounter with the witches; a cowardly, conscience-smitten criminal. No one can seriously object to a distinguished actor's taking any reasonable view of a Shakespearian character; but the auditor is quite within his rights in demanding that that conception should be made clear in the performance. Irving's "finicky" manner was hard enough to bear; but his delivery of the lines was intolerable. As Mr. J. Ranken Towse has truly said, most of the dialogue might as well have been spoken in Volapük. Even aside from this, it was easier to find excuses for Irving's Macbeth than to like it. Beside this performance, Miss Terry's Lady Macbeth seemed a masterpiece, though the reason rebelled against her idea of the character as a pale, loving wife, who entered into crime merely out of womanly love and desire to aid her husband's schemes. This revival was a great blow to the Irving prestige; it taught loyal subjects that the king certainly could do wrong, and this, in the theatrical world also, is, to say the least, unfortunate. Nevertheless, thanks to the momentum acquired by the former years, and thanks to the splendid setting, the play ran for one hundred and fifty-one nights.

ADA REHAN AS KATHARINE
From a photograph by Sarony of New York

TREE, MANSFIELD, DALY

It was three years before Irving's courage was again screwed to the producing point; that is, as far as Shakespeare is concerned. The bard, in this respect, was indebted to others. In January, 1889, Beerbohm Tree, who had for a few years been in charge of the historic Haymarket, and had acquired fame there in strong modern plays, was moved to put on The Merry Wives of Windsor, with good scenery and a good cast. This was the first of his Shakespearian revivals, and it merits emphatic mention here, in light of Tree's great service to the poet in the years to come. His Falstaff was not a remarkable performance, except in make-up, but it served for a season, and encouraged him to go on with further Shakespearian productions at the Haymarket, and beaconed him to his superb revivals in the not distant days at Her Majesty's. My respect for Beerbohm Tree grows as I read the chronicle of his courage, his devotion and his achievement in the series of memorable Shakespearian revivals at Her Majesty's, from 1897, almost to the year of his death. On him fell the mantle of Irving as producer, and for sheer splendour his settings often surpassed those of his predecessor. To excel him one would be compelled to go at the thing in an entirely different way. To complete the record of his Haymarket activities— for it is only his career at Her Majesty's that counts—I may say that he appeared as Hamlet on January 21, 1892, and as Falstaff in the first part of King Henry IV in May, 1896.

The period of Irving's inactivity was broken by two ventures from America, each of which excited considerable comment. On March 16, 1889, at the Globe Theatre, the ambitious Richard Mansfield essayed a spectacular and newly studied revival of Richard III. All who had succeeded in strong character parts in modern plays were in these days, as we have seen, likely to project themselves into the Shakespearian field, with a confidence born of popular acclaim. If Beerbohm Tree, for that matter if Henry Irving, why not Richard Mansfield? Nevertheless, the production dragged on, rather unsuccessfully, from March 16th to June 1st, and thereby offered Mansfield an excuse to take it to America in the following season.

The second American venture aforesaid was, in the language of trade, made in America. This was Augustin Daly's lovely presentation of As You Like It, produced at the home-theatre the season preceding, and now triumphantly displayed on the stage of the hospitable Lyceum. Here, on July 15, 1890, the delightful Rosalind of Ada Rehan first captivated susceptible London, and in this part she was placed ungrudgingly by critics and public on the highest pedestal. This was her crowning achievement in the British capital. From this time on Ada Rehan and Ellen Terry stood side by side as the great representatives for that generation of Shakespearian heroines; this position they still occupy without dispute in the history of the theatre. I may close this part of the history by stating that Miss Rehan's last Shakespearian success on the London stage was won in the first season of the new Daly's Theatre, when, on January 8, 1894, she played Viola in Twelfth Night, continuing for one hundred and nineteen performances.

F. R. BENSON AND MRS. LANGTRY, 1889–1890

Still two other events crowd into notice. The first was the definite appearance of F. R. Benson in the managerial field, a début still fraught with value to theatrical affairs in London. On December 19, 1889, he brought out at the Globe Theatre a pretentious scenic revival of A Midsummer Night's Dream, and followed it on January 23rd by The Taming of the Shrew, minus the Induction. Since Augustin Daly had worked such wonders with these pieces in New York during the two or three years preceding, I cannot help wondering whether coincidence or cable news of transatlantic success led Mr. Benson to the choice of these particular plays. On March 6th he played Hamlet to the Ghost of no less a person than Stephen Phillips.

The second venture was that of the ambitious stage-beauty, Mrs. Langtry. On February 24, 1890, at the St. James's Theatre, she made an elaborate revival of As You Like It (following by one month Daly's revival of the same comedy in New York, and preceding by a few months his transference of it to the Lyceum in London, as just detailed). Mrs. Langtry, however, did something far more pretentious on November 18, 1890, when, at the Princess's Theatre, she brought out a sumptuous Antony and Cleopatra, her own most inadequate Egyptian queen supported by the Antony of Charles Coghlan. In spite of the elaborate mounting, the production failed.

IRVING'S HENRY VIII AND KING LEAR, 1892

Irving's last really successful Shakespearian revival was that of Henry VIII, produced with spectacular splendour beyond anything hitherto attempted at the Lyceum. As Cardinal Wolsey he retrieved the mistake of his Macbeth; joined with him were the superb Buckingham of Forbes Robertson, the excellent King of Terriss, and the lovely Katharine of Ellen Terry. Nothing in recent years at the Lyceum had been so satisfactory, and the production—with a summer intermission—received two hundred and three performances. No one who saw it will forget the splendid pictures, the fine acting, the marvellous stage-management. After this, Shakespeare, if he did not spell ruin to Irving, nevertheless, in new productions, very nearly spelled disappointment and defeat.

The rest of his Shakespearian chapter may be briefly written. If Macbeth was beyond his physical capability, what of King Lear with its demand for superhuman power in the great scenes of the first three acts? Yet this character Irving attempted on November 10, 1892. As in the case of Macbeth, friendly critics wrote long analyses of the actor-manager's conception of the character, but failed to prove that he made of it a great, moving performance. This result was accomplished by the ineffable pathos of

Ellen Terry, who surpassed herself by a beautiful performance of Cordelia. The play ran until February 6th, and
was succeeded by one of Irving's greatest characterisations,
that of Becket, in Tennyson's tragedy of the same name.

LAST YEARS OF IRVING

Three attempts at restoring Shakespeare are to be accredited to Irving's last years. On September 22, 1896, he
brought out, with the customary care, Cymbeline, not
acted for many years previously. This revival was probably a tribute to Ellen Terry, who was, indeed, as perfect
an Imogen as any one who had followed her career knew
she would be. This was her last great part on the Lyceum
stage; one can only regret that it had not come earlier in
her career. The play itself failed, with but little help from
Irving's Iachimo; Miss Terry's Imogen is a fragrant memory. In the same season—was Irving becoming feverish as
the end approached, and trying to make up for past delin-
quency?—Richard III was revived, on the evening of
December 19th. Ellen Terry says that every one knows
the period of Irving's misfortune dates from the first night
of this production. On reaching home after the performance, he slipped and fell, injuring himself so much that he
was unable to play again for two months. It was not till
February 27th that the second performance of Richard III
was given; the run terminated on April 7th, a pitiful record
in comparison with the earlier Shakespearian revivals. I
suspect the performance received about what it deserved
in the way of approval. Irving could have played Richard
if the part had been written in prose and had been more
modernly subtle. As it was, Genevieve Ward's Queen
Margaret was the outstanding feature of the performance.

Irving lost control of the Lyceum in the autumn of 1898;
nevertheless he played there frequently until July 19, 1902,
when he left that stage forever, after a performance of
Shylock. On April 15, 1901, moreover, he had the courage
to bring out at his old theatre a condensed version of Cori-

TWO SCENES FROM IRVING'S PRODUCTION OF KING LEAR
From the Souvenir of the Play published by the Offices of *Black and White* of London

olanus, in which he was foredoomed to failure. Ellen Terry's Volumnia was a mistake in every sense of the word. This was the last of Irving in the theatre he had made so renowned.

FORBES ROBERTSON

Meantime, in those last melancholy years, two other Shakespearian interpreters firmly established themselves. The King is dead—long live the King! I need hardly say that the two men I refer to were Forbes Robertson and Beerbohm Tree. The first of these never had a home, in the sense that Irving, Tree and the non-Shakespearian Wyndham had homes in the theatres they so long directed. But Forbes Robertson has a glory denied to them: he was the accepted Hamlet of his time, and in all personal qualities that fix the actor's rank he was superior to them all. His great Shakespearian parts were played in special engagements in theatres rented for the occasion; but his home was wherever he set up his stage. Trained in the Irving school, he was no novice when, on September 21, 1895, he appeared at the Lyceum as Romeo to the pretty, appealing, very modern and wholly un-tragic Juliet of the popular Mrs. Patrick Campbell. Forbes Robertson's Romeo was the best I have seen, even back in 1885, when he played in America with Mary Anderson; what it had lost in youth, in 1895, it had gained in authority and poetic fervour. This performance was popular, but a mere episode compared to the lasting results of Forbes Robertson's next revival—that of Hamlet on September 11, 1897. The world had longed for a new great Hamlet, one that would be willing to let the poetry speak for itself, and not be eternally and finically striving for "points" and new readings. And here at last such a Hamlet arrived; lacking in force in the last act, perhaps, but conceived in the very spirit of poetry. This performance was probably the very last great Shakespearian representation of international fame made known in our times. The same actor played Macbeth at the Lyceum on September 17, 1898, and Othello at the Lyric, in December, 1902. But neither impersonation rivalled his Hamlet and, though scholarly and to some extent moving, neither is now likely to be remembered. To have been the Hamlet of one's time, however, is a great glory; and such glory belongs to Forbes Robertson.

BEERBOHM TREE

Tree was first and foremost the actor-manager, with the latter element stressed. He lacked poetry, he was not even gifted as an actor, but every particle of talent he possessed was brought into play to make Her Majesty's a theatre of brilliant reputation. This house, built on the site of Vanbrugh's old theatre in the Haymarket, which had been more latterly a home of Italian opera, was opened, new from the ground up, in 1897, and became at once the battleground of Tree's activities. Here, until his death in 1917, he produced a large number of Shakespeare's plays, on a scale of scenic magnificence sometimes beyond anything Irving had dreamed of. Against him, as usual, was frequently raised the old cry about smothering Shakespeare in scenery. Tree began his career as a producer of Shakespeare with his revival of Julius Cæsar on January 22, 1898. This was the first attempt for many years to stage the great Roman tragedy in London; the Saxe-Meiningen performances had been but visitant and temporary. In this Tree inaugurated a habit he never afterwards altered, of engaging the best available actors. In Julius Cæsar he himself elected to enact Antony, Lewis Waller was Brutus (and a very good one) and Franklin McLeay, Cassius (the best performance in the play). The Calpurnia was Lily Hanbury and the Portia Evelyn Millard. Probably two more beautiful women never appeared in the parts. The play was given for considerably over a hundred nights.

Encouraged, Tree revived King John in gorgeous style, on September 20, 1899, himself appearing as the tyrant, Julia Neilson as Constance, Waller as Falconbridge and Mrs. Crowe (the Kate Bateman of long ago) as Queen

Elinor. This also was a great success. Tree now turned to the comedies, and achieved nothing short of a triumph by his magnificent production of A Midsummer Night's Dream, in January, 1900. The last of his revivals, within our period, was Twelfth Night, in which he made a great hit as Malvolio—one of his very best parts. Lily Brayton —a recruit from Benson's company—played Viola. Her Majesty's was in full popular favour when, on July 19, 1902, Irving finally took farewell of the Lyceum stage. The transitoriness of human fortune is never more pathetically illustrated than in the history of the theatre. A particularly harrowing circumstance was that during the last engagement ever played by Irving at the Lyceum—the engagement in the spring of 1902—Miss Terry, for whom there was no part in the current bill, joined, with Irving's good will, the forces of Tree at Her Majesty's, appearing with Mrs. Kendal and Tree himself in an ever-memorable revival of The Merry Wives of Windsor. Miss Terry, however, while she was rollicking through the part of Mistress Page, at Her Majesty's, continued to appear with Irving in certain matinée performances at the Lyceum. She was the Portia to his Shylock, the last time he played at his famous old theatre, on the afternoon of July 19th, as aforesaid. Meantime, two years earlier, Tree might also have reflected on the mutation of things theatrical, while he observed the success of his own right-hand man, Lewis Waller, in a very stirring performance of Henry V, at the Lyceum, the date of the production being December 22, 1900. Thus dramatic combinations break up almost with the rapidity of changes in the moon.

MR. F. R. BENSON

If Forbes Robertson and Beerbohm Tree may be assumed, in any way, to have hurried Irving from the scene, they at least to all intents and purposes carried on the Irving tradition. That tradition enjoined the producing of Shakespeare with purity of text, indeed, but with curtailed text, and with scenes transposed almost at will, to meet the demands of scene painters and stage carpenters. These latter mechanical gentlemen were the ruling factor, and elaborate spectacle, especially in Tree's theatre, became, therefore, the first requirement in a Shakespearian revival. But the parts were also to be well played, and actors must be carefully selected. Elaborateness was the order of the day. This convention Tree, especially, accepted with implicit belief in its effectiveness. To-day we discredit such procedure. With us the play's the first thing, and we must give all of it that decorum allows, in the order of scenes selected by the poet himself, and with the minimum sacrifice of any element of the original conception. Scenery, if used, must be simple and unobtrusive; preferably the stage should be undecorated and Elizabethan. At the end of Irving's career, signs of this spirit appeared. The most notable within the years we are considering was the incursion into London of Mr. F. R. Benson, who introduced his repertoire company, from the provinces, at the Lyceum on February 15, 1900—at the very turn of the century. Mr. Benson had, as we know, started at the Globe in 1889–90 with quite different ideals, but his appearance now was as a challenge to all preceding principles. No one maintained that the actors, Mr. Benson included, were individually good; in fact, the critics called them amateurish. But they at least produced several plays of Shakespeare not acted for many years, and a few of the players of this and succeeding years—Mr. Oscar Asche, Miss Lily Brayton, Mr. Henry Ainley and Mr. Matheson Lang—have forged ahead to the front places of the profession. There were weekly changes of bills in 1900, and, before April 1st, Mr. Benson had revived Henry V, A Midsummer Night's Dream, Hamlet (in its entirety, acted over a space of six hours), Richard II, Twelfth Night, Antony and Cleopatra and The Tempest. The next year Mr. Benson was in London again at the Comedy Theatre, and added Coriolanus and The Taming of the Shrew to his list. He never tried to rival the experiment of amateurs in 1881, of producing the 1603

Hamlet. But excellent as are his intentions, it now seems unlikely that he, or any one with just his aims and ideals, will restore Shakespeare to the place he once enjoyed in popular estimation.

The contrast in method between him and Tree affords ground for reflection as we close this chapter. And with it we are glad to close—it brings us so nearly to modern problems in the staging of Shakespeare. I must not, however, neglect to admit the impeachment of having overlooked many Shakespearian performances of the twenty-odd years covered by the preceding discussion. I have said nothing of Daly's brief revivals of A Midsummer Night's Dream and The Two Gentlemen of Verona, in his last season at the London Daly's in the summer of 1895, nor of George Alexander's attempt at the St. James's to do what Beerbohm Tree did at Her Majesty's. Alexander, graduate of the Irving school, was for many years the director of the fashionable St. James's and played many parts there in the most famous plays of Pinero, Henry Arthur Jones, R. C. Carton and others of that school. Lured by the Shakespearian will-o'-the-wisp, however, he reverted to As You Like It in December, 1896, and to Much Ado about Nothing on February 16, 1898. Julia Neilson played Rosalind and Beatrice, and the other actors were well known in non-Shakespearian fields. But it was too late; after years of modern plays, Alexander had forgotten how to act Shakespeare in the true spirit. It is odd to reflect that he failed where Tree succeeded, in getting out of the modern into the larger poetic drama of the past. Offhand judgment might have predicted equal success or failure for both actor-managers. These performances of Alexander's, then, I ignore in this account; as also whatever was Shakespearian in the Italian repertoire of Salvini at Covent Garden in 1884.

These things are too transitory to debate in a chronicle aiming at a study of tendencies rather than of individual actors. Even more shadowy are three outbursts of May, 1897, blighted in the bud: Wilson Barrett's Othello, at the Lyric, and Janet Achurch's Cleopatra and Nutcombe

Gould's Shylock (under management of Ben Greet), both of these at the Olympic. Of Sarah Bernhardt's Hamlet, at the Adelphi, in June, 1899, what better can I do than quote the Athenæum of June 17th? "Where everything is necessarily wrong, nothing can be right."

CHAPTER XXXI

THE PLAYS

HERITAGE FROM THE AGE OF KEAN

Two traditions were handed down by the age of Charles Kean to the age of Irving. The first was that Shakespearian representation was now become a matter of special production. Anything like the old order, of visiting stars with regular repertoire, went out with the passing of the old stock companies; actor-managers succeeded to this idea, and with the actor-manager was inaugurated the principle of magnificent offerings, put on for a run, with all the adjuncts of perfect setting, specially engaged casts, completeness of ensemble and effect. This was the first heritage from the age of Kean.

The second was concerned with the plays. We have seen that, except for the troublesome Richard III and Macbeth, all the plays presented regularly throughout the period before Irving were presented in the original language. The producer was privileged to give as much or as little as he chose of the authentic text, but whatever he gave must be genuine. It had not yet occurred to any one that probably Shakespeare, as author, was the best judge of what should be acted, and that his plays, as written, might, with only such changes as modern delicacy required, be allowed to speak for themselves. This idea would have seemed absurd to Irving or any of his school. The plays were too long to be crowded—with heavy, unwieldy scenery (which no one then would have dreamed of renouncing)—in the allotted three hours of the regulation evening in the theatre; besides, many of the scenes or speeches seemed to the manager—the court of last appeal—uninteresting or unnecessary. Hence, naturally, there were as many acting versions of Shakespeare as there were individual managers to produce his plays.

Perhaps this feeling is best expressed by Mary Anderson in her preface to The Winter's Tale (1887): "The following stage-edition of 'A Winter's Tale,'" she says, "like its various predecessors, may be said to aim at keeping as close to the original play as is compatible with the requirements of the theatre and the no less exacting demands of modern taste. Of the larger excisions it is unnecessary to speak, they are unavoidable; no audience of these days would desire to have the 'Winter's Tale' produced in its entirety. . A literal adhesion to the text as it has been handed down to us would in any case savour of superstition." But the critics as well firmly believed this doctrine. The Athenæum of September 26, 1896—very near the end of our period, it will be observed—asserts regarding Cymbeline, then freshly revived by Irving: "To produce the play in its integrity would have been impossible. Apart from the fact that the mere question of time would prohibit such a plan, there are large hunks of 'Cymbeline' wholly unsuited to stage exposition as at present understood. Sticklers for the whole text may censure. . ." With such encouragement, who could blame the actors for blandly tailoring the text to suit their personal whims or peculiarities—or vanity?

CONFLICTING VIEWS AND VERSIONS OF HAMLET

How completely Shakespeare was at the mercy of these factors may be seen in a history of Hamlet on the stage in the last quarter of the century. Of Irving's Hamlet, Dramatic Notes (1878) informs us that "the most novel point in his conception of the character lies, in presenting the Prince as under the influence of an overmastering love for Ophelia. That love, albeit most rudely torn by the passionate steadfastness of his purposes of revenge, is very eloquently and gracefully shown in the delivery of the speeches to Ophelia in the third act. In this the mocking tone does not for a moment hide the profound emotion under which Hamlet labours, and while repelling her affectionate sympathy his whole frame seems to tremble with heartfelt longing."

This sentimental, popular view of the character naturally forces into the background the revenge-motive, and greatly subordinates, in the Irving version, the King, whose opening speech, for instance, in Act I is cut to fifteen lines, and whose speech beginning "'Tis sweet and commendable" is reduced to fourteen. The test-scene in the King's closet is, to be sure, given through the royal prayer, but, as in earlier editions, the crucial revenge-soliloquy of Hamlet is omitted. How could so gentle a Hamlet as Irving's harbour such horrible thoughts? Never mind about Shakespeare's Hamlet! After the killing of Polonius, Irving's version omits every one of the hurried, feverish scenes of the bestowing of the body, the King's shipping Hamlet to England, the episode of Fortinbras's army on the plains of Denmark, etc. The plot of Laertes and the King, likewise, is reduced to the scantiest limits, tucked in between the two mad scenes of Ophelia so modestly as to be almost lost to sight. As a matter of fact, the fourth act is practically nothing but one long mad scene for the loving, heart-broken girl. If Hamlet's love for Ophelia is the main motive of the play, obviously the fate of the best-beloved must loom large in the dénouement. Granting this conception of the play, Irving has tailored with skill.

Minor differences in his version involve the restoration of the wild and whirling words about "the old mole," "truepenny" and "this fellow in the cellarage," which previous actors had regarded as unfit to bestow upon a father's spirit; and a half-dozen lines in which Reynaldo is sent off to spy upon Laertes. The speedy running together in one unbroken scene of the "To be or not to be" soliloquy, the "Get thee to a nunnery" episode, the advice to the players, the request to Horatio to watch the King at the play, and the performance of the play itself makes a busy hour for any prince. The play ends with Hamlet's

> The potent poison quite o'er-crows my spirit:
> The rest is silence.

Irving's view of Hamlet was obviously Hamlet with as much as possible left out except Hamlet; consequently, when Hamlet was dead, nothing else mattered. While he lived, though, he was allowed to speak all his soliloquies, practically uncut.

This was Irving's version; it must be admitted that Wilson Barrett's (1884) was far more self-sacrificing. It subordinated the love for Ophelia and even for the queen; the all-devouring love of Hamlet was for his dead father. Hence the miniature portrait he wore about his neck; but hence, most importantly, the accentuation of the revenge-motive. In this version, for the first time in two centuries and more, the character of Claudius was restored to the position in which Shakespeare had placed it—that of chief antagonist, villain, thwarter of the hero. The brilliant E. S. Willard played the part for the first time in all those years as a great character part, and scored heavily. Claudius was thus for the first time seen to be a great "acting" character. This was a more valuable contribution than Barrett's "finicky" new readings—"a little more than kin and less than kĭnd" (provincial English for child); "kĭnd-less villain"; "the air bites shrewdly; is it very cold?", "a siege of troubles" (Theobald's emendation); "the Mouse-Trap, Marry, how? Trapically" (the reading of the first quarto). The restoration of the King was even more important than the scholarly research that, by taking the text of the first quarto, allowed Hamlet to appear as a youth in his teens, and justified the love of Claudius for the queen, now no longer a woman of fifty, but a captivating siren in the middle or late thirties. All these things the reader will find in the following account quoted by Dramatic Notes from The Stage magazine:

He has made his Hamlet a youth scarcely out of his teens. . . . The quarto of 1603 gives Yorick's skull as having lain in the earth only twelve years. . . The chief objections to this passionate, youthful Hamlet, apart from the question whether the actor is, or is not, representing Shakespeare, are that after he had seen his father's spirit, this Hamlet would have killed Claudius without more ado, and there would have been no need for the play to proceed beyond the second act. Nor is it probable that this Hamlet would have inspired such an ideal and heart-breaking affection for him as that of Ophelia. . . Ophelia in this case is older than Hamlet. . . . By his manner, Hamlet is convinced, in his own mind, of the King's guilt, and he regards his mother with no filial devotion. Indeed, Mr. Barrett's Hamlet shows no tenderness for his mother or any one else in the play. When Hamlet is left alone he delivers his speech beginning "Oh, that this too, too solid flesh would melt," with his gaze attracted, in the direction whither the King and Queen had gone, by the sound of laughter at the words, "That it should come to this." Here, also, he produces the medallion of his beloved father, which he fondly regards. He is quite prepared for the supernatural visitation. This previous belief in the appearance of his father's ghost robs the meeting of Hamlet with the ghost of all awe and terror. . . . He is not terrified at its appearance. In the scene with Ophelia in the second act, he is quite free from all tenderness. . . . The play scene, acted, as we have already intimated, outside the castle, is where Mr. Barrett makes the only 'point' in his impersonation, by standing aloft on the mimic stage, as he declaims on the confusion and departure of the King, and then sinks exhausted into Horatio's arms. Mr. Barrett is careful to avoid point making, and he studiously avoids all traditional business. . . . . Mr. Barrett's Hamlet is a quick, passionate, impetuous piece of acting, and, if we are to accept Hamlet as being nearer twenty than thirty years of age, it is a fine rendering of the character. . . . But the sad, dreamy, poetical Hamlet is lost sight of in Mr. Barrett's terribly earnest, determined, and youthful hero. . . . Has Mr. Barrett given us the true Hamlet? If so, all the Hamlets we have seen must be wrong. . . . Apart from Mr. Barrett's acting of the character, one or two of his readings . . . . are likely to provoke discussion.

For the rest, Mr. Barrett deserves the sincere praise of every lover of the drama for giving to the stage, for the first time, the tragedy as Shakespeare wrote it, in as perfect a form as is possible within the limits of the stage. Fortinbras, of course, has to be excluded from the play, but Mr. Barrett has shown great intelligence and considerable generosity in his arrangement of the scenes. It has always been the custom to end the second act with Hamlet's "The play's the thing wherein I'll catch the conscience of the King." But, in the Princess's version, the action continues until after the scene with Ophelia, the act ending with the King's "Madness in great ones must not unwatched go." The third act is principally occupied by the play scene and the closet scene, the King again ending the act. The remainder of the play is, in arrangement, much the same as the ordinary acting versions. Mr. Barrett has here presented the play in the most perfect form that it has ever been acted on the stage . . . and has given Hamlet simply as one character out of many . . . and has not sacrificed the poet's meaning in order to make Hamlet the central and only figure in the great tragedy. . . . Mr. E. S. Willard, as the King, has the advantage of having in his hands, thanks to the arrangement of this version, opportunity never before afforded the impersonator of this character of giving a very fine piece of acting. . . . The triumphant bearing of Claudius in the first act is a fine contrast to the dismay pictured so vividly by the actor, when the King hears of Hamlet's return to Denmark.

One can only regret that this very interesting new version of Hamlet was not supported by a greater actor than Wilson Barrett; if it had been supported by the Forbes Robertson of the next decade, for instance! Forbes Robertson's day came in 1897, and, of course, his individual preference guided the scissors and the glue-brush in making up his stage version. His chief restoration was that of the entry of Fortinbras (a novel stage figure after nearly two centuries and a half of elimination), to close with a living presence the scene in which death had played so great a part. In Forbes Robertson's interpretation, otherwise, poetry was chiefly stressed; the Athenæum of September 18, 1897, says the performance was "all that is princely, scholarly, interesting." But, "concerning the sanity" of this Hamlet, "there is no question. So sweetly reasonable is he that one marvels at the uneasiness of the King." The Times of September 13th also thinks him "perhaps the sanest of all Hamlets who have ever trod the boards." On another head the Times remarks that Mr. Robertson's Hamlet might pass for twenty-five or less, and wonders why the grizzled ghost does not profit by the general process of rejuvenation inaugurated by Wilson Barrett. "But," says this paper, "most important innovation of all is the introduction at the end of the play of the gallant helmeted soldier, young Fortinbras who . . . then pays military honours to the dead Prince. This . . episode . . has been invariably cut . . . probably from some fear of . . . an anti-climax. That the effect is excellent we are bound to say. . . . . The King and Queen being dead, Hamlet is necessarily for a few moments the Sovereign of Denmark. In his last agony he seats himself on the throne and it is there he expires, to be borne thence in state on the shields of Fortinbras's soldiers. It is . . a stirring and enlivening ending."

These are the great Hamlets of the age just passed; youthful critics, bred in the latest school, that demands the play as a whole, will curl a superior lip at these changes of text and scene, inspired by the fancy of individual managers. Let them feed their whimsy on the knowledge of a surprising attempt in 1881 to out-Benson even Benson in the presentation of the original text. In April of that year —St. George's Hall the place—a company of amateurs "took pains," according to Dutton Cook's Nights at the Play, "to commit to memory the muddled and mangled text" of the 1603 Hamlet, which was "denied scenery and musical accompaniment," and acted on a stage before a group of *cognoscenti*, then for the first—and only time— regaled by hearing Polonius called Corambis, Laertes Leartes, and Rosencrantz and Guildenstern, Rosencraft and Gilderstone! And this in 1881, in the dark age of Irving and Daly! Verily the mangled versions of Hamlet produced by Irving, Barrett and Forbes Robertson are somewhat atoned for by this heroic, if "absurd and reprehensible" attempt to stage the very most original text of the masterpiece. Surely Benson's six-hour performance of the complete Folio version was even less praiseworthy!

ROMEO AND JULIET IN VARIOUS REVIVALS

The three important revivals of Hamlet presented at intervals throughout nearly the entire period of Irving well illustrate habits of actors as to the stage-versions employed. In the case of Romeo and Juliet, however, Irving was particularly fair to the bard. For the first two acts he "cuts" but little of the original, opening with the Chorus, and retaining even twenty-two of the Friar's lines on the medicinal power of herbs. The entire sonnet-duet of the lovers is given in the ball-room scene. In Act III, the entry of the Prince and the Capulets and Montagues after the duel scene is strangely omitted, probably to bring down the curtain effectively on Romeo's "O, I am fortune's fool!" But, to atone, Juliet's "banished" scene, omitted by Adelaide Neilson and Mary Anderson, is restored, as are also some of those short, scattering scenes in this and the following acts, involving the parents of Juliet, Paris, the Nurse and the servants. Yet, after the discovery of the supposed dead body of Juliet, Irving retains the scene of the Capulets, Friar Laurence and Paris. Both he and Mary Anderson kept the scene in Act V between Friar John and Friar Laurence, a scene which, though necessary for expository purposes, is rather dull dramatically. Irving's play ends with a grand tableau of the Montagues and Capulets at the tomb, reconciled to the accompaniment of this fragment of the Prince's original speech:

> A glooming peace this morning with it brings;
> The sun for sorrow will not show his head:
> For never was a story of more woe,
> Than this of Juliet and her Romeo.

Mary Anderson's version differed but little from Irving's. The London Graphic of November 8, 1884, spoke but truth in stating that "The merit of the present Lyceum stage copy is that it neither transposes scenes nor interpolates anything, though, after a custom which has become a paramount consideration, the dialogue has been considerably reduced, and certain scenes altogether omitted." The most important scene altogether omitted was that in which the nurse announces to Juliet the killing of Tybalt, with the subsequent sending of the message and the cord-ladder to the despairing Romeo. It was felt that this scene detracted from the dramatic effect of Romeo's "banished" scene, by letting the audience know beforehand that help was on the way. Of course the omission naïvely assumes that the audience had never read or previously seen the great love-tragedy.

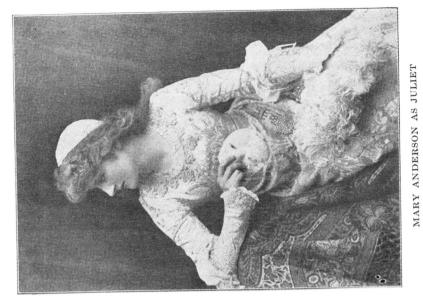

MARY ANDERSON AS JULIET
From copyrighted photographs by W. and D. Downey of London

HELENA MODJESKA AS JULIET

OTHER PLAYS

I cannot afford to weary the reader much further on this head. All the stage versions of the period were arranged according to individual judgment of the producer. In The Merchant of Venice (1879), for instance, Irving once more banished the Prince of Arragon, restored by Charles Kean and Bancroft; he also eliminated the scenes between Jessica, Lorenzo and Launcelot, immediately after Portia leaves Belmont. In Much Ado about Nothing (1882), he did not allow Beatrice to waken Hero on her wedding day, but, for the first time in my knowledge, he restored the scene in which Claudio does penance at the supposed monument of Hero. Of the Kendals' As You Like It (1885), the Athenæum of January 31, 1885, elegantly but cryptically informs us that "the alterations in the arrangement of the text are chiefly noteworthy in that they change the character of Jaques, who becomes much more reasonable and less pragmatical," surely an unwarranted managerial liberty! Mary Anderson, more than two years later, blandly left out from The Winter's Tale a very considerable amount of the befooling of the Shepherd and the Clown by Autolycus (and candour compels me to admit that nobody regretted it), as well as the scene between Dion and Cleomenes. She also took from Autolycus the speeches regarding Leontes's finding of Perdita, and divided the scene between a Gentleman and Rogero. Finally, at the end of the rustic festival, for curtain-effect the scene ends with a speech for Florizel, transposed from its proper place far earlier in the scene. This sort of thing we now consider despicable.

IRVING'S LAST PRODUCTIONS

I may close this phase of the matter by referring to Irving's latest revivals. His Henry VIII (1892) goes through the first three acts without reprehensible change, in fact, with commendable scrupulosity, even to the retaining of such inconsequential bits as that about proposed measures for the reformation of travelled gallants (Shakespeare's Act I, Scene 3). But fragments merely of the remainder are given. Just enough of the speeches of the Gentlemen in Act IV is preserved to bring in the coronation of Anne Bullen; and in Act V only enough of Cranmer's speech of prophecy to allow for the gorgeous ceremony of the christening of the infant Elizabeth. All the matter pertaining to the conspiracy against Cranmer is omitted; who can say unjustifiably, the stage and audience being what they are? The King Lear of 1892 reduced Shakespeare's 26 scenes (Cambridge text) to 16; but it left out no highly important matter. According to the Times of November 11th, though "considerably reduced," it is otherwise "in the condition in which it left the author's hand. Among the excisions . . . is the dreadful episode of the plucking out of Gloster's eyes." From Cymbeline (1896) Irving removed the vision of Posthumus, much of the tediousness of Iachimo in the last acts, some of the inconsistencies in the character of Cloten. This I learn from the Athenæum of September 26th, which concludes with the astonishing statement that the effect of the alterations is "to establish Cymbeline as a pastoral play after the fashion of 'As You Like It,' and even as a formidable rival to that loveliest of comedies." Cymbeline is, of course, all that, but to reduce it to nothing but that is to take from it, as the Athenæum not too elegantly says, "large hunks" of Shakespeare's play. The revival of Coriolanus in 1901 necessarily—Irving being a slight, unsoldierly man—removed from the first act much of the fighting in and around Corioli; as a whole the play was transmuted from the heroic to the domestic and political arena, becoming thereby the history of Coriolanus in his relations with his family and two rather antagonistic tribunes. The Athenæum of April 20, 1901, tells the story:

Somewhat mistrustfully Sir Henry Irving has carried out a long-cherished purpose of producing Shakespeare's Coriolanus. We say mistrustfully, since the changes that have been made in the disposition of the scenes amount to a virtual reconstruction of the play; and some of the characters, notably Volumnia, are much altered. In the case of Caius Marcius the omissions consist principally of scenes of action. The interrupted fight with Tullus Aufidius disappears, as does the scene in which, entering Corioli alone and having the gates shut on him, Caius Marcius earned his cognomen of Coriolanus. Against the banishment of these things nothing needs be urged. Their due presentation calls for a robust style, which is not always a desirable possession and has never been an attribute of Sir H. Irving. . . . . . Rendered as Coriolanus now is, its interest is purely psychological.

TRANSPOSITION OF SCENES

But curtailment or elimination of scenes was not all. Every actor felt justified, in view of the exigencies of heavy scenery, in running together scenes that Shakespeare separated in point of time and location, or in transposing scenes far out of their natural sequence. It was all for scenery and the play well lost. Of offenders in this respect Augustin Daly was the most flagrant. Yet that Irving was not guiltless we learn from the London Graphic of July 12, 1884, which rather severely arraigns him for his dealing with Twelfth Night: "The version which has been prepared for this revival makes little scruple regarding suppressions and transitions; hence, as it is not printed, the visitor to the Lyceum, who takes with him for reference a volume of 'Knight' or the 'Cambridge Shakespeare' will only be laying up for himself weariness and vexation."

Whatever Irving's sins in this respect, however, Daly's were as scarlet in comparison. It began with The Taming of the Shrew, in which Act IV starts by joining together Shakespeare's Scenes 2 and 4, all pertaining to Hortensio and Tranio, the elopement of Bianca, and Tranio's hiring the Pedant to impersonate the father of Lucentio. This running together of matters thus divergent in time allowed Daly to make the most absurd scene-amalgamation of which I have any knowledge; the amalgamation of Shakespeare's Scenes 1, 3 and 5 of the same act. By this welding, Petruchio—or as Daly, like Benjamin Webster, spelled the name, Petrucio—brings home his bride, bothers her about the food and the tailor, starts with her back home again, and meets on the way the old man, whom Katharine is forced to greet as "young, blushing virgin," the "virgin" aforesaid conveniently passing Petruchio's door instead of being met on the road. All this crowded together without intermission! As often as I saw the Daly revival of this comedy, I was seriously disconcerted by this ridiculous "speeding up" of the action; I could not help wondering why Katharine had been brought to her husband's house merely to spend a few minutes and depart again for the place whence she had just come.

The transpositions in Daly's As You Like It are few and defensible. Act II, for instance, begins with Shakespeare's Scene 3, that in which Adam and Orlando start for the forest of Arden. By this device all preliminary scenes are disposed of, and the action thereafter can take place uninterruptedly in the woodland glades. Of course the little scenes involving the rage of Duke Frederick are not given. Daly's greatest service in this play consisted in giving back to the First Lord those speeches about Jaques so long appropriated by Jaques himself. But it was in Twelfth Night that Daly performed his most astounding feats. After a great deal of storm business, his first scene begins, and turns out to be the first of Shakespeare's second act— the landing of Sebastian and Antonio. This, of course, destroys all dramatic suspense as to the fate of Viola's brother. But it allowed the star (Miss Rehan) to enter after the audience was seated, and the putting the storm scene first allowed an elaborate set to be arranged, later, for the Duke's Palace. Scene 2 therefore began with Orsino's soliloquy on music and love, but, being so elaborate a setting, it had to be utilised for a considerable time, and therefore Viola (who has entered the duke's service, apparently) comes on to be sent with her message to Olivia. Daly's Scene 3 is a running together of Shakespeare's Scenes 3 and 5, and his second scene of Act II—that in which Malvolio gives Viola the ring. This was possible because of a colonnade at the back, across which Viola passed in her exit from Olivia's house. To give the reader a graphic account of the liberties that a manager permitted himself in those not far-off days, I may summarise by saying that

DALY'S	SHAKESPEARE'S
Act I, Scene 1	= Act II, Scene 1 + Act I, Scene 2
Act I, Scene 2	= Act I, Scene 1 + Act I, Scene 4
Act I, Scene 3	= Act I, Scenes 3 and 5 + Act II, Scene 2

This is the worst that Daly attempted, and in that day, for so well-known a play, it was censured. The comedy was given in four acts. Daly's Midsummer Night's Dream and his Two Gentlemen of Verona, produced briefly in London in 1895, I dismiss without comment further than a statement to the effect that, both in curtailment of speeches and in transposing of scenes, they adhered to the standard then considered permissible. There was no such violent dislocation of members as in The Taming of the Shrew and Twelfth Night.

INCLUSION OF LINES NOT IN THE ORIGINAL

But I must return to my text; all presented in any play was at least found in the original. Some exceptions go to prove the rule. Ellen Terry, in The Story of My Life, states that Irving ended the church-scene of Much Ado about Nothing with the old traditional "gag" found in stage-versions from Oxberry to Charles Kean:

Beatrice. Benedick, kill him—kill him, if you can.
Benedick. As sure as I'm alive, I will!

She begged him to leave out this stuff, but he wanted a good "curtain-scene." The amusing part, as Miss Terry admits, was that the critics never noticed it at all! Later, Irving discarded the silly bit. In the same connection, I may note that Mary Anderson, as her preface states, ended The Winter's Tale with a couplet from All's Well that Ends Well, "for the simple reason that it offered, from the stage point of view, a more effective climax than the general conversation with which The Winter's Tale comes to an end." Of course the actress knew better than the author how to end the play! Still, in fairness, let us admit she knew the conditions of the theatre in 1887 far better than any one who wrote before 1616.

More reactionary was the conduct of Richard Mansfield when, in 1889, he revived Richard III. His idea was to stress the progress of Richard in crime from youth to age, and therefore his acts were all meticulously dated on the bill, to apprise the auditor of the comparative age of the royal criminal. In pursuit of his object, he, like Cibber, introduced from Henry VI, Part III, those scenes in the Tower-precincts involving the murder of the poor, weak monarch. It is to be noted, moreover, that he omitted the dream and the murder of Clarence, and the great character of Queen Margaret. Yet, oddly enough, he included the comparatively insignificant scene involving the children of Clarence. In these latter respects, the play falls under the first head of my discourse—the inclusion or suppression at will of scenes in the original play; but in the patching in of scenes from another play of Shakespeare's, it fell in line with a usage long since obsolete. William Winter, in his Life of Mansfield, gives a good account of this version as a whole:

He used a five-act version of the tragedy, preserving the text of the original, much condensed, and introducing a few lines from Cibber. It began with a bright processional scene before the Tower of London, in which Elizabeth, Queen of Edward IV, was conspicuous, and against that background of "glorious summer" it placed the dangerous figure of Glo'ster. It comprised the murder of Henry the Sixth, the wooing of Lady Anne,—not in a London street, but in a rural place, the road to Chertsey; the lamentation for King Edward the Fourth; the episode of the boy princes; the condemnation of Hastings,—a scene that brilliantly denotes the mingled artifice and cruelty of Shakespeare's Glo'ster; the Buckingham plot; the priest and mayor scene; the temptation of Tyrrel; the fall of Buckingham; the march to battle; the episode of the spectres; and the fatal catastrophe on Bosworth Field.

Quite analogous was Irving's retention of lines of the old Davenant witch-verse in his Macbeth of 1888. These were very few, and were introduced, obviously, for scenic and musical effect. The advertisement of the revival in the London Times of December 29, 1888, tells the story sufficiently for my purpose:

The introduction of this music into Shakespeare's tragedy has been the subject of much discussion, but as far as regards the two songs, Come Away and Black Spirits and White, we find these clearly indicated in the First Folio edition of Shakespeare's Works (1623). In Act III, Scene 5, at the end of Hecate's speech, we find, "Musicke and a Song, Blacke Spirits, &c.," and later on, in the same scene, when the witches go off, we have, "Musicke, the Witches dance and vanish." It is difficult to believe that these musical features and songs were introduced into the play without the sanction of Shakespeare. These songs have now been set to music by Sir Arthur Sullivan, to whom I am greatly indebted for composing the whole of the incidental music of this production. The only lines, therefore, introduced into this stage arrangement of Macbeth are the four lines of the song Black Spirits and White, and the ten lines of the song, Come away, come away. With these two exceptions, all the text is taken from the First Folio.

With this close approach to Davenant, the reader will not be surprised to learn that Lady Macduff and her son were removed from the list of characters, although the drunken porter was restored and played by the inimitable comedian, Johnson.

THE INTRODUCTION OF SONGS

Beyond the restoration of Davenant and Cibber, respectively, in the two plays involved, introduction of other Shakespearian matter, in any given play, seems to have concerned itself with song, for sensuous effect. Daly particularly loaded down his revivals with singing. In the last scene of The Taming of the Shrew, the guests were entertained by "Should he upbraid." In As You Like It and Twelfth Night every one of the songs provided by Shakespeare was well sung, including, for the former, the verses of Hymen and the seldom-given "It was a lover and his lass," and for the latter, an introduced "Who is Olivia?" to Shubert's music intended to ask that question about Sylvia. Also, "Come unto these yellow sands" was bodily transported from The Tempest to the first scene of Twelfth Night. A Midsummer Night's Dream was rich with song.

But Daly was not alone. Beerbohm Tree, in his early revival of The Merry Wives of Windsor, in 1889, did not scruple to insert a song, "Love laid his weary head," for Mrs. Tree, who played Anne Page. So late as 1896 Alexander allowed Julia Neilson as Rosalind to sing the discredited "Cuckoo song" in his revival of As You Like It, but was regarded as very generous in restoring "It was a lover and his lass." Before and after this, the utmost advantage was derived from the lyrics, and, as we see, if necessary, other plays were called on to supply them. Sir Arthur Sullivan, German, Sir Alexander Mackenzie, Raymond Roze, and other talented musicians supplied the music, vocal and orchestral, demanded by audiences more and more exacting in such matters.

NUMBER OF ACTS REDUCED

One other aspect of the stage-versions requires consideration. This is the increasingly frequent habit of producing the plays in fewer than the ordinary five acts. Daly's Twelfth Night was in four, but Beerbohm Tree, beginning with Julius Cæsar (1898), reduced the number to three. His object, apparently, was to get within the boundaries of any given rise and fall of a curtain all the material constituting a unified whole in action. Thus the first act of Julius Cæsar, as he arranged it, comprised all the matter of the conspiracy up to and including the murder of Cæsar, with Antony's apostrophe to the bleeding "corse"; this brought about a huge act two hours long. The second act was thus concerned only with the forum and mob scenes. The last act was made up of the events involving the quarrel of Cassius and Brutus and the episodes of the battle of Philippi. I reproduce the scene-synopsis for the reader:

Act I.   Scene 1. A Public Place. Scene 2. Brutus's Orchard.
          Scene 3. Cæsar's House. Scene 4. A Public Street
          Scene 5. The Senate House (Joseph Harker).
Act II.   The Forum (Walter Hann).
Act III. Scene 1. Brutus's Tent. Scene 2. The Plains of Philippi
          (Walter Hann).

This arrangement allowed Tree (who played Antony) to have in each case the tableau curtain entirely to himself, and made Antony decidedly the leading part, which he assuredly is not in Shakespeare. It vastly reduced the number of scenes, also; but that Tree gave most of the play is proved by the fact that in the *dramatis personæ* are included Caius Ligarius and Cinna the Poet, whose big scenes had been deleted from preceding stage-versions.

Similarly for his King John (1899) Tree arranged the play in a three-act episodical order. The first dealt with the fortunes of Arthur up to the end of the battle in France; the second, with his imprisonment and death; the third, with the subsequent distractions of the kingdom. For this revival Tree took a leaf out of the note-book of Charles Kean and interpolated a gorgeous dumb-show of the granting of Magna Charta. The synopsis for this play I also reproduce from the playbill:

ACT I

Scene 1. Room of State in Northampton Castle. Scene 2. Before the Walls of Angiers (France). Scene 3. The French King's Tent. Scene 4. Battlefield near Angiers. Tableau. The Fight. Scene 5. Another part of the Field.

ACT II

Scene 1. The French King's Tent. Scene 2. Crypt in Northampton Castle. Scene 3. Room of State in Northampton Castle. Scene 4. The Walls of the Castle.

ACT III

Tableau. The Granting of Magna Charta. Scene 1. Templar Church, Northampton. Scene 2. A Plain near St. Edmundsbury. Scene 3. The Same. A Field of Battle. Scene 4. Near Swinstead Abbey. Scene 5. The Orchard of Swinstead Abbey.

Both Twelfth Night (1901) and The Merry Wives of Windsor (1902) were also thus solidly blocked off into three-act plays.

This three-act theory Irving adopted in his revival of Coriolanus in 1901. In it the first act dealt with Corioli and Coriolanus's first "standing" for the consulship; the second, with his bitter contest with the tribunes and his banishment; the third, with the union with Aufidius and its consequences. By comparing the synopsis of scenes with that in the Cambridge Shakespeare, the reader may see how much of the original play Irving retained, and how much he abandoned.

Act I.	Scene 1.	Rome. The Forum. J. Harker.
	Scene 2.	A Room in Marcius's House. J. Harker.
	Scene 3.	Near Camp of Cominius. H. Craven.
	Scene 4.	Rome. A Street. H. Craven.
	Scene 5.	Rome. A Street; the Forum. J. Harker.
	Scene 6.	A Street. H. Craven.
	Scene 7.	The Capitol. W. Hann.
Act II.	Scene 1.	Rome: the Forum. J. Harker.
	Scene 2.	A Street. J. Harker.
	Scene 3.	Room in Coriolanus's House. J. Harker.
	Scene 4.	The Forum. J. Harker.
Act III.	Scene 1.	Antium. Before Aufidius's House. H. Craven.
	Scene 2.	A Hall in Aufidius's House. H. Craven.
	Scene 3.	Rome: the Forum. J. Harker.
	Scene 4.	A Camp near Rome. H. Craven.
	Scene 5.	Rome. The Forum. J. Harker.
	Scene 6.	Antium. A Public Place. H. Craven.

MR. F. R. BENSON'S HAMLET, 1900

This is the last case of such mutilation that I have to record. An entirely new principle of presenting Shakespeare as written, with the maximum of the text possible, was introduced by Mr. F. R. Benson in his first London season, beginning at the Lyceum on February 15, 1900, literally at the end of the century that had devoted so many of its hundred years to driving the bastard stage versions of the dramatist from public view. Having less scenery to manipulate, Mr. Benson could give more of the text. On March 1st he cast discretion to the winds and produced Hamlet entire, *à la* Bayreuth with Wagner, in afternoon and evening session, the whole lasting six acting hours, with an hour and a half for dinner. The first session ran from 3.30 to 6.30, the second from 8 to 11 o'clock. Yet the critics were not wholly pleased, and the Athenæum, of March 10th, is rather aggrieved: "A certain academic interest," it admits, "attends the presentation of an un-abridged version of Hamlet. Mr. Benson at least has dealt fairly and squarely with the play, and has gone as near to giving the recognized text of the Folio as the condi-tions of the modern stage permit. . . Genuine enjoyment is derived from the restitution of passages never previously heard upon the stage. Again, while there is much that is inadequate and amateurish in the performance, there is nothing jarring or offensive. Mr. Benson is but a colour-less and an uninspiriting Hamlet, and the characters gen-erally are feebly portrayed. . . That it pays the expendi-ture of time involved will scarcely be said. . . We can all of us read the whole of Hamlet at our ease and leisure, and the amount of illumination afforded is not sufficient to justify the substitution for one's easy-chair of the crowning discomfort of a Lyceum stall, and the devotion to the theatre of what is practically the whole of a working day."

These performances were not good, but they were the first on the theory that we now consider desirable as an actuating motive in Shakespearian production. Shake-speare as written (so far as possible), not Shakespeare as adapted, is the slogan of recent managers. Even so, with-out the great interpreters—the Booths, the Neilsons, the Irvings, the Terrys—Shakespeare's plays, in whole or in part, have been suffering the saddest of eclipses.

THE NEW METHOD OF ACTING SHAKESPEARE

And this brings me to the final comment. Throughout the later years of the Irving period arose the so-called

"naturalistic" method of acting Shakespeare. His poetry
was to be read more like prose than verse; action was to be
toned down; everything was to be refined and gentle. This
may have been the result of the passage of so many actors
from modern plays to the Shakespearian. At any rate the
change has been noted, and synchronised with the decline
of Shakespeare on the stage; it is really with difficulty that
one refrains from using the fallacy of *post hoc, ergo propter
hoc.* The critic of the Athenæum in the decade of the '90's
very frequently calls attention to the change then taking
place. As regards Forbes Robertson's Romeo and Juliet
(1895), he writes on September 28th:

> Never more shall we, apparently, hear the representative of Mac-
> beth or Othello strive with swelling breast to "out-roar the lion-
> throated seas" or to "out-Herod Herod." . . . Since the days of
> Fechter's Hamlet, the movement has been in progress. Slowly and
> unassertively it has worked its way, facing occasional discourage-
> ment, but keeping straight on, until now there is not an actor left
> who dare in London, on a solitary occasion, do what a generation and
> a half ago was done constantly by Phelps, Charles Kean, and a host
> of imitators. . . Not only are there no tragedians . . . . there are
> none coming. Realism has conquered convention even in tragedy,
> and instead of instructing, like Constance, "our sorrows to be proud,"
> we have to teach them to be humble.

Even Irving's Richard III (1896) was subject to the
same charge, and the Athenæum for December 26th reit-
erates: "All that is conventional in tragedy is gone, leaving
us musing whether after all we were wise in demanding its
removal. . . . Convention is, in fact, as indispensable to
tragedy as it is to opera. . . We have . . . a polished
presentment of Court manners in which nothing offends
and all is artistic and as nearly as possible real. Where,
however, is tragedy? It is gone. Richard III is not now
a tragic *rôle.* It is what is conventionally called 'a character part' . . . . We are gratified, tickled, amused. . . .
Once and again a ripple of merriment passed over the
house as Richard announced his intentions or uttered his

asides. . . . We are simply stating a fact, and will at the same time express a belief that it will be always so when realistic acting in Richard is substituted for conventional. . . . All we maintain is that . . the play does not grip us."

The critic had not changed his mind in 1898 when Forbes Robertson played Macbeth; I have not yet—in 1920— changed my mind, which is still of his persuasion. "Our actors in tragedy," he repeats, "now 'speak in a monstrous little voice,' are most courteous and well bred and loth, apparently, to do anything that might not decently be done in a modern drawing-room. We are never now offended to the soul by any robustious periwig-pated fellow. . . . That tragedy has, in a sense, gained thereby, and that a performance of a Shakspearean masterpiece may be welcomed with gratification and delight. . . Pleased as we are, however, we have ceased to be thrilled. To our pursuit of the beautiful we are sacrificing the terrible and the grotesque. Mr. Forbes Robertson is at once the priest and the deity of the latest school. . . . Take the opinion of playgoing London, and you will be told—and justly told —that his Hamlet is the most beautiful and poetical that the stage has seen. The same may now be said of Macbeth. It fulfils every requirement. Macbeth is under the spell of destiny; he has the fatefulness so rarely assigned any tragic character. The witches—the same as furies— have him in their clutches. We watch with pleasure and artistic content the degradation of a not ignoble nature, and we sympathize even with one whose darkest deeds were the product of his age. . . . But we are not moved. No need is there to stop and count our pulse. . . . Macbeth, in Mr. Robertson's hands, whether in his martial gear or his kingly robes, with his red hair and beard, is the image of a Scottish Viking. His performance is beautiful and noble. Are we unreasonable that we want to be appalled?"

I end by calling attention to the small number of Shakespearian plays produced throughout the Irving period—twenty-five in all, counting Benson's Richard II. Phelps, alone, at Sadler's Wells in his eighteen years of management produced—and well produced—thirty-one!

CHAPTER XXXII

SCENERY AND STAGE DECORATION

It is undisputed that the chief interest in the greater number of productions during the age of Irving was pictorial. I fear there is no doubt that the major part of any audience at the Lyceum or elsewhere went out primarily "for to see" Shakespeare, lured by promises or accounts of amazing spectacle. For better or worse, this is the mark of the period. The progression from the days of John Kemble had been steady; Charles Kean had brought the mounting to a high state of excellence; and it remained for Irving merely to perfect Kean's method by all the appliances of a more modern science and mechanism. In principle the men were at one; of course Kemble could not do with lamps and candles, nor Kean with gas, what Irving's contemporaries—Beerbohm Tree, especially—could do with electric light. The mass of machinery for manipulating scenery which to-day makes the purlieus of a modern stage seem almost like the engine-room of a man-o'-war was of course undreamed of by Kemble, to a less degree also by Kean; but, I repeat, they did for their patrons what Irving and Tree did for theirs. The proper decoration of Shakespeare was the goal toward which they were striving.

This being so, it will be interesting to trace the progress of Irving toward perfection of scenic investiture. In the years of Bateman's management of the Lyceum he was, as we know, but another man's man; a salaried actor, though the leading one. Whatever he may have suggested, Bateman controlled the treasury. The Shakespearian revivals of that *régime*, therefore, are not to be charged against Irving. He was even content to employ for his noted first performance of Hamlet, on October 31, 1874, a graveyard set that had been used a short time before in Eugene Aram.

Yet we know from the Autobiography of Salvini that the great Italian in the spring of 1875 was much impressed by the moonlight effects in the ghost scenes of the first act. No doubt the mounting was adequate, but the play was the thing, and the actor.

IRVING'S HAMLET, 1878–1879

At the beginning of his career as independent manager, he produced, we remember, the same tragedy. For this and the next few succeeding plays, Irving proceeded cautiously. His great formula was not worked out at once; there was nothing of the birth of a full-armed Athena about it. This we learn from the unimpeachable testimony of both Ellen Terry and Austin Brereton, the friend and biographer of Irving. Miss Terry says of Romeo and Juliet (1882), "This was the first of Henry Irving's great Shaksperian productions. Hamlet and Othello had been mounted with care, but, in spite of statements that I have seen to the contrary, they were not true reflections of Irving as a producer." Mr. Brereton has much to say of the inexpensiveness of The Merchant of Venice, which followed Hamlet; this evidence I shall soon reproduce.

But if the second Hamlet was not lavishly set upon the stage, it was adequately and attractively set. Taste would govern any production of Irving. The Theatre for February, 1879, gives a pretty account of the pictures. From this we see that Irving did not "fuss" about strict archæological accuracy, and aimed merely at harmonious effect. The reader will, I am sure, agree with me in liking Irving's use of the very remote part of the battlements for the strange impartment of the ghost, and the winding upward path for Ophelia's funeral cortège. Says the Theatre:

The intelligent manner in which the tragedy was produced, in regard to its stage-management and its decoration, received high praise in all quarters. In regard to costume . . . Hamlet, it may be presumed, lived in the fifth or sixth century. Yet the story is treated by the dramatist as one of the Elizabethan age. . . . . The

Danish costume of the dark ages was far from picturesque, and the adoption for this revival of dresses of a sixteenth century character was the wiser of two courses. These costumes, it need hardly be said, were in good taste and agreeable contrast. The scenery, without being pretentious, marked a distinct advance in the decoration of the stage. Two scenes were especially beautiful. The first was that in which the ghost makes the revelation to Hamlet. The Prince of Denmark has followed the spirit of his father to

> ' That dreadful summit of the cliff,
> That beetles o'er his base into the sea.'

Standing among a number of massive rocks, the ghost proceeds with the supernatural impartment. The soft light of the moon falls upon the spectral figure; not a sound from below can be heard; the faint flashes of the dawn are stealing over the immense expanse of water before us. The weird grandeur of the scene can hardly be appreciated from description. Equally striking in its way is that of the burial of Ophelia. The churchyard is on a hill near the palace, and, as night comes on, the funeral procession winds slowly up the ascent. Never before have the "mained rites" been so exactly and impressively performed. The scene on the battlements of Elsinore, with the illuminated windows of the palace in the background, and the star alluded to by Bernardo, glistening in the northern sky, is also very satisfactory.

This pleasing but unobtrusive scenery exactly conforms to the requirements laid down by Irving in his preface to his acting version of the tragedy. So interesting is this statement, at the outset of his career, of his conception of the function and the proportionate value of scenery in Shakespearian production, that I need crave no indulgence for reproducing it *verbatim:*

It is but natural that, in attempting to place one of Shakespeare's works on the stage in a manner worthy of the great master, the utmost care should now be exercised with regard to the scenic decorations and other accessories of the play. We live in an age remarkable for the completeness of its dramatic representations in this respect at least; and it would be showing very scant honour to the poet . . . . were we to treat his works with less generosity and less artistic care . . . . than the works of inferior authors. The first object of a manager, no doubt, should be to obtain capable representatives of the various characters; but . . their efforts will be aided and not hampered by a due attention to the effectiveness and beauty of their scenic surroundings. Shakespeare, if well acted on a bare stage, would certainly afford great intellectual pleasure; but that pleasure will be all the greater if the eye be charmed, at the same time, by scenic illustrations in harmony with the poet's ideas. . . . . .

Without attempting to overburden the play with spectacular effect, and to smother the poet under a mass of decoration, it has been the object of Mr. Irving, in the present production of Hamlet, to obtain as much effect from . . . . the scene-painter's art as the poet's own descriptions may seem to justify.

It would be a pleasure to quote the preface entire, but I may refer only briefly to the assertions that the painter, in the first act, "must try and convey the impression of on-coming dawn," and that in the last scene of this act "Hamlet is supposed to have followed the ghost to a spot at some distance from the castle," thus allowing for the weird effect described in the Theatre magazine. As to the scene in the Queen's closet, the placing of the Osric episode in the open, and as to the suitable setting for the last scene of all, the Preface must simply be allowed to speak for itself:

The next point . . . is in the last scene of Act III, the Queen's Closet. This has been represented, as usual, as an ante-chamber to her bed-chamber, hung with tapestry, and one portion of it fitted up as an oratory. The Ghost enters not in "armour," but in a kind of dressing-robe (the "night-gowne" of the stage direction in the first quarto): this is more consonant with Hamlet's exclamation:—

'My father in his habit as he lived!'

He passes through the door leading into the bed-chamber, just as he might have done in his life-time.

Irving in this scene, let me say, saw the two pictures on which he bade his mother look, merely in his mind's eye; they were verbal portraits, not realities. The Preface, after describing the hill-side burial of Ophelia, with the stars "beginning to shine faintly" on the mourners, proceeds:

. . . The second scene of this act, in which Osric appears, is supposed to take place out of doors, in the garden of the Castle. It is singular that neither Capel, Rowe, nor Theobald, when they placed the scene in "A Hall of the Palace," should have remarked on the inappropriateness of Hamlet's request to Osric to put his hat on.

. . . . The last scene takes place in . . "a hall" or "vestibule" of the palace. . . Through the arches at the back of the stage are seen the trees of what may be supposed to be the "orchard" in which the good King Hamlet met his death at his brother's hand. The spot is a fitting one for the execution of that vengeance so long deferred, and the contrast between the soft green foliage of early summer and the deepening gloom of the tragedy is not inconsistent. . . . .

The reader who has followed thus far will have no inadequate impression of the staging of that Hamlet of December, 1878. He derives from the various accounts an impression of intellectual grasp and poetic suggestiveness which will go far to soften the angularities of Irving's own acting of the Dane.

IRVING'S MERCHANT OF VENICE, 1879

The second Shakespearian presentation—The Merchant of Venice (1879)—was mounted with equal care and with equal unobtrusiveness. Everything was pleasing to the eye. That the production at first was inexpensive we may learn by the following extract from Austin Brereton's Life of Irving:

The first night of the Merchant of Venice at the Lyceum was Saturday, 1st November, 1879. The general effectiveness of the production was a revelation. But it was made so by intelligence and admirable acting, not, as some people seem to think . . . . by the scenery. In 1896 . . . Henry Irving had publicly stated that the total cost of the production was £1,200. Yet, in a book published two years later, we are told that the revival "was on a scale entirely unparalleled in its magnificence" . . . . a statement . . a little unfair to the productions by Charles Kean. . . . But to descant upon the revival of "The Merchant of Venice" as though the manager had spent a fortune on the scenery was the outcome of a false impression. There was really nothing in the scenery to rave about.

.   .   .   .

From time to time during the run, there were additional expenses for new scenes and costumes, but the total production account for

"The Merchant of Venice" only amounted, at the end of July, 1880, to £2,061—a wonderfully small sum for a "magnificent" Shakespearian production. The truth of the matter was that the beautiful pictures presented in the course of the play were the result of art —the scene-painters, Mr. Hawes Craven, Mr. Walter Hann, and Mr. William Telbin, working for the general purpose which was expressed by Henry Irving in the prefatory note to his acting version of the play: "In producing 'The Merchant of Venice' I have endeavoured to avoid hampering the natural action of the piece with any unnecessary embellishment; but have tried not to omit any accessory which might heighten the effects. I have availed myself of every resource at my command to present the play in a manner acceptable to our audiences."

This is conclusive. Miss Terry corroborates: "The Lyceum production of The Merchant of Venice," she says, "was not so strictly archæological as the Bancrofts' had been, but it was very gravely beautiful and effective. If less attention was paid to details of costume and scenery, the play itself was arranged and acted very attractively and always went with a swing." That the world was satisfied, and hopeful for the future, may be inferred from the statement in the Athenæum of November 8, 1879, to the effect that "as a sample of the manner in which Shakespeare is hereafter to be mounted, it is of the highest interest. . . . . It lends itself to the kind of additions now made, and the revels in the Venetian streets and the pictures of a gay and frolic life are altogether in keeping."

Mr. Brereton tells us that new scenery was supplied occasionally during the first run of the piece; in the years that followed, during which the play was constantly in repertoire, the production was undoubtedly renewed from time to time. But that it ever became a mere spectacle all who saw it—and I am sorry for those who did not—will emphatically deny. Irving always employed the best scenic artists of his time—Hawes Craven, Telbin, J. Harker—and their work for any play was in the highest degree beautiful. Their landscapes were extraordinarily natural and illusive, and their buildings, mediæval, renaissance or modern, were apparently of solid brick or stone or marble. I have never seen anything approaching them in verisimilitude. And yet nothing was overcrowded; the actors—unlike Daly's at times—always had ample moving-space. Of the setting of The Merchant of Venice I retain memories of a real Venice, with real palaces, real canals and real gondolas—above all, real Venetian crowds. But above all, I remember the Shylock of Irving and the Portia of Ellen Terry.

Irving of course carried on the Kean tradition of practicable bridges built over the canals, and in the third act he gained wonderful effect by this. Shylock's house was near one of these bridges, and the elopement of Jessica during the carnival celebration was accompanied by the greatest possible animation of masked crowds arriving in gondolas, running across the bridge, etc. But, after it was all ended, the return of Shylock over the bridge, across the silent stage, and his knock at the door of the deserted home! "For absolute pathos, achieved by absolute simplicity of means, I never saw anything in the theatre to compare with it," says Ellen Terry. The arrangement of the trial scene was very imposing. The magnificoes, seated to the auditor's right in scarlet and ermine robes of state, the excited crowds, the gorgeous scarlet-clad Portia contrasting with the dull-hued Oriental appearance of Shylock, stamped an indelible impression. Irving made a point in this scene by introducing among the spectators a crowd of Jews, who took the greatest interest in the fate of Shylock, laughing at his mordant jests, hanging on the words of Portia, and despairing over the final decision of the court. No one, finally, will ever forget the moonlit loveliness of the gardens at Belmont, with Portia's return to love and happiness. In this scene soft hidden music lapped the senses in delight.

VISIT OF THE SAXE-MEININGEN COMPANY, 1881

In what I have said here of the early production undoubtedly effects of later years have crept in; but I end by repeating that originally Irving's great Merchant of Venice was not an elaborate spectacle. Nor was his brief revival of Othello on May 2, 1881, with Edwin Booth as guest-star. Of this I say nothing. Meantime, just as Booth was ending his engagement, occurred that memorable visit of the Saxe-Meiningen company, so productive of result for Shakespeare on the London stage. Was Irving's later method influenced by this visit? It would seem certain that it was, in view of the fact that his next revival was that very Romeo and Juliet which Miss Terry characterises as his first great production.

The chief asset of the Meininger was their management of stage crowds. They opened at Drury Lane on May 30, 1881, in their *cheval-de-bataille*—Julius Cæsar—which, of course, offered them unlimited opportunity for this specialty. According to the Telegraph of the following day, the mob-scene was "the most startling effect ever seen—those forests of hands and arms, those staccato shouts, that brilliancy of emphasis, the whirl and rout and maddened frenzy of an excited mob." Yet admiration was not unmixed. The Times of the same date thinks that the crowd was too excited before the entrance of Cæsar in Act I, though the scene of Antony's oration was magnificently handled. "There is," it admits, "a total absence of that lumping of masses, that rigidity of form and feature which chills the spectator at ordinary performances. The German actors, if anything, fail by an excess of pantomimic gesture. Even a southern crowd is not always in the fever of excitement presented, for example, at and before the first entrance of Cæsar. The speech of Antony before the corpse of Cæsar was, on the other hand, a masterpiece of scenic arrangement, such as has seldom been witnessed on the stage. The gradual change in the feeling of the crowd, the lessening approval at the mention of the name of Brutus and the other honourable men, the final outburst of popular fury—all this was indicated with a delicacy of gradation which fully warranted the enthusiasm elicited."

The Athenæum of June 4th also thinks "the violence of the outbreak seemed . . . . out of keeping with the quasi-

symmetrical arrangement of the tableaux." Yet even this
exacting critic (Joseph Knight?) admits the splendid effect
of the mob-management in the trial scene of The Winter's
Tale, produced on June 13th. Says the Athenæum of five
days later, "an effect even finer than in 'Julius Cæsar,'
which still furnishes a subject of conversation, is obtained,
and the influence upon the spectator of the excited mob,
greeting with tears, cries, and acclamations the acquittal
of the Queen by the verdict of Apollo, is absolutely thrilling.
It is difficult to resist the impression that gay colour, especially red, is too lavishly employed in the decoration."

I have allowed of design the quotation to shade up to
the red of the costumes, because, in that day of exquisite
fabrics and colour-designs of the school of William Morris,
the crudity of colouring in the dresses of these German
visitors hurt sensitive eyes. Of Twelfth Night, also, produced on May 31st, the Times considers the dresses crude
in colour. But aside from this, archæological correctness
was to be highly extolled. Of Julius Cæsar, the Times of
May 31st asserts that "the costumes are evidently designed
by artists of the first class. . . . Fasces, signa, and vexilla
are the exact copies of antique originals." The Morning
Post also believes that "all that money can procure—costumes, decoration, historical preciseness, &c. is at hand."
Yet the Athenæum of June 4th asserts roundly that in
such respects as costume and scenic effect, "the superiority
of which we have heard is over the English stage of yester-
day, not that of today. No one would dream of saying
that the dresses . . . . . are handsomer than those to
which we are accustomed at the Lyceum."

Nevertheless, the Athenæum admits that "no spectacular
play of Shakespeare . . . has ever been put upon our stage
in a manner equally effective" with that of Julius Cæsar.
Of Twelfth Night "what remains most noteworthy is the
harmony of the whole. . . The *ensemble* is superb." No
one will ever forget the Malvolio of Phelps or the Viola of
Adelaide Neilson, *but*—"the *ensemble* is superb." This, of
course, was the lesson inculcated by the Meininger, and this

lesson Irving and his English contemporaries learned. 1 had not the opportunity to attend performances by this company, but I can assert that what has come down in talk is chiefly their handling of stage-crowds. This is all I ever heard of them until I began searching the archives. Silence on other matters implies, I think, a negligibility of accomplishment therein; I am strengthened in this conviction by the assertion of the Athenæum of June 18th that in The Winter's Tale, aside from the work of Fräulein Haverland (Hermione) and Fräulein Werner (Chorus), nothing in the performance rose above the dead level of a uniform and rather aggressive excellence." Verily, as a theatrical aristocrat, I prefer one Phelps or one Adelaide Neilson to many stage-mobs. Even the Meininger brought Ludwig Barnay as "guest."

IRVING'S ROMEO AND JULIET, 1882

The Meininger left London in 1881. Whatever the effect of their visit on Irving, it is certain that his first typically Irvingesque production came on March 8, 1882. Of the scenic details of this, one would require no better description than that in the yearly publication, Dramatic Notes, started by Pascoe, and in 1882 continued by Austin Brereton, who graphically writes:

Mr. Irving's arrangement of the scenes may best be noted by rapidly running over the order in which they appear. After the appearance of Chorus, attired after Dante, the tableau curtains divide and show the market place of Verona, a splendid stage picture. Here we have a quarrel between the rival factions of the Montagues and Capulets, which is an admirable instance of stage grouping, and Romeo enters by the sloping bridge at the back. We are then shown the loggia of Capulet's house, in which Juliet and Lady Capulet and the Nurse appear. The painting representing the exterior of the Capulets' mansion serves for the delivery of the Queen Mab speech of Mercutio, and the passage within of Romeo and his companions. The hall in Capulet's house—one of the richest and most brilliant scenes that has been witnessed, even at the Lyceum—introduces the ball, at which Romeo first meets Juliet and here, too, we notice the

presence of Rosaline. The commencement of the second act is laid
before a wall adjoining Capulet's garden, from which we pass to the
balcony scene. The balcony is solidly built up with marble pillars,
shaded in front by quivering foliage. The next scene of importance
is the garden where Juliet receives Romeo's message from the Nurse,
and the interior of the Cloisters, with the lovers kneeling to receive
the Friar's blessing, terminates this act. A ruined street—one of
the best scenes in the play, artistically considered—is where the
fight betwen Romeo and Tybalt is brought about; and the secret
place in the monastery may be instanced. as a very artistic scene.
Juliet's chamber, where the lovers part, at the end of this act, is,
perhaps, too gorgeous in its colouring. This room also serves for
the delivery of the potion scene; and here Juliet is discovered apparently dead. One might have thought that scenic art could go no
further, but the street in Mantua, in the fifth act, revealed a picture
of great beauty; and the tomb scene, with its entrance down several
flights of steps, leading from the roof, was a marvel of scenic success,
and the tableau at the conclusion of the play brought to a close one
of the grandest spectacular representations of a Shakespearian play
that has ever been presented.

What more does one desire? Miss Terry adds a few
recollections of Irving: "His whole attitude before he met
Juliet was beautiful. He came on from the very back of
the stage, and walked over a little bridge with a book in
his hand, sighing and dying for Rosaline. . . . His clothes
were as Florentine as his bearing. He ignored the silly
tradition that Romeo must wear a feather in his cap. . . .
And he wore in his hat a sprig of crimson oleander." . . .
He "chose with great care a tall dark girl to represent
Rosaline at the ball. Can I ever forget his face when suddenly in pursuit of *her* he caught sight of *me ?*

. . . .

"Again in this play he used his favorite 'fate' tree. It
gloomed over the street along which Romeo went to the
ball. It was in the scene with the Apothecary. Henry
thought that it symbolized the destiny hanging over the
lovers."

This strikes me as a poetic touch, and warrants Miss
Terry's statement that "according to his imagination"—
however physically incapable—"Henry Irving was Romeo."

Another admirable stage effect Miss Terry describes at length. "It is usual," she says, "for Romeo to go in to the dead body of Juliet lying in Capulet's monument through a gate on the *level*, as if the Capulets were buried but a few feet from the road. At rehearsals Henry Irving kept on saying: 'I must go *down* to the vault.' After a great deal of consideration he had an inspiration. He had the exterior of the vault in one scene, the entrance to it down a flight of steps. Then the scene changed to the interior of the vault, and the steps now led from a height above the stage. At the close of the scene, when the Friar and the crowd came rushing down into the tomb, these steps were thronged with people, each one holding a torch, and the effect was magnificent."

IRVING'S MUCH ADO ABOUT NOTHING, 1882

Sumptuous as was Irving's Romeo and Juliet, his next attempt surpassed it. Of this, one of the loveliest memories of my play-going career, I shall speak not in words founded on my own recollections, keen as they are, but in the extraordinarily specific accounts of two authoritative critics of the time. Their very specificness must be my excuse. This revival—Much Ado about Nothing—was bathed in sunlight and youth and beauty. I quote lavishly from George Augustus Sala in the Illustrated London News of October 28, 1882:

Such rare intelligence and such scenic splendour have not hitherto been seen since the days of the noblest of Charles Kean's Shaksperean revivals at the Princess's. And, undeniably superb as those revivals were, both in their acting and in the strict archæological accuracy with which they were presented, they have been surpassed, so far as *mise-en-scène* and costume are concerned, by those Lyceum revivals of which "Much Ado about Nothing" is undeniably the finest. Mr. Hawes Craven, Mr. W. Cuthbert, and Mr. William Telbin are not more highly endowed scene-painters than Mr. F. Lloyds and Mr. Gordon, the leading painters of the Kean managements; but modern scenic artists have at their command facilities of which their predecessors five-and-twenty years ago were destitute. They are able to model as well as to paint their scenes, to introduce really cylindrical columns and really plastic bas-reliefs, and in rural tableaux to simulate trees and plants, the leaves of which are corporeally agitated by the air. Draperies, again, are much more freely used on the modern stage . . . and manufacturers are ready to supply the theatre with a vast number of new fabrics of practically novel colours; and the designs of these fabrics, offering as they do, evidence of the study now of Japanese and now of mediæval art, have effected a complete revolution in the embellishment of a play, and have vastly enhanced the prevalence of harmony and symmetry in form and hue. The same may be said of the dresses. The costumiers have new models to work from, new materials to confect, new ornamentation to apply; and from such a theatre as the Lyceum the old barbarous style of bedizening the subordinate characters—the plastering of girdles with zinc "logies," the coarse tinselling of breastplates and shields, the smearing with yellow ochre of the gauntlets and russet boots of the "supers," and the substitution of glazed calico for real satin in "back grooves" court dresses have been wholly banished. All is handsome, appropriate and honest. Again, that department known in French theatres as that of "accessoires," and in England as "properties," has been thoroughly reformed under the auspices of Mr. Irving. . . . It was William Charles Macready, at Drury Lane . . . . who was the first to introduce really artistic "properties"; but coarse, slovenly, clumsy, and often grotesque accessories yet disgrace many of our theatres; and it is only at the Lyceum and at the Haymarket that we never see the minor details, be they weapons or toys, goblets or lanterns, or chairs or stools, or table-furniture, failing to harmonise completely in comeliness in design and tastefulness of execution with the scenery and the dresses. Finally, modern science has amazingly increased the means of lighting both the auditorium and the stage. It is expedient to mention these matters of detail, because . . . . they materially conduce to such a triumphant success as that which has been achieved at the Lyceum by "Much Ado about Nothing." It would be churlish . . . to withhold well-deserved praise on such stage-management as Mr. H. J. Loveday has brought to bear on the service of his Chief.

The reader will agree that this article is specific; but its specificness is in a way general, so to speak. There can be no doubt, however, of the definiteness of the account of the revival found in Brereton's Dramatic Notes for October, 1882. Every detail of the performance lives in his glowing words. As I read I again recall the captivating Beatrice in her flowing soft-tinted Italian robes, the courtiers, slim and silken-clad, the rush of masked dancers across the hall in Leonato's house, the Italian gardens, the magnificent church scene, the air of romance enveloping all. When shall we behold its like again? But no such melancholy thought came to Brereton as he drew that series of superb pictures for his Dramatic Notes:

Much Ado about Nothing was revived at the Lyceum on the 11th with all that splendour and magnificence which are to be seen only at Mr. Irving's theatre. It is, both in respect to acting and scenery, the most perfect representation of a Shakespearean play that the stage has seen. It is a feast for the eye and the mind. . . . . Let me try and convey some slight idea of the arrangement of the scenes. The scenery used in this revival has been marvellously well done. . . . Some of the solidly built-up scenes are unexampled in their splendour. The opening act displays the exterior of Leonato's house. The building is erected at the left-hand side of the stage, and is a classic structure, supported by columns and steps of yellow marble. In the distance is the blue sea and sky, and at the right a wealth of foliage. The house is situated on an eminence close to the harbour, and behind this building, up an incline, Don Pedro and his followers presently approach, amidst a clamour of greetings and a waving of silken banners. . . . And here, when the guests are almost all retired within, we see Borachio sneaking behind a pillar and overhearing the dialogue between Don Pedro and Claudio relative to Hero. This dramatic incident closes the first act, and the next scene presents Don John and his determination to use Borachio's information to wreak his displeasure upon Claudio. The second scene of this act is another fine example of artistic and skilful arrangement. It is the ball-room in Leonato's house, and is a brilliant scene stretching across the entire breadth of the stage. It is decorated in crimson and gold, relieved by soft tapestry hangings, and the dazzling glare of the light is softened by the appearance of rose trees placed in odd corners of the room. . . . . The plot against Claudio is again pursued in the third act, and we then come to the garden scene. Here in the glow of the setting sun Benedick is drawn into the love-trap, and after the tableau curtains have descended for a moment, the same scene is presented under the morning light, and Beatrice is led into the belief that Benedick is in love with her. The dramatic tension is again touched in another scene, the cedar walk, where Don John slanders Hero to Don Pedro and Claudio. The fifth and last scene of this act represents a street by the harbour, where Conrade and Borachio are arrested for their perfidy. The fourth act is played in one scene, the church, which is one of the grandest stage-pictures that has ever been presented. The altar stands at the left hand side of the stage, and the beautifully ornamented roof is supported by massive pillars. These accessories, the massive pillars, the figured iron gates, the decorated roof, the pictures, the stained glass, the elaborate and costly altar, the carved oak benches, the burning lights, and the perfume of incense, all combine to render this a scene of such richness and grandeur as at first to arrest all thought of the play and to delight only the eye with the beautiful sight. . . . . In the last act there is nothing particularly noticeable in the way of new scenery, but due attention should be paid to the restoration of the scene in Leonato's monument, where Claudio comes to mourn for the supposed loss of Hero, and where the hymn, "Pardon, goddess of the night," is sung to the music of the Rev. Canon Dunscombe.

A word of praise should be given to the scenic artists of the Lyceum. Mr. W. Cuthbert is responsible for the scenes representing the ball-room and the prison. Mr. William Telbin has done the church and monument scenes, and Mr. Craven has painted the remaining pictures. The magnificent costumes are from designs by Mr. Alfred Thompson, and the overture and incidental music have been chiefly composed by Mr. J. Meredith Ball, the experienced musical conductor of the Lyceum. The stage management, under the direction of Mr. H. J. Loveday, is simply perfect.

IRVING'S TWELFTH NIGHT, 1884

This, as I say, seems to me to have been the moment of Irving's happiest success; its run was interrupted by his first winter in America, and resumed on his return to the Lyceum. It is obvious that his next Shakespearian revival, Twelfth Night, was not the result of such care. Brought out at the end of the summer season of 1884, it had but a brief life, and died forever out of the repertoire. Even Ellen Terry confesses "it was one of the least successful of Henry's Shakespearean productions"; it was "dull, lumpy, and heavy." Sala, in my faithful *vade-mecum*, the Illustrated London News, of July 19th, points out the scenic beauties of the show, but concludes with the damaging statement that it was "not so brilliant nor so imposing" as its predecessors. His account of the scenery will speak for itself; I include it for completeness of record:

Mr. Irving has chosen the Venetian period as best suited for the illustration of "Twelfth Night," and although there is a slight suggestion of Orientalism in the garb of the minstrels . . . and there is an element of Sclavonic wildness and uncouthness in the array of the guards who make their appearance in the last scene, the costumes and the architecture belong essentially to the period of the Venetian domination; that is to say, sumptuous garments in which Mr. Irving has clad his company are such of which the analogues might have been found in England when the Court of Elizabeth had reached its apogee of splendour. Orsino's palace and Viola's [sic] scarcely less palatial villa are sumptuously Palladian in style; while the art of landscape gardening, as pursued in Illyria three hundred years ago, appears to have reached a very high pitch of excellence. The sea-coast scenes, the court-yard of Olivia's house, the terrace, Olivia's garden, are painted by Mr. Hawes Craven; Orsino's palace, the road near Olivia's house, and the cloisters thereof are from the pencil of Mr. W. Telbin; while Mr. W. Hann has painted the orchard scene; Mr. T. W. Hall the last scene before Olivia's house; and Mr. J. Selby Hall the scene including the dungeon in which Malvolio is immured. As a succession of beautiful pictures, the *mise-en-scène* of "Twelfth Night" is equal to any of the far-famed Lyceum revivals; but as a spectacle it is certainly not so brilliant nor so imposing as "Romeo and Juliet," "Much Ado about Nothing" or the "Cup." As regards stage-management, one of Mr. Irving's highest claims to commendation must be that he has not overloaded a merry comedy . . . with superfluous ornament.

WILSON BARRETT'S HAMLET, 1884

And this was the last Irving was to do for Shakespeare for over three years. Wilson Barrett's Hamlet comes next; by its departure from accepted standards of interpretation and mounting, it has received more attention than its dramatic value merited; my own chronicle must bow to the imputation of lengthy discussion of it from various angles. As regards scenery, however, I may be brief; the story is told to no inconsiderable extent by the group of pictures of scenes in the play from the Illustrated London News of November 1, 1884. They show what critics of the time complained of, a super-sensitive attempt to dress the play in habits of a supposably early Danish pattern. Anything for novelty! Dramatic Notes, for October, 1884, is rather severe in its comment:

We have no doubt, that Mr. Godwin's archæology of the costumes and furniture is strictly correct, but picturesque effect has been sacrificed. . . . Some of the costumes are positively ugly. . . . Nothing could be worse than the dresses assigned to Laertes and, in the last act, to Horatio. Most of the scenery has been provided by Mr. Walter Hann, but Mr. Beverley is seen at his best in an admirable bit of painting which forms the first scene of the third act.

The Illustrated London News of October 25th goes further and asserts that

with the exception of Hamlet and Polonius, I have seldom looked upon such a set of guys as those whom historical accuracy has placed upon the stage of the Princess's.

So much for making the archæological conscience arbiter in the court of beauty! A peculiarity of the production consisted in representing the mock-play out of doors in the late afternoon; what would a Hamlet be unless he wore his rueful scenery with a difference? Finally, Barrett's Hamlet always carried on a chain about his neck a miniature of his father; on this he bade his mother look while for contrast he picked up from her table a framed picture of her present lord. This and other matter may be gleaned from the London Graphic of October 25, 1884.

I saw this much-discussed performance of Hamlet in later years in America. All the original scenery had been brought from London, and the cast in most cases was the same. And the sad fact remains that I cannot remember anything about the performance, except the queernesses! Shut my eyes, and concentrate as I may, I cannot recall a glimpse of Barrett, how he looked, or dressed, or spoke—except the "kin" and "kind" line, and that sort of thing. During the same season I saw Booth and Modjeska together as Hamlet and Ophelia, and without the slightest effort on my part, perfectly accurate photographic impressions of them arise in my consciousness. What is the cause of this? Probably it is a question of art. Great acting needs no help of eccentric novelty, and I, for one, am always suspicious of artists who are constantly "fussing" to be different. At any rate, this Hamlet was Wilson Barrett's sole incursion of importance into the Shakespearian field. Years afterwards, he attempted Othello.

MARY ANDERSON'S ROMEO AND JULIET, 1884

Whatever may be said against Mary Anderson's artistic quality, she was moulded in the grand style. Person, voice, gesture, gait—all these united to produce an effect of a glorious womanhood of classic beauty. She was self-conscious and at times declamatory; but her faults were faults of exuberance. One never had to complain of her performances that they were too quiet or too "naturalistic." And how melodiously she read the verse! If I have forgotten Wilson Barrett's Hamlet, I shall never forget Mary Anderson's Juliet, nor the superb setting in which it was placed at the Lyceum and afterwards in America. The best scenes were painted by Hawes Craven and others of Irving's artists; the entire production was designed by Lewis Wingfield. Consequently it had all the beautiful characteristics of an Irving revival in seemingly solid masonry, lovely gardens, exquisite dressing, fine music, etc. That this was the general impression the reader may gather from contemporary accounts. In fact some critics were again beginning to fear that too much stress was laid on scenery and too little on the drama and the acting. This is the note of Clement Scott's ill-natured review, as quoted in Dramatic Notes of November, 1884:

> We are gradually overdoing spectacle so much that poetry must suffer in the long run. The question is no longer how this or that character in Shakespeare ought to be played, but how much money can be spent on this or that scene. The stage decorator, the costumier, and the carpenter are in the ascendant. Silks and satins, stuffs and tapestry, the shape of a shoe, the cut of a gown, the form of a lamp, the topography of a street are preferred to the interpretation of any one given part. . . . Acting is more and more made subordinate to mere scenic success . . . That the play is superbly mounted no one can doubt. . . . Stage machinery has become a miracle. Houses change into gardens, palaces are whirled into prisons, cloisters are transformed into tombs. It is a lovely panorama, and little else.

The testimony as to the sliding transition of scenery is more specifically supported by the Times of November 3,

1884. "The setting," it declares, "is a thing of beauty for the eye . . . and some wonderful feats are accomplished with revolving scenes. The friar's cell and Juliet's chamber are alternately turned inside out, in full view of the house. Whole sets are also dragged bodily across the stage." To-day we should darken the stage while these "feats" were performed. The London Graphic of November 8th gives the best account of the beauties of the production:

If the patience of profound archæological learning has broken down —if promises of original pictures of houses in Old Verona, all certified to be of no older date than the year 1300, together with costumes &c., warranted to be appropriate, because copied from Carpaccio's famous pictures of the legend of St. Ursula—a work belonging to the fifteenth century, have proved, as was inevitable, to be little more than idle words, there is still room to admire the beauty of the pictures which Messrs. Hawes Craven, O'Connor, Hall, Bruce Smith, and Perkins have prepared for this occasion. Nor should Mr. Lewis Wingfield be denied his meed of praise for the picturesque qualities of the dresses and other archaic details. After all, the search for correct costumes in relation to a Shakespearian legendary play is very much like the search for the absolute, or the true and infallible mode of squaring the circle. . . . Mr. Wingfield is not to be blamed for looking more to the picture than to the consistency of his dresses.

Comparing this revival with Irving's, the critic proceeds:

Some of the scenes of the earlier revival—the ball room and the churchyard—were certainly more effective than those of the present revival, which otherwise may compare favourably with anything that has been achieved . . . in recent years. The Garden Scene in particular, with its terrace upon terrace descending by flights of stone steps far away into the moonlit haze, is as beautiful and poetical, as the same scene in the Irving revival, overcrowded as it was with horticultural and arboricultural displays, was commonplace and pretentious.

THE KENDALS' AS YOU LIKE IT, 1885

While Irving was in America, and while Wilson Barrett and Mary Anderson were enjoying the triumphs won as aforesaid, the St. James's revival of As You Like It was revealed—on January 24, 1885. All that the performance lacked was poetry, but scenically it averaged up to the finest things of the decade. The now popular fetich of historical accuracy was god of the machine, but aside from some hideous concessions to the idol, the production merits a scenical descant altogether out of proportion to its dramatic achievement. Austin Brereton's Dramatic Notes for January, 1885, is none too kindly toward the effort; evidently accuracy can be overdone:

Mr. Lewis Wingfield, who was responsible for the adornment of the play, laid the action in the time of Charles VII of France, and dressed it accordingly. His guards were doubtless attired with perfect accuracy; and I do not dispute the statement that Celia "might have walked out of one of Froissart's illuminated pages." But the appearance of the guards was certainly grotesque, and Celia's headdress was exceedingly trying to the actress. However, these blemishes belong to the first act only. Thereafter the costumes were rich in material and exquisite in design, although, Mr. Wingfield's opinion notwithstanding, the spirit of the comedy was not sustained by the abolition of the customary suits of Lincoln-green. When Orlando saw the courtly and gaily-caparisoned foresters, he would not have delivered himself so roughly. . . . The same light touch belonging to the scenery and costumes was attached to the new vocal and instrumental music specially composed by Mr. Alfred Cellier. It is no disparagement . . . to say that his music did not evince the Shakespearean spirit, or assist the words. It was far too light, and suggestive of comic opera, and not to be compared for a moment to the compositions for the same play by Dr. Arne.

The Athenæum of January 31st is far more genial, and rather makes one envious of the privilege of having seen the pretty effects. According to this article, stage grass must have sprouted for the first time in this production. Says the Athenæum:

The surroundings at the St. James's Theatre are all gain. A picture of mediæval life such as is supplied in the first act, which passes in a terraced garden in front of a gate of what is . . . the Château d'Amboise is in itself pleasant to contemplate; and the glade in which the dwellers in Arden take their meals, with the brook rippling among the sedges, and making "sweet music with the enamelled stones," to lose itself among leaves and herbage, renders easier the task of the imagination and enhances the pleasure of the spectator. Mr. Wingfield's task has, indeed, been admirably accomplished. He has for the first time put on the stage what looks like grass, and he has presented a series of pretty tableaux.

MARY ANDERSON'S WINTER'S TALE, 1887

For her beautiful revival of The Winter's Tale at the Lyceum, in September, 1887, Miss Anderson engaged the best of Irving's scenic artists—Hawes Craven, Telbin, Hann. Some of the scenes were of extraordinary charm. The first one—the Palace of King Leontes—by Telbin, was a superb Grecian pillared hall, open the entire back width of the stage; through noble columns, rear, could be seen the garden of the palace, terminated by a view of azure seas and distant hills. The stage was divided midway, for its entire width, by three steps that led to a higher level on which were the columns just mentioned. This upper space or terrace was delimited toward the sea by marble benches, much used in the action. It was a sumptuous setting, assisted by velvet draperies at both sides of the room. The scene of the trial was a severely simple Grecian hall, of solid masonry, with a door, and pilasters, for half the back set; as to the other, through pillars, one looked out into an open court or peristyle. On the auditor's left, on a high elevation, were Leontes and the judges. Hermione sat on a stone bench, which was partly covered by a tiger's skin. The next great effect of the play was in the rustic festival, a built-up scene with flowery banks and shady trees; down the incline dashed the dancers, led by Miss Anderson as Perdita, for that captivating dance which lives still in the memory of all who saw it. For the statue scene Miss Anderson arranged a high flight of marble steps, at the top of which the statue was placed. As red velvet curtains were drawn, displaying the image, one had an impression of almost illimitable space, white marble steps leading up and up and up, the vista terminated by the statue. And what a statue! Mary Anderson in the prime of her classic beauty, posed as only she could pose! As she slowly came down those steps, she presented a picture given to any generation to behold hardly more than once.

Miss Anderson's synopsis of scenery calls for thirteen sets; some of these were repetitions, but she, like Irving, expedited matters by the not infrequent use of "drops." Irving was a great believer in this device; personally, I never receive from them much sense of illusion, especially if the subject be a landscape. Miss Anderson, then, employed this expedient; hence her rapid shifts of scenery. None of her productions, or Irving's, could have changed scenes so often without some such method of alternating "drops" and "set-scenes." Perhaps it was inevitable for that kind of Shakespearian performance. I will close the discussion of The Winter's Tale by quoting from the Illustrated London News of September 17, 1887, in regard to the wonderful pictorial effects created by Miss Anderson in her management of draperies during the trial scene of Hermione:

At the close of Hermione's trial, when the oracle has spoken, when the crash of the thunderstorm has broken over the false judgment-seat, when the lightning has played about the affrighted spectators, and when the news has been whispered round that the son of Leontes and Hermione is dead . . . Miss Anderson gives us an instance of her power in dumb acting infinitely finer than anything she has ever attempted before. In dignity it is incomparable, in terror it is grand. . . . She is not one picture, but at least a dozen. The tableaux change with incomparable variety, and each one is better than the last. We can recall three. One where Hermione crouches during the thunderstorm at the altar; one where, with veil averted and with terror-stricken countenance, the mother learns of her boy's death; the last where, with true Grecian and tragic grandeur, the outcast and desolate woman covers her face and falls a mass of wrecked humanity on the floor of the judgment hall. . . . Rachel and Ristori could have done nothing more picturesque and admirable than this.

DALY'S TAMING OF THE SHREW, 1888

The last pictorial delight to be recorded before Macbeth —the fatal line of demarcation—is Daly's Taming of the

TWO SCENES FROM THE TAMING OF THE SHREW
From photographs

Shrew (May, 1888). This production was transported
bodily from its home in New York. Only two of the scenes
call for special comment. The first—the interior of Bap-
tista's house—was a very handsome room, with a superb
old rug covering most of the floor, and with a set of massive, heavily carved gold furniture, said to have been
brought from an old Italian palace. The second was the
last great scene—the banquet wherein all warring elements
were appeased; this set was one of the finest I have ever
seen, and assuredly justified the managerial boast that it
suggested a great picture by Paul Veronese. The costumes
and the grouping were beautiful, as may be judged from
the pictorial reproduction. Miss St. Quentin and a choir
of boys very sweetly sang "Should he upbraid." Daly
never did anything to equal this supreme achievement.
The rest of the scenes were not important, but the costumes
were pleasing, and Miss Rehan's sumptuous. No one will
forget the gorgeous mahogany-red brocade and the fiery
wig in which she made her first tiger-like entry. "Magnificent" is the only word to describe her appearance and
her action.

IRVING'S MACBETH

Whatever the estimate of Irving's acting in Macbeth,
it is impossible to deny the impressiveness of the scenic
equipment of the play. It anticipated modern methods by
casting the stage in an almost impenetrable gloom, out of
which arose vast walls of storm-beaten castles or bare
northern mountains, and through which one peered into
murky interiors of solid masonry lighted only by the flare
of torches. By retaining some of the songs of the witches,
Irving was enabled to show what he could do in the management of supernatural effects. The first appearance of
the demoniac beings flying through the air was startling,
but the chief spectacle was that of the great host of singing
witches holding revel by misty moonlight "over woods,
high rocks, and mountains." No one else ever managed
ghostly appearances as did Henry Irving; and this hell-

brood in the non-Shakespearian episode referred to seemed literally to thicken the air as they dimly appeared and disappeared in that weird light of which Irving alone seemed to be master. Those who saw the ghosts that vanished in the prison-scene of Irving's Robespierre will know what I mean.

I wish to stress the fact that the witches were played by women, and that Banquo's ghost was visibly represented, though the dimming of the lights at every appearance must have seemed odd to the normal guests at the banquet. Probably the audience was to conceive that they were lowered only to the conscience of Macbeth. In this, the most perfect of his stagings of Shakespeare, it is interesting to note Irving reiterating the artistic creed formulated at the time of his production of Hamlet (1878). In the advertisement of Macbeth published in the Times on the day of the first performance, Irving says, "With regard to scenery I have endeavoured to adhere to the principle which has always guided me, namely, that to meet the requirements of the stage, without sacrificing the purpose or the poetry of the author, should be the aim of those who produce the plays of Shakespeare; and I trust that any change which I have ventured to introduce on this occasion in the ordinary scenic arrangements has been made in the spirit of true reverence for the works of our greatest dramatist. All such changes have been suggested either by the text of the play itself or by the descriptions of the chroniclers from whom we know that Shakespeare derived most of his incidents. As to the period chosen for the costumes, we read that Macbeth was slain by Macduff on December 5th, 1056; I have, therefore, taken the 11th century as the historical period of the play."

Looking back, I believe that Irving spoke no less than the truth in these statements as to his motives; Shakespeare was first with him, and all the adornment served only to the proper interpretation of the plays. In this particular revival, the scenes, involving seventeen tableaux, were painted, as usual, by Hawes Craven, Harker, Walter Hann, and others. Sir Arthur Sullivan composed act-preludes and incidental music for the production.

I shall not dwell upon the scenery of a few productions spoken of previously, that were shown between the run of Macbeth, and that of Irving's next Shakespearian offering, the Henry VIII of 1892. Of Richard Mansfield's Richard III exhibited at the Globe in March, 1889, I remember utter appropriateness, even impressiveness of staging, but the production was ephemeral and it made no mark. Of another American offering, Daly's As You Like It, the Athenæum of July 19, 1890, was correct in saying that "as far as regards . . . the *mise-en-scène* the performance is not to be told from an average English representation." Galling as this may be to American pride, my memory assures me that it is correct. There was nothing remarkable about Daly's surroundings for Ada Rehan's sprightly Rosalind. The second scene comes back to me as I read the description in the acting-version, and it revives pleasing memories: "The Terrace and Court-yeard before the Duke's Palace; an arched gateway at the L.; steps leading to the terrace at R. U. E.; an old tree and seat at R. As the scene opens, distant shouts and murmurs are heard through music of a distant march, off R. U. E." For the fight, the Duke and a group of lords and ladies went up on the terrace, and from this, also, Rosalind watched the departure of Orlando, coming forward, later to sink on the seat aforesaid. As for the forest scenes they made no impression on me; I remember that all of Shakespeare's songs were sung, and sung well, but somehow the scenery was palpable scenery and not a wood; unlike that of the Kendal woodland, it was not real grass that we saw.

I will anticipate by referring briefly to the last Shakespearian efforts of Augustin Daly on the London stage. Twelfth Night (1894) was really a great success, and the scenery was cited favourably in contemporary notices. As given at Daly's in New York I did not admire the production; it seemed overweighted with business, with music, with heavy velvet dresses. Miss Rehan's page dress of heavy crimson damask velvet seemed to me to smother the pensive, poetic, humorous Viola; her later green dress— to match Sebastian's—was rich with the same oppressive heaviness. There were too many courtiers, and they likewise sagged under a pall of velvet richness. The first set, of the sea-coast after the storm, was attractive, but too many happy villagers dashed by, warbling "Come unto these yellow sands." And there was too much song in Olivia's kitchen and in her garden. Moonlight was brought into play as never before in this comedy; Viola dreamed on a bench as Orsino's minstrels warbled Shubert's "Who is Olivia (Sylvia)?" By aid of this moonlight, however, Daly explained Olivia's mistake of Sebastian for Viola—a reasonable device employed by the Meininger in 1881. Ada Rehan's Viola and James Lewis's Sir Toby availed, more than all mechanical adjuncts, to set the piece forward on its long London career.

A Midsummer Night's Dream (a huge success in New York in 1888) and The Two Gentlemen of Verona failed in the last summer (1895) of Daly at his theatre in London. The fairy play was beautifully done in New York; The Two Gentlemen of Verona less well. They caused hardly a ripple on the London season of 1895. The vogue of Daly's had passed.

Beerbohm Tree began as a great producer only after he assumed control of Her Majesty's in 1897; I therefore pass over without comment his revivals of The Merry Wives of Windsor (1889), Hamlet (1892), and the first part of Henry IV (1896). Adequate, but not great, they paled their ineffectual fires before his Julius Cæsar of 1898 and the successive revivals in years to come.

Oddly enough, Mr. F. R. Benson, in recent years rather pluming himself on mere adequacy, the humble handmaid of dramatic representation, first burst on the London world in December, 1889, with a very elaborate production of the difficult Midsummer Night's Dream. This surprising fact, with the impressions of the critic, may be gathered from Dramatic Notes for the same month. "For beauty of scenery," says the article, "correctness in costume, and general perfection in stage-mounting it would be difficult to surpass the production. . . The arrangements for spectacular display in both the exterior and interior views of Theseus's Palace, the exquisite beauty of Titania's Bower, with its numerous elves tripping here and there, and peeping forth from all sorts of nooks and crannies, the twinkling lights of the glow-worms, and the excellent setting of 'A Wood near Athens' will long be quoted . . . Mendelssohn's music was well executed . . I ought certainly to mention most favourably the dances arranged by Mr. Ozman, and the truly artistic scene-painting by Mr. Hemsley."

Mr. Benson obviously had not yet discovered where his strength lay. A similar remark could not be applied to Mrs. Langtry in the gorgeous revival of Antony and Cleopatra (November, 1890). She knew only too well that it could not be in her acting, and therefore she lavished money on the scenery. The results were magnificent, as may be learned from Dramatic Notes for December, 1890:

It will not be for the acting . . . that the Princess's production will be specially remembered, but for the gorgeousness of its pageants. On these the expenditure must have been enormous, and the Hon. Lewis Wingfield, if he erred, did so on the score of liberality. The pictures he presented to us in the "Alexandrian Festival," and the "Triumphal Reception of Antony by Cleopatra," were magnificent and faithful reproductions of the Eastern displays of the period. Whilst retaining Shakespeare's text, and only transposing a scene or two, Mr. Wingfield gave us processions of Egyptian soldiery and Roman legions, and Egyptian dances in the form of ballet, which feasted the eye, but detracted from the attention that should have been devoted to the play, which, on the first night, occupied over four hours in representation. Such pictures as "The Exterior," and "A Hall in Cleopatra's Palace," "The Banks of the Nile," and "The Interior of an Egyptian Monument" were in the very best style of scene-painting, and, with the general accessories, attracted the public for a time, independently of the merits of the performance.

IRVING'S HENRY VIII, 1892

Undoubtedly the greatest—if not the only—Shakespearian "spectacle" that Irving ever attempted was that of Henry VIII, which, with its opportunity for gorgeous costume, pageantry and procession, had attracted every manager since Booth, Cibber and Wilks spent so much on the coronation of Anne Bullen, in 1728. Irving neglected none of these adjuncts, and the result lives in theatrical history as the greatest in its own line to the time of its appearance. Dramatic Notes, the invaluable publication on which I have already largely drawn, describes the effects far better than my memory could do, full as is my memory of the marvels of the show. Say these Notes:

Henry Irving's revival of *Henry VIII* at the Lyceum will be ranked in dramatic history as his greatest achievement. . . . As the various scenes are displayed to us, we, for the time being, live in the epoch in which they occur. For this, Mr. Irving is in a great measure indebted to Mr. Seymour Lucas, A. R. A. and Mrs. Comyns Carr, who between them designed the dresses; nor must we forget Mr. H. J. Loveday, whose untiring stage management caused everything to go off without a hitch. . . Scene I shows us the interior of the Palace at Bridewell, where Buckingham is the only one who will not doff his hat to the proud Cardinal, on his arrival with his almost kingly retinue. In Scene II we have the arrest of Buckingham; and Scene III is the Council Chamber of the Palace, where are seated bluff King Hal and Katharine, in all the pomp of state. "A Hall in York Place" (Scene V) is the representation of a superb banquet given by Wolsey. Presently some masquers request admittance, the leader of whom is none other than Henry, who is here first smitten with the charms of Anne Boleyn, whom he takes out to dance. The measure is a dainty one, and is followed by a wild dance executed by men in bizarre costume, with whirling lighted torches. The second act opens with a beautiful set, "the King's Stairs, Westminster," rich in colour from the diversity of the costume, where Buckingham . . . . passes on his way to execution. . . . Two comparatively unimportant changes take place, and then comes Scene IV, "a Hall in Blackfriars," a magnificent scene. Here are the Cardinals Wolsey and Campeius. On the left is Henry on his throne, and in the body of the hall is Queen Katharine, surrounded by her maids, and the sumptuously-robed supporters of her cause. Act III gives us the

"Queen's Apartment," where she yields to the persuasion of the Cardinals, and in this an exquisite trio is introduced. Scene II, in the "Palace at Bridewell," shows us the downfall of the great Cardinal. . . . Act IV is the sensation act so far as spectacle is concerned. The first scene gives us a genuine reproduction of old London, "A Street in Westminster," with its three-storied wooden-beamed houses, at every casement of which are citizens and their wives and daughters. Below are the prentices indulging in horse-play, beggars and street-players, the halberdiers and men-at-arms clearing the way for the attendants on Anne Boleyn going to her coronation. Preceded by a gorgeous procession, which includes every dignitary in church and state, with her bridesmaids and girls strewing flowers immediately in advance of her, seated in a gorgeous palanquin, and borne aloft on her retainers' shoulders, passes by lovely Anne Boleyn in the person of Violet Vanbrugh. The second scene in this act takes us to Kimbolton, to show us the dying moments of Katherine, and here . . . Henry Howe as Griffith delivered his eulogy on Wolsey. . . . Then, in the Queen's sleep, came the vision of the angels inviting her to a celestial banquet. The last act (the fifth) is occupied entirely by a reproduction of the Church of Grey Friars at Greenwich, an exquisite piece of work by Hawes Craven, with its ancient stained glass windows and time-worn stones. Here there is another pageant showing the christening of the baby princess . . . and here Arthur Stirling . . . as Cranmer . . . prophesies the future greatness of the Virgin Queen.

That such extravagance must be its own reward, Irving was to prove. Austin Brereton, in his Life of the actor, shows us something of the price paid the piper; yet, somehow, I believe that without these costly surroundings this particular play could never be depended on to "draw"—it is too spineless, too scattering in interest. But as to the cost, according to Mr. Brereton:

The production was, indeed, lavish. Independent of the ordinary working expenses of the theatre, it cost £11,879 1s. 10d. The revival took place on 5th January, 1892, and it lasted until 30th July, when the one hundred and seventy-second performance was given. . . The actors' salaries for this seven months' season amounted to £18,356 8s. 10d. and the wages of the supernumeraries to £2,221 4s. 10d., a total of over £20,000 on this head alone. The end hardly justified the means, for, although the house was crowded at each performance, and the receipts amounted to the enormous sum of £58,639 10s., the running expenses were several thousand pounds beyond that enormous sum. This was the first, and last, occasion upon which Irving ever went in for mere pageantry—and he found that it did not pay.

IRVING'S KING LEAR, 1892

No wonder Irving never again attempted such pomp and circumstance! Yet his loving-care for appropriate adornment of Shakespeare did not leave him. His next venture —with King Lear—came ten months after Henry VIII, and was heralded in the public prints with the usual advertising pother about chronology, archæology, and all other bugbears so dear to the scholarly mind. The only account I shall give is that selected from the London Times of November 11, 1892. To this, and to reproductions of pictures from his Souvenir of the play, I trust for imparting necessary impressions to the reader. Says the critic of the Times:

On the fall of the curtain last night at the Lyceum, Mr. Irving . . . . expressed his thanks for one of the most cordial receptions which it has been his lot to acknowledge. For there was but one opinion in the house—namely that *King Lear* had obtained a representation entitled to rank in some respects as one of the greatest and most memorable. . Not that the new *King Lear* is entitled to a place among the greatest of Mr. Irving's spectacular achievements. . . *Henry VIII* was a beautiful spectacle.

Mr. Irving . . . in a short preface to his acting edition . . . . observes:—

"As the period of King Lear, I have chosen, at the suggestion of Mr. Ford Madox Brown (who designed three scenes in the first and second acts), a time, shortly after the departure of the Romans, when the Britons would naturally inhabit the houses left vacant. ."

The new Lear consequently appears in rich, flowing robes which might have graced a Roman emperor, while his retainers attire themselves in rude, but serviceable garments of varying cut, evidently copied from the dress of Roman soldiers, and bear shields and spears of a more native origin. A party of the King's retainers returning from the hunt in one of the earlier scenes wear a species of head-gear consisting of bullock's horns, which appear to have been a badge of servitude. . . In another scene a painted cloth shows us huge stones roughly laid upon each other in the Stonehenge fashion. . . Of Mr. Ford Madox Brown's scenes, the most typical, perhaps, is an exterior

TWO SCENES FROM IRVING'S PRODUCTION OF HENRY VIII
From the Souvenir of the Play published by the Offices of *Black and White* of London

view of Roman dwellings, though doubtless his castle interiors, in
which the early action of the play passes, are as authentic as may be,
albeit conveying little of a distinctive character to the uninstructed
eye.   Upon the mechanical effects an equal amount of care has been
bestowed. . .   The storm which rages at the Lyceum . . . is a
storm indeed.   The scene is a desolate heath, swept, as we feel, by
furious blasts and beating rain, and illumined by coruscating lightning as dazzling in its brilliancy as the rolling thunder that accompanies it is terrifying.

.   .   .   .   .   .   ,   .

From the moment of his entrance the striking personality of Mr.
Irving's Lear rivets attention.   His unkempt locks and patriarchal
beard are not of the snowy whiteness . . . but a tawny gray, indicative of an octogenarian virility, and the regal air with which he plans
the division of his kingdom.

IRVING'S CYMBELINE, 1896

At the risk of some violence to chronology, I will pass to
the next two of Irving's Shakespearian revivals, a rather
unlucky pair of the autumn of 1896. Of Cymbeline, the
first, I can give a specific idea of the show and its chief
artists by quoting from the advertisement in the Times of
September 22nd, the first day of performance. It will be
remembered that Ford Madox Brown was artistic director
for King Lear, and Seymour Lucas for Henry VIII; no
less a man than Alma-Tadema was chosen for Cymbeline.
Truly, if Irving failed on the artistic side, it was not for
lack of famous and authoritative advisers. The synopsis
of scenes follows:

ACT 1

Scene 1. Britain. Garden of Cymbeline's Palace. Hawes Craven.
Scene 2. Rome. Philario's House. The Triclinium. J. Harker.

ACT 2

Scene 1. Britain. Room in the Palace. J. Harker.
Scene 2. Britain. Before the Palace. Hawes Craven.
Scene 3. Britain. Imogen's Bedchamber. J. Harker.

ACT 3

Scene 1. Britain. Garden of the Palace. Hawes Craven.
Scene 2. Rome. Philario's House. The Atrium. J. Harker.
Scene 3. Britain. Room in the Palace. J. Harker.

ACT 4

Scene 1. Wales. Before the Cave of Belarius. Hawes Craven.
Scene 2. Wales. Near Milford Haven. Hawes Craven.
Scene 3. Britain. Cymbeline's Palace. J. Harker.
Scene 4. Wales. Before the Cave. Hawes Craven.
Scene 5. Wales. Near the Cave. Hawes Craven.
Scene 6. Wales. Before the Cave. Hawes Craven.

ACT 5

Scene 1. Britain. Near the Roman Camp. Hawes Craven.
Scene 2. Britain. The Field of Battle. Hawes Craven.
Scene 3. Britain. Another part of the Field. Hawes Craven.
Scene 4. Britain. Cymbeline's Tent. Hawes Craven.

> Mr. L. Alma-Tadema has kindly acted as adviser in the production.
>
> The Costumes, under the direction of Mr. Carl and Mrs. Nettleship.
>
> Incidental Music composed by Mr. Hamilton Clarke (including the Madrigal, "Hark! the Lark" in Act III).

From the Times, once more, I quote for impression of the result. The reader will note that the hue and cry after accuracy was now beginning to entail the expected result—weariness to the flesh. The formula, perfected from Kemble to Macready to Kean, to Irving, was bearing fruit—the system was dying of dropsy. Alas, that at the moment of perfection all tends to decline! the rose's full beauty lasts hardly a moment of time. But to the Times review:

> An ancient British background, of course, is one thing, and the magnificent early Celtic *mise-en-scène* of the Lyceum another. . . . . It is obvious that any attempt to obtain archæological consistency in such a hotch-potch of history, fiction and period must fail, and the question suggests itself whether . . . for such plays as *Cymbeline* . . . it would not be well to adopt on the stage a more or less fantastic setting, with something of that indefiniteness of place, period, and costume, which the modern stage-manager for some reason will only allow to comic opera. Perhaps after all there is not much more reality in these picturesque kilted Britons who fill the Lyceum picture, excelling the Romans themselves in refinement and luxury, as well as war. . . . The introduction of a dancing scene in one of the two Roman interiors, Philario's house, where the fateful wager is

made, conveys some notion of Roman luxury; but for the most part the scenic splendours of the Lyceum *Cymbeline* are early British—in fact, their period is fixed by the playbill as the "first century"; and it will be pleasing to the masses to learn, as they will do here for the first time, that their Celtic forefathers were so eminently refined and cultured a race. Is this, by the way, the boasted education of the stage? Are we to believe that the early Celtic royalties wore golden crowns in their daily life as well as the richest costumes, and that Princesses like Imogen had thus early acquired the bad habit of reading in bed and turning down the page—of an apparently printed book? Because, if so, it is clear that the methods of the other schools frequented by the public stand in need of some revision with regard to the manners and customs of the early Britons.

So much for Cymbeline. The revival with which time factitiously paired it in the Irving schedule—Richard III— may be dismissed almost summarily. "As an historical pageant with accompaniment of action," the Athenæum of December 26, 1896, declares, "the representation is all that can be desired. The views of Renaissance London are striking and picturesque, the Court proceedings have all possible truth, and the scenes of combat are as realistic as is possible when the combat is mimic." What then was wrong? Joseph Knight, in this article, states it positively. The spirit of tragedy is dead—choked to death by "naturalism"—the false god of these later days. "We have," says the Athenæum, "a polished presentment of Court manners in which nothing offends and all is artistic and as nearly as possible real. Where, however, is tragedy? It is gone. Richard III is not now a tragic *rôle*. It is what is conventionally called 'a character part.'" Of this we have spoken elsewhere.

FORBES ROBERTSON AND GEORGE ALEXANDER

Before Irving's next (and last) revival of a Shakespearian play, Forbes Robertson and George Alexander attempted the Shakespearian field. Of neither shall I speak here at length. Forbes Robertson's productions made an effort toward simplicity; he wished, apparently, that his settings should be not only unobtrusive but modest. They were tasteful and accurate enough—they could not be otherwise, since Hawes Craven painted them—but no one remembers them. Perhaps that is the ideal condition. Of Hamlet (1897 and later) I seem to remember chiefly the interior of the castle, with a fine Norman effect and vast spaces within and without. Yet in this revival, as the London Times of September 13, 1897, informs us, a novelty was that of having Ophelia's mad scene placed in an orchard, the trees laden with apple-blossoms. Again, anything to be different! Forbes Robertson was the first to bring Fortinbras into the last act, largely, I think, for the great tableau allowed, of bearing off the dead body of Hamlet on the shields of the warriors. This device was followed by Mr. E. H. Sothern.

Of George Alexander's As You Like It (1896) and Much Ado about Nothing (1898) I say practically nothing. Both were excellently and ambitiously mounted—the latter, according to the Times of February 17, 1898, holding "first rank" for *mise-en-scène*. "Very picturesque," continues the Times, "are the interiors and exteriors of ancient Messina; the masked ball in Leonato's house is a dream; the dresses are sumptuous to a degree. . . . Perhaps the culminating picture is the church interior with its realistic acolytes, its chanting friars, its candles, its crosses, its altar, its music, and its heavy incense-laden atmosphere, vividly recalling the same scene as represented at the Lyceum. . . The play . . . is a feast for the eye." Alexander, then, tried; but he had been too long associated with the plays of the school of Pinero to hope for rehabilitation in the Shakespearian drama. His revivals are forgotten, though similar attempts of the Bancrofts and the Kendals are remembered.

BEERBOHM TREE ARRIVES

With Tree's production of Julius Cæsar at Her Majesty's, January 22, 1898, began a new epoch in the history of

Shakespeare on the London stage. No one, considering Tree's previous record, could have predicted this. Highly spiced modern drama, melodrama, romantic comedy, plays "with a purpose," do not usually lead to Shakespeare. After all, it is a matter of human spirit; and Tree, despite serious drawbacks as an actor, possessed indomitable ambition to succeed. From this time (1898) till the outbreak of the war in 1914, his theatre was the only "home" of Shakespeare in London. Revivals became more and more frequent, until at times, in the fashionable season of the year in the last two decades, a scanning of the bills for His Majesty's (as it had then become) gives almost the effect of old days at Drury Lane or Sadler's Wells, so many and so varied are the Shakespearian offerings. Tree frequently surpassed Irving in the massive splendour of his settings; against him came to be hurled with particular virulence the charge of burying Shakespeare under scenery.

And what were Tree's productions? To judge by Julius Cæsar and from such as I saw, they were gorgeous and generally artistic affairs. For Julius Cæsar the chief artists were our old friends of the Lyceum, Walter Hann and Joseph Harker; the whole production was designed and supervised by Alma-Tadema. In the management of the mob-scenes some thought this production surpassed that of the Meininger in 1881; since their visit much water had flowed under Thames bridges. In the account of Tree's beautiful Julius Cæsar I can add nothing to the statement of the Times of January 24th, and I reproduce it in large part for the delectation of the reader. Can he conceive of a more perfect setting of the great Roman play?

The busy streets of Rome, the Senate, the assassination of Cæsar, the Forum, the wayward passions of the mob, the battle of Philippi —all these are inviting subjects for pictorial treatment; and Mr. Tree, calling in the aid of Mr. Alma-Tadema, has produced a succession of scenes of unexampled beauty and effect. Not only the marble palaces of the eternal city beginning to abandon itself to luxury are here; not only senators and patricians; not only the pomp of a dawning imperialism. The plebs are on view. As Cæsar's procession passes through the streets the workmen throng to see it, in their habit as they lived and, in many cases, with the tools of their craft in their hands. Mr. Alma-Tadema has not forgotten even the umbrellas or parasols of the period. In short, the Rome of 2000 years ago . . . lives before us. A statue of Cæsar is moulded upon one in Berlin. . . . Here and there one notices some pretty, though purely fanciful illustrations of the text. After the soothsayer's warning "Beware the Ides of March" girls throw a handful of blood-red roses in Cæsar's path, and the Dictator starts at the omen. The assassination scene is composed with all a painter's skill. High on a chair of state sits Cæsar, with the conspirators as his friends grouped around him. He is stabbed in the back as he sits; he stumbles forward and down the steps that lead from the dais, receiving dagger-strokes on either side as he comes, until he falls into the arms of Brutus, who deals him the finishing blow. . . He falls to the ground, muffling his face in his cloak as he falls. At this juncture the arrival of Antony and his dissembling with the conspirators, some of whose hands are red with Cæsar's blood, make an effective act-drop scene, Antony being in Mr. Tree's dramatic scheme the central figure in the play. . . .

The Forum scene establishes the dramatic ascendancy of Antony, and it is here that the management of the mob reaches its highest point of excellence. If the Saxe-Meiningen company had something to teach us in this respect, they may now themselves come to London for a lesson. . . . This is an impressively real crowd that first Mr. Lewis Waller as Brutus, and then Mr. Tree as Antony, harangues. Their excitement is contagious to the house; their execrations thrill; one feels the irresistible force of this seething and surging mass of humanity. And always the picture—the elements, the grouping, the colouring, in a word the composition—is that of an artist. In this . . . one feels the plastic hand of Mr. Alma-Tadema. . . . The now unchained passions of the mob, clamouring for vengeance upon the conspirators and brandishing their avenging torches lighted at the pyre that has been prepared for the dictator's remains, combine to produce a scene which, for its moving effect upon the house, has probably never been surpassed upon the stage. . .

The closing episodes of the play are tame by comparison. . . The battle itself seems ineffective. . . . It necessarily partakes of the nature of . . alarums and excursions. . One sees no tactics, no generalship. . . But the costumes are highly picturesque, the designer exhibiting here, as throughout the play, a predilection for warmth of colour. Nor is it solely the Plain of Philippi that we see, but a picturesque ravine, from either side of which the combatants, to begin with, hold parley, and in the centre of which both Cassius and Brutus meet their death.

TREE'S KING JOHN, 1899

Turning to English history, Tree carried on the traditions of Charles Kemble in 1823, and with the same play—King John. His production was, as the Athenæum of September 23, 1899, states, "in all respects worthy of our modern stage. . . It is long since a Shakespearean performance has been more picturesque or illuminating."

Those who contemplated King John on his throne . . . saw a picture of life under the Angevin Kings as correct and as splendid as is ever likely to be realized. Equally excellent were the scenes before Angiers or at St. Edmundsbury."

The Times, of September 21st, is equally laudatory. It calls attention to a gorgeous interpolated tableau of the granting of Magna Charta, which, of course, Shakespeare does not provide for:

The artistic setting. . . Costumes, armour, heraldic bearings and banners, all designed by Mr. Percy Anderson, are a feast for the eye; while the scenery, from the massive interior of Northampton Castle, at the rise of the curtain, to the fresh and delicate beauty of the orchard at Swinstead Abbey, at its fall, is always in perfect taste, satisfying the mind without distracting it. As a "spectacle," then, this revival of King John is beyond all reproach. Possibly there may be some misgiving . . . . over the interpolated tableau showing the granting of Magna Charta. . . . The addition, being one merely of dumb show, leaves the text intact, it completes the chronicle aspect of the play, and it supplies in itself a striking stage-picture.

TREE'S MIDSUMMER NIGHT'S DREAM, 1900

But splendid as were these things, they were eclipsed by the magic of A Midsummer Night's Dream, in 1900. On this Tree lavished the very last possibilities of stage craft, and with it he produced for the last year of the century the utmost scenic marvels toward which that century had steadily progressed. Perhaps the year 1900 was the very high-water year in Shakespearian production of the Kemble-Charles Kean-Irving-Tree formula. Both the

Times and the Athenæum are enthusiastic. Says the former, under date of January 11th:

No scene has ever been put upon the stage more beautiful than the wood near Athens. . . . With a carpet of thyme and wild-flowers, brakes and thickets full of blossom, and a background seen through the tall trees, of the pearly dawn or the deep hues of the night sky. . . . The mind in recalling it seems to dwell upon some actual beauty of nature, instead of a painted arrangement of canvas and pasteboard. . . The costumes . . . designed by Mr. Percy Anderson. . .

The Clowns' ridiculous performance is given in a splendid Duke's palace, which, as soon as the mortals have retired, is filled with the fairy throng. There they dance, and, as they wind in and out, gradually the pillared hall glows with mysterious light, every pillar a shaft of fire, with little points of light starting out here and there at the touch of Oberon's wand. Then the fairies are dismissed . . . they troop off, and slowly the hall darkens again. The glow dies away, the stage is swallowed up in gloom, the lights in the house are suddenly turned up, and the play is over. It is as if the audience were rudely awakened from a pleasing vision. . There is a quick shifting of lights, and they find themselves blinking at the curtain, wondering whether it has not really all been a dream. A fitting ending to a performance full of charm.

And says the Athenæum, under date of January 20th:

In presenting the poetic aspects of a Midsummer Night's Dream, Mr. Tree has not only gone beyond precedent and record, he has reached what may, until science brings about new possibilities, be regarded as the limits of the conceivable. No spectacle equally artistic has been seen on the English stage. The glades near Athens in which the action passes are the perfection of sylvan loveliness, the palace of Theseus is a marvel of scenic illusion, the dresses are rich and tasteful as they can be, and the entire spectacle is of extraordinary beauty. What in it is best moreover, is that the fairy revels, unlike anything previously seen, are not mere ballets of children, but seem to be spontaneous ebullitions of mirth and joyousness. Many of the children were so youthful as to be all but incapable of supporting themselves, yet all took part in actions that seemed dictated by individual volition, rather than concerted purpose. . . As Oberon, Miss Julia Neilson, richly clad and with an electric coronal and breastplate . . . Mrs. Tree in clinging robes and with willowy grace of movement, realized Titania well. The effects of twinkling

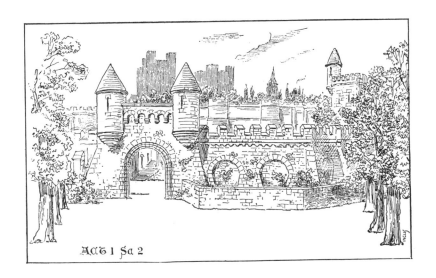

Act 1 Sa 2

Act 1 Sa 1.

TWO SCENES FROM TREE'S PRODUCTION OF KING JOHN
From the Souvenir of the Play printed by the Nassau Press

lights and floating shapes were magical, and the whole, for the first time on record, merited its name, A Midsummer Night's Dream. High as is this eulogy, it is fully merited—stage illusion and stage splendour being capable of nothing further.

It is scarcely too much to say that a play of Shakspeare's has never been given in equally artistic fashion. . . A strikingly pleasant feature is the restitution of passages not ordinarily spoken. . . The rendering of the whole of Mendelssohn's charming music added to the grace of the play.

This strikes me as the ultimate seal of approval, placed at the end of the century, on the last great production of the century. The goal was reached as the clock struck twelve. The last two productions of Tree before the retirement of Irving from the Lyceum in 1902—the limiting date I have arbitrarily fixed for this period—were Twelfth Night (1901) and a new Merry Wives of Windsor (1902). The former—if in 1901 like what it was in 1913, when I saw it—was notable for the most extraordinary single setting I have ever beheld. It was the garden of Olivia, extending terrace by terrace to the extreme back of the stage, with very real grass, real fountains, paths and descending steps. I never saw anything approaching it for beauty and *vraisemblance*. The actors were literally in an Italian garden. Of course the disadvantage lay in the fact that, once put up, this scene could not easily be removed, and it was perforce used for many of the Shakespearian episodes for which it was absurdly inappropriate. There were necessarily other sets, of course, but they were few in number, and largely "front"; all evening this lovely garden appeared and reappeared, always, I think, to the delight of the audience.

And the last of Tree's revivals, before the curtain rang down on Irving at the Lyceum—The Merry Wives of Windsor—was very well dressed and mounted; but who could think of scenery when Mrs. Kendal and Ellen Terry were disporting as the wives? Of Mr. Benson's many revivals between 1900 and 1902, I am freed from the necessity of speaking; his pretensions lay elsewhere—not in mounting.

IRVING'S CORIOLANUS, 1901

But the Lyceum curtain had not yet quite fallen on Henry Irving, and it is now my sad task to give the signal for that event. The last Shakespearian revival of his career was that of Coriolanus in April, 1901, directed and designed by Alma-Tadema, painted, as usual, by Harker, Hann, and Hawes Craven, under the stage-management of the faithful H. J. Loveday, and with music specially composed by Sir Alexander Mackenzie. Externally, everything was prepared for a success of the olden kind; internally things were awry. Irving was a sick—a doomed man; he had lost heart. Besides, he could never have been Coriolanus. Miss Terry was in all ways ill-fitted for Volumnia. Scenically, and from the point of view of stage-management, however, the piece was finely "got up," and the reader shall see, for the last time, what the critic of the Times had to say about a stage-production of the Victorian era:

The Coriolanus of Irving is to the Coriolanus of his predecessors as the classicism of the Davids in the Louvre is to the classicism of the Alma-Tademas at Burlington House.

.   .   .   .

And what a crowd it is! As every one knows, the crowd is a protagonist in this play, and everything depends upon the power of the stage-management to give it life, individuality, diversity. That power is certainly not lacking at the Lyceum. Whether the crowd is hooting or acclaiming Coriolanus, listening open-mouthed to its Tribunes, or arguing fatuously with itself, we are made to feel that it is a genuine mob and no mere pack of "supernumeraries."

The glories of the procession are here somewhat abbreviated in order not to delay the scene at the Capitol, one of the very finest pictures in the play, with its tier after tier of white-robed senators seated in concentric semi-circles round the altar. It is a thrilling moment when they rise to their feet as one man to proclaim their new Consul, and with their shout "To Coriolanus come all joy and honour!" the curtain descends on the first act.

.   .   .   .

It has occasionally been said that *Coriolanus* is an uninteresting play, but the Lyceum performance . . . is brimming with life. . .

And amid all the swaying to and fro of the mob, the pageantry of
Forum and Capitol, the clash of arms, the Coriolanus makes a splendid
central figure.

Exit from the chronicle Irving, the most conspicuous, in
many ways the most gifted stage-figure of his time. He
had fought the good fight, and had had his days of glory as
well as his days of disquietude. He had, moreover, won
for himself a great niche in the artistic history of his country. What could man wish more?

Would the reader know the cost and the reward in terms
of money? He shall hear upon the authority of Austin
Brereton, in his Life of the actor.

The following [says Brereton] is the statement of Henry Irving's
gross receipts and his expenses from the period when he took possession of the Lyceum Theatre, 31st August, 1878, until the end of
his season in London, 10th June, 1905:—

Gross Receipts:—

London Admissions and (Rent of Lyceum)	£1,177,734	1	1
America and the Provinces (Admissions)	1,049,729	7	5
Rent of Saloons, etc.	13,584	13	4
Sale of Books and Pictures	7,955	7	2
Miscellaneous receipts	12,634	1	1
Total Receipts	£2,261,637	10	1

Deduct Outgoings:—

Working Expenses	£1,877,028,	0	6
Production Account	221,178,	15	5
Expenditure on House	59,862,	9	9
Law Expenses and Audit	3,948,	19	0
Cost of Books, Pictures, etc.	6,272,	1	5
Total Expenditure	£2,168,290,	6	1

This leaves a net profit of £93,347 4s 0, which, extended over the
period from August 1878 to June, 1905, brings an average yearly
profit of £3,457 6s. 1d.

Total receipts from all sources	London	£1,221,281	0	11
	America	711,016	18	4
	Provinces	329,339	10	10
	Total	£2,261,637,	10	1

EPILOGUE

RECENT TENDENCIES

In 1900 we saw that Mr. F. R. Benson emerged in London with a company trained to perform Shakespeare with the use of the maximum of text and the minimum of scenery and accessories—modest though satisfactory. This ideal of adequacy of presentation Mr. Benson has carried throughout the years that have succeeded. In 1901 he was again in London, this time at the Comedy Theatre; in 1905 he was at the Coronet Theatre for four weeks in February and March, with almost nightly changes of bill. One weakness of his scheme lies in the fact that neither he nor Mrs. Benson is very good in the great rôles. They have, however, been able to train a number of men and women who have achieved success in various theatrical activities.

This of Benson's was the first effort to break the long reign of the magnificent and costly production of Shakespearian plays—the ideal, in other words, of Irving and Tree. In 1903, the year after Irving passed forever from the Lyceum, it happens, by curious coincidence, that two other very modern ways of presenting Shakespeare were forcibly impressed on London playgoers. The first was an experiment of Ellen Terry's, largely brought about, I should suppose, by her desire to start her son on his chosen career of stage decorator and director. Mr. Gordon Craig has become well known in later years by his publications, his drawings for stage-settings, and his few activities in the theatre. He has been much "written up," so much so, indeed, that it is unnecessary here to describe his aims and accomplishments. He is the great apostle of that "new" method of stage-setting which consists in suggestion rather than reality. By screens and arrangement of lights, and the minimum of painting, he has attempted to steep the stage in mysterious and majestic gloom or in airy radiance beyond the conception of mere earthly decorators. His ideal is said to be a wordless drama with one vision beatific after another. Of course, in 1903 he was beginning on this form of German and Russian dyspepsia, but his mother good-naturedly spent much money on his setting for Ibsen's Vikings, and followed it, on May 23, 1903, with a revival of Much Ado about Nothing. Critical opinion was naturally divided. The Times of May 25th speaks of the play as relieved of "the over-gorgeous trappings" that had burdened it at the Lyceum, and gives us a hint of the effects in saying that "Mr. Gordon Craig has designed a quaint formal garden"—in spite of the fact that there is nothing quaint or formal about the play—"and a church scene of real beauty." But the Athenæum, of May 30th, dislikes it heartily: "We do not speak of Mr. Gordon Craig's scenery, much of which, especially the scene of Leonato's garden, with an enormous structure of apparent wicker-work, fails to convey to us any intelligible idea." This revival, at any rate, was the first of a line that terminated, for the present at least, in the eccentricities of Mr. Granville Barker, ten years later; the first of the cult of "modern" stage-setting. It came close on the withdrawal of Irving from the Lyceum.

The second form of innovation—even more of a cult— was that illustrated by the activities of the Elizabethan Society. This organisation, advised by Mr. William Poel and Mr. Ben Greet, hired vacant halls or theatres, and produced Elizabethan plays on something like a Shakespearian stage, with no attempt at scenery, other than a representation of the architectural bounds of that Shakespearian stage itself. This kind of thing enabled the directors to produce the piece without "cuts"—now grown to be a matter for nervous apprehension—and without intermission, except possibly at the end of the third act. In 1901 the Society had so played Henry V in the Lecture Theatre at Burlington Gardens; now—in 1903—it brought out Twelfth Night at the Court Theatre. For our day and generation there is something academic, not to say "precious," about this plan, but it has advantages not to

be overlooked. It enables students, at least, to get into
the spirit of the Elizabethan performances, and gives to
the presentation something of the charm of a romance read
continuously through. This was the second novel type of
production presented to London playgoers in the year following Irving's departure from the Lyceum.

Adequate representation, scenic, dramatic, textual, *à la*
Benson; "new" staging, *à la* Gordon Craig; Elizabethan
representation, *à la* Ben Greet and William Poel: all three
of these births of time London saw within a year after the
passing of the Lyceum, and before the death of Irving.
Meantime, Beerbohm Tree and others went on serenely in
the old way, reaping success, and undisturbed by talk of
theorists, amateurs and visionaries. The revivals of Tree
for the next few years increased, if possible, in beauty and
massive effect. Let us here lay a wreath on the tomb of
the brave believer in Shakespeare and the theatre. In
September, 1903, Tree brought out Richard II, even more
superbly mounted than had been his previous revivals of
historical plays, and again divided into three acts or groups
of events—his now invariable formula. The first of these
groups is naturally composed of the episodes pertaining to
the banishment of Hereford and Norfolk and the death of
John of Gaunt, and shows Richard at the height of his
power, preparing to start for Ireland, and confiscating the
estates of Lancaster; the second shows the arrival of Bolingbroke, with the nobles flocking to his standard, the
return of Richard from Ireland, the discovery of the deser-
tion of his nobles, the surrender of Flint Castle, and his
being led a captive in the train of the victor (a memory of
Charles Kean); the third group is devoted to Richard's
surrender of the crown and his murder at Pomfret. It was
almost a stroke of genius that enabled Tree to see the three-
fold grouping in any Shakespearian play; not only did it
solidify interest, but it enabled the scene-shifters to work
most effectively. It literally, also, followed the Aristotelian
dictum about a play's having a beginning, a middle and
an end.

Tree's next great effort was The Tempest in September, 1904, also in three acts; he revived Much Ado about Nothing in the same season. In September, 1906, came The Winter's Tale, with Ellen Terry as Hermione. Of this, the Athenæum of September 8th informs us: "Like most Shakespearean revivals at His Majesty's, the piece is presented in three acts. . . Act I simply contains the whole of the scenes in Sicily, and ends with the vindication of Hermione by the oracle of Apollo, and her supposed death after hearing of that of Mamilius. The second act passes in Bohemia and includes the appearance of Time as prologue, the pastoral scenes of Florizel and Perdita, and the display of the wiles and wares of Autolycus. Act III is re-transferred to the Court of Sicily.

.   .   .   .

"This arrangement is not only pardonable—it is expedient and the play thus obtained is dramatic and effective."

A gorgeous Antony and Cleopatra (in four acts) came at the beginning of 1907. This surpassed all of Tree's previous efforts and awoke the Athenæum to rapture in its issue of January 5th: "As regards the mounting, it is not only the best that has ever been given to this play, it may also be regarded as the best that has ever been bestowed upon any work of the author. . . To have produced it is the chief glory of the management, establishing the house as foremost among theatres, English or foreign, private or supported by subventions."

The Merchant of Venice in April, 1908, Henry VIII in September, 1910, and Macbeth in September, 1911, complete the list of Tree's great revivals of Shakespeare. Henry VIII, seen in America in 1916, was a revelation of old-time splendour in theatrical mounting, and still lives in memory as perhaps the most gorgeous thing ever attempted in this country in that line of staging. It was so regarded in London. This play also was arranged in three acts, omitting everything pertaining to the conspiracy against Cranmer, and the christening of the royal infant.

Tree, it will be seen, waged a good fight. More than any other man of the last ten or fifteen years, he kept alive interest in Shakespeare on the stage. Others, however, deserve a word of praise. Mr. Oscar Asche, graduate of the Benson school, and trained more recently by Tree, "commenced manager" in December, 1904, with a fine revival of The Taming of the Shrew, his wife, Lily Brayton, making a great "hit" as Katharine. Mr. Asche is a very large man, physically, and impressed, physically, as Petruchio. This revival was followed in November, 1905, at the same theatre—the Adelphi—by an equally successful Midsummer Night's Dream, with a good cast and very pleasing setting. By this time Mr. Asche had won recognition. In March, 1906, he pursued his course with the seldom-acted Measure for Measure (discarded since the days of Phelps, and, later, of Adelaide Neilson). Finally, in 1907, in October and November respectively, during Tree's temporary absence from His Majesty's, Mr. Asche produced As You Like It and Othello. These were all careful revivals, and gave Mr. Asche a place of no mean note in modern theatrical history. Mr. Walter Hampden —recently a very successful Hamlet in America—and Mr. Henry Ainley were conspicuous in his support, and in every revival Mrs. Asche (Lily Brayton) won applause as possibly the best actress of her day in Shakespearian parts.

Other experiments in the old way, inherited from Irving and perpetuated by Tree, were Mr. Arthur Bourchier's revivals at the Garrick Theatre of The Merchant of Venice (October, 1905) and Macbeth (December, 1906). His success was moderate, the chief reward coming in the engagement of himself and his wife (Violet Vanbrugh) to assist in Tree's revivals of Henry VIII and Macbeth. Yet no one could maintain that Miss Vanbrugh was a great Queen Katharine or Lady Macbeth. I cannot close without calling attention to the appearance of Mr. H. B. Irving in his father's old part of Hamlet at the Adelphi, in 1905. This performance excited favourable comment, and was especially liked, several years later, when it was revived with a

newly arranged text that restored much material hitherto
omitted in representation. A visit of Mr. and Mrs. E. H.
Sothern (Julia Marlowe) to London in the spring of 1907
failed to secure for their Shakespearian repertoire—Hamlet, Romeo and Juliet, Twelfth Night, As You Like It—
the acclaim with which it was greeted in America. Finally,
at the New Theatre in September, 1911, Miss Phyllis Neilson-Terry (daughter of Fred Terry and Julia Neilson)
appeared, after years of careful preparation, as Juliet.
Obviously she did not efface, in the part, memories of that
other Neilson—the beautiful Adelaide of 1870–80. Miss
Neilson-Terry played Viola in Beerbohm Tree's Twelfth
Night in 1913.

This is the main trend of Shakespearian production in
London in the years following Irving's retirement from the
Lyceum. On the whole it looms up, when thus collected,
more impressively than pessimists might have believed
possible, till confronted by facts of arithmetic and nomen-
clature. It leads us to believe that Shakespeare is still
alive in the midst of dying cohorts of modern plays and
musical "shows." Of course the extremists also have been
busy, and modern stage societies and exemplars of the new
staging have done their best—and their worst—with the
deathless one. Mr. Granville Barker at the Savoy Theatre
in September, 1912, brought out The Winter's Tale on his
specially constructed stage, and with fantastic costumes
that can be imagined by those who witnessed his Midsummer Night's Dream at Wallack's Theatre, in 1915, and his
two Greek tragedies at the Stadium of the College of the
City of New York in the spring of 1916. This Shakespearian stage of Mr. Barker's consisted of a huge apron, extending half-way into the parquet of the theatre, with the
space behind the proscenium serving something as the
inner stage of the Elizabethan playhouse. It was modern
staging with a vengeance. The Athenæum, of September
18, 1912, says of The Winter's Tale, "Mr. Granville Barker,
in a distressful striving after the artistic, has achieved that
mingling of discordant, ill-related elements, that impossible

jangling of different keys, which can never be removed
from vulgarity. . . . The rich simplicity of the first scene
emphasizes the tawdriness of the second. Caparisoned for
the most part in attire which should wring pity from the
stoniest critic, and in more than one instance surmounted
by head-gear which would have earned a well-merited curse
from even an early nineteenth-century grenadier, the rest
of the company deserve commendation for their attainment of seemliness under difficulties. Mr. Barker is capable of being wearisome."

As to the Midsummer Night's Dream, produced some
time after, I beg leave to quote some words I wrote after
the reproduction of the work at Wallack's Theatre, New
York:

On February 16, 1915, Mr. Granville Barker presented at Wallack's Theatre his London production of Shakespeare's play. . . .
Let it be said that it represented the last cry in the new stage decoration.

Mr. Barker divided his play into three parts; the first dealing with
the "mortals"—Theseus and his court, Quince and the other hard-
handed men; the second running together without break the fairy
episodes and the affairs of the perplexed lovers, as well as the transformation of Bottom; the third showing all the characters again in
the palace of Theseus. The stage was built out far into the auditorium, and the huge apron thus formed was used as a place for
posing actors in effective groups; the part behind the proscenium was
used for whatever "decoration" was required. The fairy scene was
built up to a round mound in the middle of the stage, and covered
with bright green velvet carpet. Just above the mound was suspended a large terra-cotta wreath of flowers that would have been
the envy of a German pastry cook, and from it depended a veil of
white gauze, lighted within by vari-colored electric bulbs, hanging
at irregular lengths. At the back and sides of the stage fluttered
curtains of chintz or silk, designed to suggest forest branches. Like
forest branches they waved vigorously in the breeze, so that one
felt disposed to ask some one to shut the windows of heaven in order
that the trees might not blow out so violently into Titania's bower
(the gauze canopy aforesaid). The scene of Theseus' palace in the
last act, however, was a very solidly-built affair, with steps and many
heavy columns of black and silver, and with a door at the back letting in much red light. It was evidently quite Egyptian in its mass

and design. The other changes of scene were indicated by curtains that waved, to the loss of all illusion. The first, Theseus' palace, was of white silk, with conventional gold design. The Quince curtains were of salmon pink silk, with steel-blue masses supposed to represent the roofs of the city. There was another curtain of electric blue, heavily spangled with silver stars and moon. This was all supposed to be very much more artistic than the kind of thing Augustin Daly aimed at, and far more suggestive. It was thought to be full of illusion. Of course, it was not. Any one who has imagination can get the poetic illusion by seeing these things acted on a bare stage or on a stage hung with curtains or with just a conventional unchanged setting, such as Mr. Ben Greet has used. No human being, however, can be expected to be anything but worried and annoyed by pink silk curtains that are supposed to be the roofs of houses, or green silk curtains that are supposed to be forest trees; especially when they blow and stream out in the gales of the stage. . .

Perhaps no feature of this "show" awakened more discussion than Mr. Barker's fairies. From head to foot they were differentiated by a coat of bronze paint, that made them look precisely like something you might buy to set up in the corner of the parlor; their dresses exactly corresponded. These fairies clanked as they walked. Viewed just as decoration, without regard to time, place or sense, they were very pretty; groups of them were novel and interesting. Their dancing under and around Titania's gauze bower was really a pleasing sight. By the aid of their bronze you could tell at a glance whether any person in the play was a fairy or a mortal, and as Mr. Barker evidently had no faith in Shakspere or the imagination of the audience, this was an advantage. Let it be admitted, then, that in his way he solved the problem of making the fairies seem different. He also gave the part of Oberon and Puck to men, for which I thank him; I hope the silly custom of the Nineteenth Century, in this regard, has been broken forever.

With the time-saving device of the curtains Mr. Barker was able to give the play entire. The verse was delivered at a rapid pace. None of it was spoken well . . . . And when one grew weary of trying to understand what Puck was saying, he could find solace in wondering why the sprite was not gilded like the other fairies but made to look like a toy Loge in the Rheingold, flaring, flaming hair and all. I hope this is not indicative of what will happen when stage setting ceases to be scenery and becomes only decoration.

I hope, also, that this silly and vulgar way of presenting Shakespeare died with all other vain, frivolous, un-simple things burnt up by the great war-conflagration. Some good may be found in the residuum, but not in the utter affectation of such "simplicity" as this.

It would require a brave man to predict the future manner of presenting Shakespeare on the stage. I suspect it will not be wholly Tree's way, nor Mr. Ben Greet's; I hope it will not be Mr. Granville Barker's. Meantime managers are at sea in these contending theories, and trim their sails warily. On one conviction we rest: Shakespeare is not dead, and the way will be devised for presenting him so that he shall not spell ruin, but the fullest measure of success. Signs of a revival are even now visible in England and America. Perhaps it will be on the wave of a great democratic impulse that the dramatist who knew most about all kinds of men and women will be carried to new life in the very near future.

INDEX